"In a period of time that questions the place of confession in religious practice, Annemarie S. Kidder offers a thorough and easy-to-read study of confession in the Christian tradition, rooting it in its biblical ground. She gives us helpful knowledge of its theological foundations, good insights into the forms of its development, and practical ways of entering into the exercise or sacrament of confession. Her book is a rich treasure to be valued by all readers, especially coming from the various Christian traditions."

—David L. Fleming, SJ
Editor, *Review for Religious*

"This historically well-informed and pastorally sensitive book, written from an ecumenical perspective, will be helpful to both clergy and laity in all the churches. Accessible in its style, it gently challenges us to give confession, no matter what form it might take, the place it deserves in our spiritual lives as Christians."

—John W. O'Malley, SJ
Professor of Religion, Georgetown University
Author of *The First Jesuits* and
What Happened at Vatican II

"Nothing is more useful for reinvigorating the practices of Christian tradition than a thorough and penetrating knowledge of their history, pursued with ecumenical openness. By recognizing the relationship between personal confession of sins, charisms of spiritual discernment, offices of pastoral care, and public rituals bonding the church in its members, Kidder has achieved a historical tour de force demonstrating how confession—in various forms—is anything but moribund for present and future Christianity. With its combined theological, pastoral, and historical resources, this book has no peer in the English-language literature treating penance, reconciliation, and spiritual direction."

—Bruce T. Morrill, SJ
Boston College

"Community. Confession. Penitence. Reconciliation. Spiritual formation. Annemarie S. Kidder presents a meticulous historical study of these five strands, which have been interwoven and separated variously through Christian history. She supports the study with substantial theological reflection. *Making Confession, Hearing Confession* will be a valuable addition to the libraries of theological schools, graduate schools—and the bookshelves of reflective Christians."

—Mary Ann Donovan, SC, PhD
Professor of Historical Theology and Spirituality
Jesuit School of Theology at Berkeley

"Kidder brings to life the monastic process of spiritual fathering and mothering that evolved into the sacrament of penance, illuminating the history of penitential practices with amazing detail. She amply demonstrates how Christian thinkers of all ages, whether Catholic or Protestant, have been concerned with moral conversion and spiritual development. In the process, she assembles a wealth of information on confession as a means of spiritual growth from the Middle Ages to the present, pointing the way to a renewal of th⋯

—Joseph Martos
Author of *The*
An Interdisc

"This engaging book on the practice of confession in the life of the church brings together historical and spiritual theology in a wonderful way. Annemarie Kidder shows how confession, rooted in the Scriptures and the great tradition of Christian faith through the ages, is still relevant for the life of faith today. Well researched and well written, we have here a welcomed resource for both academic theology and spiritual direction."

> —Timothy George
> Founding Dean of Beeson Divinity School
> of Samford University
> Senior Editor of *Christianity Today*

"I was absolutely stunned on first reading *Making Confession, Hearing Confession.* Annemarie Kidder integrates the many expressions of the subject that honor the basic human need for disclosure, to respond to the hunger for forgiveness, ranging from confession to spiritual direction during these 2,000 years. She expertly discerns the common thread that keeps all these various ways recognizably coherent in their historical and theological underpinnings and their rootedness in the Gospel. I welcome this as a critical and timely gift for today's church—its congregations and pastors."

> —Eugene H. Peterson
> Professor Emeritus of Spiritual Theology,
> Regent College, Vancouver, B.C.
> Author of *The Message*

"An extraordinary achievement. A book for conservative bishops and liberal academics, for pastors Catholic and Protestant, spiritual directors religious and lay, for anyone interested in using a time-honored means for growing in the spiritual life.

"At a time when psychologists and 12-step programs alike recognize that confession is essential to the treatment of troubled souls, Kidder demonstrates brilliantly why confession matters.

"An extraordinary work of historical, ecumenical, and sacramental theology, encyclopedic in its treatment of penance, confession, and spiritual direction. From its biblical roots to the most contemporary reflection on the pastoral healing of souls, Kidder allows the tradition to speak for itself.

"When public, once-in-a-lifetime penance died in the early middle ages, the laity sought spiritual healing by bearing their souls to monks and religious women like Brigit. Can the work of a knowledgeable, wise, Presbyterian woman pastor-theologian help revive what appears like a moribund if not dead Catholic sacramental practice? As Kidder brilliantly demonstrates, stranger things have happened in the history of confession. With meticulous scholarship made accessible for any interested reader, this may well be the most important book of academic and pastoral theology in a decade."

> —Ronald Modras
> Professor of Theological Studies
> Saint Louis University

Making Confession, Hearing Confession

A History of the Cure of Souls

Annemarie S. Kidder

A Michael Glazier Book

LITURGICAL PRESS

Collegeville, Minnesota

www.litpress.org

A Michael Glazier Book published by Liturgical Press

Cover design by David Manahan, OSB.
Photo © Arekmalang/Dreamstime.com.

Excerpt from Martin L. Smith, *Reconciliation: Preparing for Confession in the Episcopal Church* © 1985, Cowley Publications. Used with permission.

Excerpts from the English translation of *Rite of Penance* © 1974, International Committee on English in the Liturgy, Inc. All rights reserved.

Excerpts from documents of the Second Vatican Council are from *Vatican Council II: The Basic Sixteen Documents*, by Austin Flannery, OP © 1996 (Costello Publishing Company, Inc.). Used with permission.

Scripture texts in this work are taken from the *New Revised Standard Version Bible* © 1989, Division of Christian Education of the National Council of the Churches of Christ in the United States of America. Used by permission. All rights reserved.

1   2   3   4   5   6   7   8   9

Library of Congress Cataloging-in-Publication Data

Kidder, Annemarie S.
    Making confession, hearing confession : a history of the cure of souls / Annemarie S. Kidder.
        p. cm.
    "A Michael Glazier Book."
    Includes bibliographical references (p.   ) and index.
    ISBN 978-0-8146-5497-2
    1. Confession.   I. Title.
BV845.K48 2010
234'.166—dc22

2009037611

To
Timothy George
and
Robert Hater

Contents

Acknowledgments

The modest question someone asked me in an adult education class at a Presbyterian church in Ann Arbor was: "How can I experience God's forgiveness?" The question would eventually send me off on the meandering paths of the history and practice of private and public confession. Had I known of what lay ahead in order to be able to produce a reasonably adequate answer, I would have gladly admitted ignorance and left it at that. But the more I read, the more the question became my own. Many people have assisted me during the nearly four years of research and writing, especially the parishioners at the church I serve and the seminary students I teach.

Gratitude must also go to those who gave initial encouragement to my germinating ideas, namely, Roy Carlisle, the late David Noel Freedman, and Ursula King. Two scholars were constantly working from behind the scenes in this book through theirs; they are the late John T. McNeill, who with his *History of the Cure of Souls*, published in 1951, showed me how it should be done; and Kenneth Leech, whose *Soul Friend*, first published in 1977, still is the standard work on the history of spiritual direction. I benefited from the library services at the Athenaeum of Ohio, the University of Innsbruck, the Karl-Rahner archive at Innsbruck and Munich, Sacred Heart Major Seminary in Detroit, and the University of Michigan in Ann Arbor. I thank those who read the manuscript or portions of it and those who offered helpful pointers, especially Andreas Batlogg, Margaret Brennan, John Burgess, Margaret Gaffney, Robert Hater, Joseph Martos, Eugene Peterson, John Schwarz, and Roman Siebenrock. And I thank the team at Liturgical Press for their support: Hans Christoffersen and his enthusiastic endorsement of the proposal, Linda Maloney for the tedious reference and fact-checking labors, and Mary Stommes for managing copyrights and tying up loose ends.

This book is dedicated to two "fathers in the faith" who by their theological acumen, scholarly rigor, and pastoral integrity have been and are to me signs of Christ's presence in the world: Timothy George, founding dean of Beeson Divinity School and Reformation scholar extraordinaire who over two decades ago lit the flame that kindled my passion for historical theology and has been teaching me ever since; and Robert J. Hater, professor of pastoral and systematic theology at Cincinnati's diocesan seminary of Mount St. Mary's and longtime mentor in all things Catholic.

Introduction

A book on confession may seem like an archaic undertaking. It conjures up images of monastic self-chastisement and penance, darkened confessionals with a concealed priestly presence, and a trembling and squirming sinner waiting to be absolved. Why revisit what the Protestant Reformation had dismissed and eliminated as a sacrament and what Catholics, in the wake of Vatican II, practice only on occasion, if at all? The fact is that incidences of confession, albeit concealed and innocuous, are a regular occurrence in most our lives. For example, on a flight to Philadelphia some years ago I was looking forward to studying my conference book and selecting the seminars I would be attending, hearing speakers of national renown in the world of theology and biblical studies. But even before takeoff I saw my hopes crumble. "Where are you headed?" my seat neighbor asked gregariously as soon as I settled into my seat. "To a convention on religion," I said. "Oh, then you must be a theologian or a pastor," came his immediate reply. "Yes, I'm a pastor," I said, hoping that would intimidate him enough to be quiet. Instead, it encouraged him to launch into a monologue about the church, the hypocrisy of members, his longstanding involvement there, and then his misgivings about the pastor that had led him to resign from his post on the church board and quit church altogether. Was I thinking that a bad thing, he asked, and I, still hoping to be able to read, lamely conceded that at times it was good to take a break. But this only spurred him on to elaborate on his church upbringing, his marriage, his children who were in college, and his sense of wanting to quit his job, too. I wasn't paying much attention until he got to the part about a woman he had met and the fact that he was thinking of leaving his wife of thirty-some years. "I feel guilty about that, you know," he said, "but life can get away from you if you don't watch out."

After my return I attended an AA meeting with a friend who had begged me to come along to ease her first-time jitters. No one could have prepared me for what was to ensue. One by one, members introduced themselves as alcoholics, some sober for months, some for years, until it was my turn to say that I was "just accompanying my friend," as if I had no problems whatsoever. By the end of the meeting I had become privy to stories of panic attacks, misplaced anger, and hapless exchanges with workmates and family. Everyone felt better, it seemed, but me.

Then another friend called to report on her latest dispute with her boss. "I hate him and there is nothing I want more than to see him fired," she said. I waited for her to elaborate on the most recent incident, but all she said was that she was tired of going to work, dreaded his presence, even hated herself. She was finally looking for another job.

Locked into captivity by an airplane seat, a kindly disposition of keeping a friend company, or a telephone connection, we become ex officio confessors to those with troubled consciences and traces, or bold footprints, of guilt. Confession seems to make us feel better, to lift burdens, to restore our self-confidence. I notice it when church members come to see me for pastoral counseling in my office. Often I can tell that what they name as the reason for the appointment is something entirely different from the real cause: they need to admit to a failure of the past, a slip of their temper, a careless word or precipitous deed, even drug abuse, abortion, attempted suicide, or a resentment harbored for years. "I feel better now that I told you," they say as they get up from the chair. "Thanks for listening and understanding." Yet, while I am grateful for their relief and appreciation of me as unofficial confessor, I cannot help but feel that something is missing: a biblical word of forgiveness and direction, a litany of repentance and absolution, an assurance on my part to pray for them that they may resist future temptation, and a verbal or visual pledge on their part not to slip again. Moreover, I find myself stretched in making a plausible connection between their act of confession and the biblical concept of repentance, of turning from the old ways and reconciling with God in Christ and the church so as to be born anew and made anew.

This book results from my own need for private confession and self-examination in a safe and sacred context that bears upon my Christian convictions as a child of God through baptism. I ask myself: where do I go to share my troubles and receive forgiveness? Who will hold me accountable and what pledges and offerings can I bring to demonstrate true repentance in hopes of a new beginning? The book results from my discontent with a church that used to consider itself a hospital and sanatorium for sinners and now functions as an elitist enclave for those who seemingly have it all together. And it results from puzzlement over why churches are not providing more intentionally for occasions of confession, forgiveness, and conversion when outside groups have successfully adopted these practices, thus facilitating members' wholeness and recovery. Finally, I have observed a discrepancy between how people act within and outside the church, and I have wondered about that. On the one hand, people long for assurance by sharing their most intimate fears and failures, sometimes asking forgiveness, more often affirmation— even from disengaged strangers who make every effort to look bored. On the other hand, most people—with the exception of a few bold or trusting souls—are hesitant to divulge their failures and sins to a member of the clergy, either because they fear repercussions ("Will I get nominated for a church function next year?" "Will I still be respected around the church?") or because church leaders are tentative or bumbling guides in listening to, absolving, and holding accountable those who have come to us with their burdens of guilt and shame. Of course, Christian denominations differ in their histories regarding the practice of confession, which plays a role in members' awareness of the practice and its use. Some, such as the Roman Catholic Church, consider it a sacrament, the sacrament of reconciliation, to be observed prior to partaking of the Eucharist or at least annually during Holy Week. Others, such as the Episcopal Church, commend confession to their members as a perennial rite of reconciliation with God, neighbor, and the church. And still others, such as churches in the Reformed tradition, have communal acts of confession during Sunday liturgy or on special days, providing confessional litanies printed in the bulletin. Members of denominations without a sacramental practice or a rite of confession, along with those who could participate in confession but fail to do so, are left to take their burdens elsewhere: to a friend, stranger, self-help group, journal, or directly to God. They are on their own when it comes to preparing the setting and beginning the process of introspection and self-examination.

The practice of confession in the context of a liturgy or in a private ecclesiastical setting has declined drastically over the past fifty years, and in particular since the Protestant Reformation in the sixteenth century. Has the need for forgiveness diminished? Or have we forgotten that our search for wholeness begins with a contrite heart over past wrongs and the willingness to allow God to restore and guide us? I don't think so. The need for hearing the words spoken as if they were Christ's is everyone's need, and the need for restoration and correction, for a turning and a remembering of the ways of God is the basis of the church's existence and ministry. Knit together as individual members of Christ's body, we are both sinner and saint, broken and redeemed, aware that we "have sinned and fall short of the glory of God" (Rom 3:23) and can be renewed by the Spirit of forgiveness. This means that if we recognize and act upon our need for ongoing forgiveness and God's grace we will be renewed, and so will the church as a whole.

The saying goes that confession is good for the soul, and in the particular understanding of the church it is a way of the soul's coming clean before God in Christ. While psychotherapists readily admit to the healing dimension of confession and most twelve-step programs incorporate it explicitly in the fifth step, churches are less likely to make provision for this practice. I suspect that the reason for today's disuse of confession as a spiritual discipline may be twofold: people are not sure whether they want to or can trust the clergy—or another church member— charged with listening; and pastors and laypeople in most denominations are not sure how best to draw on this ancient rite and relate their fundamental human need for forgiveness to the biblical concept of repentance, *metanoia*, and the new birth in Christ. Fortunately there is ample assistance for recovering the central place and the varied contexts of confession in the biblical story and the church's history of practice—and even its malpractice. The question is: How can we today reap the benefits of what was once a commonplace and vital spiritual discipline with significant transformative effects? How do we select a confessor with whom to enter into this process of self-examination? And in what ways can we adopt this practice today in a postmodern era that holds in suspicion ecclesial, biblical, and clerical authority? A word concerning terminology is in order. I use the term confession not in the strict sacramental sense it has assumed in later centuries, but as a way of describing an interpersonal exchange or private meeting between two people that involves remorse, repentance, and conversion to God. While diverse means and contexts set the stage for facilitating confession and forgiveness, it is the actual transformation in the person that matters: the burden of guilt and shame is lifted and one finds forgiveness, cleansing, and a restored self.

It is my hope that this brief historical survey of confessional practices in the church's history will commend confession as a spiritual practice to all Christians, regardless of denominational affiliation. Part I will explore the origins of public and private confession in the church, the rising popularity of private confession among the laity and its emerging sacramental status, and developments resulting from the arrival of the friars, beguines, members of third orders, and the movements of the Friends of God and *devotio moderna* involving mutual confession and spiritual direction among the laity. Part II will address the changes begun with the Protestant Reformation and the Council of Trent, and the subsequent use or disuse of confessional practices among various denominations. And Part III will sketch the biblical antecedents and historical developments up to today in the areas of preaching, worship, and confessional litanies, small and accountability groups, and private confession and spiritual direction; it will explore the reasons for the decline of private confession in churches; and it will seek to formulate a theology of confession that draws on contemporary Christian theologians and spiritual writers from both the Catholic and Protestant traditions. The Conclusion offers practical suggestions for preparing for and making private confession today, choosing a confessor, and hearing confession from another. Appendices include additional tools for an examination of conscience and confessional litanies for use by the laity.

PART ONE

Biblical Beginnings
to the Middle Ages

Tracing the history of the church's practice of confession can be a daunting undertaking. Given the complexities of the topic, it seemed prudent to initially follow historical chronology (as in parts 1 and 2), rather than topical arrangement (as in parts 3 and 4). But even with a chronological approach, the intricacies needed to be streamlined and detail condensed so as to allow for recognizable strands and patterns to emerge. In tracing the various stages of confession from its biblical beginnings through the church's history up to the present day, I have tried to highlight decisive developments, caesuras, and significant turning points.

Part 1 will chronicle the gradual unfolding of confessional practices from its biblical beginnings to its flowering during the High Middle Ages. Practices that are apparent in the Old Testament are considered in their continuity and contrast with those in the New. New Testament beginnings are seen as setting the stage for public confession, which will come to be replaced in time by private confession and spiritual direction. And the unfolding of private confession is seen in the context of its beginnings among early monastic communities and later within the larger church where it is commonly accompanied by counsel, exhortation, and spiritual direction on the confessor's part. At private confession's flowering stage and at its height, not only priests as male clergy are engaged in hearing confession, but also women, most often third-order members of religious communities who lived among the people, beguines, and female members of spiritual circles and pious societies, who served as both "unofficial" confessors and spiritual directors. Not surprisingly, the popularity of private confession among Christians by that time saw the steady rise and burgeoning of abuses by those administering the sacrament, while the variety of "clandestine" confessors emerging from among the laity resulted in ecclesiastical measures aimed at curbing potentially "illicit" activity within the ministry of the cure of souls.

CHAPTER ONE

Setting the Stage

The Need for Confession
and Its Biblical Beginnings

The history of repentance is as old as humankind. We each carry the remembrance of wrongdoing in burdensome satchels, hoping that eventually someone will ease them off our back. We each know the feeling of self-reproach, self-criticism, and self-blame. And we each continue to enjoy the vast landscape of free will by doing what is wrong, harmful, and unjust, and by refusing to aim for what is good, life-giving, and fair. Repentance and confession release our high-piled debts and scrub clean a sullied conscience. The Hebrew word used in the Old Testament to express repentance means "to turn," reflecting the notion of journeying and pilgrimage and an attitude and relationship between YHWH and ancient Israel that required constant vigilance and intentionality. The Greek word used in the New Testament is *metanoia*, basically denoting a "change of mind," with only subtle nuances of regret or remorse. When we repent we "turn" and "change our mind" about who we thought we were and the acceptability of what we have done. We recognize the difference between our ways and the ways God intended for us and find that we have drifted off course and out of line with the divine current. Confession, on the other hand, comes from a Latin word meaning "to agree" and "to give consent." It describes an oral activity, a moment in time when we "agree" to the difference observed between what should have been and was not, due to our actions, when we verbally lay bare and make public our off-course dealings and doings. Underlying this oral statement is an instinctual knowledge that confession might relieve us of the burdensome satchels that pull us under and that there is the vague hope of obtaining relief, forgiveness, and appropriate instructions

3

on how to make amends. While confession is the moment of disclosure, repentance and remorse have generally preceded it. An attitude of introspection and self-examination has produced the inclination to confess. This may mean that self-examination is at least as important as the act of confession itself.

In his devotional guide on preparing for the rite of confession in the Evangelical Lutheran Church, the nineteenth-century Danish philosopher Søren Kierkegaard says that true repentance from the perspective of the Eternal One "is a silent daily anxiety."[1] When we abandon the practice, terror may seize us at unexpected moments and keep us frozen and stuck in our relationship with God. Kierkegaard illustrates what he means through the story of a man who had served a sentence in prison:

> After he had suffered for his wrong acts he went back into ordinary society, improved. Then he went to a strange land, where he was not known, and where he became known for his worthy conduct. All was forgotten. Then one day there appeared a fugitive that recognized the distinguished person as his equal back in those miserable days. This was a terrifying memory to meet. A deathlike fear shook him each time this man passed. Although silent, his memory shouted in a high voice until through the voice of this vile fugitive it took on words. Then suddenly despair seized this man, who seemed to have been saved. And it seized him just because repentance was forgotten, because the improvement toward society was not the resigning of himself to God, so that in the humility of repentance he might remember what he had been.[2]

Because the man had flung away his sense of wrongdoing, his repentance was only temporary and of no lasting redemptive value. Contrary to popular belief, says Kierkegaard, we need to continually meditate on our wrongdoing, for "the longer and the more deeply one treasures [repentance], the better it becomes,"[3] and the more transformative it is on the soul. Repentance resulting from self-examination is a lifelong endeavor, occasionally surfacing in the public or private act of confession as an act of "courageous memory"[4] in recalling one's past.

---

1. Søren Kierkegaard, *Purity of Heart Is to Will One Thing: Spiritual Preparation for the Office of Confession* (New York: Harper & Brothers, 1938), 45.

2. Ibid.

3. Ibid., 47.

4. The Presbyterian pastor Thomas Long calls the confession of sins "the courage of memory" and speech, employed both inside and outside the sanctuary; see Thomas G. Long, *Testimony: Talking Ourselves Into Being Christian* (San Francisco: Jossey-Bass, 2004), 61.

In the Old Testament the acts of confession and penance occur collectively for the most part, and in dramatic fashion. The cycle follows a predictable pattern: the people of Israel sin and violate God's commandments, they experience various sorts of pestilence and calamity, they remember their wrongdoing and repent in sorrow over their wrongdoing, and they make amends by offerings and expressions of thanksgiving in cultic rituals. The first of such cultic acts of confession occurs as a result of Israel's deliverance out of Egyptian bondage. In time, several liturgical traditions emerge as marked annual periods of fasting, almsgiving, and reconciliation. Such liturgies of repentance are preserved in Isaiah 63:7–64:12, Daniel 9:4-19, and Hosea 6 and 14. Rituals of repentance typically include the tearing of one's clothes, fasting, putting on sackcloth, and sitting in ashes. In addition, the prophets, as preachers of exhortation, appear on the scene on various occasions to alert people to their wrongdoing and their perverted ways. Often their message contrasts genuine penitence with one marked by merely outward ritual. Such genuine repentance leads to obedience, rejection of idolatry, and a refusal to lean on human understanding and help. The Psalms are enlisted in worship to be sung, enacted, and used for meditation and thanksgiving, and they serve as an ongoing mnemonic tool for day-to-day reflection and exhortation. Later, during the postexilic period, it is individual confession that takes on a more prominent role. Litanies of confession, which are personal and individualistic, include Psalms 22, 33, 34, 40, 55, and 116. The penitent prays in Psalm 40: ". . . evils have encompassed me without number; my iniquities have overtaken me, until I cannot see; they are more than the hairs of my head, and my heart fails me" (v. 12). Hymns of penitence are Hannah's prayer (I Sam 2:1-10), the prayer for health and restoration of King Hezekiah (Isa 38:10-20), and the prayer of Jonah in the belly of the fish (Jonah 2:2-9). On occasion one finds stories of a personal call to repentance, such as the prophet Nathan confronting David for his adultery and the calculated murder of his mistress's husband (I Samuel 12). The story of Job serves as an example of private confession gone awry: despite Job's fierce self-examination, in which he scrutinizes his past for moral failures and offenses against the divine, he does not confess because, to his mind, there is nothing that warrants it. His so-called comforters, or self-appointed confessors, come away empty-handed. No coaxing, cajoling, insinuation, and insult can elicit from Job a confession of wrongdoing, in spite of the many ills and losses he has suffered, which suggest to his confessors the gravity of Job's concealed and unconfessed sin.

In the New Testament the cycle of confession of sin, divine deliverance, and gratitude and praise persists. However, the centrality of Jesus and developments in the early church add significant changes to the meaning and practice of confession. John the Baptist emphasizes confession of sins as a sign of repentance. Moreover, people are to show their remorse by submitting to baptism in the Jordan River. This dramatic enactment of their repentance is a form of penance and self-humiliation. The new ritual is an outward sign of an inward disposition, a public message of a privately wrought change of heart. Like the prophets of the Old Testament, John stresses that baptism is to result in changed behavior. "Even now the ax is lying at the root of the trees," he says; "every tree therefore that does not bear good fruit is cut down and thrown into the fire" (Matt 3:10). The baptized are not merely to join the crowd but to show inner conviction and a shift of attitude, a reorientation toward God in light of the Messiah's coming and the inbreaking of a new, divine order. Thereby baptism functions as a preparation for the coming kingdom and a symbol of the forgiveness of sins.

Jesus proclaims the urgency of repentance in his initial preaching. Following his temptation in the wilderness and John's arrest, Jesus' first sermon is a call to repent: "The time is fulfilled, and the kingdom of God has come near; repent, and believe in the good news" (Mark 1:14). Again, repentance is to involve the whole person, not simply outward gestures and rituals: "The tree is known by its fruits . . . For out of the abundance of the heart the mouth speaks" (Matt 12:33-34); "First clean the inside of the cup, so that the outside also may become clean" (Matt 23:26; cf. Mark 7:15). Jesus elaborates on the call to repent by giving concrete examples of what such repentance and turning entails. Anything that stands as an obstacle between the person and God is to be renounced: possessions, family ties, and human loyalties (Luke 14:33). Entrance into the kingdom involves becoming another person, someone who makes an effort at loving one's enemies, shows forgiveness and self-sacrifice, and takes on the attitude of helplessness, lowliness, and dependence on God. "Unless you change and become like children, you will never enter the kingdom of heaven" (Matt 18:3). Unless one is willing to associate and identify with the despised and lowly of society, the sinners and tax collectors and prostitutes, one cannot be part of the new heavenly rule. Jesus associates with those whom society marginalizes and even enlists them in his work: fishermen and tax collectors are his companions on an itinerant ministry and women his coworkers in spreading his teachings and the message of his resurrection. He finds acceptance and welcome largely among those who know that their lives are not what they should be: "Those who are well have no need of a physician, but those who are sick; I have come to call not the righteous but sinners" (Mark 2:17). Among his most responsive audiences are those who acknowledge their yokes and burdens, their shortcomings and failures, their disorientation and disarray; they are willing to draw near and lay bare what they lack. A socioeconomically oppressive condition had put them at an advantage in regard to repentance: they could more easily admit to and confess what was wrong in their lives and in their souls. The other side of repentance is to trust that one will be forgiven. The humiliation accompanying admission of wrongs involves courage and faith. Repentance and faith in being forgiven are coupled. Thus the Great Commission that concludes Luke's gospel reads: "Repentance and forgiveness of sins is to be proclaimed in his name to all nations" (24:47). Failure to repent, confess, and trust in God's forgiveness is not an option: either repent or "perish" (Luke 15:7, 10), either repent in this life or suffer "torment" in "hell" thereafter, either yield and listen to the warning signs or end up "in agony" (Luke 16:23-30).

In the preaching of the early apostolic church the call to repentance and confession of sins is central. Echoing John the Baptist, Peter urges the people gathered in Jerusalem during the festival of Pentecost: "Repent, and be baptized every one of you in the name of Jesus Christ so that your sins may be forgiven . . . . For the promise is for you, for your children, and for all who are far away, everyone whom the Lord our God calls to him" (Acts 2:38-39). The apostle Paul says on the Areopagus that God "commands all people everywhere to repent, because he has fixed a day on which he will have the world judged in righteousness by a man whom he has appointed, and of this he has given assurance to all by raising him from the dead" (Acts 17:30-31). For Paul this type of repentance requires faith, leading to union with Christ, the death of the old nature, the putting on of the new humanity, resurrection to newness of life, and a new creation. Repentance is turning away from evil and returning to God.

Another New Testament development is that confession of sin is equated, or often coincides, with confessing Christ. The disciple pronounces loyalty to Jesus as a way of being transformed and being allowed to enter into the new birth and the new life with Christ. This pronouncement is a public event "in the presence of many witnesses" (I Tim 6:12), presumably in connection with baptism. At the beginning of his ministry John the Baptist made confession, saying of Jesus: "Here is the Lamb of God who takes away the sins of the world!" (John 1:29). At Caesarea Philippi, Simon Peter confessed Jesus as Messiah, saying: "You are the Messiah, the son of the living God," and in turn is promised "the keys of the kingdom of heaven" that would unlock the "gates of Hades" and give power to bind and loose, to forgive and retain sins (Matt 16:16-19). Martha of Bethany did so after the death of Lazarus, saying to Jesus in response to his question whether she believed that he himself was "the resurrection and the life": "Yes, Lord, I believe that you are the Messiah, the Son of God, the one coming into the world (John 11:25-26). And the apostle Paul did so during his two-year imprisonment by Felix, the governor in Caesarea (Acts 24:14-27).

The apostolic church emphasized that confessing Jesus as Lord was a way to salvation, providing entry into the kingdom of heaven and access to life everlasting. The apostle Paul writes, "If you confess with your lips that Jesus is Lord and believe in your heart that God raised him from the dead, you will be saved. For one believes with the heart and so is justified, and one confesses with the mouth and so is saved" (Rom 10:9-10). The need for catechetical instruction encouraged the development of confessional formulas in preparation for baptism. This becomes evident in a later manuscript addition of verse 37 to the story of the Ethiopian eunuch, who upon his confession of Jesus as Lord is baptized, saying, "I believe that Jesus Christ is the Son of God" (Acts 9:37). While the quotation may not be part of the original text, it shows that the practice of linking a confessional statement regarding Jesus with baptism is a rather early development. At the same time it raises the question whether confession of Jesus as Lord was beginning to be equated with and substituted for confessing one's sins, repentance, and conversion. Another question is whether confessing Christ allowed room for postbaptismal confession with an opportunity and incentive for ongoing self-examination, or whether the new creation begun at baptism was seen as potentially equipping believers to henceforth lead a life pleasing to God.

Both the gospels and the epistles are primarily concerned with a first-time confession of sins. This is understandable since the apostolic church was mainly interested in evangelism and conversion, proclaiming the good news of Jesus, making disciples, and baptizing them in the name of the triune God. The call to conversion seemingly bypasses repentance as a preparatory step, as do the Gospel of John and the Johannine letters, which make no mention of the word repentance. Instead, the focus is on a new life, a fresh beginning, a clean slate that occurs when one meets and hears Jesus. "He told me everything I have ever done," the woman of Samaria announces to her people, so that "many Samaritans from that city believed in him because of the woman's testimony" (John 4:39). Then "many more believed" because they heard Jesus speak, and they said to the woman: "It is no longer because of what you said that we believe, for we have heard for ourselves, and we know that this is truly the Savior of the world" (John 4:41-42). Another example of rebirth and new beginning is the woman caught in adultery. After her accusers have left, too ashamed to throw the death-dealing stone at her, Jesus asks: "'Woman, where are they? Has no one condemned you?' She said, 'no one, sir.' And Jesus said, 'Neither do I condemn you. Go your way, and from now on do not sin again'" (John 8:10-11). While repentance is implied, the focus in John's writings is on the believer's movement from death to life, from darkness to light, from falsehood to truth, from hatred to love, from living for the world and oneself to living for God.

Only a few passages in the New Testament point to the problem of postbaptismal transgressions. The letter of James advises that the transgressor seek out the elders of the church for forgiveness and renewal. "The prayer of faith will save the sick, and the Lord will raise them up; and anyone who has committed sins will be forgiven. Therefore, confess your sins to one another, and pray for one another, so that you may be healed" (Jas 5:15-16). Here sickness of body and sickness of the soul are linked, both requiring outside help through intercessory prayer and confession. In fact, the one hearing confession and extending forgiveness will be privileged by God and will be forgiven in turn: "You should know that whoever brings back a sinner from wandering will save the sinner's soul from death and will cover a multitude of sins" (Jas 5:20)—presumably one's own. Another approach to postbaptismal sin is to write off those Christians who have continued sinning and not made progress toward perfection in their conduct. In the letter to the Hebrews the author instructs: "Let us go on toward perfection, leaving behind the basic teaching about Christ, and not laying again the foundation: repentance from dead works and faith toward God, instruction about baptisms, laying on of hands, resurrection of the dead, and eternal judgment. . . . For it is impossible to restore again to repentance those who have once been enlightened, and have tasted the heavenly gift, and have shared in the Holy Spirit, and have tasted the goodness of the word of God and the powers of the age to come, and then have fallen away" (Heb 6:1-5). Such people are like "worthless" soil producing only "thorns and thistles" and drinking up the rainwater, "on the verge of being cursed" and about "to be burned over" (Heb 6:7-8). The first letter of John echoes this view: "Everyone who commits sin is a child of the devil; for the devil has been sinning from the beginning. . . . Those who have been born of God do not sin, because God's word abides in them; they cannot sin, because they have been born of God" (John 3:8-9). Committing sins after baptism is considered inexcusable, and repentance that would restore one's relationship with God is not possible.

While in exile, John of Patmos issues report cards to the seven churches he may have helped found, commending two (Smyrna and Philadelphia) and calling five of them to repentance. The nature of the sins of the five churches differs enough to deserve a closer look. To the church in Ephesus, John writes: "I know your works, your toil and your patient endurance. . . . But I have this against you, that you have abandoned the love you had at first. Remember then from what you have fallen; repent, and do the works you did at first" (Rev 2:2-5a). To the church in Pergamum he writes: "I know where you are living, where Satan's throne is . . ." and that "you are holding fast to my name. But I have a few things against you: you have some there who hold to the teaching of Balaam," eating food sacrificed to idols and practicing fornication, and "some who hold to the teaching of the Nicolaitans. Repent then" (Rev 2:13-16a). To the church in Thyatira he writes: "I know your works—your love, faith, service, and patient endurance. . . . But I have this against you: you tolerate that woman Jezebel," who teaches the members to practice fornication and eat food sacrificed to idols. "Those who commit adultery with her I am throwing into great distress, unless they repent of her doings" (Rev 2:19-22). To the church in Sardis he writes: "I know your work; you have a name of being alive, but you are dead. Wake up, and strengthen what remains and is on the point of death, for I have not found your works perfect in the sight of my God. Remember then what you received and heard; obey it, and repent" (Rev 3:1-3). And to the church in Laodicea he writes: "I know your works; you are neither cold nor hot. I wish that you were either cold or hot. So, because you are lukewarm, and neither cold nor hot, I am about to spit you out of my mouth. For you say, 'I am rich, I have prospered, and I need nothing.' You do not realize that you are wretched, pitiable, poor, blind, and naked. . . . I reprove and discipline those whom I love. Be earnest, therefore, and repent" (Rev 3:15-19). While the churches, and more precisely the angels of the respective churches, are addressed, the individual members and leaders are responsible for the church's misguided behavior, the violating of Christian conduct, the attitude of permissiveness. It is significant that the particular sins of each church are a representative sample of the grave sins that two hundred years later would require Christians who were found guilty of any of them to enroll in the order of penitents. The sins listed in Revelation are: a sagging love for Christ or a falling away (apostasy), idolatry, sexual immorality, and pride (the root cause of all other sins), respectively. But all is not lost for the churches: There are available remedies and measures of penance that will restore members to God: "Do the works you did at first" (Rev 2:5); "hold fast to what you have until I come" (Rev 2:25); "wake up, and strengthen what remains and is on the point of death" (Rev 3:2); "buy from me gold refined by fire so that you may be rich; and white robes to clothe you and to keep the shame of your nakedness from being seen; and salve to anoint your eyes so that you may see" (Rev 3:18). From the letters of Ignatius, the second-century bishop of Antioch, we know of the ministry of one of these churches in need of repentance: the church at Ephesus, which Ignatius praises repeatedly for its members' courage in opposition to false teachers, their devotion to God, and their maturity in Christ.[5] We can assume that the Ephesians had yielded to John's call to repentance and confession, most likely as a community at large.

---

5. Ignatius, *Epistle to the Ephesians*, in *The Ante-Nicene Fathers*, vol. 1, eds. Alexander Roberts and James Donaldson (Repr. Peabody, MA: Hendrickson, 1999), 49–58.

CHAPTER TWO

The Early Church and the Rise of Public Confession

The early theologians and teachers of the church held that salvation began with one's baptism. Upon the baptismal confession of Christ, the sins one had committed up until then were forgiven, and one entered into a rebirth with Christ as a new creation, born of water and the Spirit, with a clean slate before God. People feared, however, that they were likely to continue sinning, especially in light of civic pressures and the persecutions of Christians. Many compromised on their Christian witness, for example, by submitting to pagan rituals or emperor worship. This meant that increasingly converts and catechumens began to put off baptism until shortly before their death: they refused to risk losing their salvation and being denied by Christ in the afterlife as a result of denying him in the face of civic threats in the here and now. Still, the problem of postbaptismal sin remained and the question became how to deal with it effectively, what sins qualified for forgiveness, and how often one could be forgiven. According to Clement of Alexandria, writing in the mid-second century, one needed to distinguish between two types of repentance: the first is the one obtained in baptism, the second is that of living in the fear of the Lord. "He, then, who from among the Gentiles and from that old life has betaken himself to faith," writes Clement, "has obtained forgiveness of sins once. But he who has sinned after this, on his repentance, though he obtain pardon, ought to fear; "for there is no more remaining sacrifice for sins left," only "a certain fearful looking for of judgment and fiery indignation."[1]

---

1. Clement of Alexandria, *Stromata* ("Miscellanies"), in *Ante-Nicene Fathers*, vol. 2, eds. Alexander Roberts and James Donaldson (Peabody, MA: Hendrickson, 1999), 360–61.

In general, the early teachers of the church agreed that Christians could receive forgiveness of minor postbaptismal sins. According to Origen, Clement's former student, to quickly recognize one's error was key. "If a brief lapsus" were to "take place, and the individual quickly repent and return to himself, he may not utterly fall away, but retrace his steps, and return to his former place, and again make good that which had been lost by his negligence." Such speed allowed one to "repair those losses which up to that time are only recent, and recover" the knowledge that had only slightly slipped from the mind.[2] Regarding major sins, however, there was no wavering: members were excommunicated without hope for restoration in accordance with the church's teachings since apostolic times.[3] A case in point is the presbyter Hippolytus (160–235), who insisted that Christians be saints in the literal sense of the word, with the effect that his church in Rome was frequently purged of those showing unsaintly qualities. In the opinion of his fellow presbyter Callistus, on the other hand, sinners could do postbaptismal penance, so that Callistus not only retained members but kept adding to his flock those who had been previously excommunicated by Hippolytus. According to church historian Burton Scott Easton, "This decision of Callistus was nothing short of revolutionary, and it was destined to change the ideal of church membership for all time,"[4] so that in the interest of church growth the standards for church membership were relaxed.

Christians who had committed grave sins such as idolatry, adultery, murder, and apostasy were no longer excommunicated, but were allowed to make public confession: they were to enroll in the order of penitents, keep separate from the other members in worship, and undergo a course of prayer, fasting, and almsgiving. After penance, which could last several years or decades, they were restored to the communion of the church and welcomed back to the Eucharist. An early fourth-century litany, patterned perhaps after a second-century church order, has members pray for the assembled penitents during the imposition of hands: "Look

2. Origen, *De Principiis*, in *Ante-Nicene Fathers*, vol. 4, eds. Roberts and Donaldson, 256.

3. This view is largely based on the letter to the Hebrews: "For if we willfully persist in sin after having received the knowledge of the truth, there no longer remains a sacrifice for sins" (10:26); "for by a single offering he has perfected for all time those who are sanctified" (10:14).

4. Burton Scott Easton, "Introduction," *The Apostolic Tradition of Hippolytus*, translation, introduction, and notes by Burton Scott Easton (Cambridge: Cambridge University Press, 1934, 1962), 23.

down upon these persons who have bended the neck of their soul and body to Thee; for Thou desirest not the death of a sinner, but his repentance, that he turn from his wicked way, and live. Thou who didst accept the repentance of the Ninevites, who willest that all men be saved, and come to the acknowledgment of the truth; who didst accept of that son who had consumed his substance in riotous living, with the bowels of a father, on account of his repentance; do Thou now accept of the repentance of Thy supplicants: for there is no man that will not sin."[5] During times of persecution, apostasy was not uncommon, but during the Decian persecution of 250–51, North Africans were able to buy certificates saying they had offered sacrifice in a pagan temple, thus hiding the fact that they were Christians. Cyprian, the bishop of Carthage at the time, has stern words for these deceivers, and he calls them the "lapsed."[6] They falsely imagined themselves martyrs, saying: "My mind stood firm and my faith was strong, and my soul struggled long, unshaken with the torturing pains; but when, with the renewed barbarity of the most cruel judge, wearied out as I was, the scourges were now tearing, the clubs bruised me, the rack strained me, the claw dug into me, the fire roasted me; my flesh deserted me in the struggle, the weakness of my bodily frame gave way—not my mind, but my body, yielded in the suffering" (440). In truth, says Cyprian, these Christians had "defiled their consciences with certificates," and were now no less polluted than those who had engaged in pagan sacrifices (444). Urging them to submit to public repentance, he says: "Let us turn to the Lord with our whole heart, and, expressing our repentance for our sin with true grief, let us entreat God's mercy. Let our soul lie low before Him. Let our mourning atone to Him. Let all our hope lean upon Him. He Himself tells us in what manner we ought to ask. 'Turn ye,' He says, 'to me with all your heart, and at the same time with fasting, and with weeping, and with mourning; and rend your hearts, and not your garments'" (445).

Initially, repentance was allowed Christians only once in a lifetime following baptism. This view found practical expression in the penance process, popular between the late second and the fifth centuries, in which one enrolled only once and that came to be known as the "second

---

5. *Constitutions of the Holy Apostles,* in *Ante-Nicene Fathers,* vol. 7, eds. Roberts and Donaldson, 485.

6. Cyprian, *Treatise III: On the Lapsed,* in *Ante-Nicene Fathers,* vol. 5, eds. Roberts and Donaldson, 440–45.

baptism"—not of water but of tears. In his treatise *On Repentance,*[7] dating from the late second century, Tertullian provides the rationale: People "in general, after escaping shipwreck" will "declare divorce with ship and sea; and by cherishing the memory of the danger, honour the benefit conferred by God," namely their deliverance (662). However, that "most stubborn foe of ours" assaults Christians through "carnal concupiscence," "worldly enticements," "fear of earthly power," and lures into "perverse traditions." Even though "the gate of forgiveness has been shut and fastened up with the bar of baptism," God has allowed a small crack: "In the vestibule He has stationed the second repentance for opening to such as knock: but now *once for all*, because now for the second time; but never more because the last time it had been in vain" (663). Tertullian calls this process a second (and only) repentance, or *exomologēsis*, an "outward confession," because it involves external acts of penance and "may not be exhibited in the conscience alone" (664). It is "a discipline" for "prostration and humiliation," marked by extended periods of prayer and fasting and by the simplicity of the penitent's dress (sackcloth) and food. While such a discipline "abases the man, it raises him; while it covers him with squalor, it renders him more clean; while it accuses, it excuses; while it condemns, it absolves" (664). To those deterred by the severity of penance and hesitant to confess publicly, Tertullian responds: "Is it better to be damned in secret than absolved in public? . . . Miserable it is to be cut, and cauterized, and racked with the pungency of some (medicinal) powder: still, the things which heal by unpleasant means do, by the benefit of the cure, excuse their own offensiveness" (664–65).

As more and more "lapsed" Christians enrolled in the program of making public penance, a system of grades or degrees evolved, modeled on the gradual admission of catechumens for baptism. According to Monika Hellwig,

> The five grades of penitents were named and defined by their relation to the liturgy. The "mourners" were those altogether outside who pleaded with the faithful for their prayers and for readmission. The "hearers" were those permitted to stand just within the entrance hall of the church and only during the "mass of the catechumens," that is, during the Scripture readings and homily. The "fallers" (prostrators) were allowed outside the nave of the church in a posture of self-abasement . . . [and] allowed in the nave only as long as the catechumens [were] . . . . The "bystanders" were

7. Tertullian, *On Repentance*, in *Ante-Nicene Fathers*, vol. 3, eds. Roberts and Donaldson, 662–65.

permitted to be present for the whole liturgy of the faithful, but were not admitted to communion. The "faithful" were those admitted to full communion.[8]

This gradual process could stretch out over a period of several years, even decades, depending on the gravity of one's sin.

One might wonder to what degree penitents had the opportunity for oral confession. In addition to the outward signs of penance, such as wearing sackcloth and ashes, being relegated to a certain place within or outside the church during the liturgy, and exercising penance in self-examination and extended periods of prayer, what were the oral signs of penance and what the occasion that preceded enrollment in the order of penitents? Most likely it was during an official meeting between bishop and penitent that the nature of the offense and the thoughts of the penitent were assessed. According to John T. McNeill and Helena M. Gamer "it is incredible that *exomologēsis* did not at the outset, in accordance with the primary meaning of the word, involve explicit and frank confession." While bishops and presbyters controlled the penitential process, it would have been only "natural that private consultation should precede the *exomologēsis*," so that this consultation was regarded as "the official confession."[9] Other instances distinguish private soul guidance from official confession. For example, both Clement and Origen recommended private pastoral consultations for the faithful, while Ambrose of Milan heard the confessions of penitents and "told none but God" what he had learned.[10] In addition, Christians could confess everyday, lighter sins by open acknowledgment in worship. As indicated by the *Teaching of the Twelve Apostles* (*Didache*), dating from the early second century, faults of this nature were confessed as part of mutual and public confession preceding the Eucharist each Sunday.[11]

8. Monika K. Hellwig, *Sign of Reconciliation and Conversion* (Wilmington, DE: Michael Glazier, 1982), 36; her description is based on an account by Gregory Thaumaturgus (213–270), *Canonical Epistles*, canon 11.

9. John T. McNeill and Helena M. Gamer, *Medieval Handbooks of Penance: A Translation of the Principal* Libri Poenitentiales *and Selections From Related Documents* (New York: Columbia University Press, 1938, 1990), 11.

10. Ibid., 10; the quotation is from Ambrose's biographer, Paulinus.

11. Ibid., 6; see also *Didache* 4: "But every Lord's day do ye gather yourselves together, and break bread, and give thanksgiving after having confessed your transgressions, that your sacrifice may be pure. But let no one that is at variance with his fellow come together with you, until they be reconciled, that your sacrifice may not be profaned," in *Ante-Nicene Fathers*, vol. 7, ed. Roberts and Donaldson, 381.

Beginning with the fifth century, Christians could repent, confess their sins, and be forgiven on several occasions and eventually an unlimited number of times. With the rise of desert monasticism in Egypt and Syria and the subsequent activity of the Irish monks and the Celtic church, the practice of public confession in the West was eventually transformed into private confession and gave rise to the accompanying practice of spiritual direction and counsel.

CHAPTER THREE

The Rise of Private Confession and Spiritual Direction

When Augustine, bishop of Hippo, published his *Confessions* in 397, the Mediterranean world took note: Here were private confessions and sexual sins made public in what could be called the first autobiographical confessional work of a Christian. Augustine's primary concern had been that "a craving for sexual gratification" fettered him "like a tight-drawn chain."[1] His release was occasioned by a visitor named Ponticianus, who had come to his house on a business matter and shared with Augustine and his friend Alypius his knowledge of the life of the monk Antony of Egypt. Unfamiliar with monasticism, including the fact that a monastery existed right outside Milan under the auspices of his mentor Ambrose, bishop of Milan, Augustine heard how two men at Trier, upon meeting some monks and reading from *The Life of Antony*, had resolved to call off their marriages and, along with their fiancées, had committed themselves to a life of celibacy. In the course of Ponticianus's story Augustine was forced to recognize "how despicable I was, how misshapen and begrimed, filthy and festering."[2] In his conversion he was influenced by a tradition that valued private confession, namely, that of the desert fathers and mothers of Egypt.

In the early fourth and fifth centuries many Christians had become disenchanted with the institutionalized church and its alignment with the local and civic authorities and power structures. Some left the cities for a life of solitude and silence in the wilderness of Egypt, Syria, and Palestine

---

1. Augustine, *Confessions*, in *The Works of Saint Augustine—A Translation for the Twenty-first Century*, vol. 1/1, trans. Maria Boulding, ed. John E. Rotelle (Hyde Park, NY: New City Press, 1997), 196–97.
2. Ibid., 198.

in hopes of recovering the essence of the Christian faith. Antony (d. 356), whose life had been chronicled by Bishop Athanasius of Alexandria between 355 and 362, was one of them: for more than forty years he lived in a cave in Egypt with a minimum of food and sleep, devoted to prayer and self-examination in a community of like-minded solitaries and ascetics. These desert fathers and mothers, or *abbas* and *ammas*, as they were called, soon became known for their wisdom, counsel, and purity of faith. While they regarded themselves as "sinners in need of mercy," outsiders viewed them as holy people, "nearer to heaven than earth, and therefore available as intercessors."[3] As a visitor wrote, "It is clear to all who dwell there that through them the world is kept in being, and that through them too human life is preserved and honoured by God."[4] As the news of their lifestyle spread, bishops from nearby towns and from far abroad came to visit and were impressed with the Christian life they observed, so that they wished to share what they saw. A saying attributed to Pachomius sums it up: "If you see a man pure and humble, that is a great vision. For what is greater than such a vision, to see the invisible God in a visible man."[5] Since visiting bishops could not bring the entire community of ascetics to the people of their parish, they resolved to introduce some of the ascetics' practices in their parishes during set times of the church year: the practices of sustained prayer, fasting, self-examination, and penance during the weeks before Easter, later known as the season of Lent.

One of the central virtues of the holy men and women of the Eastern desert was discernment. Disciples who would come to live in the community were asked to seek out a spiritual father or mother in whom they could confide their struggles and transgressions and joys so as to gain a better understanding of themselves. "If he is able to, a monk ought to tell his elders confidently how many steps he takes, and how many drops of water he drinks in his cell, in case he is in error about it."[6] The purpose of such a close relationship was that the younger learn from the elder by example and observation, while developing a trusting and intimate relationship that was conducive to confession and dialogue. For example,

---

3. Benedicta Ward, "Introduction," in eadem, *The Desert Fathers: Sayings of the Early Christian Monks* (New York: Penguin Putnam, 2003), xi.

4. *The Lives of the Desert Fathers*, trans. Norman Russell, introduced by Benedicta Ward, SLG (Kalamazoo: Cistercian Publications, 1981), 50.

5. Ibid., 45.

6. *Apophthegmata*, Alpha Antonii, n. 38, in *The Sayings of the Desert Fathers: The Alphabetical Collection*, trans. Benedicta Ward (Kalamazoo: Cistercian Publications, 1975), 7; quoted in Kenneth Leech, *Soul Friend: Spiritual Direction in the Modern World* (Harrisburg, PA: Morehouse, 2001), 37.

a monk would confess to an elder that he could not find any peace in his cell. The advice given was: "Go attach yourself to a man who fears God, humble yourself before him, give up your will to him, and then you will receive consolation from God."[7] In general, the counsel of the elder or spiritual guide given upon confession or inquiry was no trifling matter; rather, it was considered a charismatic word that, when obeyed unfailingly, would put the sinner back on the road to salvation.

The purpose of confession in the desert communities was to find remedies for the cure of the disciple's soul rather than conveying judgment and sentencing. Both major and minor sins were confessed, with larger offenses drawing on the collective wisdom of the elders. Topics addressed in conversation between disciple and elder ranged from matters of charity, hospitality, patience, and humility to greed, ostentatiousness, lewdness, and lust. The relationship of trust is evident in a story of a brother attacked by lust. "He began to struggle and to fast more, and for fourteen years he guarded himself against this temptation and did not give in to it. After that he went to the community and told to them all what he was suffering. A decree was made, and for a week they all fasted on his behalf, praying to God continually; and so his temptation ceased."[8] Sin was not kept secret but laid before the community as a plea for help.

Another story illustrates the compassion shown a sinning brother and the resistance to dividing members into sinners and saints. "At that time a meeting was held at Sketis about a brother who had sinned. The Fathers spoke, but Abba Pior kept silent. Later, he got up and went out. He took a sack and filled it with sand and carried it on his shoulder; then he put a little sand into a small bag that he carried in front of him. When the Fathers asked him what this meant he said, 'In this sack which contains much sand, are my sins which are many; I have put them behind me so that I might not be troubled about them and so that I might not weep. And behold, here are the little sins of my brother which are in front of me, and I spend my time judging them. This is not right. Rather, I ought to carry my sins in front of me and concern myself with them, begging God to forgive me.' The Fathers stood up and said, 'Verily, this is the way of salvation.'"[9] Not punishment for sins committed but the soul's

---

7. Thomas Merton, "The Spiritual Father in the Desert Tradition," *Cistercian Studies* 3, no. 1 (1968): 3–23, at 17; quoted in Leech, *Soul Friend*, 38.

8. *The Desert Fathers: Sayings*, 37.

9. See "Sayings of the Desert Fathers. Selected Sayings from the *Apophthegmata patrum*," trans. M. C. Steenberg, at www.monachos.net/content/patristics/patristictexts/99 -sayings-of-the-desert-fathers-selections.

healing and restoration was the purpose of confession. Not the handing out of concrete advice, but patience in waiting until the penitent could see his or her faults was the confessor's task. Abba Poemen is reported to have said, "If a man sins and denies it, saying, 'I have not sinned,' do not correct him, or you will destroy any intention he might have of changing. If you say, 'Do not be cast down, my brother, but be careful about that in future,' you will move his heart to repent."[10]

The length of penance differed drastically from the penitential system in which penitents could be enrolled for years and even decades. When a monk in the desert volunteered to do penance for three years, Poemen replied: "'That is a long time.' The brother said, 'Are you telling me to do penance for one year then?' Again he said, 'That is a long time.' Some of the people nearby suggested, 'A penance of forty days?' Again he said, 'That is a long time.' Then he added, 'I think that if someone is whole-heartedly penitent, and determined not to sin that sin again, God will accept a penance of even three days.'"[11] Viewed against the backdrop of Western penitential practices, discipline in the desert community seems more bearable and humane. The release of the soul's burdensome and oppressive forces was paramount and the penitential process less rigid than that of the West.

The desert monks strove to be repentant even before their concrete actions would warrant it. This meant searching the heart for times when one had strayed from good in thought only and being sorry for it. Abba Poemen said, "Grief is twofold: it creates good and it keeps away evil."[12] Hyperichius said, "The watchful monk works night and day to pray continually: but if his heart is broken and lets tears flow, that calls God down from heaven to have mercy."[13] And Ammon advised a monk, "Go and meditate like the criminals in prison. They keep asking, where is the judge, when will he come? and because they are waiting for him they dread their punishment. The monk should always be waiting for his trial, chiding his soul, saying: 'Alas, how shall I stand before the judgement seat of Christ? How shall I give an account of my actions?' If you always meditate like this, you will be saved."[14]

Primary among the monk's spiritual tasks was self-examination. Abba Antony advises: "Now daily let each one recount to himself his actions

---

10. *The Desert Fathers: Sayings*, 100.
11. Ibid., 98–99.
12. Ibid., 14.
13. Ibid., 15.
14. Ibid., 12.

on the day and night, and if he sinned, let him stop. But if he has not sinned, let him avoid boasting . . . and persist in the good" until the coming of the Lord.[15] As an aid for self-examination and a device to curb sinful behavior and thought Antony counsels the monks to imagine themselves as being continually at private confession: "Let each one of us note and record our actions and the stirrings of our souls as though we were going to give an account to each other. And you can be sure that, being particularly ashamed to have them made known, we would stop sinning and even meditating on something evil. For who wants to be seen sinning? Or who, after sinning, would not prefer to lie, wanting to remain unknown? So then, just as we would not practice fornication if we were observing each other directly, so also we will doubtless keep ourselves from impure thoughts, ashamed to have them known, if we record our thoughts as if reporting them to each other."[16] Such an exercise of imaginary confession was as if one were continually guarded by an extra set of eyes, even the eyes of God.

Unlike in later monastic communities in the West, the desert monks' life was marked by physical labor and less by the study, memorization, and exposition of Scripture. Still, it is likely that the monks of the desert used the Psalms as a tool for private and communal worship, reflection, self-examination, and repentance. Athanasius, the author of *The Life of Antony*, in his letter to Marcellinus cites the reasons for the longstanding, habitual use of the Psalms in worship and their memorization by Christians: "For the Psalms comprehend the one who observes the commandment as well as the one who transgresses, and the action of each. And it is necessary to be constrained by these, and either as a keeper of the law or as its transgressor, to speak the words that have been written."[17] Moreover, hearing and reciting or singing the Psalms allows "these words to become like a mirror" of one's conscience, for "he who hears the one reading receives the song that is recited as being about him, and either, when he is convicted by his conscience, being pierced, he will repent, or hearing of the hope that resides in God, and of the succor available to believers . . . he exults and begins to give thanks to God." Thus, in addition to serving as a teaching tool about the life of Christ as foreshadowed in the Psalms, they serve "for a remembrance of the emotions in

---

15. Athanasius, *The Life of Antony* and *The Letter to Marcellinus*, trans. and intro. by Robert C. Gregg (New York: Paulist Press, 1980), 72.

16. Ibid., 73.

17. Ibid., 110.

us, and a chastening of our life."[18] The use of the Psalter would become a staple among later monastic communities in the West, as well as in the life of Christians intent on searching their own consciences and willing to seek forgiveness for their sins from the Lord and one another. The practice is illustrated by the early Irish books on penance, prescribing the Psalter as the chief liturgy of penance and listing the repeated singing of psalms[19] or portions of them as a favorite assignment.

By the end of the fourth century, monks from Ireland introduced the desert fathers' and mothers' practices to their homeland, among them the practice of private confession, and incorporated them into their monasteries. According to David L. Fleming private confession "seems to have grown out of the practice of [Irish] monks who sought direction for their spiritual development by telling their faults as well as virtues to a spiritual father," so that "eventually, this monastic practice became common among all church members" in the West.[20] By the fifth century the renewal was ripe to happen, since "penance, if practiced at all, occurred largely on one's death-bed" and "penance in time of health was nearly lost."[21]

---

18. Ibid., 111.

19. The "Penitential of Cummean" (ca. 650) says: "He who is willingly polluted during sleep, shall arise and sing nine psalms in order, kneeling. On the following day he shall live on bread and water; or he shall sing thirty psalms, kneeling at the end of each" (104); or "if anyone, diligently garrulous, injures his brother's good name, he shall do penance in silence for one or two days; but if he did it in conversation, he shall sing twelve psalms" (110); the "Penitential of Columban" (ca. 600) says about monks: "If anyone holds a conversation with a secular person without an order, twenty-four psalms. If anyone when he has completed his task fails to ask for another and does something without an order, he shall sing twenty-four psalms"; see John T. McNeill and Helena M. Gamer, *Medieval Handbooks of Penance: A Translation of the Principal* Libri Poenitentiales *and Selections From Related Documents* (New York: Columbia University Press, 1938, 1990), 264.

20. David L. Fleming, SJ, "Reconciliation," in *The Complete Library of Christian Worship*, vol. 6, ed. Robert E. Webber (Peabody, MA: Hendrickson, 1993), 321–25, at 323.

21. Oscar D. Watkins, *A History of Penance*, vol. 1 (London: Longmans, 1920), 465.

The Practice of Private Confession

The rigors of public penance may have contributed to its decline both from the perspective of the laity, who had to endure its humiliation, and the clergy, who had to administer it. At the same time the waning popularity of public penance coincided with the church's rapid growth, the social prestige associated with church membership, and an increasing number of members who were Christian in name only. About the middle of the fifth century Salvian of Marseilles observes: "How changed is the Christian people now from its former character."[1] Citing Peter's measures against Ananias and Sapphira (Acts 5:1-5) and Paul's expulsion of a sinner from the church (1Cor 5:5), Salvian attests to a state at the time in which almost all church members are guilty of some grave offense. "Some of them, I suppose," he writes, "are relying on a foolish assurance of long life, or the intention of eventual penitence."[2] In the words of John McNeill and Helena Gamer, "There are a few sincere ascetics and a small minority of respectable clergy, but lay life is little affected by religion and quite untouched, it would appear, by any systematically practiced penitential discipline."[3] The result is that crimes and immoral acts go unpunished, and offenders are only on occasion forced to make amends in accordance with Germanic law. Gregory the Great, for example, looks primarily to God rather than the state or the church to right the wrongs

1. Salvian, *On the government of God; a treatise wherein are shown by argument and by examples drawn from the abandoned society of the times the ways of God toward His creatures. Indited by Salvian as a warning and counsel* 6, trans. Eva M. Sanford (New York: Octagon Books, 1966), 158; quoted in John T. McNeill and Helena M. Gamer, *Medieval Handbooks of Penance: A Translation of the Principal* Libri Poenitentiales *and Selections From Related Documents* (New York: Columbia University Press, 1938, 1990), 20.

2. Salvian, *On the government of God*, trans. Sanford, 195; quoted in McNeill and Gamer, *Medieval Handbooks*, 20.

3. McNeill and Gamer, *Medieval Handbooks*, 21.

of his flock, and the rare mention he makes of penitent sinners and ex-communication imply the absence of a functioning system of repentance for healthy persons. In the fourth century Ambrose could still describe penitents "whose tears had hallowed a furrow on their faces, and who prostrated themselves on the ground to be trampled upon by the feet of everyone."[4] By the fifth century such scenes were apparently rare, and still more so by the sixth.

The practice of private confession is closely linked with the monks of Ireland and Wales, who had learned the practice from the desert fathers and mothers in Egypt, Syria, and Palestine. However, it is unlikely that the monks had visited these desert sages. More probable is that the monastic ideals of Egypt had spread to Palestine, Syria, Mesopotamia, and Greece, then into the west to Africa, Italy, and Gaul, whence they were carried to Britain, then Scotland and Ireland.[5] The sea routes along the coasts of Europe connecting with those of the Eastern Mediterranean enhanced not only the exchange of goods but also of ideas and Christian practices. Today the visual link between Celtic and desert spirituality still remains. According to Esther de Waal it is "visually represented by the dominating presence of the figures of St. Antony of Egypt and St. Paul of Thebes on so many of the Irish high crosses."[6] The biographies of these saints, one written by Athanasius, the other by Jerome, had become widely popular among the Irish by the sixth century. Despite the time gap separating the beginnings of desert spirituality in the fourth century and Celtic spirituality originating in the sixth and seventh centuries, many similarities exist. These are noticeable in the groups' emphasis on solitude and the ascetic life, the need for a mentor or spiritual guide, and the call to become a spiritual mentor for others in turn. In addition, Celtic descriptions of saints, or hagiographies, were inspired by and some of the contents borrowed as a whole from such writings as Athanasius's *Life of Antony*, Sulpicius Severus's *Life of Martin* (of Tours), and John Cassian's *Conferences.*[7] These writings describe the early stages

---

4. *The Life and Times of St. Ambrose, by P. de Labriolle,* trans. Herbert Wilson (St. Louis: Herder, 1928), 286; quoted in McNeill and Gamer, *Medieval Handbooks,* 22.

5. According to John R. Walsh and Thomas Bradley, "Monasticism in Ireland came, then, indirectly from France and directly from Britain, but definitely along two distinct veins, one from northern Britain and the other from Wales"; see John R. Walsh and Thomas Bradley, *A History of the Irish Church 400–700 A.D.* (Dublin: Columba Press, 1991), 53–54.

6. Esther de Waal, "Introduction," in *Beasts and Saints,* trans. Helen Waddell (Grand Rapids: Eerdmans, 1934, 1995), xxii.

7. See Edward C. Sellner, *Wisdom of the Celtic Saints* (Notre Dame, IN: Ave Maria Press, 1993), 28; also Carolinne White, *Early Christian Lives* (New York: Penguin Books, 1998), xxxvi–xxxviii.

of monastic practices in Egypt and Gaul (Sulpicius) and an ever-growing concern with waging war on sin and temptation with the possibility of their treatment through confession and penance. Much like physicians who sought to describe and classify diseases and their symptoms, some of the early founders of monasticism in the desert and in the Celtic churches sought to assess and classify the sins of their charges so as to bring about treatment and relief. In private conversation the monastic guide or elder would gain an understanding of the disciple's spiritual temptations and sins by due listening, then giving counsel and offering spiritual remedies for relief.

In time several lists of sins evolved that the confessor would use for assessing the disease of the penitent's soul and finding appropriate remedies. Primary among those who wrote such lists are Evagrius Ponticus (345–99) and John Cassian (360–433). Having been ordained a deacon by Gregory of Nazianzus, Evagrius lived as an ascetic at a Jerusalem monastery and later moved to Egypt, where he became a hermit. Perhaps the first to systematically record and organize the sayings of the desert fathers, he also wrote, among other things, an influential work on practical spirituality, the so-called *Practicus*. Cassian, who was ordained a deacon by John Chrysostom, may have spent some time in a monastery in Bethlehem, where he was acquainted with Jerome. Later he, together with his friend Germanus, visited several monastic desert communities in Egypt, moving on eventually to Constantinople and Rome before settling in Gaul, where he founded two monasteries. Cassian's two major works on Christian spirituality are the *Institutes* (420–429) and the *Conferences*. Both Evagrius and Cassian provide detailed advice in their works for disciples and aspiring monks, and both distinguish eight principal vices or sins, the forerunners of the seven capital sins of Roman Catholicism and the predecessor of a sin-based personality type indicator, the Enneagram, which lists nine sin types. Cassian's order of the eight principal vices is as follows: gluttony, fornication (lust), avarice, anger, dejection (*tristitia*), languor (*accedia*), vainglory, and pride. Foremost among the sins is pride because it is the source of all the others. Most of the later Celtic lists were compiled on the basis of this list. On the other hand, Gregory the Great revised Cassian's order of treatment of the deadly sins, reducing them to seven. He emphasizes pride and lust, of which the first "is a revolt of the spirit against God" and the second "a revolt of the flesh against the spirit."[8] Again the primary sin is pride, from

---

8. Cf. Sirach 10:13; quoted in McNeill and Gamer, *Medieval Handbooks*, 19.

which derive vainglory, envy, anger, dejection, avarice, gluttony, and lust, along with a host of sub-sins associated with each of these strands. Gregory's list is followed by most medieval writers and appears in the penitential literature of the ninth century and onward.

Having lists of sins was designed to help the confessor, even the most inexperienced and uneducated, match the sin with the appropriate remedy of penance. These lists developed into books, also known as penitentials, and circulated initially only in the early Celtic monasteries. By the late sixth century these penitentials were in use in Frankish lands, by the late seventh century in England, by the late eighth century in Italy, and by the early ninth in Spain.[9] Celtic monks had been carrying the practice of private confession to the continent and elsewhere.

The spread of the penitential books is due in large part to the migratory activity of Celtic monks. This had little in common with the modern missionary movement and evangelical zeal. Rather, it was ascetical in nature, a form of mortification and self-denial, of leaving one's possessions and familiar surroundings for rocky islands and fierce landscapes whose inhabitants were different in race, custom, and language. Celtic scholar Tomás Ó Fiaich points out that monks who left Ireland to set out for France, for example, "had little hope of ever seeing their native land and their family relations again, and this was the sacrifice which they embraced eagerly for the love of God"; it was "a call from God to sacrifice what was most dear to them."[10] Leaving one's home for good was considered the ultimate sacrifice one could make for Christ.[11] It was called the "green martyrdom," in recognition that initially the movement meant retreating to the woods, mountains, and islands off the coast in a solitary, hermitlike existence, a choice of lifestyle modeled after that of the desert monastics of Egypt. Thomas Cahill sees similarities of motivation between the ascetics and monks of Ireland and those of Egypt: both were "lacking the purification rite of persecution," so they "devised a new form of holiness."[12] This green martyrdom contrasted with "red martyrdom," being willing to die for the sake of one's faith, or "white martyrdom," in which one joined a monastic community (whose members might have worn white robes) as a lifelong act of penance. Typically

9. McNeill and Gamer, *Medieval Handbooks*, 26.

10. Tomás Ó Fiaich, "Irish Monks on the Continent," in *An Introduction to Celtic Christianity*, ed. James Mackey, 103–4 (Edinburgh: T & T Clark, 1989).

11. The Celts even had a word, *hiraeth*, for this extreme longing for home associated with the green martyrdom; see Sellner, *Wisdom of the Celtic Saints*, 23.

12. Thomas Cahill, *How the Irish Saved Civilization: The Untold Story of Ireland's Heroic Role From the Fall of Rome to the Rise of Medieval Europe* (New York: Random House, 1995), 151.

these missionaries or so-called *peregrini* traveled on foot in groups of twelve plus a leader, emulating Jesus and the twelve apostles; they wore a white tunic covered by a cowl, were tonsured, and carried a staff, a water bottle, and perhaps a gospel book. Often groups included women also. Once they reached such lands as France, Belgium, and Germany, the monks were moved by compassion for the people and spurred on to share the good news of the gospel: they began preaching to their pagan neighbors and to the many Christians who had fallen into immorality, grown lukewarm, or lapsed in faith. As the hermit's cell expanded into a monastery, the practices of the Irish church became more widely known among its neighbors. In addition to the monks' emphasis on self-sacrifice, the duty of hospitality, the linking of the monastery with pastoral work, and the study of the Scriptures and especially the Psalms, they also brought with them the practices of private confession and the use of penitential books with prescribed penances.

Among the first Christian writers to explore and commend at great length the practice of private confession is John Cassian. According to Edward C. Sellner, his "writings on desert elders were among the most influential of all writings about desert spirituality in the early Celtic Church."[13] After his stay with the desert monastics in Egypt, Cassian had moved to Gaul to become abbot of St. Victor's at Marseilles, convinced of the importance of a wise, holy, and experienced teacher, soul guide, and confessor in the life of every Christian. In his *Conferences* Cassian describes how in Egypt he had observed students and teachers meeting in so-called conferences to openly and honestly acknowledge to each other their struggles and sinful behavior. The primary task of the elder during these meetings was not to give advice or pronounce judgment, but to evoke an emotional response in the disciple leading to repentance, remorse, and change of heart. The modeling of such self-examination and confession on the part of the elder was crucial, as it invited the disciple to follow suit. To that end the elder would disclose personal struggles and attempts at finding a cure, so that often, according to Cassian, "we were cured without any shame or confusion on our part, since without saying anything we learnt both the remedies and the causes of sins which beset us."[14] In turn the younger monks were expected to acknowledge

---

13. Edward C. Sellner, *The Celtic Soul Friend: A Trusted Guide for Today* (Notre Dame, IN: Ave Maria Press, 2002), 74.

14. John Cassian, *Institutes*, II.3, in *A Select Library of Nicene and Post-Nicene Fathers of the Christian Church*, vol. 11, ed. Philip Schaff and Henry Wace, 234 (Grand Rapids: Eerdmans, 1986).

their own secret sins, but not without first taking a preliminary inventory of them by thorough, private self-examination. "All the corners of our heart," writes Cassian, "must therefore be examined thoroughly," so as to "destroy the lairs of the wild beasts within us and the hiding places of the venomous serpents."[15] After this preparation the disciple was to share these insights with the elder and confess orally. Through such self-disclosure destructive behavioral patterns were brought into the open and potential remedies could be prescribed. Only after the disciple has orally acknowledged sins in confession, says Cassian, is "the grip of this diabolic tyranny" abated and "forever laid to rest."[16]

Several features of private confession as used by the Celtic monks and missionaries are noteworthy. First, confession was to take place in private at every stage, and so were the acts of penance. Unlike in the public penitential practices up to the fifth century, there was no *exomologēsis* or corporate knowledge of the sins committed and the congregation as a whole was not involved in the process. Even though the nature of some of the penances precluded secrecy, as in the case of prescribed fasting or excommunication, the penitential process itself leading up to the penitent's restoration to the church assembly and to the end of the discipline was kept private. This meant that the relationship between confessor and penitent was uniquely intimate, with the confessor assuming the role of a trusted, caring soul friend or *anamchara*, as the Irish called it, who was the personal choice of the penitent and could be retained for a whole lifetime. Second, confessors qualified for the position not on account of their ordination status as bishop or priest, but on account of their wisdom, compassion, and godly qualities. This meant that many confessors were women. According to the lives of the saints, or hagiographies, the sixth-century Celtic monk Brendan is said to have sought confession with the abbess Ita, who was known for her teaching and healing ministry and practiced hearing confession from members of her monastic community and people outside. The Celtic monastic founder Columban in his early years regularly sought the counsel and advice of a saintly woman. And the abbess Brigit, who oversaw a vast double monastery (a religious house admitting both men and women) is said to have regularly welcomed both male and female penitents who sought her out for confession, including her own monks and nuns. Other female confessors and teachers of repentance are the monastics Samthann and

---

15. John Cassian, *Conferences*, trans. Colm Luibheid, Classics of Western Spirituality (New York: Paulist Press, 1985), 57–58.
16. Ibid., 68.

Moninna, who provided soul care and guidance to those both within and outside the community. Third, confession was not reserved for the exceptionally wicked and only practiced during set periods of the year. It was an expectation of all Christians in their repeated attempts to draw near God, purify the soul, and advance in Christian virtue. Regular confession and acts of penance were not considered punishments, but a healing device and medicine for the treatment of the mind's and soul's disease. The nature of the offenses and prescribed "remedies" kept in mind the proclivities and character inclinations of the individual. Penances were adjusted to the status and rank of the sinner within the life of the community, so that those with influence and rank were held to higher moral standards and more severe measures of penance than others. Offenses of both thought and deed were addressed, and their penitential remedy was considered with discrimination and a sympathetic knowledge of the human condition. Often the cure of a malady, or sin, was seen as the practice of its opposite virtue. Columban advises in his penitential (ca. 600) that "the talkative person is to be sentenced to silence, the disturber to gentleness, the gluttonous to fasting."[17] Long penances were often carried out in monasteries, which provided penitents with relative privacy and uninterrupted focus. The monastery of Iona, for example, operated a colony on the neighboring island of Tiree where penitents where sent.[18] However, long penances could be converted into shorter ones of greater severity, based on the so-called system of commutation originating in Ireland in the early seventh century. Acts of penance generally consisted of fasting, often on bread and water, the recitation or singing of psalms, and kneeling and other physical demonstrations of remorse; the elderly or infirm could substitute for these acts the giving of alms. The objective was an inward change, a conversion and return to God, and a readjustment of character, so that "contraries are cured by their contraries,"[19] as Cassian suggested in the early fifth century, and the person could recover, for a time at least, a harmonious relationship with church, neighbor, and God.

17. See the "Penitential of Columban" in McNeill and Gamer, *Medieval Handbooks*, 265.

18. See *The Life of St. Columba, founder of Hy*, trans. with notes and illustrations by William Reeves (Edinburgh: Edmonston and Douglas, 1874), 303ff.; quoted in McNeill and Gamer, *Medieval Handbooks*, 34. Also "there was a special penitential church at Armagh" and "penitents sometimes went to stay with the Columban community on the Scottish island of Inba"; see Walsh and Bradley, *History of the Irish Church*, 124 n. 1.

19. See the "Penitential of Cummean" in McNeill and Gamer, *Medieval Handbooks*, 101; also the "Penitential of Finnian," ibid., 92.

Central to the rising popularity of private confession must have been the conviction among Christians that they stood in need of repeated, ongoing repentance. Like a patient seeking out a physician, Christians consulted with confessors concerning their moral maladies. The ensuing prescription the confessor ordered came in the form of a penance. Hence the acts of penance were the physical expression of sorrow over sins committed as well as deliberate disciplines of restitution and self-restraint. In the prologue to his penitential Cummean sums up the healing power of self-restraint in the penitential act: Since "contraries are cured by contraries," those "who do what is forbidden without restraint ought to restrain themselves even from what is allowed."[20] Summoning the courage to seek out a confessor required as much discipline as the act of penance and its completion. Christians seemed to understand that the temporary price paid in terms of the physical or mental discomfort involved in doing penance was small by comparison. They feared the spread of their soul's sickness more than its cure. In his introduction to *Celtic Spirituality*, Oliver Davies notes that one of the central themes of Celtic spirituality is "the awareness of the body as the focus of human existence, not subordinate to the mind in a torturous relation of subjection and culpability, but thematized as the locus of penance." With this view of the body, "penance itself is not self-inflicted mutilation but the reception of new life and the beginning of the transformation that leads to glory."[21] A Welsh poem dating from the thirteenth century reflects the spirituality of early Celtic Christianity by commending the benefits of penance:

> The beauty of the virtue in doing penance for excess,
> Beautiful too that God shall save me . . .
> The beauty of desire for penance from a priest,
> Beautiful too bearing the elements to the altar . . .
> The beauty of the word which the Trinity speaks,
> Beautiful too doing penance for sin."[22]

By linking penance with beauty the poet shows penance's life-affirming and life-giving power, a power resulting from self-surrender and even

20. See the "Penitential of Cummean" in *Celtic Spirituality*, ed. and trans. by Oliver Davies and Thomas O'Loughlin, Classics of Western Spirituality (New York: Paulist Press, 1999), 231.

21. Oliver Davies, "Introduction," in *Celtic Spirituality*, 24.

22. Davies calls the poem "a classic expression of the spirit of early Celtic Christianity." See "Introduction," *Celtic Spirituality*, 45; for this poem, titled "The Loves of Taliesin," see *Celtic Spirituality*, 283–85.

martyrdom ("blue martyrdom") for the sake of salvation and the health of one's soul.[23]

Initially the confessor depended on personal wisdom and experience in prescribing the appropriate penance. By the early seventh century, however, private confession had spread to the laity, so that confessors obtained help from manuals of penance. Both women and men used these so-called penitentials in the monastic communities of Ireland and Wales. Abbots and abbesses consulted these manuals to help them discern an adequate cure for those who had come for help—both members of their religious community and those outside. According to John R. Walsh and Thomas Bradley, "The practices of frequent confession (often of devotion rather than necessity) and public and private spiritual direction for monks were easily adapted to the needs of the laity."[24] As a result, repeated auricular confession and private penance among all Christians, not only members of the monastic community, were introduced in Ireland and Wales, from where the *peregrini* took the practices to the Anglo-Saxon lands and the continent. The penitentials, as a new genre of religious literature, both reflected and supported the new practices. These manuals and handbooks were intended for private circulation only among those serving as confessors. As professional manuals they helped the confessor facilitate the conversation with the penitent while matching the particular sin with its proper remedy and advising pastoral sensitivity. They also urged confessors to exercise discretion in not suggesting to penitents previously unthought-of sins that might tempt them further.

The penitentials of the Celtic church make up a large body of literature, spanning from the sixth to the eighth centuries. The first of these documents, surviving mostly as fragments and considered proto-penitential, are of Welsh origin and include "The Preface of Gildas on Penance," "The Synods of North Britain," "The Synod of the Grove of Victory," and "Excerpts from a Book of David" (the patron saint of Wales). The main penitentials of this early period, those of Finnian, Columban, and Cummean, are of Irish origin and are all written in Latin. The earliest extant Irish penitential is that of Finnian,[25] probably written between 525 and 550, and it is addressed to both monks and laity with little distinc-

---

23. See Clare Stancliffe, "Red, White and Blue Martyrdom" in *Ireland in Early Mediaeval Europe: Studies in Memory of Kathleen Hughes*, eds. Dorothy Whitelock, Rosamond McKitterick, and David Dumville, 44–46 (Cambridge and New York: Cambridge University Press, 1982).

24. Walsh and Bradley, *History of the Irish Church*, 113.

25. "The Penitential of Finnian," in McNeill and Gamer, *Medieval Handbooks*, 87–88.

tion. The first four rules, of a total of fifty-three, spell out the need for ongoing self-examination. Christians ought to examine their hearts and thoughts continually, and they need to know what to do when detecting evil thoughts in themselves or recognizing an inadvertent slip of the tongue: "If anyone has sinned in the thoughts of his heart and immediately repents, he shall beat his breasts and seek pardon from God and make satisfaction, that he may be whole" (1). But if the same person has these thoughts frequently and "hesitates to act on them, whether he has mastered them or been mastered by them, he shall seek pardon from God by prayer and fasting day and night until the evil thought departs and he is whole" (2). Moreover, "If anyone has thought evil and intended to do it, but opportunity has failed him, it is the same sin but not the same penalty" (3). Finally, "If anyone has sinned in word by an inadvertence and immediately repented, and has not said any such thing of set purpose, he ought to submit to penance . . . and thereafter let him be on his guard throughout his life, lest he commit further sin" (4). As educational manuals, the penitentials reminded Christians that they were never safe from sin and that working out their salvation began and ended with a scrutiny of their motives, introspection, and honesty with themselves and God in prayer.

The most comprehensive of the early penitentials is that by Cummean, written circa 650, which addresses the sins of both monks and laypeople and includes sections on the eight deadly sins. An epilogue reminds the confessor to give due regard to the particular circumstances of each penitent in assigning a penance. The confessor, says Cummean, is to carefully take into account "the length of time anyone remains in his faults, what education he has received, with what passion he is assailed, with what courage he resists, with what intensity of weeping he seems to be afflicted, with what pressure he is driven to sin."[26] Presumably confessors memorized portions of the penitentials as a conversation aid and to help educate the penitent to ensure that he or she had confessed all serious sins while simultaneously providing instruction on the nature and workings of sin. Unlike a legal code, this system provided degrees of penance depending on the sinner's rank in the community and other circumstances, while helping the confessor recommend a penance appropriate to the offense based on the principle that "diversity of guilt occasions diversity of penalty."[27] The "Penitential of Columban," for example, distinguishes

---

26. "The Penitential of Cummean," in *Celtic Spirituality*, 245.
27. "The Penitential of Columban," Part B, in McNeill and Gamer, *Medieval Handbooks*, 251.

between offenses by monks and all others, such as clerics (those who held positions in the faith community) and laypeople, thus lumping together the latter two under one category. For monks the mere intention to sin requires penance: "If, therefore, anyone sins by planning to sin, that is, [if he] desires to kill a man, or to commit fornication, or to steal, or secretly to feast and become drunk . . . or to do anything else of the kind, and [if he] is prepared with his whole heart to do these things, in the case of the greater crimes he shall do penance on bread and water for half a year; in the case of the lesser, for forty days."[28] For all others, namely, clerics and laypeople, only those sins require penance that have been actually committed, such as murder, adultery, fornication, perjury, magic, theft, sexual intercourse after one had become a cleric (assumed the office of deacon or other rank in the church), physical violence, masturbation, and sexual pursuits. However, there is one exception: "If any layman plans to commit adultery or to commit fornication with the betrothed [of his neighbor?] and lusts after the wife of his neighbor and does not accomplish his design, that is, is unable because the woman does not comply, yet he was prepared to commit fornication, he shall confess his guilt to the priest, and thus he shall do penance for forty days on bread and water."[29] Apparently self-examination among all Christians was considered most necessary in regard to sexual thoughts and intentions, and so was subsequent penance.

In the early penitentials, sin is frequently compared to a disease, the sinner to a patient, and the confessor to a physician. Sins are considered "the wounds, fevers, transgressions, sorrows, sicknesses, and infirmities of the souls," while confessors are "spiritual physicians," who know how "to treat all things unto cleanness, to restore the feeble to the full state of health."[30] The confessor is viewed as acting as a representative of Christ, who did not come to call the healthy but sinners (Matt 9:12), who did not come to judge and condemn the world, or the sinner, but to bring salvation and healing (John 3:17). Acts of penance were seen as medicinal measures prescribed by the confessor to realign and adjust the Christian's character. Thus they became salvific activities rather than tools for punishment and humiliation.

With the penitentials' popularity and their growing use by ordained priests on the continent, a new system of private penance evolved. This system was eventually regarded as sacramental in nature and came to

28. Ibid., A 2, 250.
29. Ibid., B 23, 255–56.
30. Ibid., B, 251–52.

include a formula of absolution, or the official pronouncement of forgiveness, by the confessor on behalf of the church and Christ. Since absolution was seen as based on Jesus' handing the keys of the church to Peter and ceding to him the power to bind and to loose, to retain sins and to absolve them (Matt 16:18-19), the Roman church reserved the privilege of pronouncing absolution to those only who were Peter's apostolic successors, namely, ordained male clergy. Women and the laity were thereby excluded from hearing confession and pronouncing absolution. Moreover, Christians could no longer seek out a guide and soul friend of their own choosing, but were limited to the priest or bishop of their particular parish, regardless of whether there existed a sense of mutual kinship and intimacy and regardless of the cleric's qualities of pastoral sensitivity, wisdom, and holiness. By confining confession and penance to the auspices of the clergy (except among monastics), the church assumed increasing influence in the shaping of the moral behavior and the spiritual formation of its members. At the same time, Christians could no longer choose their own confessors or serve as official confessors to others based on spiritual kinship, calling, and gifts of discernment. This restriction, resulting from confession's sacramental status, introduced an unnatural split whereby spiritual direction and soul guidance was severed from confession—spawning a separation of roles between clerical confessor and lay spiritual director that persists to this day.

CHAPTER FIVE

Private Confession in the Monastery and in the Church

Private confession had been introduced on the European continent and in Britain in the sixth century. Two hundred years later, the practice had become well established in the Western church. In fact, it is one of the few Celtic innovations that have entered the mainstream of church life and remained. "How different might Catholicism be today," writes Thomas Cahill, if, in addition to appropriating private penance, "it had taken over the easy Irish sympathy between churchmen and laymen and the easy Irish attitudes toward diversity, authority, the role of women . . . ."[1] What in retrospect seems plausible and desirable, in practice was complex. Some of the traditions did not easily transfer from Ireland, a tribal culture, to the continent, from monastic life to life in the larger community. For example, private confession in the Celtic church had originated with the concept of soul friendship and mentoring between an elder and a younger member of the clan, presupposing a close-knit community and intimate ties among members. The saying that "anyone without a soul friend is like a body without a head," attributed to Brigit and Comgall, may even go back as far as the druids, the wise teachers among the Celtic tribes whose customs, especially that of kinship and kingship, had to be reinterpreted in Christian terminology when Christianity was introduced. Also, during Ireland's Christianization through Patrick and his disciples—from the rise of an early ascetic movement to the missionary activities of the monks and ascetics on the continent and in Britain that led to the founding of monasteries—many practices were altered to fit the needs of Celtic Christians, their communities, and those of the peoples they sought to evangelize. Finally, what had originated

---

1. Thomas Cahill, *How the Irish Saved Civilization: The Untold Story of Ireland's Heroic Role From the Fall of Rome to the Rise of Medieval Europe* (New York: Random House, 1995), 178.

in the monastic community and was practiced there with diligence could assume new traits outside the monastery walls due to local customs, feudal tradition, and the preferences of church authorities. This is certainly true for the rule of ongoing self-examination and confession.

How, then, was confession practiced among early Celtic Christians, particularly in the monastic communities? Apart from the penitentials, the texts that shed light on Celtic monastic soul guidance and confession are the hagiographies of the Celtic saints and early monastic rules in the West. One of these hagiographies is the so-called Confession of Patrick, a testimonial of the great works God had worked through him. In it we hear of Patrick's disappointment with his confessor. Predicting initially that Patrick would be offered the rank of bishop, the confessor later betrayed him. "I am very sorry for my dearest friend, to whom I trusted my soul, that he merited to hear this [divine] revelation,"[2] Patrick writes. In private conversation he had heard from the friend: "'Behold, you are to be given the rank of bishop'—something for which I was unworthy. So how did he later come to the idea of disgracing me in public in the presence of all those people both good and bad, [regarding a matter for] which earlier he had, joyfully and of his own volition, pardoned me . . . ."[3] Patrick had shared a confidence with his soul friend and confessor from a long time past and "hinted to [my] dearest friend about something I had done one day—indeed in an hour—in my youth, for I had not then prevailed over [my sinfulness]," remaining "in death and nonbelief until I was truly punished and, in truth, brought low by daily deprivations of hunger and nakedness." Now Patrick can see these hardships—perhaps even the betrayal of his confessor, who had "fought for me in my absence"—in a positive light as being "very good for me for I was corrected by the Lord; and he prepared me for what I am today—a state I was then far away from—when I have the pastoral care, and many duties, for the salvation of others . . . ."[4]

The hagiography "The Life of St. David" by Rhigyfarch offers a detailed account of physical labor and monastic discipline among the

---

2. Patrick, "Patrick's Declaration of the Great Works of God" in *Celtic Spirituality*, ed. and trans. by Oliver Davies, and Thomas O'Loughlin, Classics of Western Spirituality (New York: Paulist Press, 1999), 75. Oliver Davies prefers this title to "confession," since it is neither an admission of one's sins nor a faith declaration; rather, the work is "Patrick's account of what God did through him," so that "his *confessio* is but another part of his own service of God, which is the preaching of the gospel to those who have not heard"; see Davies, "Introduction," in *Celtic Spirituality*, 29.

3. "Patrick's Declaration," in *Celtic Spirituality*, 75.

4. Ibid., 74.

monks of Wales. One of their practices was to confess their thoughts to their abbot, David.

> When the labor in the fields was done, they would return to the cloisters of the monastery and would pass the rest of the day until vespers reading, writing, or praying. When evening came and the bell was rung, everyone left what they were doing. Even if someone heard the bell when they had only just begun a character, or had only half completed it, he would quickly rise and leave his work, making his way silently to the church without any idle chatter. When they had sung the Psalms, in unity of heart and voice, they devoutly remained on bended knees until the appearance of the stars in the heavens marked the close of day. . . . For Saturday evening until break of day at the first hour of Sunday, they devote themselves to vigils, prayers, and genuflections, except for one hour after matins on Saturday. They make known their thoughts to the father, and even seek his permission to answer the call of nature.[5]

The abbot functioned not only as spiritual guide and confessor, but also as intercessor for the monks and others. "After matins, he [David] proceeded alone to commune with the angels. . . . He spent all day, one after another, steadfastly and untiringly teaching, praying, and kneeling, and caring for his brethren, as well as feeding a host of orphans, wards, widows, the poor, the sick, the weak, and pilgrims." In all that, the biographer says, David "imitated the monks of Egypt, and lived a life like theirs," attracting even kings and princes, who "left their kingdoms and sought out his monastery," so as to live there in "humble obedience in this father's cell."[6]

Another hagiography is "The Life of St. Brigit the Virgin," written by Cogitosus in the seventh century. Cogitosus says that the founding of Brigit's double monastery at Kildare was due to her fame as a guide of souls. Her character and good works drew people. She "drew to herself from all the provinces of Ireland inestimable numbers of people of both sexes who willingly made their votive offerings," so that her monastery's influence extended to both coasts of Ireland. For help in overseeing the male monastery Brigit enlisted "a famous hermit," asking him "to leave his retreat and his solitary life," so that "by both their merits their episcopal and feminine see spread throughout the whole island of Ireland." Brigit's aim was "to provide for the orderly direction of souls in all things and to care for the churches of the many provinces which were associ-

---

5. "The Life of St. David," in *Celtic Spirituality*, 199.
6. Ibid., 200–1.

ated with her."[7] In yet another hagiography, "The Irish Life of Brigit," Brigit leads both nuns and outsiders to repentance and confession. On one occasion Brigit has been called to the house of Brig to heal a sick woman living there. While she is there, Brig washes Brigit's feet and carries the wash water to the sick woman, who is healed instantly. Later at table Brigit sees Satan sitting on the dish in front of her, and Brig was able to see Satan, too, after making the sign of the cross. When asked what has brought him to this place, Satan replies: "I always live here with a certain virgin, whose sloth has given me a place." When the woman is called, Brigit signs her eyes with the cross, and she is able to see Satan and is filled with great fear and remorse. "Behold, you see him whom you have cherished for many years and seasons," Brigit says. By confronting the woman with the sin that allowed Satan to dwell in her heart Brigit could assure her that from now on Satan "shall not enter this house until the Day of Judgment."[8]

Two stories of Brigit's life illustrate the connection between physical healing and doing penance. One story relates to two lepers who had been following Brigit. Because they harbored jealousy toward each other and quarreled, their hands and feet had become stiff. When Brigit sees them she says, "You should do penance."[9] When they do, the lepers are freed of their stiffness and the leprosy is healed. Another story shows Brigit visiting Tailtiu, the place of Patrick's community. Great tumult had arisen because a woman had come to return her son to a cleric of Patrick's community named Brón. "I had come to Brón to have the veil blessed on my head and to offer my virginity to God. But my cleric seduced me so that I have given birth to his son," the woman said. After Patrick gives Brigit permission to speak, she asks the woman about the child's father. It is Brón's, the woman replies. "That is not true," says Brigit, making the sign of the cross over the woman's face, so that both her head and tongue swell up. Then she asks the child about his father. Though not old enough to speak, he replies: "Brón the bishop is not my father but a certain base and ugly man who is sitting at the edge of the assembly. My mother is a liar." The entire assembly now demands that the woman be burned, but Brigit objects, saying, "This woman should do penance." After the woman has done so, the swelling of her head and tongue subside, while "the people rejoiced, the bishop was freed, and Brigit was praised."[10] Though

7. "The Life of St. Brigit the Virgin," in *Celtic Spirituality*, 122–23.
8. "The Irish Life of Brigit," in *Celtic Spirituality*, 149–50.
9. Ibid., 150.
10. Ibid., 152–53.

typically embellishing the life and power of a saint, hagiographies still can show the saint's relation to peers and devotees, in this case her role as a physician of the soul: by compassionately leading sinners to repentance the saint restores the bodies and souls of those too weak, unpracticed, or inexperienced to do so on their own.

In the early Celtic church, members of monastic orders were held to higher standards of self-examination than laypeople. Nonmonastics only needed to confront their apparent faults and transgressions, while monks were expected to discern their motivation to sin long before such sin became evident in word and deed. To that end Columban's monastic rule, written around 600 CE and used in the monastic communities he founded in France and Italy, recommends confession for monks several times a day. Claiming the authority of precedent set by earlier fathers and teachers of the church, Columban says that "we should make confession [of all offenses, not only capital offenses, but also minor negligences] before eating or before going to bed or whenever it shall be convenient, since confession and penance deliver [us] from death."[11] This practice means seeking counsel in humility, a corrective measure of the heart before it transforms into visible actions and digressions and habits. It is a form of prayer that detects excesses before they take root, a form of seeking counsel before deciding on an action. The aim of self-examination leading to confession is to discern extremes. Columban puts it succinctly: "Just as error overtakes those who have no path, so for those who live without discernment excess is near at hand, always contrary to the virtues, which lie between the extremes."[12] For discernment Christians needed to seek counsel from a confessor. "For what the judge's scrutiny has already tried," says Columban, "protects from the fear of judgment" of the one making confession and seeking counsel. Even though such a discipline may seem hard to follow, "to those who are secure in their fear of God it will seem sweet and safe if it is kept wholly and not just in part, since nothing is sweeter than security of conscience and nothing safer than exoneration of the soul." No one, says Columban, can achieve such freedom of conscience "through their own efforts since it properly belongs to the estimation of others,"[13] above all to the confessor, spiritual director, or elder. True perfection in one's Christian walk

11. "The *Regula Coenobialis* of Columban," in John T. McNeill and Helena M. Gamer, *Medieval Handbooks of Penance: A Translation of the Principal* Libri Poenitentiales *and Selections From Related Documents* (New York: Columbia University Press, 1938, 1990), 258.

12. "The Rule for Monks by Columbanus," in *Celtic Spirituality*, 246–56, at 252.

13. Ibid., 254.

can only be achieved "under the direction of a single father, in the company of many, so that [the monk] may learn humility from one, and patience from another."[14] This also meant that the penance and the counsel given by the elder were to be carried out without grumbling and objection in a spirit of humility and obedience. Let the monk "be silent when he suffers wrong, let him fear the superior of the monastery as a lord, and love him as a father, believing that whatever he commands is for his own good"[15]—even if the prescribed counsel ran counter to one's desires, opinions, and personal judgment.

Rigorous obedience to the counsel of the abbot or elder is equally crucial in the non-Celtic Rule of Benedict (ca. 480–547). Written around 530, the Rule identifies twelve steps of humility, the forerunner of today's twelve-step programs, a progressive movement toward perfection in the life of faith in accordance with Christ's teachings. In writing the Rule, Benedict was influenced by the monks in the Egyptian desert. After his conversion he had initially chosen to live as a solitary in a cave, as did the early desert fathers and mothers. In his Rule[16] he commends that monks read Cassian's "Conferences," the Fathers' "Institutes" and their "Lives," and "the rule of our holy father Basil" (RB 73). Several commonalities exist between Benedict's Rule and that of the Celtic monks. They include the monks' manual labor, the daily singing of Psalms in the oratory, consultation with the spiritual father in all matters (RB 49), ongoing self-examination of the conscience and subsequent confession (RB 7), and satisfaction of one's sins and transgressions through penance (RB 23–28, 44, 46). Benedict views the Rule as "a school for the Lord's service" to the end of reaching eternal life, for doing "now what will profit us forever" (RB Prol. 44). Central to the Rule is a daily self-examination and discernment of conduct, outlined in the twelve steps of humility. Remember, writes Benedict concerning the first step, that we are "seen by God in heaven" at all times, that one's "actions everywhere are in God's sight and are reported by angels at every hour." Therefore we ought to guard ourselves "at every moment from sins and vices of thought or tongue, of hand or foot, of self-will or bodily desire" (RB 7.12-13). According to the fifth step of humility this means "that a man does not conceal from his abbot any sinful thoughts entering his heart, or any wrongs committed in secret, bur rather confesses them

14. Ibid., 256.
15. Ibid.
16. The text used here is Timothy Fry, OSB, ed., *Rule of St. Benedict 1980* (Collegeville, MN: Liturgical Press, 1982).

humbly" (RB 7.44). It also means, as the twelfth step makes clear, that one is constantly aware of standing in need for God's mercy and forgiveness. "Judging himself always guilty on account of his sins," the monk "should consider that he is already at the fearful judgment, and constantly say in his heart what the publican in the Gospel said with downcast eyes: 'Lord, I am a sinner, not worthy to look up to heaven' (Luke 18:13)" (RB 7.64-65).

The Rule of Benedict makes several provisions for private and public penance. "If a brother is found to be stubborn or disobedient or proud, if he grumbles or in any way despises the holy rule and defies the orders of his seniors, he should be warned twice privately by the seniors in accord with the Lord's injunction (Matt 18:15-16). If he does not amend, he must be rebuked publicly in the presence of everyone" (RB 23.1-3). Failing that, the monk is to be prevented from sharing meals with the others and having leadership in the singing of the liturgy, "until by proper satisfaction he gains pardon" (RB 24.7). Acts of penance are lying prostrate and facedown "at the oratory entrance at the end of the celebration" of the liturgy, prostrating oneself "at the abbot's feet, then at the feet of all that they may pray for him" (RB 44.1-4). As in the Eastern and Celtic monastic rules and documents, the role of the abbot or spiritual guide is that of "a wise physician" who acts with "all speed, discernment and diligence in order not to lose any of the sheep entrusted to him" and who realizes "that he has undertaken care of the sick, not tyranny over the healthy" (RB 27.2, 5-6). For help the abbot may send in "mature and wise brothers who, under the cloak of secrecy, may support the wavering brother, urge him to be humble as a way of making satisfaction, and 'console' him 'lest he be overwhelmed by excessive sorrow' (2 Cor 2:7)" (RB 27.2). Should this procedure of "applied compresses, the ointment of encouragement, the medicine of divine Scripture, and finally the cauterizing iron of excommunication and strokes of the rod" fail, the abbot is to "apply an even better remedy: he and all the brothers should pray for him so that the Lord, who can do all things, may bring about the health of the sick brother" (RB 28.3-5). In case even such public disciplinary measures fail, the abbot is allowed to "use the knife and amputate," urging the departure of the brother from the community, "lest one diseased sheep infect the whole flock" (RB 28.6-8). The monk is to confess the minor offenses immediately to the abbot or the spiritual elders in private; otherwise the penance, if the offense is reported by another, becomes more severe. These minor offenses are confessed in private to the abbot or elders because "they know how to heal their own wounds as well as those of others, without exposing them and making them public" (RB 46.6).

By contrast to the desert way of monastic living, Benedict stresses the involvement of the entire community in the ongoing work of sanctification. According to Esther de Waal, "The older ideal had been essentially that of the novice finding a holy man and asking to learn from him, and the monastery had been a group of individuals gathered round the feet of a sage." Now Benedict "changes this almost exclusively vertical pattern of authority by emphasizing the relationships of the monks with each other."[17] In commenting on Benedictine spirituality, Joan Chittister, OSB, elaborates on the power of community and its role in confession. "Life with someone else . . . doesn't show me nearly as much about his or her shortcomings as it does about my own. In human relationships I learn how to soften my hard spots and how to reconcile and how to care for someone else besides myself. In human relationships I learn that theory is no substitute for love."[18] Living in community involves learning to ask for forgiveness and to be reconciled to another. While the abbot remains the prime confessor, other elders are enlisted and all members of the community serve as confessors to one another by extending and receiving forgiveness, showing patience, and bearing one another's weaknesses in obedience and humility. "Obedience is a blessing to be shown by all, not only to the abbot but also to one another as brothers," says Benedict, "since we know that it is by this way of obedience that we go to God" (RB 71.1-2). Therefore monks should demonstrate respect toward one another, "supporting with the greatest patience one another's weaknesses of body or behavior" (RB 72.5). Such obedience and humility is a form of self-restraint. Indirectly it is also a form of penance and correction, the results of which benefit both the individual and the community at large.

By 600 CE a system had evolved in the Western church that promoted private confession to a priest. This system was at first more pastoral than penitential in nature, more focused on spiritual direction than on penitential practice and absolution. For example, the writings of Augustine give no evidence that private confession with absolution was administered for either grave or minor sins. If he seemed to waver from that rule it was largely to persuade a penitent to enroll in the order of penitents or, if the circumstances justified a more lenient treatment, he recommended that the sinner practice prayer and almsgiving. Similarly, the

---

17. Esther de Waal, *Seeking God: The Way of St. Benedict* (Collegeville, MN: Liturgical Press, 1984), 18–19.

18. Joan Chittister, OSB, *Wisdom Distilled from the Daily: Living the Rule of St. Benedict Today* (San Francisco: Harper & Row, 1990), 49.

writings of Gregory the Great indicate that priests served as spiritual directors or pastoral counselors rather than as confessors dispensing absolution. Gregory's own monastic life informed the advice he gave to clergy to stand by their people as an abbot would by his monks, while encouraging both clergy and parishioners to practice confession to a superior and to seek spiritual direction as was done in the monastery. In a study on the origins of private penance Robert C. Mortimer attributes the practice of private confession and absolution to the arrival of the Irish monks on the continent. "They took the old public penance and adapted it to suit the requirements of a mission field and a half-converted church," he says. "And by so doing they restored penance to its proper place as a means of renewing and deepening Christian life."[19] However, the old system was not radically discarded: The practices of the laying on of hands, fasting, almsgiving, and prayer were features of the old system as well as the new, and bishops and priests—rather than lay-people and women—continued to be the ones to hear the penitent's confession, administer penance, and pronounce forgiveness or restoration of the sinner to full communion. "What was destroyed," says Mortimer, "were the enrolment in a specified order of penitents, the continuance of obligations after the term of penance was fulfilled . . . the limitation of penance to one occasion in a lifetime." With one simple reform the lesser sins, so common and frequent in their occurrence among all people, could now be addressed "and the grace and comfort of absolution . . . was continuously bestowed upon the ordinary and humble Christian."[20] Since the custom of making confession to a priest on one's deathbed was already common, the doors were opened now to making regular private, secret confession to a priest for sins both great and small, not just at the end of one's life but throughout it.

As Christians in the West welcomed private confession, pastors faced the dilemma of being unprepared. Members were flocking to them rather than to the bishops—the earlier ministers of confession and penance—and they needed guidance. The Irish penitentials offered priests a standard procedure for functioning as confessor and guide of consciences. Despite the books' utility, bishops hesitated to approve their use. For one thing, bishops saw priests intruding upon their prerogative and ecclesial authority in absolving Christians of their sins. For another, a priest was free to use the penitential of his preference, so that widely

---

19. Robert C. Mortimer, *The Origins of Private Penance in the Western Church* (Oxford: Clarendon Press, 1939), 189.

20. Ibid., 189–90.

differing penances were prescribed for the same sin. In addition, a penitential's authority rested solely with its author, of whom little or nothing was known, while copies were almost recklessly made, often with free alterations. The fact that these penitentials had been introduced by Irish compilers and immigrant monks on the continent did not raise ecclesiastical regard for them either—in fact, it enhanced suspicion among bishops that these books were something intolerably innovative, disruptive, and uncoordinated in the life of the church. Around 800 CE several efforts at reviving the old public penitential system failed, while bishops, such as those convened by Charlemagne in several Frankish councils in 813, railed against the books: they needed to be "utterly cast out," the councils said, since they "slew souls which should not have died and saved souls alive which should not have lived" when prescribing "light and strange sentences for grave sins" and, in general, appearing to "sew cushions under every elbow."[21] Still, the use of these manuals and the spread of private confession could not be stopped. People flocked to priests and bishops with a reputation as skilled confessors. In the prologue to the "Penitential of Theodore of Tarsus," archbishop of Canterbury (668–690), the writer says that both men and women "made haste in crowds" to visit the archbishop "with inextinguishable fervor" to be healed of their sins through the act of penance.[22]

Not all Christians were eager to make use of the cure of confession by visiting a priest and doctor of the soul. Priests had to reach out to them. In "The So-Called Roman Penitential," dating from circa 830, the compiler, named Halitgar, urges priests to "be solicitous on behalf of sinners," so that "if we see anyone fallen in sin, let us make haste to call him to penance by our teaching."[23] As an incentive, the eighth-century penitential of Pseudo-Cummean promises priests who are fervently exhorting their parishioners to do penance the rewards of divine recognition; thus, the sinners' "merit may be your reward and their salvation your glory."[24] And the penitential written by the "corrector" and "physician" Burchard of Worms, dating from circa 1008–1012, enjoins priests

21. John T. McNeill, *A History of the Cure of Souls* (New York: Harper & Brothers, 1951), 125; for the Frankish councils see McNeill and Gamer, *Medieval Handbooks*, 402. Also see Peter Damian's *Liber Gomorrhianus*, written in 1051, which calls the penitentials "spiny, stinging plants of thorn" and "spurious upstarts" that lack all ecclesial authority on account of their questionable or indistinct authorship; the quotation is found in McNeill and Gamer, *Medieval Handbooks*, 411.

22. "The Penitential of Theodore," in McNeill and Gamer, *Medieval Handbooks*, 183.

23. "The So-Called Roman Penitential," in ibid., 297.

24. "The Pseudo-Cummean Penitential," in ibid., 268.

to call penitents together once a year during the week prior to Lent, so as "to require the contentious to come to peace and delinquents to penance." At this time "the priests of the parishes shall assemble the people to themselves and reconcile the contentious by canonical authority and settle all quarrels and then first give the penance to those who confess; so that before the beginning of the fast comes about, all shall have confessed and received their penance, that they may be able freely to say: 'And forgive us our debts as we forgive our debtors.'" [25] The frequency of confession differed for monks and laypeople, yet its regularity became interwoven with the sacramental and liturgical traditions of the church. Columban advised his monks to make confession of even minor sins prior to going to mass; this is done to "wash away the indeterminate vices and fevers of the sick mind" and to cleanse the mind and conscience, "lest perchance one approach the altar unworthily."[26] Four hundred years later, confession is recommended for laypeople at least annually in the course of the church year, preferably at the beginning of Lent,[27] but also whenever Christians sense a need.

The priestly duties of hearing confession could be taxing. In the words of John T. McNeill, "the priest in a parish of awakened sinners would be very busy."[28] To the burden is added the expectation of solidarity in penitential practice and proper empathy. According to the Pseudo-Roman penitential the priest joined the penitent in fasting "for one or two weeks, or as long as we are able." Pastoral empathy is prescribed in both word and deed, for "no one can raise up one who is falling beneath a weight unless he bends himself that he may reach out to him his hand; and no physician can treat the wounds of the sick, unless he comes in contact with their foulness."[29] In addition, priests were to take out time for prayer before hearing confession: When "anyone comes to a priest to confess his sins, the priest shall advise him to wait a little, while he enters into his chamber to pray." And if there is no available chamber, the priest is to pray in his heart, saying: "Lord God Almighty, be Thou

25. "The Corrector and Physician of Burchard of Worms," in ibid., 323.

26. "The Penitential of Columban," in ibid., 257.

27. John T. McNeill says that the beginning of Lent was probably Ash Wednesday, so that "prior to that" meant the preceding Tuesday, also called Shrove Tuesday "since on that day souls were shriven that they might enter the Lenten season in purity. Its 'carnival' aspect was a later secular innovation"; see McNeill, *A History of the Cure of Souls*, 132.

28. Ibid., 128.

29. "The So-Called Roman Penitential," in McNeill and Gamer, *Medieval Handbooks*, 297; the identical instructions are also included in an early penitential of ca. 800, the "Tripartite St. Gall Penitential"; see ibid., 283.

propitious unto me a sinner, that I may be able worthily to give thanks unto Thee, who through Thy mercy hast made me, though unworthy, a minister, by the sacerdotal office, and appointed me, though slight and lowly, an intermediary to pray and intercede before our Lord Jesus Christ for sinners and for those returning to penance. And therefore our Governor and Lord . . . accept my prayer, which I pour forth before the face of Thy Clemency, for Thy menservants and maidservants who have come to penance."[30] If the penitent sees the priest sad and weeping on behalf of the sinner, the penitential suggests, he or she is more likely to be moved to grieve the sins committed and be inspired to make unrestrained confession.

Examining the penitent was a delicate matter. The penitential of Burchard provides detailed instructions on how to conduct the penitential interview, which questions to ask, what answers to offer, what prayers to say. First there is the question concerning one's proper Christian belief, which is to be asked "softly and gently"; then the question of the penitent's willingness to forgive the sins of those who have sinned against him or her; and finally the address that "affectionately" encourages the sinner to be forthright and frank: "Brother, do not blush to confess thy sins, for I also am a sinner, and perchance I have done worse deeds than thou hast. Wherefore I warn thee in these things, since it is a habitual fault of the human race, as saith the blessed Gregory, both in falling to commit sin and not to bring out by confessing what has been committed, but to defend in denying and in defending to multiply that which had been disproved."[31] The priest then affirms the dictum so frequently cited by the desert monks that concealing one's sins leads to greater sins, whereas confessing them stalls the devil's powers over us. If the penitent hesitates, the priest is to proceed and to gently submit for the confessant's consideration a list of sins that are likely to have been committed. Among them are murder, perjury, blasphemy, robbery, adultery and fornication, various pagan practices and superstitious acts, theft, and the eight principal sins. In listing them, caution and discretion on the part of the priest are commended so as not to stimulate the sinner's sinful imagination. The ritual concludes with the penitent's confession and a plea for mercy, along with a physical demonstration of sorrow. Lying prostrate on the ground, the penitent says: "Both in these and in all vices, in whatsoever ways human frailty can sin against God its creator—either in thought or speech or deed or love or lust—I confess that in all I have sinned and

30. "The So-Called Roman Penitential," in ibid., 298.
31. "The Corrector and Physician of Burchard of Worms," in ibid., 324–25.

acknowledge myself guilty above all men in the sight of God. Humbly, then, I plead with thee, a priest of God, that thou intercede for me and for my sins to the Lord our Creator, so that I may deserve to obtain pardon and grace for these and all my transgressions."[32] Then the priest joins the penitent by prostrating himself while chanting a psalm and appropriate prayers. Such compassionate treatment and coaxing must have made confession an experience of profound importance to the penitent; moreover, it may have eased the penitent's swallowing of the soul's bitter remedies. From the rite one can conclude that the penitent's difficulty was less the ensuing hardships of the penance than the shame associated with having to bare one's faults and transgressions. Fasting and temporary exclusion from the table, penances prescribed by this and later penitentials, appear as relatively easy to bear compared to the initial struggle at overcoming pride and admitting wrongdoing. The priest in the role of confessor is both a counselor and a physician of the soul as well as a skilled midwife who, by coaxing and compassion, listening and empathy, seeks to deliver the penitent from sin's burden. By identifying, acknowledging, and then releasing the sin, the penitent is induced to cleanse his or her soul of the harmful contaminants, ultimately allowing, with God's help, for the soul's restoration to health. Throughout the process the priest is to mediate God's nature as merciful and benevolent, demonstrating by his demeanor that the cost of making confession and baring one's soul is well worth the ensuing gain of forgiveness and restoration.

We learn, then, that private confession in the West was a gradual process developing and establishing itself over a period of nearly a thousand years. During the times beginning with Theodore of Tarsus (d. 690) up to those of Cardinal Charles Borromeo (d. 1584), numerous penitentials were produced in such countries as England, Germany, France, Ireland, Spain, and Italy, all of them bearing the imprint of early Celtic models. As priests made use of these instruction manuals and commended confession in sermons, catechesis, and set liturgical practices during the church year, Christians learned of and even sought confession's benefits. They came to appreciate the practice as a type of spiritual hygiene. Seeking out a priest and making confession at least annually came to be seen as a soul remedy. Monasteries played a leading role in promoting the practice of private confession among Christians, either by stressing the need for an individual teacher, mentor, or spiritual direc-

32. Ibid., 342.

tor or by making plain the daily challenges of living in a close-knit community that formed the habit of examining one's conscience, confessing one's thoughts and deeds, and practicing forgiveness and forbearance toward one another. It is unfortunate that the benefits of these spiritual practices have been largely lost to us today. What remains is the ill repute of certain customs connected with confession, such as allowing the penitent to convert a physical penance into payment of money or other goods to an abbot, bishop, priest, or the parish. It is a development that largely resulted from the popularity of private confession among Christians. As priests and bishops began promoting the practice they also found themselves limited in how much time and effort they could give the individual penitent. The time of counseling and spiritual direction was cut short, its benefits relegated to the province of monastic life, and its practice enclosed behind monastery walls. Thus laypeople began to associate private confession with two main elements: the confession itself, which often was executed in a perfunctory and mechanical way, and the penances assigned, which could be converted into monetary contributions or almsgiving. It is these newer trade practices, often referred to as commutations, tariffs, and indulgences, that would become the center of dispute in the medieval church and eventually spark the tumultuous sixteenth-century uprising, called the Protestant Reformation, at whose center stood the Augustinian monk and priest Martin Luther.

CHAPTER SIX

Doing Penance
Its Use and Abuse

The penances assigned to the laity depended on the circumstances surrounding the sin committed. Priests were to take into account the person's age, moral disposition and character, educational background, rank in the community, frame of mind, and health. Was the sinner likely to reform; was there evidence of true remorse; was the sin under consideration an act of rash judgment or a premeditated and calculated deed? Many factors influenced the decision to settle for a specific penance, not least the priest's discernment of who someone was or could be in light of Christ's renewing activity. Mitigating circumstances reduced the penance or allowed for its conversion to one less severe or a monetary payment. Illness was a special factor that many of the penitentials took into account. According to John T. McNeill, "From early times there had been a considerate treatment of sick penitents, and the penitentials continued to provide for this."[1] For example, the "Penitential of Theodore" of the late seventh century advises that "the sacerdotal authority shall be modified in the case of a sick person." The Old Irish Penitential of circa 800 says twice that the penitent "who is sick is allowed to eat meals at any hour of the day or night." And the "So-Called Roman Penitential" of circa 830 makes provisions for a penitent who had fallen sick after making confession to receive communion while being allowed to postpone penitential fasting until recovery. Concerning the dying, Boniface advises at a Bavarian synod that communion and reconciliation be offered immediately, so that "he shall be reconciled by imposition of hands

---

1. John T. McNeill, *A History of the Cure of Souls* (New York: Harper & Brothers, 1951), 129.

and the Eucharist shall be thrust in his mouth."[2] Other provisions considered the penitent's age, gender, and physical disposition. The penitential ascribed to the Venerable Bede suggests "discrimination" in regard to penance, that is, "between rich and poor; freeman, slave; little child, boy, youth, young man, old man; stupid, intelligent; layman, cleric, monk; bishop, presbyter, deacon . . . married or unmarried; pilgrim, virgin, canoness, or nuns; the weak, the sick, the well."[3] And the "Confessional of Egbert" advises the priest to find out before imposing a fast whether a person is "strong or weak, rich or poor; how young he is, or how old; whether he is ordained or a layman; what kind of repentance he has; and whether he is a bachelor or a married man."[4] Provisions are offered for those "unable to do penance in the way we have stated" in the form of almsgiving, so that the prescribed fasting, singing of psalms, kneeling, and genuflecting could be converted into payment of certain sums over a period of time: "He who is not able to do penance in the way we have stated above shall expend for one year twenty-six solidi for alms and shall fast one day each week until nones, and another until vespers, and the three forty-day periods. In the second year, twenty solidi; for the third year, eighteen."[5] The "Pseudo-Cummean Penitential" makes similar provision but also allows those unable to fast to substitute a person who could fast while paying for the services rendered: To

> those who are too feeble in body or in mind we give the advice that if what
> we have said above seems grievous to them, [each] when he is due to fast
> on bread and water shall [rather] sing for every day fifty psalms, kneeling,
> and seventy psalms without kneeling, and for one week he shall chant
> three hundred psalms in sequence, kneeling, or if he is not able to kneel
> he shall sing four hundred and twenty psalms and fulfill this within a
> church or in a secret place. . . . And he who does not know the psalms
> and is not able to fast shall choose a righteous man who will fulfill this in
> his stead, and he shall redeem this with his own payment or labor; this he
> shall disburse among the poor at the rate of a denarius for every day.[6]

2. From the "So-called Constitutions of Boniface," in John T. McNeill and Helena M. Gamer, *Medieval Handbooks of Penance: A Translation of the Principal* Libri Poenitentiales *and Selections From Related Documents* (New York: Columbia University Press, 1938, 1990), 399.

3. "Selections from the Penitential Tentatively Ascribed by Albers to Bede," in ibid., 223.

4. "Selections from the So-called Confessional of Egbert," in ibid., 245.

5. "Penitential Tentatively Ascribed by Albers to Bede," in ibid., 231.

6. "The Pseudo-Cummean Penitential," in ibid., 268–69.

Following the example of Zacchaeus (Luke 19:8), wealthy penitents shall give to the churches up to half of their total assets in alms as a penance (rather than giving "fourfold" as the gospel mentions), and those with lesser means who are not able to do the prescribed fasting "for one year on bread and water" shall instead give alms.[7]

Apparently some Christians were hiring themselves out to do penance through fasting on behalf of others. "If anyone fasts for a reward and takes upon himself the sins of another, he is not worthy to be called a Christian," an eighth-century penitential warns.[8] But it was not the practice of substitutionary penance that was objectionable, in this case; it was keeping the money for oneself as income when it should have been given to the poor instead.

The authors of the penitentials distinguish among various degrees of repentance and works of penance by which sins may be remitted. According to the "Bigotian Penitential" there are seven degrees by which one may obtain forgiveness of sins: the first is baptism, the second martyrdom, the third almsgiving, the fourth forgiving one's neighbor, the fifth offering charity to others, and the sixth doing penance. A seventh remission of sins is reserved for bishops and priests alone, who by virtue of their office lead others to repentance in accordance with the letter of James (Jas 5:20), "by warning, exhortation, teaching, instruction," and are thus able to cover a multitude of their own sins—no doubt an incentive for clerics to greater fervor in carrying out their pastoral duties. Nevertheless, the painstaking enumeration of sins and their matching penances, along with various commutations to monetary offerings, introduced a flood of abuses. It is at this point that the penitentials are related to the rise of indulgences. The word *indulgentia* meant initially "the merciful mitigation of a penalty due," but it soon came to be seen as a way of waiving penitential exercises by compensation and commutation—in short, a way of using good works (and money) to obtain remission of sins. While previously penance provided the penitent with the opportunity to experience its remedial and restorative qualities, now the mechanical trading of acts of discipline offered a shortcut and spurious substitute that lacked the power to restore the person to health.

An early protest against indulgences comes from the eighth century at a council held under Cuthbert, archbishop of Canterbury. A man of wealth, "seeking to have reconciliation speedily accorded him for some grave sin he had committed, asserted in writing that this same misdeed,

---

7. Ibid., 269–70.
8. "The Judgment of Clement," in ibid., 271.

as he had been assured by many persons, was so fully expiated that if he should be able to live yet three hundred years the [requirement regarding] fasting would have been fully met by these means of satisfaction; namely, the psalmody, fasting, and alms of others, without fasting on his part . . . ."[9] The resolution of the council was that penitents were to fast and sing psalms in person, not vicariously, though they were to invite intercession from other Christians.

A word of caution is in order lest the practices be too easily condemned. The belief in shared merit was a long-standing tradition in medieval society. From a religious perspective there existed an understanding of the communion of the saints in heaven and on earth with whom one was invariably connected in spirit and through prayer and with whom one shared both joys and sorrows. From a secular perspective the solidarity of the tribe, clan, or extended family superseded individual rights and obligations, so that relatives of the evildoer, for example, could make vicarious restitution for him or her in the hope of restoring the group's good name and honor. Conversely, parents would often force a son or daughter to join a monastic order for life and regard the "offering," along with the dowry-like payment for admission, as a penitential act that would vicariously ensure the well-being of the (rest of the) family. The growth of indulgences was especially apparent in the Germanic nations, where the payment of money in place of punishment in criminal cases was common, so that the practice of paying fines instead of doing acts of penance was a natural development. In addition, substitutions or indulgences for penitential obligations could be performed not only by the prayers and good works of other church members, but also by the unused merits of the lives of saints to whom one made devotion, or by making a pilgrimage to the Holy Land or to Rome. This last form of indulgence became popular among Christians when in 1095 Pope Urban II proclaimed the first general or "plenary" indulgence at the inauguration of the First Crusade. Over the course of five hundred years penitential practices and substitutions became so widespread a custom in the churches of the West that the pope convened a council of bishops to direct and order their use.

In 1215 Pope Innocent III convened the Fourth Lateran Council, ordering the bishops in the various provinces and some eight hundred abbots and ambassadors of secular rulers to meet at the Lateran Palace in Rome. Among the issues to be resolved were transubstantiation as the interpretation of the Eucharist, disciplinary regulations of the conduct and

9. From the "Canons of the Council of Cloveshoe," circa 747, in ibid., 394.

life of clergy (such as suspension of clergy living with concubines), and ruling that all sacraments be given free of charge. The council also ruled concerning confession and the receiving of the Eucharist to affirm what was already standard practice, namely, that Christians were to confess their sins annually and to receive the Eucharist at least at Easter. According to Canon 21 of the Fourth Lateran Council,[10] "all the faithful of both sexes shall after they have reached the age of discretion faithfully confess all their sins at least once a year to their own (parish) priest and perform to the best of their ability the penance imposed." Violators of this regulation regarding annual confession and the receiving of the Eucharist were to "be cut off from the Church during life and deprived of Christian burial in death." Provision was also made for choosing a parish priest for confession other than one's own. "If anyone for a good reason should wish to confess his sins to another priest, let him first seek and obtain permission from his (parish) priest, since otherwise he (the other priest) cannot loose or bind. . . ." Moreover, detailed instructions guide the priest in how to conduct confession and choose penance. "Let the priest be discreet and cautious that he may pour wine and oil into the wounds of the one injured after the manner of a skillful physician, carefully inquiring into the circumstances of the sinner and the sin, from the nature of which he may understand what kind of advice to give and what remedy to apply, making use of different experiments to heal the sick one." If the priest needed to seek further advice before assigning a penance, it was to be done in strictest confidence and without mentioning the name of the person; otherwise, the priest risked being deposed from office and "relegated to a monastery of strict observance to do penance for the remainder of his life."

A few canons of the council give evidence of the widespread abuse of the penitential practice, particularly through the exchange of money. In canon 49, for example, priests and bishops are prohibited from using the threat of excommunication to extort money from penitents or restore them to communion through the payment of an indulgence. "Under threat of the divine judge we absolutely forbid that anyone, impelled solely by greed, dare bind one with the chain of excommunication or absolve one so bound, especially in those regions where it is customary," thus taking advantage of "pecuniary punishment." Canon 62 condemns

---

10. The canons of the Fourth Lateran Council cited are from the "Internet Medieval Sourcebook," edited by Paul Halsall, available at www.fordham.edu/halsall/sbook.html. Subsequent references to the canons of the First and Fourth Lateran Councils in this chapter are from this source.

the sale of the relics of saints, saying: "relics are not to be sold or put on exhibition, lest the people be deceived in regard to them." The practice of buying a relic of a saint and devotion to it substituted for doing a certain number of days or months of penance. Other abuses involved prelates of newly built churches granting "indiscreet and superfluous indulgences" and bringing contempt "on the keys of the Church," so that "the penitential discipline is weakened." The canon permits an indulgence of one year to be granted penitents who made a pilgrimage on the occasion of a church's dedication, but "on the anniversary of the dedication the remission granted for penances enjoined is not to exceed forty days." In general, "letters of indulgences which are granted from time to time" are not to exceed forty days, since even the pontiff customarily followed this rule.

Apparently bribes and extortion were common among clergy and monastics. The council felt compelled to address these abuses as well. One of them involved the practice of monasteries charging families who wanted to be rid of their unmarried or unmarriageable daughters or widowed female relatives by consigning them to a monastic order. Canon 64 threatens punishment of both female novice and mother superior for future violations. "Since the stain of simony has so infected many nuns that scarcely any are received into the community without a price, doing this on the plea of poverty to conceal that evil, we strictly forbid that this be done in the future"; in case of violation, both parties, "the one receiving and the one received," are to be "removed from their monastery to one of stricter observance to do penance for the remainder of their life." Those received prior to the decree were to be removed to another monastery of the same order, or in case there was no available space they were to be received anew in the same monastery, but at a lower rank. The same rule was to be applied to monks also. Another abuse involved making an appointment to ecclesiastical or monastic rank in exchange for a contribution or tax levied. Canon 63 leaves little doubt that the practice was widespread: "We have learned with certainty that in many places and by many persons exactions and base extortions are made for the consecration of bishops, the blessing [or nomination] of abbots [or abbesses], and the ordination of clerics." The council condemned such a custom as "corruption" and decreed "that neither for those conferring nor for the things conferred shall anyone presume to demand or to extort something under any pretext whatsoever." Finally, canons 65 and 66 forbid bishops and clergy to charge for services commonly part of their ecclesiastical responsibilities. The custom of some clergy was to demand and extort money "for burials, nuptial blessings, and similar things," and if they did not receive the requested amounts to "fraudulently interpose fictitious impediments" (c. 66). Similarly, bishops were keeping a church vacant following the death of its parish priest until they received payment for appointing another (c. 65). It appears that even abbots engaged in extortion, since the council condemned the practice of exacting a fee from a soldier or cleric (or their relatives), who, upon retirement or in old age, wished to join the monastic order so as to live out life and be buried there. "We absolutely forbid exactions of this kind," the council stipulates, so that violators have to "restore double the amount exacted" to the local authorities "to whose detriment the exactions were made" (c. 65). This brief overview shows that often ecclesiastical authorities and monastic communities were providing services to fellow Christian brothers and sisters from motives of greed rather than compassion or a desire to provide cures. What should have been the ministry of tending to souls and sinners, restoring them to health, had taken on the characteristics of a commercialized and mercenary activity. The process of administering penances followed a similar pattern.

A crucial aspect of the process of private confession was receiving forgiveness and absolution. In the early stages of private confession the confessor pronounced forgiveness to the sinner on completion of the penitential process. With the rise of penitential substitutions and indulgences, however, forgiveness of sins was pronounced on the spot and at the time of confession. As speedy penitential transactions were beginning to replace the lengthy disciplines of self-examination, prayer, and fasting, forgiveness was obtained at once. Such forgiveness came to be known as absolution and was typically performed by the bishop or priest through the laying on of hands and a prayer or liturgical formula patterned after the early public rite of confession. With the decrees of the Fourth Lateran Council the rite of confession and absolution was officially recognized and identified as the sacrament of penance—though commonly called the sacrament of confession in keeping with the original name given to it by the Irish.

Private confession as an ecclesiastical rite was given a somewhat imaginative, though by this time traditional, theological justification. A sacrament was considered a mystery and means of grace that Christ had given to the church. In regard to penitential rituals the authority to forgive sins was believed to rest with the successors of the apostles, that is, bishops, and those whom they ordained as priests. Only they held the authority of granting forgiveness of sins and possessed the so-called "keys of the kingdom," the power of binding and loosing, of retaining and remitting sins on behalf of Christ. The two sayings of Jesus that gave rise to this view are: "If you forgive the sins of any, they are forgiven them; if you retain the sins of any, they are retained (John 20:23), and "I will give you the keys of the kingdom of heaven, and whatever you bind on earth will be bound in heaven, and whatever you loose on earth will be loosed in heaven" (Matt 16:19). An early third-century manual, the *Didascalia*, asserted this view by urging bishops to exercise this divinely bestowed power with mercy. Objectors to this view were Origen, who in his "Commentary on Matthew" sees it as "ridiculous" that bishops who themselves are subject to sin should claim the power to bind and loose, and Cyprian, who says in his treatise "On the Lapsed" that "only the Lord can grant mercy" (17). Some third-century documents contain a prayer offered at the elevation of a bishop that he might receive the power to forgive sins. Conversely, the prayers offered as part of the public act of reconciliation during the imposition of the bishop's hands, commonly held on the Thursday preceding Easter, imply no such episcopal power and appeal only to the generous compassion and mercy of God. Until the twelfth century the formula "I absolve thee" was commonly preceded by a petition for divine absolution. And it is only during this time that one sees a decisive transition from the disciplinary to a more ritualistic view of penance, according to which only those regarded as direct successors of the apostles, namely, bishops and priests, were allowed to absolve sins as part of the sacrament.

In the early twelfth century the clerical nature of penance is affirmed by prohibiting abbots and monks from administering it. In 1123 Pope Callixtus II had convened the First Lateran Council in Rome; it sought to put an end to encroachments on the influence and offices of the church by civic rulers, nobility, laypeople, and monastics. Canon 17 of the council makes the case against monastic encroachments: "We forbid abbots and monks to impose public penances, to visit the sick, to administer extreme unction, and to sing public masses." Nearly a century later the Fourth Lateran Council found it necessary to repeat the injunction, giving more detailed reasons for doing so. Canon 60 reads: "From different parts of the world complaints of bishops come to us in regard to grave excesses of some abbots, who, not content within their own spheres, extend their hands to those things that concern the episcopal office, deciding matrimonial cases, imposing public penances, granting letters of indulgences, and similar things." The result of such activities is that "the episcopal authority is looked upon by many as something of trifling importance." In an effort to "safeguard the dignity of the bishops and the welfare of the abbots, we absolutely forbid in the present decree that abbots presume to overreach themselves." The clericalization of the penitential process meant that Christians had to seek out as their confessor the priest of their parish, who alone had the authority to absolve them of their sins. Since absolution immediately followed the act of confession, penances were considered largely debts owed to the church for the service of bestowing forgiveness, thus shortchanging the former extensive penitential process and turning it into what could be perceived as a brief business transaction. As demands on the parish priest increased with the rising number of Christians in a parish, the spiritual direction and care of souls that had previously accompanied the confessional examination between priest and penitent largely disappeared. Christians who wished to examine their consciences under the careful guidance of a doctor of the soul were left to find other venues: they could entrust their secrets to and seek counsel from God directly, find an elder in their own parish, or seek help from those who had committed themselves to the wholehearted service of God, namely, members of monastic orders. It was this need for spiritual guidance and direction in conjunction with confession that gave rise to the growth of books and manuals of lay direction in the twelfth and thirteenth centuries and contributed to the emergence and successful establishment of the Franciscan and Dominican orders as their members began serving as spiritual directors to the laity.

CHAPTER SEVEN

The Rise of Spiritual Direction among the Laity and the Role of Women in Confession

In the Middle Ages the relationships among members of monastic communities, ecclesiastical authorities, and the laity were a mix of mutual disdain, competition, and interdependence. From the times of Benedict, monastic life in the West required separation from the world and seclusion within the monastic walls for a more focused concentration on liturgical prayer, manual labor, and the prayerful reading and study of the Bible. The first departure from the traditional monastic ideal came when the Benedictines were asked to become missionaries. At the request of Pope Gregory the Great (590–604) some of these Benedictines left their monasteries to evangelize England and much of northern Europe. Under the leadership of such Benedictines as Augustine of Canterbury (d. 604), the Venerable Bede (672–735), and Boniface (680–754), the new missionary endeavor came to fruition, producing monks who were also priests so as to be able to administer the sacraments, hear confession, and tend to the souls of those within and outside the monastery. When the Benedictines changed from a lay order to a predominantly clerical institute a second shift occurred: their focus began to move from manual labor on the farm to the intellectual endeavors of study, teaching, and preaching. With the founding of Benedictine abbeys, monasteries also became schools that began recruiting and training men for the priesthood. In order to have enough time to study, pray, and follow the liturgy of the hours, the monks had to enlist people from the outside to do the work on the farm and tend to the (sometimes vast and sprawling) estate of the community. The missionary activity of the Benedictines, the education of future priests, and the employment of laypeople within the monastic community provided contact with their neighbors and allowed them to be known and consulted in spiritual matters by members of the nobility, clerics, burghers, merchants, and laborers alike.

The monks' regular contact with members of the laity, nobility, and ecclesiastical authority also created problems. Two reform movements sought to resolve the predictable entanglements. The Cluny reform addressed abuses and conflicts between religious and secular authority resulting from the acquisition by many monasteries of large and valuable holdings of land. This reform created a centralized federation of monasteries by affiliating smaller houses with larger ones. Some fifteen hundred monasteries in Western Europe enrolled in this federation, with the result that monasteries were freed from secular and episcopal control. In addition, Cluny expanded the office of the liturgy, celebrating two community Masses per day, adding psalms for the monastery's benefactors, lengthening the lessons at the night office, and laying down elaborate rules for processions to the altars, with cross, candles, incense, and reliquaries. The second reform movement began around 1100 with the rise of the Cistercians, who sought a literal interpretation of the Rule of Benedict, a return to manual labor, a stress on interior personal sanctification, and an emphasis on solitude. As a result many of the Cistercian monasteries were built in remote places in a symbolic and practical effort to renounce the property, wealth, and power associated with towns and cities, including the institutions of the cathedral and the school.

The most obvious interaction of the monastery with the world was in the area of recruitment. While previously children donated by their parents formed one group of the monastic population, by the twelfth century this had changed: the newly formed orders rejected child oblates. Peter the Venerable of the Cluny branch, for example, regarded them as a potential source of trouble. Monastic applicants now were largely adults, both clerical and lay. Recruits came from the local town or city, or from the monastic schools. No distinction was made on account of birth, as long as postulants could bring with them some form of endowment. The custom of local recruitment meant that many of the monks had relatives among the townspeople, encouraging the interchange between the outside world and the monastic confines. In the case of the Cistercians the ideal of collective poverty amid deserted and uncultivated lands led to recruitment from among the peasantry and artisans, who were mostly illiterate and served as lay brothers engaged in doing the manual labor around the holdings. The Cistercian lay brother or lay convert, called *conversus*, had taken monastic vows and wore the habit, but lived a separate existence from the choir monks. Though he attended the choral offices he took no part in singing them. By performing manual labor as plowmen, shepherds, carpenters, masons, or similar occupations, these lay brothers would constitute the permanent workforce of the monastery, allowing the choir monks the necessary time of liturgical and private prayer and study. Usually choir monks were outnumbered by lay brothers at a ratio of one to three (or four). The rising number of lay brothers the Cistercians were able to attract shows that their zeal for poverty and a return to the desert monastics' teachings had struck a chord with the common laborer: he, too, could now look at his work of service and consider it a means of sanctification and a sacrifice acceptable in the eyes of God.

While previously the road to Christian perfection was available only to those who had taken solemn vows and lived as monastics, now a way was made for lay members to participate in monastic life and its disciplines. Lay brothers could receive spiritual guidance from the monks, benefit from their learning, and participate to some degree in their way of life. What evolved from this interaction between religious and the laity is commonly called the lay movement of the Middle Ages and led to a new lay spirituality that saw sanctifying value in the labor of the commoner. The movement would shape the rise of two orders whose members' ministry was aimed directly at the laity. The Franciscans and Dominicans directed their teaching and preaching, their efforts at evangelizing and hearing of confession, at the members of a feudal society laced by heresies and luxurious living. The friars' presence with the people rather than being separated by monastery walls served as a constant reminder of Christ's presence among them, of his poverty and humility in their midst, and his calling them to turn to God anew.

Both the Dominicans and the Franciscans were mendicant orders, which meant they combined active social ministry and preaching with a refusal to own private or communal property. Their income consisted of donations in return for services rendered, and they secured a livelihood by begging and the benevolence of the townspeople or local bishops. According to George Lane the turbulent "times urgently needed friars who could go out of their monasteries and combat the world's evils and errors."[1] Humbert of Romans says in his commentary on the Rule of Dominic, "Our order has been founded for preaching and for the salvation of our neighbors. Our studies should tend principally, ardently, above everything, to make us useful for souls."[2] St. Francis makes a similar point by describing the joy he felt when hearing God, saying that "God has not

---

1. George A. Lane, SJ, *Christian Spirituality: A Historical Sketch* (Chicago: Loyola Press, 1984, 2004), 27.
2. Herbert B. Workman, *The Evolution of the Monastic Ideal* (Boston: Beacon Press, 1962), 272; quoted in Lane, *Christian Spirituality*, 27.

called him into this estate for himself alone, but to the end that he may gain fruit of souls and that many through him may be saved."[3]

The Dominicans were formally approved as an order in 1216 and the Franciscans gained papal approval in 1223. The bishops welcomed the friars' services as a way of combating such heresies as those of the Cathars and Waldensians. While the Cathars held that material things were evil, including the body, the state, and the visible church, the Waldensians emphasized poverty, Bible reading, and itinerant preaching, eventually leading to their wholesale rejection of the institutional church. Despite both orders' similar orientations toward a ministry to the laity, they differed significantly in how they went about it. The Dominicans maintained a more tempered poverty, devoted themselves to Scripture study and secular learning, and could be excused from the common liturgy for the sake of study. The Franciscans advocated a radical voluntary poverty, were initially distrustful of advanced learning and the possession of books, and engaged in the practical work of social and pastoral ministry. Dominic's was an order of priests, while Francis was never a priest and considered himself a part of the populace, calling his brothers *fratres minores*, from the *minori*, the little people of the Tuscan towns.

The Franciscans carried their mission to rich and poor alike. In their itinerant ministry of preaching and voluntary poverty they had been preceded by the Waldensians and the Humiliati of the late twelfth century. The Waldensians had been founded by Peter Waldo, a wealthy cloth merchant and banker of Lyons who had renounced his property, settled his estate with his wife and two daughters, given the rest of the money to the poor, and embarked on a preaching ministry while supporting himself by begging. Similarly, the Humiliati of Italy were a lay group dedicated to apostolic ministry and poverty, drawing their recruits from the urban patriciate, that is, merchants and bankers, and either lived in community or stayed in their own homes while practicing a life of simplicity and works of mercy. Thus the founding of the Franciscans was aided by an urban scene in which visits from wandering preachers and threadbare evangelists were not uncommon. Exchanging wealth and noble standing for poverty and a beggar's state, as Francis and others before him had done, held the promise of a more simplified life in harmony with God. Shedding their property enabled the friars to have unhindered contact with the poor. Their testimony of poverty also gave the rich the opportunity to demonstrate charity toward the poor, so that

3. *Little Flowers of St. Francis*, chap. xvi; quoted in Lane, *Christian Spirituality*, 27–28.

through the friars' mediating activity rich and poor were equally served. Francis was mostly a missionary with a zeal for winning souls for Christ. In this quest he was respectful toward the church authorities and saw himself and his friars as supporters of the overall mission of the church. The friars were to approach the prelates with humility and reverence, for only then would they be welcome to preach and convert people in the marketplaces and squares and to hear confessions. From their humble beginnings in Italy the friars eventually went all over Europe and into far lands, preaching repentance, persuading men and women to return to peaceful relations and mutual charity—especially during the Lenten season—and hearing confessions and assigning penances. In England several of the friars became scholars, and those who were not preachers or lecturers were appointed to be confessors to clerics and laypeople. Francis himself had guided the soul of Clare, who at his direction founded the Second Franciscan Order, the Order of Poor Clares, and he brought into existence the Third Order, composed of laypeople, both single and married, who had pledged themselves to follow a Christian spiritual discipline within society and among their families. These Tertiaries, or Brothers and Sisters of Penance, as they were called, formed local groups. In their principled Christian devotion they sought to serve the sick and the poor by advocating on their behalf, their neighbors by promoting peaceful relations and reconciliation, and one another by providing spiritual counsel and guidance.

The Dominicans had as their primary concern the combating of heresies and a strengthening of the orthodox faith through ecclesiastical channels such as training the clergy. They provided preaching and wrote preaching manuals and materials for sermons, produced catechetical literature, and offered pastoral care and guidance. Dominic was an Augustinian monk and priest and founded his order on the Augustinian rule. He himself was university trained and advocated rigorous studies in theology and the Scriptures, so that the order soon embarked on the course of sending teachers to the young, fledgling universities of France, Italy, and Germany. But Dominic was also concerned with the subversion of clerical and monastic integrity. He disapproved of monks and bishops flaunting their wealth in the presence of heretics who, by contrast, practiced severe austerities, so that he sought to outdo the latter by demonstrating humility, labor, and fasting. Early sources attest to Dominic's evangelistic zeal and his spirit of compassion as well as his intellectual ability to argue with his opponents so as to win them over.

From their very beginnings the Dominicans, called the Order of Preachers, were also an order of confessors. In 1221, only five years after the order's founding, Pope Honorius III commended the Dominicans to all the bishops, urging that they entrust to them the ministry of confession. Dominic's successor as master general was Jordan of Saxony, who was well known as a director of souls. His journeys throughout Europe, his legislation, his educational endeavors all point to the collective and individual direction of souls as his single aim. During the Middle Ages the royalty of several European countries found the Dominicans to be prudent advisers and enlightened confessors. The French monarchy was much attached to them. As early as 1226 Jordan of Saxony would write about his pastoral role as confessor to Blanche of Castile: "The queen tenderly loves the friars and she has spoken with me personally and familiarly about her affairs."[4] During the Middle Ages the French monarchy sought most of its confessors from the Order of Preachers. So did the dukes of Burgundy, the kings of England, several German emperors, the kings of Castile and Spain, and the kings of Portugal. The ideal of an exchange between confessor and penitent is outlined by Paul of Hungary in 1220: "Let [the confessor] be inclined to correct kindly and to bear the weight himself. He must be gentle and affectionate, merciful to the faults of others. He shall act with discernment in different cases. Let him aid his penitent with prayer, alms, and other good works. He is to help him by calming his fears, consoling him, giving him back hope, and, if need be, by reproving him."[5] Another Dominican, St. Thomas Aquinas, discusses the practice of the hearing of confessions by monks and members of religious orders. In his *Apology for the Religious Orders* he cites the various objections raised—largely by the secular clergy who felt threatened in their professional status and pastoral purview—against the friars' preaching and their hearing of confessions, and then disposes of them one by one by citing the authority of the bishops who were making use of the friars' services, and of the pope and his potentates who had issued letters to authorize their preaching and penitential activities in an effort to revitalize the parishes.

4. Pierre Mandonnet, "Order of Preachers, Part 2: History of the Order, (j): The Preachers and Civil Society," citing Emmanuel-Ceslas Bayonne, *Lettres du B. Jourdain de Saxe, deuxième général de l'ordre des Frères-Prècheurs, aux religieuses de Sainte-Agnès de Bologne, et à la b. Dianae d'Andalo, leur fondatrice (1223–1236)* (Paris and Lyons: Bauchu, 1865), 66, in *The Catholic Encyclopedia*, vol. 12 (New York: Robert Appleton Company, 1911), http://www.mb-soft .com/believe/txh/dominic.htm.

5. Jean Leclercq, François Vandenbroucke, and Louis Bouyer, *The Spirituality of the Middle Ages*, History of Christian Spirituality 2 (London: Burns & Oates, 1968), 325; quoted in Kenneth Leech, *Soul Friend: Spiritual Direction in the Modern World* (Harrisburg, PA: Morehouse, 2001), 50.

In 1215 Pope Innocent III had required that confession be made by each Christian "to his own priest." The interpretation of this phrase was soon expanded to mean that people could seek out those trained in the art of hearing confession, who were primarily the Franciscan or Dominican friars. Only twelve years after the Lateran Council, in 1227, Pope Gregory IX granted the right to both Dominicans and Franciscans to hear confessions and absolve, with or without the consent of the local bishop. Apparently against the objections of the local parish priests, the people warmly welcomed the choice and began to prefer the friars; they came to hear them preach, to make confession, and to obtain spiritual counsel. What a chronicler says of Thuringia seems to have been the case in most of Europe: "Before the arrival of the Friars Preachers the word of God was rare and precious and very rarely preached to the people. The Friars Preachers preached alone in every section of Thuringia and in the town of Erfurt and no one hindered them."[6] In 1267 the Bishop of Amiens, Guillaume de Flavacourt, declared that the people refused to hear the word of God from anyone other than the Preachers (Dominicans) and Minors (Franciscans).[7] And the English Benedictine monk and historian Matthew Paris asserts that the people in England would no longer confess to their own priests. "None of the faithful," says this chronicler, "any longer believe themselves to be saved unless they are guided by the counsels of the Preachers [Dominicans] and the Minorites [Franciscans]."[8]

The preaching of the friars prompted conversions among the people and the need for hearing confession and assigning penances. If people were moved to contrition and repentance by the word proclaimed they would want to relieve their consciences and find healing through confession and penance, a process that would reinvigorate their faith and heighten their sense of Christ's presence with them. Bishops who wished for a revival in their parishes would invite the friars to participate in both proclamation and the hearing of confession. An example is Bishop Robert Grosseteste in England, who, though associated with the Franciscans at Oxford, invited some Dominicans also to help with a series of systematic visitations for reform in his urban diocese. In the course of these gatherings he assembled both clergy and laity, describing the scene

6. "Order of Preachers 2: History of the Order, (k): The Preachers and the Faithful," quoting Ludwig Koch, *Graf Elger von Holmstein: der Begründer des Dominikanerordens in Thüringen; ein Beitrag zur Kirchengeschichte Thüringens* (Gotha: A. Perthes, 1865), 70, 72, *Catholic Encyclopedia*, vol. 12 (see n. 4 above).

7. Ibid., citing Bibl. de Grenoble, manuscript 639, fol. 119.

8. John T. McNeill, *A History of the Cure of Souls* (New York: Harper & Brothers, 1951), 142–43.

as follows: "I preached to the clergy and some friar to the people. Four friars were employed at the same time in hearing confessions and enjoining penances."[9]

It was only a short step before individual Christians began seeking out the friars for spiritual counsel and direction apart from diocesan renewal gatherings and the annual Lenten discipline of making confession. Male converts could also join either order or one of its confraternities, thereby deepening their Christian discipline. By contrast, female converts intent on practicing a life of devout Christian discipleship had few options apart from joining the cloister or convent with its small number of available and often costly slots requiring a sizeable dowry. The dearth of options for women proved to be the seedbed for the birth of lay religious societies or consororities, whose members were commonly called beguines. The initial refusal of the friars to provide sacramental services, such as confession, to these women forced them to rely on one another for spiritual guidance and counsel. It is with the rise of women's lay groups, who shared much in their focus of ministry with the friars, that confession in its strictest sacramental sense and spiritual direction began to separate into two distinct branches of pastoral ministry that were carried out and administered by different people.

Women and Confession

The role women played in the larger historical development of the practice of confession and spiritual direction is significant. Their first decisive influence occurs visibly with the rise of the lay movement in the twelfth century. Until then it was as if their joint forces had been lying dormant for several hundred years, waiting to have their say. Much of the wait had to do with the customs that governed the religious life of women. In the early eighth and ninth centuries, for example, women could pursue the path of Christian perfection only by entering a monastic community. A typical convent strictly enforced full enclosure of the nuns and allowed for only limited contact with visitors, even visiting priests. In this way the convent would shield women, especially wealthy widows, from the advances of unwelcome suitors, the pressures of political intrigue and power plays and temptation, and the prospect of marriage with someone of unequal social and economic status. The majority of women in convents came from aristocratic and knightly families, and those who joined and the families who placed their daughters there

9. Ibid., 143.

expected to be in their own company. Other women monastics were married, yet had been disposed of by their husbands (often because they did not produce male offspring), had escaped abusive or unbearable marriages, or had husbands who had entered a monastery when their wives agreed to do likewise. The social status and educational background of these women gave them a sense of self-confidence and a relative independence in governing their own affairs. This attitude is especially evident in double monasteries of the time where, in the Germanic regions, for example, the royal abbesses of Merovingian Gaul and Anglo-Saxon England governed both the men and the women of their religious communities. By the tenth century this situation had changed. According to C. H. Lawrence, "An aristocratic society, whose legal arrangements and modes of thought were conditioned by the military fief, reduced women to a strictly subordinate role," a status that was "reinforced by the male chauvinism of the Latin Church," barring women not only from sacramental acts but also from such ecclesiastical functions as teaching and oversight.[10]

In the tenth and eleventh centuries monastic communities of women had to rely for sacramental services, including the hearing of confession and teaching, on an exclusively male clergy, often ill-trained and lacking in morals. Their abbesses and members were subject in the governance and exercise of ministry to male clerics, benefactors, and monastic founders and reformers. The rise of the friars in the thirteenth century initially changed little for female monastic communities: it was still inconceivable that women should be allowed to leave the safety of their convent or assume an active role in the apostolic life of preaching, teaching, hearing confessions, and evangelizing, even within convent walls. They remained dependent on the services of outside clergy. But here the ill repute of secular clergy, lacking in morals and education, was of grave concern to the nuns, especially in the context of the privacy of confession. In his *Apology for the Religious Orders*, published in 1257, Thomas Aquinas observes "the great ignorance prevailing in some places amongst many of the clergy," making it "rare to find any who are conversant with the Scriptures." Moreover, "the ignorance which prevails among the clergy, is, also, most detrimental in the duty of hearing confessions," leading both confessor and penitent "to fall into the ditch."[11] Other writers of the

---

10. Clifford H. Lawrence, *Medieval Monasticism: Forms of Religious Life in Western Europe in the Middle Ages* (London and New York: Longman, 1984), 218.

11. Thomas Aquinas, *An Apology for the Religious Orders*, ed. and trans. John Procter, STM (St. Louis: Herder, 1902), 122.

thirteenth century allude to priests using the confession of sins for making sexual advances and soliciting their female penitents. Monks like
Caesarius of Heisterbach (d. 1240) and friars like Bonaventure (d. 1274)
believed that many parish priests were addicted to this perversion and
abuse of power.[12] Rather than resorting to parish priests for sacramental
services, women's houses preferred to affiliate with a male monastery
that could furnish them with confessors, priests, and spiritual guides.
The only problem was that male orders were reluctant to do so.

In the thirteenth century male monasteries and the newly founded
orders of friars found plausible reasons to refuse the spiritual care of, or
affiliation with, female communities. For one thing, they feared losing
patrons, who preferred to support a monastery whose members could
celebrate Mass and make intercessory offerings on their behalf within
the Mass, something women could not do. For another, affiliation could
prove a source of temptation and be the cause of moral lapses among
the monks. In addition, ascetical and theological literature was mostly
written by men, and their pastoral and ecclesiastical services were given
to the laity and the church at large, which led donors, church authorities,
and laity to regard the communities and orders of women as of marginal
importance for the perfection of spiritual pursuits, hence an unnecessary
drain on resources. Increasingly, male orders refused to provide pastoral
services to, affiliate with, or incorporate female establishments for fear
of becoming financially or morally weakened, stigmatized in the eyes
of their donors, or derailed in their mission focus. As many male orders
refused to serve those of women, the few male orders willing to accept
them experienced a boom. For example, when the Premonstratensians
put a halt to admitting any further female houses the Cistercians found
themselves inundated with women postulants. An observer, Jacques de
Vitry, writes: "The nuns who professed the religion of the Cistercian
Order multiplied like the stars of heaven and vastly increased . . . convents were founded and built, virgins, widows, and married women
who had gained the consent of their husbands, rushed to fill the
cloisters."[13] In response to this tidal wave, the 1213 Cistercian chapter in
the diocese of Liège issued a rule of strict enclosure and stressed the

12. Centuries after the abuse had been noted, Pope Benedict XIV declared in 1741 that
absolutions granted by priests who had preyed on women under the protection of the seal
of confession were invalid. See McNeill, *A History of the Cure of Souls*, 148.
13. The quotation is from Jacques de Vitry, an Augustinian abbot and priest; see *The
Historia Occidentalis of Jacques de Vitry*, ed. John Frederick Hinnebusch, Spicilegium Friburgense 17 (Fribourg, Universitätsverlag, 1972), 117; quoted in Lawrence, *Medieval Monasticism*, 228.

responsibility of abbots to supervise the newly affiliated houses of women. Only seven years later the general chapter decreed that no more women's abbeys should be incorporated; these orders were reiterated in 1228. The chapter specified that "if any convent of nuns not yet associated with the order or not yet built wishes to imitate our institutes, we do not forbid it; but we will not accept the care of their souls or perform for them the office of visitation."[14]

The same fate of strict enclosure befell the women's orders that had formed under the Franciscans and Dominicans shortly after their founding. Their common property came under the auspices of their male order, and for the greater part of the thirteenth century the Franciscan and Dominican nuns came close to being disowned and disinherited by their parent orders of friars. The argument was that ministry to the women's houses, including Dominic's own women's houses at Prouille in France and St. Sixtus in Rome, would divert the friars from their apostolic mission and urban ministry. The same argument was made concerning the Poor Clares by the Franciscans, who refused responsibility for their spiritual care and direction. The resistance to the newly formed female religious groups is especially striking in the case of the Dominican friars. In their preaching they regularly effected conversions among the laity, including women who were members of lay sisterhoods and either lived alone or in communities. But for more than half a century the friars resisted the approaches of these laywomen to affiliate with the order, even though both groups shared similar ideals. It was during the time of strict enclosure for women monastics and their near abandonment by the friars that groups of laywomen would band together in semi-religious sisterhoods patterned after the friars' ideals of the apostolic life. They lived in the world and ministered to the poor and sick through works of charity and spiritual guidance while practicing a devout life of piety, prayer, and Scripture study.

The rise and rapid spread of lay sisterhoods is one of the most startling phenomena in medieval Europe. Communities and loose associations of women sprang up in northern France, Germany, and the Low Countries in the late twelfth and early thirteenth centuries. They constituted an alternative to the strict observance of enclosure and allowed women to maintain contact with other members of the laity. Practicing an experimental type of religious life, the groups' members took no solemn,

---

14. In A. Trilhe, *Statuta Capitulorum Generalium Ordinis Cisterciensis*, ed. Joseph Marie Canivez (Louvain: Bureaux de la Revue, 1933), 517; cited in Lawrence, *Medieval Monasticism*, 228.

irrevocable vows, but committed to observe celibacy while they belonged to the community. They gave up personal wealth while cultivating a frugal lifestyle that benefited the community at large. They attended Mass and the canonical hours in the local parish church while freely moving about the village or city to tend to the needs of the poor and the sick. In imitation of the friars some groups supported themselves exclusively through begging; they wanted to remain unencumbered by worldly possessions and be able to focus on study, prayer, and works of mercy. The majority of them, however, earned a living by their own work, such as weaving, sewing, embroidery, and brewing. It was these groups that their contemporaries called beguines and who would shape the development of confession and spiritual direction among Christians in significant ways.

Beguines: Hadewijch, Mechtild of Magdeburg, and Marguerite Porete

The beguines had formed in the late twelfth century as groups of laywomen who had united in their commitment to a life of simplicity, Scripture study, prayer, celibacy, and active Christian discipleship and service. Their practices were modeled on those of the apostolic church and they lived at home or in small communities while using the town church as the center of their association. By the early thirteenth century some beguines occupied houses in the towns of northern France, Flanders, Germany, and even England. With many of their members belonging to the aristocracy, at least in the early stages of the movement, they gradually secured recognition from the authorities of the church and the state, forming small, self-contained settlements within towns, with streets, gardens, houses, a cemetery, a brewery, a church. In some cases the houses were purchased with the funds new members brought to the communities; in others the buildings had been donated to them by members of the nobility, their own relatives, or friends. By the end of the thirteenth century the city of Cologne, for example, the biggest and most populous in northern Germany, had fifty-four beguinages, in many cases with their own chaplain and confessor. Other beguines continued living at home with their families or as solitaries.

The first to promote the beguines with the papal authorities was the future Augustinian canon and bishop Jacques de Vitry. He saw the beguines in the way reforming popes and bishops saw the friars: as a sign of new life for a church beleaguered by heresies and scarred by the ignorance and immorality of its secular clergy. Jacques had come to visit the beguine Mary of Oignies, whose fame as a holy woman and leader of a group of other holy women and educated clerics had reached him in Paris. The meeting would shape his life, leading him to commit to the vocation of ordained priest, joining the community at Oignies, becoming Mary's official ecclesiastical mouthpiece in preaching, and writing her biography after her death in 1216. Since in Mary the young Jacques de Vitry had found a mentor and teacher, he defended the new communities of women against their detractors and persuaded Pope Honorius III (1216–1227), who would approve the mendicant orders of the Franciscans and Dominicans, to authorize the beguines' way of life. Another advocate was Robert Grosseteste, bishop of Lincoln and considered one of the most learned men of the Middle Ages, who, when lecturing to the Franciscans at Oxford, said that "the Beguines have attained the highest perfection of holy religion, for they live by their own labour and do not burden the world with their demands."[15] And Master Robert of the Sorbonne conjectured that the beguines would fare better at the Last Judgment than many of the masters and theologians of Paris.[16] Objections to the beguines' lifestyle were voiced with equal fervor. Clifford H. Lawrence observes that "the spectacle of laywomen, without the sanction of any religious order, engaging in an active apostolic role was offensive to both male chauvinism and to clerical professionalism."[17] Objections focused on the women's lack of enclosure and their refusal to seek the services of and submit to secular clergy for teaching and counsel.

By the end of the thirteenth century most beguinages had managed to attach themselves to houses of Franciscan or Dominican friars, who provided them with spiritual directors and confessors. The process of affiliation and its inherent difficulties can be gleaned from history. Repeatedly the friars refused the beguines' request to affiliate with them even though friars served more or less covertly as confessors to individual beguines, including the group's spiritual guide, overseer, or "mistress." The decrees of the Dominican general chapters of 1228 and 1229, for example, prohibited giving the habit to any woman or receiving her profession, or giving spiritual direction to any community of women not subject to some authority (or monastic rule) other than that of the order. It would take nearly sixty years for the women's requests to be

---

15. Thomas of Eccleston, *Tractatus de Adventu Fratrum Minorum in Anglicam*, ed. Andrew G. Little (Manchester: Manchester University Press, 1951), quoted in Lawrence, *Medieval Monasticism*, 233.

16. Herbert Grundmann, *Religiöse Bewegungen im Mittelalter* (Hildesheim: G. Olms, 1961), 305, in Lawrence, *Medieval Monasticism*, 233.

17. Lawrence, *Medieval Monasticism*, 233.

granted with the founding of the Penitential Order of St. Dominic in 1285, for which beguines provided the main clientele, and of which Catherine of Siena (1347–1380) was a member. In light of this and similar delays and obstacles the women were forced into self-sufficiency and, consequently, into relative autonomy. They learned to rely on one another for the cure of souls and matters of confession and spiritual guidance; they recovered the monastic practice of examining one's own conscience, adapted the venue of confession to their own living situation, and made possible the increased availability of spiritual direction among the laity.

The thirteenth century marks a turning point for confessional practices and related theological and spiritual developments in the church. This was largely due to the influence of women in lay religious communities on their contemporaries. They were in regular contact with the laity and exemplified by their life, ministry, and teachings the claims of the Gospel and Christ's transforming powers. Some of these women were tertiaries, so called for their affiliation with the Third Order of St. Francis, founded by St. Clare. Their contact was limited, due to the enclosure requirement, but less so than for other women's orders, such as the Cistercian nuns. Others were beguines, living under no monastic rule, who had established unofficial and often covert connections to Franciscan or Dominican friars who would serve as the women's confessors and spiritual directors. Some friars recorded the lives of these women or supported them in writing down their teachings, often serving as their secretaries. In a patriarchal society being authenticated by male supporters and ecclesiastical authorities was not only crucial for the rise of communities, but also for the dissemination of religious literature written by women. Bernard McGinn calls these foundational writings "the earliest large-scale emergence of women's voices in the history of Christian thought,"[18] and Caroline Walker Bynum says: "For the first time in Christian history certain major devotional and theological emphases emanated from women and influenced the basic development of spirituality."[19] These writings were also among the first vernacular writings on spiritual and pastoral theology in Western Christianity. By their broad appeal they helped fill the perceived need among penitents to prepare for the sacrament of confession, they met a quest among Christians to deepen their

18. Bernard McGinn, *Meister Eckhart and the Beguine Mystics* (New York: Continuum, 1994), 1.
19. Caroline Walker Bynum, *Jesus as Mother: Studies in the Spirituality of the High Middle Ages* (Berkeley: University of California Press, 1982), 172.

spiritual lives, and they proposed a type of spiritual perfection possible apart from the monastery and open to all believers.

Several of these lay religious women, called beguines or *mulieres religiosae*, helped shape a new model of discipleship and of spiritual direction, contributing to the flowering of lay manuals for spiritual directors emerging in the late thirteenth and fourteenth centuries. What makes this model new is that the women's texts of instruction are written not in the customary Latin but in the vernacular, seemingly aiming at the laity at large and signaling a newly broadened audience. By implication all Christians, rather than only the few able to read Latin, are encouraged to serve as spiritual directors to one another. Three beguine authors in particular stand out as the leading Christian writers and "female evangelists"[20] of the thirteenth century. They are Hadewijch of Antwerp (thirteenth century) in the Low Countries, Mechtild of Magdeburg (1208–1297) in Germany, and Marguerite Porete (d. 1310) in France. Their writings examine the state of the soul in preparation for repentance and confession. They could be classified as mystical writings, as they speak of the author's burning desire for God and an intense consciousness of God's love and presence in all things, and the possibility of divine union. They differ markedly from the treatises of their male contemporaries, such as the Franciscans Bonaventure and Alexander of Hales or the Dominicans Raymond of Penafort and William of Auvergne, by bypassing debates on confession and penance as sacrament along with the various preparatory stages and distinctions of attrition and contrition. Rather, the women's writings speak of personal experiences and visions of the divine, generously employing the literary devices of paradox, poetry, and metaphor. In recent years these spiritual writings of the period have been classified as "vernacular theology,"[21] forming a distinct third strand of literature in addition to those of the scholastic and the monastic traditions written by men. Originating from and complementing the other two strands, the literature of vernacular theology places women and men, laity and clergy, on equal footing as an audience by

---

20. Bernard McGinn identifies four women as the "female evangelists" of thirteenth-century mysticism; they are a Franciscan tertiary, Angela of Foligno, in Italy, along with the three beguines Hadewijch, Mechtild of Magdeburg, and Marguerite Porete; see Bernard McGinn, *The Flowering of Mysticism: Men and Women in the New Mysticism—1200–1350*, vol. 3 of his *The Presence of God: A History of Western Christian Mysticism* (New York: Crossroad, 1998), 141.

21. See Saskia Murk-Jansen, *Brides in the Desert: The Spirituality of the Beguines* (Maryknoll, NY: Orbis Books, 1998), 41–42; also Bernard McGinn, "Introduction," in *Meister Eckhart and the Beguine Mystics*, 1–14.

eliminating the hierarchy between those who knew Latin (monastics and the clergy) and those who did not (the laity). It emphasizes a spiritual inwardness and mystical experience that is uniquely personal and experiential, while insisting on its universality and availability to all. And it uses "image language," in contrast to discursive language, engaging the imagination to make fluid connections rather than employing rational logic to obtain final and often static answers.

The aim of beguine literature is to help Christians practice humility and repentance in everyday life and to prepare for union with Christ in this life as a foretaste of the life to come. The early vernacular theology of the beguines points to two movements in Christian discipleship or the *vita apostolica*, the apostolic life. These are: first, the ongoing examination of the self in light of Christ's life and passion, leading to outward tears and inward repentance; and second, the return of the soul to Christ, the supreme lover and bridegroom, leading to intimate contact or mystical union with him and frequently resulting in ecstatic visions. For examining one's conscience, the writers contemplate themes of Jesus' life and passion, his rejection by the people, his humility, and his self-giving love. These themes would find extensive treatment in a later genre of vernacular devotional literature flourishing at the beginning of the fourteenth century and urging the believer's imitation of Christ. A representative example of this new lay devotion is the *Imitation of Christ*, a book ascribed to Thomas à Kempis but possibly penned by the Carthusian monk Ludoph of Saxony (d. 1377). In addition to the *Imitation*, he also wrote the *Life of Christ* that contains recommendations on prayer and became the *Biblia pauperum*, the Poor People's Bible. This book, containing extensive woodcuts and passages on the life of Jesus, circulated widely in the fifteenth century. The founder of the Jesuits, Ignatius of Loyola, read the *Life of Christ* in 1521 and would incorporate the book's recommendations on prayer and the practice of meditating on Jesus' life in his *Spiritual Exercises*.

Other books related to the beguines' emphasis on self-examination and repentance were collections of anecdotes, or *libri exemplorum*, for use by preachers in sermon preparation. One variety of these collections is the *speculum*, or mirror, so called because the story is a mirror of the soul, contrasting good and evil behavior and illustrating sins and virtues. Much of this material passed from the clergy's hands to the laity, prompting the creation and circulation of books on moral guidance written in the vernacular. Collections of *exempla* stem largely from Dominican friars or those affiliated with the Dominican tradition, such as Jacques de Vitry, Jordan of Saxony, and John Bromyard. A growing theme in this type of

devotional literature is the notion of spiritual progress and its stages.
Thomas Aquinas (1225–1274) speaks of beginners, proficients, and the
perfect, dividing the spiritual journey into three "ways," namely, the
purgative, the illuminative, and the unitive. Catherine of Siena uses
the metaphor of the "three stairs" leading to perfection, the first of which
represents the Christian in the role of a mercenary, the second in that of
a faithful servant, and the third in that of a child who shows unreserved
love toward a parent. She also speaks of these stages as a subsequent
dwelling at the feet, the heart, and the head of Christ crucified. According to Benedict M. Ashley these three stages of spiritual growth are
portrayed by Dominican writers in the tradition of John of the Cross
(1542–1591) as separated from each other by spiritual nights, the "dark
night of the soul," and they mark "the transition from the purgative to
the illuminative" or "unitive phase."[22]

The second central theme in women's literature of this period is that
of mystical union, often using bridal and courtly imagery. Contemplating
and identifying with the suffering Christ creates awareness of one's sinful acts and thoughts, both spiritual and corporeal. In turn, such self-
examination leads to remorse and sorrow, a self-abandon and surrender
that trusts in God's forgiveness and mercy and the possibility of union
with the divine manifested in ecstatic visions and revelations. Among
the earliest collections of revelations written in the vernacular is the *Book
of Visions*, composed in the 1240s by the Dutch beguine Hadewijch of
Antwerp. Little is known of her, including the years of her birth and
death, and her writings were not widely circulated during her lifetime.
She is credited with being one of the creators of Dutch lyrical poetry and
employs courtly imagery throughout her writings. Based on her thirty
extant letters, Hadewijch knew Latin and French, was widely read and
of possibly aristocratic lineage, served as the head and spiritual guide
of a community of beguines near Antwerp, and was a sought-after spiritual guide among the laity. Many of her letters are addressed to those
seeking her spiritual guidance. In her *Book of Visions* the descriptions of
her encounters with Christ, the divine bridegroom, contain accounts of
ecstasy and joy, but they are portrayed as only the beginning of the
contemplative life steeped in a self-abandoning love for God, or *minne*,
as she calls it, rather than its end. *Minne* compels one, according to her,
to seek the shedding of one's will and all images and illusions so as to
attain to a "pure and naked Nothingness," the ground of the divine. This

22. Benedict M. Ashley, OP, *Spiritual Direction in the Dominican Tradition* (Mahwah, NJ:
Paulist Press, 1995), 89.

nothingness is the meeting place and the proverbial marriage bed of the soul and God. The language employed is that of courtly love, the knight's honorable pursuit of the noble lady whom he woos and eventually wins. Along with the traditional interpretation of the allegory, as found in Bernard of Clairvaux's numerous expositions on the Song of Songs, Hadewijch's interpretation contains a nontraditional approach as well: she reverses the roles of God as the lover and the soul as the lady. Since *minne*, love, is a feminine noun, representative of God, Hadewijch is free to mix metaphors and describe God as female and the soul as male. Thereby the soul (and the Christian) is viewed as the humble, valiant male knight who by persistent wooing and steadfast courage prompts the lady, God, to open her doors to the soul. According to Saskia Murk-Jensen this inversion of metaphorical roles for God and soul "represented the many reverses of the mystic life"; it encouraged "those for whom she was writing to identify with steadfastness" and placed on her readers "the duty to act" and "obey the dictates of their lady."[23] This duty to act differs from the traditional concept of a righteousness obtained through good works and acts of penance. It consists no longer of the highest stages of virtue and moral perfection, but rather of a plunge into limitless unknowing, into the abyss of *minne*. Such acting encourages the experience of the "wild desert" in the midst of trials and suffering, a remaining steadfast in the absence of love. It also encourages the abandonment of self-will and reason's self-reliance so as to prepare for the inbreaking of and union with the divine.

The themes of self-abandon leading to union with God and God as the ground of nothingness were further developed by the Dominican priest Meister Eckhart (1260–1327), who may have learned of them when visiting the houses of beguines in the Rhineland and the Low Countries and serving there as preacher, spiritual director, and confessor. The bridal mysticism of Hadewijch also provided an inspiration to Jan van Ruysbroeck (1293–1381). In his book *The Spiritual Espousals*, sometimes called *The Adornment of the Spiritual Marriage*, the Flemish priest and Augustinian monk appropriated Hadewijch's themes of the primacy of love for God, its joys and sorrows, and the dynamic participation of the believer in the life of the Trinity. Ruysbroeck's most famous disciple was Geert de Groote (1340–1384), who founded a movement of spiritual reform in the Low Countries known as Brethren of the Common Life, or New Devotion (*devotio moderna*). The religious tradition of *devotio moderna*

---

23. Murk-Jansen, *Brides in the Desert*, 51.

shaped the teachings of the Dutch theologian and Augustinian monk Erasmus of Rotterdam (1466–1536), who was educated by the Brethren, and it would also have its influence on the Augustinian monk and priest Martin Luther in sixteenth-century Germany.

Another representative of the earliest vernacular theology is the German beguine Mechtild of Magdeburg. She recorded her visions and spiritual union in *The Flowing Light of the Godhead*, composed between 1250 and 1280 at the urging of her Dominican spiritual director, who remains unnamed. Already during her lifetime the book was widely circulated, and the Italian poet Dante (1265–1321) may have read it, to judge from the striking similarities with passages in the *Divine Comedy*. For the greater part of her forty-year stay with the beguines Mechtild appears to have held a position of authority among her group. However, in 1270 she was forced to flee to the community of Cistercian nuns at Helfta, an important center for female spiritual writing. *The Flowing Light* presents itself as of quasi-scriptural status, intended for public reading and discussion not just among beguines and other lay orders, but for all Christians. More than a sequence of visions, the book uses the key images of "flowing," "courting," "playing at love," and "sinking" in reference to the soul's relationship with the deity, and especially the Trinity. Mechtild's visions are rooted in the soul's participation in Christ's passion, leading to union with the divine, where the soul meets the divine lover in emptiness, pain, God-estrangement, and humble service to others.

Hadewijch's and Mechtild's theme of detachment and nakedness before God finds expression in the works of the Dominican Meister Eckhart, who was the first to systematically promote it in his commentaries, treatises, and sermons. Eckhart taught at the universities of Paris and Cologne and frequently preached in the beguine communities of France, Belgium, and the Rhineland. His contact with these devout and educated women leaders of a new lay devotion certainly shaped his theology. Rather than stressing the human sinful nature and a scrupulous self-examination in regard to one's sins, followed by confession, penance, and absolution, Eckhart raises up a vision of the soul and God as one. To obtain divine union, according to Eckhart, one was to purge the soul of earthly thoughts and desires by practicing "detachment" (*Abgeschiedenheit*) and "releasement" (*Gelassenheit*). Such detachment and emptying of self, exemplified by Christ's passion and death on the cross, allowed the divine word to settle and penetrate the soul as if into a vacancy and to find resonance and union with the "divine spark" (*Seelenfünklein*) existent in each person. "I praise detachment above love," writes Eckhart in his treatise on the subject, "because . . . [it] leads me to where I am receptive to nothing except God."[24] Eckhart's followers, the Dominicans Heinrich Suso (1295–1366) and Johannes Tauler (ca. 1300–1361), continued to promote the notion that the human soul could unite with the divine by the practice of detachment. Tauler's collected sermons, or *Conferences*, became immensely popular in Germany and, in their Latin translation, in Spain. Recorded by nuns to whom Tauler may have served as spiritual director, the sermons stress "the uncreated ground of the soul" that is present in all human beings, the soul's hunger for God, and the need for passivity so as to allow for God's transformative work. Suso's works include the *Little Book of Truth* and the *Little Book of Eternal Wisdom*, which were widely read in the fourteenth and fifteenth centuries, stressing the abandonment of self, the human and divine oneness, and the knowledge of and union with God resulting from a contemplation of Christ's passion and one's dying to self in this life. Like Tauler, Suso was valued as a spiritual director in many women's convents, especially those of the Dominican order,[25] and his works were translated into Spanish, influencing the spirituality and writings of the Carmelites Teresa of Avila (1515–1582) and John of the Cross (1542–1591).

The focus on ongoing self-examination in the beguine movement was intended to complement the annual practice of confession to a priest. Christians, especially those living in community or affiliated with a lay order, could regularly gather to read Scripture and devotional books, pray, examine and reveal their consciences to one another, and practice the kind of self-abandonment, surrender, and detachment that Hadewijch, Mechtild, and later Eckhart were proposing. Christian perfection, often equated with salvation, was no longer reserved for members of monastic communities but could be attained in lay communities and was accessible to the many. Thus the direction and definition of religious piety among the laity shifted from doing to being. Doing penance, along with its accompanying acts of fasting, almsgiving, or other sacrifices, was interpreted to mean a form of surrender, a gradual annihilation of the will. One no longer scaled the heights of perfection or gathered divine favors by works of supreme self-sacrifice and abstinence but found God's immanent presence, peace, and consolation in the act of "being," such

24. Meister Eckhart, "On Detachment," in *Meister Eckhart: The Essential Sermons, Commentaries, Treatises, and Defense*, trans. and introduced by Edmund Colledge, OSA, and Bernard McGinn (Mahwah, NJ: Paulist Press, 1981), 286.

25. Ursula King, *Christian Mystics: Their Lives and Legacies Throughout the Ages* (Mahwah, NJ: Paulist Press, 2001), 113.

as in persevering in one's trials, identifying with the life and passion of Christ, and allowing the love thus experienced to overflow into good works.

As the teachings on mystical union through detachment and surrender gained prominence in Germany, France, and the Low Countries, church authorities became increasingly concerned about their own status and influence with believers, more so, perhaps, than about the good these teachings produced and the resulting charitable activity among the flock. The tendencies of mysticism, stressing the inner life of the individual, appeared to rival and conflict with the communal liturgical practices, sacramental rites, and an established church order that reaped considerable (financial) benefits from sinners' guilt. But the beguine communities did not wish to sever their relationship with the established church or eschew sacramental practices, as had members of the societies of the Free Spirit, for example. Instead, beguines insisted on receiving the Eucharist and practicing confession to a priest, relying for these services on friars ordained to the priesthood, mostly Dominicans, or clergy members they knew and who were kindly disposed toward them and supportive of their ideals, ministry, and teachings. Often friars and clerics risked criticism, reproach, and even censure by their provincial or bishop for their pastoral support of and friendship with the women. But they also received significant benefits from informal association and visits with these female lay communities and their members. The passionate zeal, apostolic activity, and reinterpretation of monastic teachings that members embraced and practiced had to leave an invigorating and enlightening effect. As some commentators put it, "The men served the women and gained spiritual nourishment from doing so,"[26] in addition to receiving new insights and the otherwise rare opportunity of "sustained and serious conversation with a member of the opposite sex."[27]

It is telling that the beguine writings do not mention the practice of hearing one another's confession or providing spiritual direction, even though such practices are likely to have occurred in the close-knit communities in which some lived. It is possible that as ecclesiastical criticism of the beguine movement mounted, beginning with the second half of a roughly one-hundred-year span of thriving activity, authors and perhaps editors, such as their own male spiritual directors, became increasingly cautious about how much of their devotional practices it was

---

26. Murk-Jansen, *Brides in the Desert*, 81.

27. Jodi Bilinkoff, *Related Lives: Confessors and Their Female Penitents, 1450–1750* (Ithaca: Cornell University Press, 2005), 18–19.

deemed safe to share with the public. Moreover, visiting friars, preachers, and clergy are rarely identified by name, even though a lively exchange existed. This may have been to protect the communities' monastic or clergy friends from appearing to assume ecclesiastical functions that could have brought them into conflict with their own order's chapter or diocesan authorities. Finally, these male friends are alternately referred to as both confessors and spiritual directors, which could mean that the ministry of spiritual direction and the "cure of souls" (*cura animarum*), so called in the decrees of the Lateran Council, had become a value-neutral descriptor of varying aspects of soul care, which included preaching and teaching, emphatic and sympathetic listening, hearing confession, exhortation, assigning penances, and offering absolution. It is at this point, in the late thirteenth to the early fourteenth centuries, that a tentative blending of confession and spiritual direction occurs. This blending gave rise to a subsequent clear role separation, widely common by the fifteenth century, whereby priests serving as confidants, chaplains, and advisors to individual members of the laity would explicitly label themselves "spiritual directors" rather than confessors[28]; the parish priest and the spiritual director might be two different people.[29]

The reorientation in spiritual practice and theological doctrine advanced by the women evangelists and teachers of the thirteenth century was not without consequence. Aimed at the laity at large and written in the vernacular, the women's teachings stood to rival those orally presented by the local parish priest. Most certainly they threatened the established hierarchy of the church and sacramental practices, especially those of confession, penance, and absolution. In 1310 the beguine Marguerite Porete was executed by the Dominican Inquisitor of Paris, William Humbert. The major objection to her teachings in *The Mirror of Simple Annihilated Souls*, written in the 1290s, involved her seeming indifference to the ecclesiastically administered and controlled means of salvation. In addition, Marguerite had insisted on "wandering, preaching, and disseminating material from her book."[30] While Hadewijch had recorded years earlier that a beguine had been killed by another Dominican inquisitor, Marguerite's is "the first documented case of an execution for mystical heresy in Western Christianity."[31] Despite the fact that Mar-

28. Ibid., 17.

29. Leech, *Soul Friend* (2001), 53.

30. Abby Stoner, "Sisters Between: Gender and the Medieval Beguines," at http://userwww.sfsu.edu/~epf/1995/beguine.html.

31. McGinn, *The Flowering of Mysticism*, 244.

guerite's book, along with her body, was burned, *The Mirror of Simple Souls* survives in six versions and four languages (Italian, English, and Latin, besides French), making it one of the more widely read vernacular mystical texts of the Middle Ages. Meister Eckhart almost certainly knew and used the book in his own preaching and writings, as did Jan van Ruysbroeck.

Central in Marguerite's *Mirror* is the idea of the human soul as one with God in essence. The soul may recover and experience eternal pre-existence in God through the negation of self-will and by the ongoing practice of humility, leading to infinite freedom and a transcendent being. Traversing several stages, the soul is invited at each stage to undergo a form of death, from the first death to sin, to the second death to one's desires of the body, to the third death of the will, and so on. It is at the fifth stage that the death of the spirit takes place, the death of reason, self-will, self-direction, as a preparatory stage for the soul's "annihila-tion." The book is aimed at those "simple souls" who have been practic-ing the surrender of reason and self-will for some time. With them the soul has, according to Marguerite, no concern for herself, for her neigh-bors, or even for God. Instead, the soul "swims and bobs and floats" in eternal peace "without any movement in her interior and without any exterior work."[32] The book is a trialogue among the persons of Reason, Love, and the Soul, with Reason and Love the main protagonists. The representatives of Reason are the clergy, who will never grasp the mes-sage that Love teaches the simple souls. The representatives of Love are those who by ascetic practices, self-abandonment, and lowly service have come to regard themselves as simple souls, who know their sinful nature and their shortcomings and regard their own efforts as futile in drawing near to God and becoming God's vessels. Because they have little else on which to fall back, such souls own nothing and have sur-rendered themselves to the abyss of a nothingness of the will, thus be-coming truly unencumbered and free. The Soul is representative of one's conscience and the inner voice of truth as well as the place of God's presence in the human heart. The role of Christ is that of example, a first manifestation of the soul's descent into nothingness, where his descent is primarily meant to "amaze" the soul into a similar loss of self. Such a union with God, resulting from the descent, means that the soul "loses her name in the One in whom she is melted and dissolved," similar to a river, which has a name as long as it flows by itself but which loses its

32. *The Mirror of Simple Annihilated Souls*, chap. 81, as quoted in McGinn, *The Flowering of Mysticism*, 264.

name and all its labor once it returns to the sea.[33] No outside help is needed, no mediator, apart from reason (and the teachings of the *Mirror*) as an aid to release and annihilate reason and allow for an aperture to God's abiding presence and goodness and peace. Such autonomy in reaching for and finding God disconcerted the ecclesiastical authorities enough for them to press for Marguerite's execution. Sometime between 1296 and 1308 Marguerite's book was condemned to be burned, while she continued to disseminate the text and seek counsel and endorsement from various friars and bishops. One of the endorsers noted "that he did not advise that many should have" the book on account of its advanced teachings and the danger of their becoming "deluded," while affirming that "the Soul is not able to attain divine life or divine way of being until she has reached the way that this book describes."[34] In 1308 Marguerite was arrested. During her two-year imprisonment and trial she refused to speak to her inquisitors, a commission of twenty-one theologians of the Sorbonne, or make any other statement in her defense, dying as a condemned heretic at the stake in 1310.

Marguerite's teachings are slowly being rediscovered and appreciated by modern scholarship. Her theological concepts of an immediate God-experience by laypersons apart from ecclesiastical mediation and the equality of believers before God, including their role as "confessor" to one another without regard for ordination or social status, seemingly anticipate the sixteenth-century Protestant Reformation. Among the Reformation principles are the priesthood of all believers, a radically reduced and simplified sacramental system and a diminished authority of the clergy, the autonomy and freedom of conscience of the Christian believer before God, and the individualizing of spiritual practices and penances, such as Scripture study in the vernacular to aid in self-knowledge, and works of charity and almsgiving as concrete expressions of penance. First, however, other laywomen of the fourteenth century would carry on Marguerite's vision of how simple souls, namely, lay members of the church, could strive for spiritual perfection by surrender and obedience and serve as preachers, teachers, lay confessors, and spiritual directors. Two prominent examples are the Italian Dominican tertiary Catherine of Siena, who lived at home, and the English anchoress

---

33. *The Mirror of Simple Annihilated Souls*, chap. 82, as quoted in McGinn, *The Flowering of Mysticism*, 264.

34. Marguerite Porete, "Approbatio" (The Approbation of the Three Clerics), in Emilie Zum Brunn and Georgette Epiney-Burgard, *Women Mystics in Medieval Europe*, trans. Sheila Hughes (New York: Paragon House, 1989), 163–64.

Julian, who may have lived bricked into her quarters adjacent to St. Julian Church in Norwich.

Tertiaries: Catherine of Siena

The founding of the third order among Franciscans and Dominicans had given women the opportunity to follow the *vita apostolica*. They could practice a devout life and pursue Christian perfection while living in the world. The advantages of the tertiary life for women included freedom to move about and carry out ministry among a wide range of people. This freedom and the immediate influence on large numbers of people are especially apparent in the case of the Dominican tertiary Catherine of Siena (1347–1380). From an early age Catherine had devoted herself to the pursuit of a holy life. One of twenty-five children of the family of a dyer in the Siena district, she took a vow of celibacy at the age of seven and, overcoming the pressures of her parents to marry, became a Dominican tertiary at the age of sixteen, while living at home. For three years Catherine practiced the life of a solitary, reminiscent of the desert fathers and mothers in Egypt, speaking only to God in confession, following a monastic schedule of prayer, fasting, and penances, and leaving her room only to attend Mass. Then, in 1366, she experienced a vision of her "mystical marriage with Christ," often depicted in Renaissance paintings, which prompted her to gradually leave her cell to go and help her neighbors and to minister to the terminally ill, the sick, and prisoners. Before and during this time of transition her confessor was her foster brother Tommaso della Fonte, who had become a priest and who brought to the home other Dominicans such as Tommaso Caffarini, a teacher at the University of Siena, and the priest Bartolomeo Dominic, who became her subsequent confessor. Catherine's earliest teachings were recorded during these conversations with visitors. Despite the lack of a formal education, Catherine drew a host of followers—members of religious orders, secular priests, and laypeople—who sought her out for spiritual direction and counsel. Their company included Dominican, Augustinian, and Franciscan friars, who also penned her numerous letters and correspondence with popes, bishops, the nobility of Italian city-states, and townspeople. More than four hundred of these letters have survived. The friars also took dictation for her book *The Dialogue*,[35] recorded in only five days in 1370 while

---

35. Catherine of Siena, *The Dialogue*, trans. and introduction by Suzanne Noffke, Classics of Western Spirituality (New York: Paulist Press, 1980); quotations in this chapter are from the online version, *Dialog of Catherine of Siena*, at www.ccel.org.

Catherine was in a trancelike state. The book chronicles Catherine's dialogues with God in visions of mystical union and illustrates her view that true knowledge of God and of the self is found only in ongoing self-examination and humility within one's "inner cell." Those who through confession and penance have searched themselves "are another Myself, inasmuch as they have lost and denied their own will, and are clothed with Mine, are united to Mine, are conformed to Mine."[36] In words similar to those of Marguerite, Catherine describes the experience of divine union as the soul's descent into an "abyss," where the "selfish will" is drowned and the desire for God increases, for "the deeper I enter the more I find, and the more I find the more I seek; the soul cannot be satiated in Your abyss, for she continually hungers after You."[37]

All Christians share equally in being counselors to one another, in Catherine's view. Each may retreat to the inner cell and perfect one's walk on the model of Christ. God has "given you the Bridge of My Son, in order that, passing across the flood, you may not be drowned, which flood is the tempestuous sea of this dark life. See, therefore, under what obligations the creature is to Me, and how ignorant he is, not to take the remedy which I have offered." Keeping to this bridge at all times allows one to find "true happiness," partake of God's being, and "taste my supreme and eternal sweetness and goodness." In short, "the height of the Divinity, humbled to the earth, and joined with your humanity, made the Bridge and reformed the road."[38] In like manner all Christians are in a position to provide spiritual counsel and direction to one another. The good spiritual director understands the distinction between outward acts of penance and true contrition of the heart. This means that "the works of penance, and of other corporal exercises, should be observed merely as means, and not as the fundamental affection of the soul."[39] They are "instruments of virtue," not an end in themselves; and unless they spring from true self-awareness they should be abandoned because they are offensive to God. The apostle Paul instructs us to "mortify the body and destroy self-will, knowing, that is to say, how to keep the rein on the body, macerating the flesh whenever it should wish to combat the spirit, but the will should be dead and annihilated in everything, and subject to My will."[40]

36. Catherine of Siena, "A Treatise of Divine Providence," in *Dialogue*.
37. Catherine of Siena, "A Treatise of Obedience," in *Dialogue*.
38. Catherine of Siena, "A Treatise of Discretion," in *Dialogue*.
39. Ibid.
40. Ibid.

Central to confession and penance are self-examination and discernment, according to Catherine. Such knowledge of self produces "hatred and disgust of [the soul's] offenses and sensuality." Knowledge of self "is the knife which slays and cuts off all self-love founded on self-will"[41] and produces a multitude of good works that are pleasing to God. True good works flow from knowledge of self and our connectedness to one another in the body of Christ. All Christians "are obliged to help one another by word and doctrine, and the example of good works, and in every other respect in which your neighbor may be seen to be in need; counseling him exactly as you would yourselves, without any passion of self-love."[42] Thereby Christians function as workers in their own and in their neighbor's souls and in the "mystic body" of the church. Working on oneself involves virtue and subjecting one's will in surrender to God, serving as an example to others and teaching them. This is especially important since the church has "become leprous, on account of her filthiness and self-love, and [is] swollen with the pride and avarice of those who feed on their own sin."[43]

Christians are free before God in their conscience. Catherine considers this freedom as essential to happiness because "the soul can, by her free will, make choice either of good or evil." Our freedom is so great that "no demon or creature" can force us into sinning. Rather, we are freed from slavery to govern our own "sensuality" and obtain the end for which we are created.[44] The freedom we have in Christ knows no outward laws, but urges the conscience to become attuned to God and to function as a "body guard." When enemies are "coming to attack the city of the soul," the conscience acts like a "watch-dog," which "warns the sentry of reason, and the reason together with the free-will know by the light of the intellect whether the stranger be friend or enemy."[45] True merit before God, then, does not result from good works and acts of penance and supreme sacrifice. Instead, it springs from having trained the conscience to flee temptation and allow for the soul's union with God, resulting "in the virtue of love alone, flavored with the light of true discretion, without which the soul is worth nothing."[46]

41. Ibid.
42. Catherine of Siena, "A Treatise of Divine Providence," in *Dialogue*.
43. Catherine of Siena, "A Treatise of Discretion," in *Dialogue*.
44. Ibid.
45. Catherine of Siena, "A Treatise of Prayer," in *Dialogue*.
46. Catherine of Siena, "A Treatise of Discretion," in *Dialogue*.

In 1374 the Dominican chapter in Florence summoned Catherine to address accusations made against her. Both friars and Dominican laywomen were among her opponents. The charges made against her had to do with her close contact with men and her increasingly public role as a preacher, spiritual guide, and confessor. Instead of being censured Catherine was given the well-known Dominican scholar Raymond of Capua as her spiritual director and confessor, which lent her even greater credibility both in Siena and in the wider church. In his chronicle about Catherine's life, known as the "Legend," written in 1395, Raymond recounts his initial skepticism of her and their first meeting: "She kept on speaking on the subject she had begun. And as she spoke my sins came before my mind with a clarity I had never before experienced. The veil was torn from my eyes, and I saw myself standing at the bar of my Divine Judge . . . I burst out into such a torrent of tears and sobs as, I must reluctantly confess, made me fear my very breast and heart would be ruptured. Catherine discreetly said not another word, as though this was the very purpose for which she had come."[47] The year after their first meeting, Raymond encouraged Catherine to begin an evangelistic preaching tour in the regions of Tuscany and Lombardy. Raymond accompanied her, serving as her chaplain and coworker and hearing the confessions of numerous converts brought to repentance by Catherine's preaching. During the tour additional priests had to be enlisted to help hear confessions and baptize converts. In Pisa so many people came to the church to hear her preach that penitents lined up outside the church and beyond the city gates. It was in Pisa also that Catherine received the stigmata, the wounds of Christ impressed on her hands and feet when praying and contemplating the passion of Christ before a crucifix, much as had St. Francis before her. While Catherine's preaching brought many to repentance, her letters appear to have been equally effective; they address plainly the sin and spiritual ailments of her charges and those to whom she provided spiritual counsel. "I want you to be the sort of true and good shepherd," she writes to Pope Gregory XI, "who, had you a hundred thousand lives, would be ready to give them all for God's honor and other people's salvation." For those in authority are bound to "do evil when holy justice dies in them because of their selfish self-

47. Raymond of Capua, *The Life of Catherine of Siena*, translated, introduced, and annotated by Conleth Kearns, OP, preface by Vincent de Couesnongle, OP (Wilmington, DE: Michael Glazier, 1980), 81–82.

centeredness and their fear of incurring the displeasure of others."[48] To Charles V, king of France, she writes: "I want you to follow Christ cruci- fied and be a lover of your neighbor's salvation."[49] And to her own spiritual director, Raymond of Capua, who at their first meeting had found repentance and to whom she, in turn, served as spiritual director,[50] she says: "I want you to keep the good, holy, and true faithful will that I know God in his mercy has given you."[51]

Anchorites: Julian of Norwich

The public life of Catherine's ministry of preaching, teaching, and providing spiritual guidance in Italy contrasts sharply with the ministry of another laywoman, namely, Julian of Norwich (1342–1416). Despite her chosen life of self-enclosure, Julian became one of the best known and most popular spiritual directors of her time. As an anchoress she lived walled into a cell adjacent to the church of St. Julian in Conesford at Norwich. This way of life had become popular in England by the late thirteenth century, mostly among women. It was modeled on that of the hermits and solitaries in the desert of Egypt, who had inhabited caves or small huts. Yet, unlike these men and women eight hundred years earlier, anchorites in the fourteenth century were solitaries in the midst of the town center, the marketplace, the hub of city and village activity. Their quarters were attached to the church, often with a small opening to the inside, where Mass could be observed and the Eucharist received, and another opening to the street outside. Unlike the desert monastics who could leave their cell and community at any time, anchorites were pre- sumably walled into their living quarters without doors or, more symboli- cally, had made a commitment to long-term stability of residence. In fact, a solemn rite of enclosure existed, involving the sacrament of extreme unction, a sprinkling of dust reminiscent of a burial, and "the sealing of the doorway to the living tomb."[52] Food and daily necessities would be handed through the window by a servant, while in turn the anchorite

---

48. Letter 54, in Catherine of Siena, *Letters of St. Catherine of Siena*, trans. Suzanne Noffke (Binghamton, NY: Medieval and Renaissance Texts and Studies, 1988), 167–68.

49. Letter 78, in ibid., 239.

50. In her letters Catherine did not hesitate to counsel, exhort, or chide her confessor; in his "Legend" on Catherine's life Raymond refers to several incidents of such a role re- versal, when she served as his spiritual director; see Bilinkoff, *Related Lives*, 30–31.

51. Letter 70, in *Letters of St. Catherine of Siena*, 220.

52. The ritual is preserved in Bishop Lacey's *Pontifical*; see "General Introduction" in *Ancrene Riwle: Introduction and Part I*, ed. and trans. Robert W. Ackerman and Roger Dahood (Binghamton, NY: Medieval and Renaissance Texts and Studies, 1984), 16.

would provide the members of the parish and townspeople with intercessory prayers and spiritual counsel. As resident "saints" and solitaries, anchorites devoted themselves to a life of penitential practices, Scripture study, reading, and prayer, which in turn equipped them to serve as spiritual guides and physicians of the soul. As stationary intercessors and "anchors," they were living models of piety holding up the church "with their holiness of life and their blessed prayers."[53] Even though anchorites could be those who had not professed vows, a rule existed, called the *Ancrene Wisse*, dating from the thirteenth century and initially written for three women. Presumably authored by a Dominican or Augustinian monk and heavily borrowing from "A Rule for Life for a Recluse" by the English Cistercian abbot Aelred of Rievaulx (1109–1167), the *Ancrene Wisse* spells out the contractual agreement by which the anchoress makes herself available to those who "come to them at the window"[54] and are seeking guidance about the dilemmas of life and Christian conduct. The eight chapters into which the rule is divided give instructions on prayer, protection from the influence of the senses, the life of the interior world, and mundane matters such as clothing, diet, visitation, and work. The core of the *Ancrene Wisse* is section 4, an enumeration of temptations, vices, their distinctions and consequences, and appropriate penances and remedies, along with a description of the role of confession and penance as a sacrament in sections 5 and 6. While the rule appears to help discern sins among those who live by it, for the sake of their doing penance, it is striking that the sins enumerated tend to require conditions that entail communal living and contact with others, something the anchoress would not have had available to her. At the same time the role of the priest is limited, as he appears only in the sidelines. It is conceivable, then, that the rule served both as a manual of self-examination and self-discipline and as a veiled penitential book for hearing confessions from those seeking council through the window. The few sources available to us leave much room for conjecture. About a hundred women may have been practicing the anchoritic life in England at the time, and their existence would have been largely forgotten had it not been for the book of visions produced by one of them, the *Showings* of Julian of Norwich.

Julian's work enjoyed none of the popularity of that of other fourteenth-century English mystics, such as the Augustinian canon Walter Hilton, the hermit Richard Rolle, or the anonymous author of *The Cloud*

---

53. "Ancrene Wisse" in *Anchorite Spirituality: "Ancrene Wisse" and Associated Works*, trans. Anne Savage and Nicholas Watson (New York: Paulist Press, 1991), 101.

54. Ibid., 206–7.

of Unknowing. But her life, wisdom, and spiritual guidance must have made a considerable impression on her contemporaries. Four wills of the time mention Julian as beneficiary, and one woman, Margery Kempe (ca. 1373–after 1439), recounts in her own book a visit to the anchoress for spiritual guidance in about 1410, making it the only other outside reference to Julian's life. Margery had wanted to find out about her own mystical visions and their validity, so she and her husband went "to many other places, and spoke with God's servants, both anchorites and recluses," along with "clerics, doctors, and bachelors of divinity."[55] They sought out Julian, "for the anchoress was expert in such things and could give good advice." As it turned out, Julian affirmed Margery in her quest to discern the spirits during their extensive conversations that lasted several days, saying, "I pray God grant you perseverance. Set all your trust in God and fear not the language of the world."[56] No mention is made of Julian's book in Margery's brief account of the visit.

Little is known about Julian's life. Her writings point to an extensive education. She read Latin, had a profound knowledge of the Scriptures, and was familiar with the foundational spiritual writings of the monastic tradition of the Western church. Probably educated by Benedictine nuns at Carrow Priory, she later served as a catechism teacher at a monastic school for boys. When Archbishop Arundel of Canterbury prohibited women from teaching theology she was forced to change course. Julian became an anchoress at St. Julian's at the age of thirty-one, taking on the name of the church. Several months earlier, in 1373, she had recovered from an illness that nearly took her life and received sixteen visions, which she recorded. The resulting work, titled *Showings*, or *Revelations of Divine Love*, is the first book known to be written by a woman in English. About twenty years later she wrote a second, longer version of the book in which she reflects and elaborates on the meaning of these visions, and in 1413 she may have completed a revision of the earlier short text to dispel potential suspicions of heresy.

As in previous books by lay religious women of this period, contemplation of the passion of Christ is prominent. Such contemplation forms the general outline and central theme of the *Showings*, and it invites the reader to examine the conscience, practice repentance, and demonstrate humility before God and neighbor. Though the book remained largely unknown to the wider public until the middle of the seventeenth century,

---

55. "Booke of Margery Kempe," trans. B. A. Windeatt, in Monica Furlong, *Visions and Longings: Medieval Women Mystics* (Boston: Shambhala, 1996), 183.

56. Ibid., 185.

everything Julian writes "I mean to apply to all my fellow Christians . . . and to the comfort of us all."[57] According to Julian, the life of spiritual perfection is open to all Christians and is intimately connected with the way one treats one's neighbor, for "if any man or woman withdraws his love from any of his fellow Christians, he does not love at all, because he has not love towards all."[58] Similarly, the experience of intimate union with God is meant to be shared with others, and one's own happiness is interconnected with helping others reach that state, for the more "I love in this way whilst I am here, the more I am like the joy that I shall have in heaven without end."[59]

The idea that a small part of the soul is inalienable from God is a recurring theme in the *Showings*. "For in every soul which will be saved there is a godly will which never assents to sin and never will," Julian writes. "Just as there is an animal will in the lower part which cannot will any good, so there is a godly will in the higher part, which will is so good that it cannot ever will any evil, but always good."[60] This divine spark or "godly will" in the human soul is reason to give us hope while we live in this body. We need to "know it in our faith and our belief, and particularly and truly that we have all this blessed will whole and safe in our Lord Jesus Christ, because every nature with which heaven will be filled had of necessity and of God's rightfulness to be so joined and united in him that in it a substance was kept which could never and should never be parted from him."[61] The consequences of this inalienable spark in the human soul are twofold: first, the "godly will" unites all Christian souls "as it were [into] one soul,"[62] which should govern our relations with others; and second, knowing this "godly will" to be innate to our nature will give us hope regarding God's forgiveness of the sins we have committed and should prompt us to practice forgiveness and compassion toward our neighbor.

Central to the *Showings* is an exploration of the nature of human sin, its consequences, its forgiveness, and ways to cure it. Repeatedly Julian wrestles with the origins of sin and asks God "why the beginning of sin was not prevented," for then "all would have been well."[63] The answer

---

57. Julian of Norwich, *Showings*, trans. Edmund Colledge, OSA, and James Walsh, SJ (New York: Paulist Press, 1978), 133 (short text); 191 (long text).
58. Ibid., 134.
59. Ibid.
60. Ibid., 241–42.
61. Ibid., 283.
62. Ibid., 241.
63. Ibid., 224; cf. 148.

she receives is simple: "Sin is necessary, but all will be well, and all will be well, and every kind of thing will be well."[64] At the mention of "this naked word 'sin,'" the passion of Christ is brought to her mind, along with the spiritual and physical pains of the entire creation. Among them, Christ's passion is "the greatest and surpassing pain," but its sight turns to consolation, because God does not want to frighten the soul "by this ugly sight." More importantly, sin remains invisible, "for I believe that it has no kind of substance, no share in being, nor can it be recognized except by the pain caused by it." This pain that sin causes persists only for a while, "for it purges and makes us know ourselves and ask for mercy." Meanwhile, God stands by most readily to provide comfort, "showing no kind of blame to me or to anyone who will be saved," indicating that "it is true that sin is the cause of all this pain, but all will be well, and every kind of thing will be well."[65]

The consequences of sin plague the human soul so that one is prompted to make confession. When one seems to "sink into hell" by one's awareness of sin, "contrition" may seize the human heart "by the inspiration of the Holy Spirit and turns bitterness into hope of God's mercy," so that "the wounds begin to heal and the soul to revive." It is at this point that sinners are brought to confession and "nakedly and truthfully" reveal their sins with sorrow and "great shame." They then accept willingly "the penance for every sin imposed by [their] confessor," which is "one meekness which greatly pleases God," along with other expressions of meekness, such as bodily sickness, sorrows and shame, and "all kinds of affliction and temptation into which we are cast, spiritually and bodily."[66] It is due to such meekness that God raises us up, delivers us "from sin and pain," and makes us "equal with the saints." For Julian the remedies of sin and its "medicines" begin with God's initiative among those who humble themselves before God. In the utmost crisis God pours out contrition upon the sinner and instills in the soul compassion and a longing for God, making the path to salvation threefold: "By contrition we are made clean, by compassion we are made ready, and by true longing for God we are made worthy. These are the three means, as I understand, through which all souls come to heaven, those, that is to say, who have been sinners on earth and will be saved."[67]

64. Ibid., 225.
65. Ibid.
66. Ibid., 244.
67. Ibid., 244–45.

Given the inevitability of sin, Julian advises the reader to remember the great compassion God shows us and the completeness of love God bestows on us, despite our wrongdoing. Sin will not produce lasting shame but everlasting honor before God for those who confess in humility: "Just as various sins are punished with various pains, the more grievous are the sins, so will they be rewarded with various joys in heaven to reward the victories over them, to the degree in which the sin may have been painful and sorrowful to the soul on earth."[68] For in the same way that "sin is punished here with sorrow and penance, in contrary fashion it will be rewarded in heaven by the courteous love of our Lord God almighty, who does not wish anyone who comes there to lose his labours." The more we understand this paradoxical principle, the more we will "hate to sin."[69] Therefore we should not be too troubled when we sin inadvertently, but know that God "loves us endlessly, and we sin customarily, and he reveals it to us most gently."[70]

Penance is not only an annual act performed at the priest's direction following confession, but an ongoing, daily discipline. All our earthly life is penance, Julian says. Regardless of what we do, we will have troubles and woes. But this should not make us despair, because such penance is profitable to us and contains an inbuilt remedy. "This place is prison, this life is penance, and he wants us to rejoice in the remedy," she says. The remedy for us is to seek refuge with God and recall the knowledge "that our Lord is with us, protecting us and leading us into the fullness of joy."[71] Pain and penance are profitable, then, because they drive us to God for comfort and greater familiarity with him.

Julian shapes her work in the form of a revelation she receives on her deathbed when the priest administering last rites holds up the crucifix to her. But the form of her book is merely a frame for teaching the catechism on the sacraments, especially penance. The anchoress is both a teacher and a doctor of souls. Based on her daily dealings with those who came to see her for spiritual advice by her window, she conveys in her *Showings* a new treatment of confession and penance. Sin is manifested by human pain, enduring one's pain is a form of penance, and penance carried out with patience and humility is a remedy for our sin that drives us back to God and prepares for us a place of heavenly honor. In her reinterpretation Julian is careful to uphold the sacramental nature

---

68. Ibid., 242.
69. Ibid., 155.
70. Ibid., 338.
71. Ibid., 331.

of confession and penance and ecclesiastical authority without compromising the inner workings of the Holy Spirit in the human heart. Her caution is also evident in her repeated qualification of the audience to whom her counsel applies: those only "who will be saved." Moreover, the Scripture quotations in the vernacular are unlike those of the Oxford scholar and reformer John Wycliff (1325–1384), whose popular Bible translation into the vernacular, along with the religious movement of Lollardy he represented, had come under serious attack by 1380. It is likely that Julian knew of the execution of Marguerite Porete in 1310, the Council of Vienna's condemnation of the beguine way of life in 1312, and the execution of Margery Kempe's curate, William Sawtre, burned in chains as both heretic and traitor in London in 1399. Also possible is that the Benedictine monk Adam Easton, a Hebrew scholar and theologian, had been Julian's spiritual director for some time and advised her to use caution. Easton, who had served as cardinal in Rome, had been forced to return to his home town of Norwich, where he had written a defense of the *Life* of Birgitta of Sweden and her *Revelations*, effecting her canonization, at the same time that Julian was writing the Long Text of the *Showings* (between 1388 and 1393) in Norwich. Most likely is that he brought to her from the continent the works of Marguerite Porete, Henry Suso, Jan van Ruysbroeck, and Catherine of Siena. His biography notes that he also wrote many contemplative, vernacular treatises on the spiritual life of perfection, no longer extant, and had a large library of spiritual writings that included a rare copy of the teachings of Pseudo-Dionysius, one of the proponents of the idea that a part of the soul remained undefiled by sin and one with God.

What makes Julian's work unique, compared with other English manuals of confession of the time, such as the *Memoriale presbiterorum* of the mid-fourteenth century, is that it is aimed at the laity. Written in the vernacular and probably circulated among a loosely knit group of men and women, both lay and cloistered, who called themselves the Friends of God, the book opens up the possibility of a mutual cure of souls administered by the non-ordained. In the preface to an early manuscript edition of the *Showings*, the so-called Amherst Manuscript dating from about 1435, the scribe notes the book's function as a manual for confession, designed to help probe and heal the wounds of the soul and giving "comfortable words to Christ's lovers," both women and men.[72]

72. See the Amherst Manuscript project web site www.umilta.net/amherst.html by Julia Bolton Holloway.

The Friends of God

Julian's manual for soul care and confession fits into a larger, loosely organized movement that had arisen during the thirteenth and four-teenth centuries, mainly in German-speaking countries. This Dominican-inspired movement was called the Friends of God (*Gottesfreunde*), and began between 1339 and 1343 in Basel, Strasbourg, and Cologne. Its members were both clergy and laity, women and men, those within and outside monastic orders, all seeking to cultivate the interior life of spiri-tual perfection by contemplation and self-examination, and working toward the conversion and repentance of sinners through preaching, teaching, and spiritual guidance. The two most prominent representa-tives of this circle were Meister Eckhart's disciples, Dominicans Johann Tauler, an eloquent preacher, and Henry Suso, a contemplative writer. Their teachings had been influenced by the view of the annihilated soul as the locus of God's unhindered activity in the person, explored by Marguerite Porete and shaped, in part, by Pseudo-Dionysius of the fifth century, and the notion that the human soul desired to know God in perfect love, advanced by the Benedictine abbot and chronicler of Ber-nard of Clairvaux's life, William of St. Thierry (1085–1148), who was a native of Liège, the birthplace of the beguine movement.

The Friends of God movement was aimed at empowering the laity in attaining to spiritual perfection. From German-speaking countries it may have spread to England through the dissemination of contemplative writings. According to Bernard McGinn, the term "friends of God" had been employed for centuries for the devout, but now "this general term seems to have acquired a more specific social connotation, describing actual circles of people who met together, conversed, prayed, and wrote each other about their desire for loving union with God." While even "more amorphous than the early beguines," the movement constituted "a force in the democratization of mysticism,"[73] spreading among the clergy and laity through the dissemination of vernacular writings, and demonstrating and affirming that divine gifts and mystical union with God were available to all Christians.

The Amherst Manuscript is an example of the kinds of writings the Friends of God read. A compilation of several texts by diverse authors, it contains the shorter text of Julian's *Showings* dated 1413, Margaret Porete's *The Mirror of Simple Souls*, Jan van Ruysbroeck's *Sparkling Stone*, an extract from Henry Suso's *The Little Book of Eternal Wisdom*, and works

---

73. McGinn, *The Flowering of Mysticism*, 310.

by Richard Rolle. According to Julia Bolton Holloway the Amherst Manuscript was written for contemplative women and "may include translated texts originally in Julian's own contemplative library, then recycled by copying it out for a later anchoress. One can envision Julian herself leaving instructions as to what it should contain."[74] Written for the anchoress Margaret Heslyngton, as the manuscript states, and compiled by a single scribe, the collection points to the practice of sharing and disseminating contemplative works among a circle of like-minded Christians. The manuscript's inclusion of the works of Porete, Suso, and Ruysbroeck relates it to the Friends of God.

Members of the Friends of God are portrayed as skilled spiritual directors. Explicit references to them are found mostly in Johann Tauler's sermons. Other references come from the letters exchanged between the Dominican nun Margaret Ebner (d. 1353) and her spiritual director, the secular priest Henry of Nördlingen, who had introduced Tauler to Mechtild of Magdeburg's *Flowing Light of the Godhead*. Tauler describes the Friends of God as not an isolated group of esoteric thinkers but those who annihilate their own will and live for God alone and among God's people. They had allowed their will to merge with the divine will, so that others could see in them models of the oneness between the love of God and the love of neighbor. "These folk are trustful and merciful toward all; they are not severe or hard-hearted, but full of graciousness," Tauler writes. "One cannot think that such a person can ever be separated from God."[75] The Friends of God are fully surrendered to God, especially through the endurance of repeated trials and suffering and dark periods in the soul, and they are like pillars in the mystical body of Christ, the church. The union and friendship those Christians have with God makes them transparent images of God's nature. About the experience of such a union Tauler says: "In this stage the Lord lifts a person up out of self and into him. He consoles him for all his suffering and heals his wounds. God raises him from a human mode of life to a divine one, out of all sorrow into divine security, and a person becomes so divinized that everything he is and does, God is and does in him. He is lifted up so far beyond his natural mode of being that he becomes by grace what God

---

74. Amherst Manuscript project web site www.umilta.net/amherst.html.

75. Johann Tauler, Sermon 41, in Ferdinand Vetter, *Die Predigten Taulers*, Deutsche Texte des Mittelalters 11 (Berlin: Weidmann, 1910); quoted in Bernard McGinn, *The Harvest of Mysticism in Medieval Germany, 1300–1500*, vol. 4 of his *The Presence of God: A History of Western Christian Mysticism* (New York: Crossroad, 2005), 413.

is by nature."[76] Since these Christians know God as friend, they make for the best spiritual guides possible. "People should seek out an experienced Friend of God a hundred miles away, one who knows and can direct them in the right path,"[77] for the Friends of God can strengthen other Christians and help them discern the ways of God. Ultimately it is they, rather than the pope and the clergy, who ensure the survival of the church.

Brethren and Sisters of the Common Life and *Devotio Moderna*

A movement related to the Friends of God, those highly regarded spiritual directors, is that of the Brethren of the Common Life in the Low Countries. Founded by Geert de Groote (1340–1384), the group included both secular clergy and laity, resembling in purpose the now declining beguine communities of a century earlier. Influenced by the German Friends of God and the writings of and personal friendship with Jan van Ruysbroeck, de Groote had studied for the priesthood at Cologne, the Sorbonne, and Prague. After some years of living at a Carthusian house and reading widely in spiritual authors, de Groote obtained ordination as a deacon and a license to preach, carrying his message of repentance and conversion throughout the diocese of Utrecht for four years, until his death in 1384. By then both secular clergy and laity, men and women, had been drawn to his preaching and had begun meeting in private homes to cultivate their interior life by study, prayer, and other devotional disciplines. Members lived in houses designated for either women or men, shared their work wages or ecclesiastical incomes, and remained active in their local parishes. This reform movement within the Roman Catholic Church came to be known as *devotio moderna*, drawing members largely from the middle and lower classes of urban and nearby rural areas and spreading rapidly throughout the Netherlands and into northern Germany and the Rhineland.

Like the beguines before them, the brothers and sisters made use of the vernacular in Scripture study, spiritual readings, and private devotion. They valued the church's monastic traditions, such as the liturgical hours, and read from the church fathers and other monastic and devotional writers during gathering times, meals, and chapel meetings. And they provided spiritual counsel and direction to one another and the townspeople, though mostly in group sessions rather than one-to-one.

---

76. Tauler, Sermon 39, quoted in McGinn, *The Harvest of Mysticism*, 289.
77. Tauler, Sermon 49, quoted in McGinn, *The Harvest of Mysticism*, 412.

The similarities in lifestyle between the Sisters of the Common Life and the beguines often led to confusion of the two. Both lived in voluntary community without a rule, practiced celibacy without taking solemn vows, and sought to deepen their Christian faith through study, modest living, and charity. The difference was that sisters could not own houses, property, or personal items. This communal emphasis affected the spiritual climate as well, so that sisters not only worked together but also mutually exhorted, corrected, and advised one another on matters of the spiritual life. Originally begun in de Groote's own home as a place of refuge for women in crisis, the women's houses quickly multiplied, consistently outnumbering the brothers' houses. By 1460 there may have been more than thirty houses for women in the Netherlands and about sixty in Germany, many of them eventually joining the third order Franciscans or the Augustinians as the two most closely affiliated monastic alternatives. While one of the brothers served as the women's chaplain and priest, the communities were financially self-supporting and governed by a "rectrix" or "mistress," who had charge of the sisters' communal and devotional life.

The emphasis on communal life among the brothers and sisters resulted in unique approaches to and variants on the practices of preaching and confession. Keenly aware that both preaching and confession were, strictly speaking, reserved for the clergy, friars, and clerics who had the bishop's permission and license to carry out these functions, the brothers and sisters added a novel twist. During their gatherings they would hold so-called collations, a form of expository and evangelistic preaching on the Scriptures that would seek to edify and exhort the sinner and bring him or her to repentance. They also opened up their gatherings to townspeople, usually on Sunday afternoons, and later enforced mandatory chapel for the students attending their schools in hopes that, through the hearing of the Word read and proclaimed, souls would be won to Christ. The brothers and sisters managed to appease local curates and mendicant friars by insisting that their collations were no substitute for church services or sermons, rather had as their origin the monastic practice of an abbot addressing his community, and they carefully avoided calling these collations "sermons" or "homilies," even though that is what they were. The communal emphasis also had consequences for matters of discipline and the practice of the virtuous life. A portion of their gathering time was dedicated to "fraternal correction," which involved the unreserved individual confession of members' faults, admonition and exhortation, and the penitent's willingness to accept such admonition and guidance. Subjecting oneself to communal scrutiny and receiving correction required humility, which was regarded as an essential trait for developing a deepened spiritual life. According to John van Engen the process of correction "probably functioned partially" as "a substitute for the canonically required confessional," and raised suspicion among the clergy who were not part of the movement.[78] In response, the brothers and sisters sought to scrupulously meet the church's standard obligation of making annual confession to their own parish priest in addition to practicing regular, perhaps weekly, communal confession and mutual correction during their gatherings—submitting to more than a double dose of confessional practice, as it were.

The goal of preaching and frequent confession and correction among the Brothers and Sisters of the Common Life was the ongoing conversion of the self to Christ. Conversion was seen as the only sure path to salvation and involved intentionally submitting to the divine will as expressed by the community. The means by which the brothers and sisters effectively realized or followed up on the conversion process consisted of various forms of penances or "exercises." Three of them in particular are worth mentioning: making a resolution (*resolutio* or *intentio*) to carry out what was expected of them in the way of prayer, work, and growth in virtue; the exercise (*exercitium*) and training of their spiritual selves, as by study, obedience, fasting, submission to correction, and scrutiny of their consciences, not unlike the "methodical meditation" Ignatius of Loyola would prescribe for his fellow Jesuits in the *Spiritual Exercises* a century and a half later; and a love born from the contemplative reading of Scripture, particularly the life and passion of Christ, that was directed primarily toward members of their own community, students at their schools, and those who were associated with the houses and came under their influence. A distinguishing feature of the *devotio moderna* is its reforming effect on the lower-class urban clergy, who represented the great mass of clerics in the Late Middle Ages and whose common reputation marked them out as ignorant and immoral. Many of these urban clerics, barred from cathedral chapters or monasteries for lacking the status of nobility and the funds required for entrance, became affiliated with or joined the Brethren. Thus they, too were allowed to take part in the communal process and practices of inward conversion and become educated and practiced in the virtues of the Christian life.

The Brethren and Sisters of the Common Life also founded several monastic communities under the Augustinian rule, such as those at

---

78. John van Engen, "Introduction," in *Devotio Moderna: Basic Writings*, translated and introduced by John van Engen (Mahwah, NJ: Paulist Press, 1988), 17.

Windesheim and Deventer, and numerous schools that became centers of spiritual and intellectual life in the Low Countries. They operated a scriptorium and a press, copying and printing missals, Bibles, hymnals, and *florilegi*, or compilations of spiritual writings, such as *The Imitation of Christ* by Thomas à Kempis, who was one of their better-known members and the author of a life of de Groote. By the middle of the fifteenth century the Brethren of the Common Life had well over a hundred religious monastic houses for both women and men, along with non-monastic gathering places. They also operated numerous schools in Germany and the Netherlands. One of their pupils was the Augustinian theologian Erasmus of Rotterdam (1469–1536), who was educated by the Brethren of the Common Life at their schools in Deventer and Bois-le-Duc, and who would play a leading role in the Protestant Reformation of the next century.

As a reform movement the *devotio moderna* affected the working classes and the lower secular clergy both inside and outside the monastery walls. The brothers and sisters did this by what Heiko A. Oberman calls a "meditation technique" aimed at "the reformation of the soul and the rejuvenation of the spirit as the basis for renewal of the communal life."[79] The movement's strength lay in the practical reforms of Christian devotion and communal discipline. Unlike the subsequent Protestant Reformation with its antimonastic and anticlerical sentiment, members sought to work renewal from within the monastic system and among the clergy. The emphasis was less on the intellect and logic and more on the heart and religious sentiment. Devotional study, contemplation, and preaching were to effect conversion, repentance, confession, and a re-forming of the soul in accordance with divine will. Despite the movement's anti-intellectualism and decline in the early sixteenth century, *devotio moderna* would provide practical inspiration for later reform movements aimed at conversion and repentance, such as Puritanism with its conversion focus and the Catholic Reformation with its rise of new monastic foundations.

The fourteenth and fifteenth centuries present us, then, with two strands in the practice of confession and penance: the sacramental, on the one hand, marked by penance and absolution administered by a priest; and the contemplative/mystical, on the other, marked by self-examination, meditation on the life and passion of Christ, and an abandonment or surrender of the individual's will to the divine will, potentially leading to union with the divine apart from a priestly agency.

---

79. Heiko A. Oberman, "Preface," in *Devotio Moderna: Basic Writings*, 4.

These two strands are reflected also in the role definitions of the confessor and spiritual director, who, as separate people, come to have distinct functions in the ministry of the cure of souls. While the office of confessor is reserved for clerics due to its sacramental nature, spiritual directors may include laypeople, both men and women, who carry out a ministry of "preaching" and teaching, exhortation, and spiritual guidance, either in the context of the community (as did the Sisters of the Common Life) or one-to-one (as did the beguines and anchorites). The rise of distinct lay or third orders for women living the religious life outside the monastery and in regular contact with the laity seems to have forced the new role definition of spiritual director. Initially these associations allowing women to exercise their spiritual gifts and to be examples of a deeply felt piety and apostolic fervor were seen by the church's hierarchy as a welcome antidote to lax morals and a nominal faith. However, they also blurred what women, and by extension all the laity, could and could not do in regard to soul care, effectively blending the roles of confessor and spiritual director. Predictably, this blending would not last; in fact, it came to be seen as heretical or potentially threatening to the sacramental means of salvation and its agents, the clergy. A clear role distinction was needed between clergy and laity and its gauge would be the church's sacramental system. As the church sought to strengthen clerical authority over the laity it also exposed the church's appointed servants, clergy and monastics alike, to greater visibility, inadvertently bringing into full focus their vices of immorality, ignorance, abuse of power and privilege, and exploitation of the masses' superstition. It is the tension, then, between the roles of the clergy and the laity in regard to care for and cure of souls, the heightened distinction between the sacrament of penance and the ministry of spiritual direction, and the marks of an exterior versus an interior piety that Martin Luther would address in his sacramental reforms, especially with regard to penance. To this reform and its effects on the next five hundred years in the church's practice of confession and penance we will now turn.

PART TWO

Confession, the Protestant Reformation, and the Council of Trent

The Protestant Reformation of the sixteenth century is mainly remembered for the controversy over indulgences, the exchange of money for absolution from sins, and the inherent abuse of church power and privilege regarding the sacrament of penance. At the center of the controversies giving voice to centuries of struggle stood the Augustinian monk and priest Martin Luther (1483–1546), who seemingly carried the torch for sacramental reform. However, many of his reforms had begun centuries earlier. In the late twelfth century, for example, a synod of bishops had ruled against the habit of confessors imposing penances consisting in the purchase of Masses from the confessor himself. Over twenty synods forbade the practice between 1195 and 1446, prohibiting the so-called *Beichtgeld*, as it was called in German lands, or the "alms" given to the confessor, who counted on it as part of his regular revenue. In the early thirteenth century the Fourth Lateran Council had addressed in several canons the widespread abuse of indulgences and commutations by prelates, bishops, and clergy. In the late fourteenth century John Wycliff had criticized the use of indulgences by Pope Urban VI to finance the Crusades, and in the early fifteenth century John Hus had denounced a similar abuse of indulgences, with the effect that the people of Prague publicly burned the papal bull authorizing their use. By the early sixteenth century the public revolt and opposition could no longer be suppressed, and the controversy over a sacramental system that took advantage of the masses' superstition found a ready hearing.

Part 2 will chronicle the developments of confessional practices during the time of the Protestant Reformation and its resulting movements, along with the Roman Catholic Church's response and new initiatives. Due to Martin Luther's prominent role in this reform movement, precipitating the unfortunate split of Protestant churches from the Roman Catholic Church, his theological views on confession will be examined in greater detail. Also examined are movements emerging from Luther's doctrinal stance on confession, namely, Lutheran Pietism and Methodism in their emphasis on the priesthood of all believers. Other Protestant movements examined here and arising during the time of the Protestant Reformation, though only indirectly influenced by Luther, are the Reformed tradition, spearheaded by Martin Bucer, Ulrich Zwingli, and John Calvin, and the newly formed Church of England. The two concluding chapters offer an overview of the Roman Catholic Church's response to the Protestant Reformation in regard to confession and spiritual direction as formulated at the Council of Trent. Chronicled here are also the rise and the mission of the Society of Jesus, founded by Ignatius of Loyola at that time, with its aim, among others, of promoting among Catholics the practice of making frequent confession, examining the conscience, and frequent partaking of Communion.

Martin Luther and Confession

On the eve of All Saints in 1517 Martin Luther posted ninety-five theses, or a "Disputation of the Power and Efficacy of Indulgences," on the door of the castle church at Wittenberg. This action would launch a controversy that shook the Western church to its foundation, eventually leading to the split of Protestant churches from the Roman Catholic Church, a development Luther himself did not foresee or ever intend. The first four propositions addressed the two prongs of inward and outward, sacramental and internal penance, and read as follows:

1. Our Lord and Master Jesus Christ, when He said *Poenitentiam agite*, ["Repent"], willed that the whole life of believers should be repentance.
2. This word cannot be understood to mean sacramental penance, i.e., confession and satisfaction, which is administered by the priests.
3. Yet it means not inward repentance only; nay, there is no inward repentance which does not outwardly work divers mortifications of the flesh.
4. The penalty [of sin], therefore, continues so long as hatred of self continues; for this is the true inward repentance, and continues until our entrance into the kingdom of heaven.[1]

Luther had charted the potential tension of the Christian life between inner and outer repentance. On the one hand, there was a lifelong inner obligation to seek repentance and to turn to God in Christ after baptism;

---

1. "Disputation of Doctor Martin Luther on the Power and Efficacy of Indulgences," in *Works of Martin Luther*, translated and edited by Adolph Spaeth, L. D. Reed, Henry Eyster Jacobs, and others, vol. 1 (Philadelphia: A. J. Holman, 1915), 29–38, available at www.iclnet .org/pub/resources/text/wittenberg/luther/web/ninetyfive.htmlwww.iclnet.org.

on the other, there was the necessity of faithful communion with the church as the visible body of Christ through the sacramental means of grace. Luther had unearthed this tension through his own personal struggles with sin, scruples, and the sacramental efficacy of confession. Born on November 10, 1483 in Eisleben, the son of a silver miner and destined for the study of law, Luther had turned to the monastery to appease his own scruples and the tension he experienced between a wrathful God and a God who pardoned sinners. Convinced of the popular notion that becoming a monk was a form of second baptism, restoring the sinner to the state of innocence, Luther had entered the Augustinian monastery at Erfurt in 1505 to make his peace with God. But then the troubles began. When he was celebrating Mass for the first time in 1507, terror seized him at the altar in light of God's holiness so that he was barely able to utter the words of institution. In addition, his father, present at the time and still not convinced of Luther's choice of vocation, questioned whether Luther had truly followed God's call in taking up the cowl and had not yielded to the devil's apparition and voice instead. To appease his doubts and scruples Luther threw himself into the monastic disciplines of perfection in excess of the required vigils, fasts, and austerities. "I was a good monk," Luther would write later about his heroic feats, and "if ever a monk got to heaven by his monkery it was I."[2] But even these austerities did not offer him the longed-for peace and a sense of worthiness before a righteous God. It was his good fortune that in 1508 Luther was temporarily transferred to the newly founded village university at Wittenberg to lecture on moral philosophy. The elector, Frederick the Wise, was trying to secure better teachers to boost his academy to rival the well-established University of Leipzig and had invited the Augustinians and Franciscans to supply three new professors, Luther among them. It was here that Luther met Johann von Staupitz, the vicar general of the Augustinian order in Germany and dean of Wittenberg University, who in 1509 initiated Luther's studies for the doctoral degree in theology. A recall to Erfurt and being sent on foot to Rome by the Augustinian chapter delayed Luther's academic career by a full year, but in 1511 he was permanently transferred to Wittenberg. Von Staupitz took an interest not only in Luther's academic career but also in his spiritual well-being, and served as Luther's confessor and spiritual guide. Had it not been for von Staupitz and his wisdom and patience, Luther admits, "I should have sunk in hell."[3] Luther made ample use of

---

2. Roland Bainton, *Here I Stand: A Life of Martin Luther* (Nashville: Abingdon, 1950), 45.
3. Ibid., 53.

von Staupitz's services, seeking him out for confession at least weekly, often daily, and on one occasion for as long as six hours.

Luther's scrupulosity is well known, yet what is often considered evidence of his somewhat morbid spiritual disposition may have been primarily a product of the social ideal of the time. Much had changed since the 1215 decree of the Fourth Lateran Council that required annual confession of church members prior to Lent. Now Christians were urged to confess their sins as often as possible and to delay *no longer* than Lent. In addition to the liturgical season of Lent, four new occasions had been introduced that necessitated confession: First, Christians in the state of sin had to confess immediately if they were in danger of dying or of facing some grave peril; second, they were to confess prior to receiving the Eucharist, prior to partaking of another sacrament (except baptism), and prior to performing a solemn religious act, such as saying Mass; third, they were to confess if they were likely to be without the opportunity of confessing for the coming year; and fourth, if their conscience dictated it at the time, they must confess. By the sixteenth century the sacrament of penance with private confession was a commonplace and well-regarded ritual, and parishioners and monastics alike made use of its presumed healing and medicinal power, or at least were aware of it. According to Thomas Tentler, to both "the tepid as well as the fervent, the confessional symbolized discipline and reconciliation. It was the place of forgiveness, not just for scrupulous monks who ran to it continually, but also for worldly laymen who stayed away." Consequently, "the call to frequent confession at the end of the middle ages was loud and insistent,"[4] and Luther, among many others, yielded to it with great fervor.

In addition to making frequent confession, Luther was concerned also with the completeness of the sins enumerated and confessed. Only sins orally confessed could be absolved, and those withheld from the confessor, even if by accident or lapse of memory, would presumably also withhold God's mercy from the penitent. Luther scrutinized his conscience and memory as best he could. According to Roland Bainton, "Luther would repeat a confession and, to be sure of including everything, would review his entire life until the confessor grew weary and exclaimed, 'Man, God is not angry with you. You are angry with God.'"[5] After Luther had appeared once more with some leftover sin that had escaped his prior scrutiny, von Staupitz exclaimed in exasperation, "If

---

4. Thomas N. Tentler, *Sin and Confession on the Eve of the Reformation* (Princeton, NJ: Princeton University Press, 1977), 78–79.

5. Bainton, *Here I Stand*, 54.

you expect Christ to forgive you, come in with something to forgive—patricide, blasphemy, adultery—instead of all these peccadilloes."[6] But to Luther they were no peccadilloes but real and vivid obstacles and hindrances to receiving God's favor and salvation. He knew what the teachings of the church and the manuals on confession popular at the time said, namely, that a good confession was a complete confession. The responsibility of being forgiven and made clean rested mainly with the penitent, less with the confessor, and still less with God. Guidelines existed for making a good confession. According to the *Summa* of Thomas Aquinas, such a confession entailed sixteen conditions: "Let the confession be simple, humble, pure, faithful, and frequent, unadorned, discreet, willing, ashamed, whole, secret, tearful, prompt, strong, and reproachful, and showing readiness to obey."[7] In addition to manuals for confessors and priests mostly written in Latin, there now also existed manuals for the laity and those making confession written in the vernacular. In the fifteenth century a popular and widely circulated book on confession for the laity was the three-part work *Opus tripartium* by Jean Gerson (1363–1429), chancellor of the University of Paris. It contained an exposition of the Ten Commandments, a treatise on confession, and a preparation for death, advising "the sinner to accuse himself humbly, and not derisively; honestly and not deceitfully; purely, and sincerely, avoiding irrelevancies; and above all discreetly, so that he does not reveal those who were his companions in sin."[8] If the penitent wanted to make complete confession, a thorough examination of the conscience was required, generally following some categories of sin, as outlined by the Ten Commandments or the list of the seven deadly sins. The manuals advised additional helps in recollecting one's sins, such as a review from one's youth to the present of various "companions, occupations, habitations, ages, and so on."[9] Gerson's manual makes preparation and careful examination of one's conscience the necessary requisite for the penitent to move from the state of sin to the state of grace, which involved mining the memory and conscience in such a way "as if he expected to find some great treasure there."[10] Penitents were saved by a general statement of sorrow over forgotten sins, but should they remember additional sins

6. Ibid.

7. Tentler, *Sin and Confession*, 106–7.

8. See Jean Gerson, *Opus tripartium II* (Cologne: Ulrich Zell, [1470?]), 1.446A; quoted in Tentler, *Sin and Confession*, 109.

9. Tentler, *Sin and Confession*, 110.

10. Ibid.

at a later time they were required to confess them immediately. Luther did what manuals of confession commended: he sought out von Staupitz as soon as a previously forgotten sin sprang to mind.

Mining one's memory and conscience for hidden sins became Luther's obsession. The voice of a troubled conscience haunted him, and he sought ways to appease it, means of finding refuge from it, and discernment between the alarmed voice of the conscience as God's instrument and the damning and accusatory voice of God's adversary, the Devil. So penetrating is Luther's treatment of a troubled, negative conscience that, according to Erik H. Erikson, he accepted it "for his life work" and made it its "circumscribed locus." This negative conscience, represented as an auditory threat, was the voice of wrath of what Luther called a "false Christ," who says, "Again, you have not done what I told you"—a statement burning itself into the soul as a *conscientia cauterisata*, a branded conscience bearing the mark of sin.[11] It was von Staupitz who would try to divert Luther's branded and burdened conscience to the way of the mystics. Inclined to mysticism, von Staupitz encouraged Luther to practice surrender to the abyss of God's unknowable presence. Luther tried releasing his self-will and relinquishing his meritorious, perfectionist efforts at self-discipline and asceticism. But relying on God's grace alone seemed to him an impossibility. The sight of a crucifix caused him distress, the flight from a judgmental Son to a merciful Mother was in vain, and the twenty-one saints he had selected as his particular patrons— three for each day of the week—brought no help either. When von Staupitz counseled Luther to understand God as a loving God, it was more than Luther could handle. "Love God?" Luther exclaimed. "I hate him."[12] In light of such words of blasphemy the only recourse von Staupitz could think of was to occupy Luther's mind with study, Scripture reading, and pastoral work. By commissioning him as a teacher, preacher, and counselor of sick souls he hoped that delegating to him the cure of others' souls would help him find a cure for his own. In September of 1511 von Staupitz offered Luther the chair of Bible, a chair von Staupitz himself had held for many years. By doing so he placed before Luther the task of searching for his soul's remedy not in the books of the scholastics, but in Scripture. Following the conversation Luther pursued his studies and received his doctorate in theology on October 18, 1512, being appointed for life *lectura in Biblia* at the University of

11. Erik H. Erikson, *Young Man Luther: A Study in Psychoanalysis and History* (New York: W. W. Norton, 1958), 195.
12. Bainton, *Here I Stand*, 59.

Wittenberg. In the winter of 1512 he began preparation for his lectures on the Psalms, given between 1513 and 1515, continued with the apostle Paul's epistle to the Romans in 1515 and 1516, and treated the epistle to the Galatians in 1516 and 1517. The course of these studies in the Augustinian monastery proved to be a Damascus Road experience for him. No works of merit, excessive penances, painstaking scrutiny of the conscience for nearly forgotten sins to be confessed in order to be forgiven had brought him any peace. That came only from a faith that was born in the hearing and study of God's word. About his conversion experience Luther says: "I did not love a just and angry God, but rather hated and murmured against him. Yet I clung to the dear Paul and had a great yearning to know what he meant" by the phrase "the just shall live by faith alone." Night and day he pondered the phrase and its connection with the justice of God. And then one day "I grasped that the justice of God is that righteousness by which through grace and sheer mercy God justifies us through faith," upon which "I felt myself to be reborn and to have gone through open doors into paradise."[13]

The new perspective on God and Christ as merciful and forgiving gained by Scripture study would make Luther the great reformer of the church. His preeminent insights, containing the essence of his mature theology, were shaped between 1513 and 1516, so that, according to Roland Bainton, everything thereafter "was but commentary and sharpening to obviate misconstruction."[14] Luther's goal was to make plain the Scriptures and allow the Gospel to be proclaimed for the salvation of souls. As Timothy George puts it, "Luther did not become a reformer because he attacked indulgences. He attacked indulgences because the Word had already taken deep root in his heart."[15] Central to Luther's preaching, writings, commentaries, and treatises was the insight gained from Scripture that forgiveness of sins came by the unmerited grace of God through the cross of Christ, which triumphed over sin and death, enabling people to die to sin, being resurrected to a new life in Christ, and allowing sinners to be reconciled with God. In the words of Bainton, "Luther envisaged no reform other than that of theological education with the stress on the Bible rather than on the decretals and the scholastics."[16] However, he soon began to unearth the discrepancies between his theological insights gained from Scripture study and pre-

---

13. Ibid., 65.
14. Ibid., 68.
15. Timothy George, *Theology of the Reformers* (Nashville: Broadman Press, 1988), 54.
16. Bainton, *Here I Stand*, 68.

vailing ecclesiastical practices. In his lectures on Romans, Luther repeatedly strikes out against the greed and ignorance of the clergy and their undue use of power and privilege, and in his 1516 sermons he speaks critically on three occasions about the practice of dispensing indulgences, generating significant revenue that benefited his own parish, the Castle Church at Wittenberg, and his place of work, the university. The occasion for his criticism was the profuse display of relics on All Saints Day at the church, relics ambitiously collected by the elector of Saxony over a lifetime in an effort to make Wittenberg the Rome of Germany and draw pilgrims willing to pay for the "holy sight." Those who viewed these relics on the appointed day and made the stipulated contributions received a papally approved indulgence for the reduction of the sufferings owed in purgatory equivalent to the benefits of doing penance for the specified length of time.

According to an illustrated catalogue by painter Lucas Cranach, Frederick's relic collection at Wittenberg contained more than five thousand particles by 1509, and by 1520 it included more than nineteen thousand pieces. Much to the chagrin of Elector Frederick, Luther preached publicly against the indulgence traffic at Wittenberg in 1516 and early in 1517, warning parishioners that the practice of purchasing indulgences could easily hinder interior penance, consisting of contrition, confession, and satisfaction (as in fasting, prayer, and almsgiving). Through indulgences "nothing is accomplished except that the people learn to fear and flee and dread the penalty of sins, but not the sins themselves."[17] It was an insight Luther had reached earlier, in the autumn of 1514, when denouncing indulgences in the university's lecture hall, even though, according to Heiko Oberman, "good works still constituted the treasure of the Church for him at the time."[18] In 1517 a new crisis arose, precipitated by Prince Albert of Brandenburg, who had secured the rights from the pope to raise funds through the sale of indulgences to pay for the purchase of his post as cardinal of Mainz. (He also held the offices of archbishop of Magdeburg and vicar of Halberstadt.) Half of the sale was to pay the pope, Leo X, desperately in need of money for the construction of St. Peter's Basilica in Rome; the other half was to go to Albert and his lenders, the Fugger family. Even though Frederick the Wise had not

---

17. Martin Luther, "Sermon on St. Matthew's Day, Matt 11:25-30, February 24, 1517," in *Luther's Works*, gen. ed. Helmut T. Lehmann, vol. 51, *Sermons I*, edited and translated by John W. Doberstein (Philadelphia: Muhlenberg Press, 1959), 31.

18. Heiko A. Oberman, *Luther: Man Between God and the Devil*, trans. Eileen Walliser-Schwarzbart (New Haven: Yale University Press, 1989), 191.

granted Albert permission to sell indulgences in his territory, to preclude competition with the indulgence traffic benefiting Wittenberg, Albert's fundraisers came close enough for Luther's parishioners to simply cross over the nearby border and return with stunning concessions: they would be restored to the state of innocence enjoyed in baptism, could avert the pains of purgatory, and could help loved ones escape purgatory without any effort at internal contrition or private confession.

Chief of the vending campaign in Germany was the Dominican priest John Tetzel, who upon entering a town was met by the local dignitaries, who joined him in procession and then listened with rapt attention to his sermonizing. "Listen now, God and St. Peter call you. Consider the salvation of your souls and those of your loved ones departed. You priest, you noble, you merchant, you virgin, you matron, you youth, you old man, enter now into your church, which is the Church of St. Peter," Tetzel would say. "Consider that all who are contrite and have confessed and made contribution will receive complete remission of all their sins. Listen to the voices of your dear dead relatives and friends, beseeching you and saying, 'Pity us, pity us. We are in dire torment from which you can redeem us for a pittance.'"[19]

When on the eve of All Saints the relics were again on display at the Church of All Saints at Wittenberg generating revenue through indulgences, Luther posted ninety-five theses on the door of the Castle Church of Wittenberg, according to university custom. The 1517 theses were written in Latin, meant for disputation among scholars and dignitaries, and called for financial relief and an ongoing repentance of the self in surrender to Christ. Luther had invited an open discussion on these topics, but no one came at the suggested time and day. Instead, the theses were quickly transmitted by word of mouth and translated into the vernacular with unfortunate results: The theses' call to crucifixion of the self was given scarcely any attention, while the financial relief for the masses from the extortionist sale of indulgences became the prime exhibit for exposing a penitential system in need of reform. Repeatedly Luther tried to stress the full import of internal penance and due preparation for the sacrament of confession, the meaning of conversion, and Jesus' call to ongoing repentance in the Christian life. It was less the extortion through indulgences that Luther bewailed and feared than the havoc such practices had wrought in his parishioners' souls. Indulgences, he maintained, were fraught with false promises. They were a spurious substitute for

19. Bainton, *Here I Stand*, 78.

appeasing a troubled conscience and were apart from internal penance devoid of eternal effects. They robbed the sacrament of penance of its intended purpose, discrediting its officiants—the clergy, bishops, and the pope—and the church, and giving believers a false sense of security in regard to their own and their loved-ones' standing with God. Moreover, they ignored the life of the spirit and the internal growth that came with the examination of one's sins, the surrender of one's will to God, and a contemplation of the cross of Christ in submission, humility, and contrition. Rather than primarily seeking to attack a sacramental system gone awry, Luther meant to recover the scriptural foundation of Christian discipleship, Jesus' call to the faithful to return to him, and the essence of the Gospel message. For "the true treasure of the church is the most holy gospel of the glory and grace of God," he says in Thesis 62, and it "is not very well known to a large part of the church." This Gospel "is a preaching of the incarnate Son of God, given to us without any merit on our part for salvation and peace. It is a word of salvation, a word of grace, a word of comfort, a word of joy . . . When the sinful conscience hears this sweetest messenger, it comes to life again, shouts for joy while leaping about full of confidence, and no longer fears death, the types of punishments associated with death, or hell."[20] Luther concludes that those "still afraid of punishments have not yet heard Christ or the voice of the gospel."[21] Not a temporal rectifying of outward conditions drew his attention and energies then, but a refocusing of believers' attitudes regarding the state of their souls in light of the saving word of God.

In his preaching and writing Luther sought to recover and proclaim the Gospel message for the salvation of souls. In the context of the controversy over indulgences this is made particularly clear in the first of his ninety-five theses. According to Harold J. Grimm, the first thesis is "the core of all the others," saying "that penance is not a mechanical act but a permanent inner attitude."[22] The first thesis reads: "When our Lord and Master Jesus Christ said, 'Repent' [Matt 4:17], he willed the entire life of believers to be one of repentance."[23] As misunderstandings and misinterpretations by his opponents mounted, von Staupitz encouraged Luther, against the explicit order of the bishop, to write "Explanations

---

20. Martin Luther, "Explanations of the Ninety-Five Theses," in *Luther's Works*, vol. 31, *Career of the Reformer I*, ed. Harold J. Grimm (Philadelphia: Muhlenberg Press, 1957), 230–31.

21. Ibid., 231.

22. Harold J. Grimm, "Introduction," in *Luther's Works*, vol. 31, 22.

23. *Luther's Works*, vol. 31, 25.

of the Ninety-Five Theses" in late 1517. These "Explanations" were published in August of 1518, with a preceding "declaration" in which Luther affirms his intent to say "absolutely nothing except" what is found in "Holy Scriptures and can be maintained from them; and then what is in and from the writings of the church fathers and is accepted by the Roman church and preserved both in the canons and the papal decrees."[24] In his elaboration on the first thesis Luther says that Christ is our great teacher of repentance, who calls all people, regardless of their station in life, continually and throughout their life to repent and be displeased with themselves, praying "forgive us our debts." In commenting on Jesus' injunction to repent, Luther maintains that the Greek *metanoeite* used here does not mean "do penance," so as to support the act or the activity of doing. The Greek word's meaning, says Luther, is that we should "assume another mind and feeling, recover one's senses, make a transition from one state of mind to another, have a change of spirit."[25] Luther had made this glowing discovery by comparing the Latin Vulgate to the Greek New Testament of Erasmus, finding that the Vulgate's rendering of Matthew 4:17 as *penitentiam agite* was a mistranslation; the correct Latin word should have been *transmentamini*, meaning to come to one's senses and have a change of heart. "I venture to say," he wrote to von Staupitz in the dedication, that "they are wrong who make more of the act in Latin than of the change of heart in Greek."[26]

Luther's ensuing three theses are directly related to his first. In the second thesis he distinguishes between real repentance and sacramental repentance. In that he follows the scholastics, who "[consider] real penance as the material or the subject of sacramental penance." Sacramental penance is "only external" and presumes "inward penance." While inward repentance can exist without sacramental penance, the reverse does not apply. Therefore sacramental penance "can be a sham," while inward penance cannot.[27] In the third thesis Luther affirms that inward penance needs to find expression in outward works, in so-called acts of satisfaction such as fasting, prayer, and almsgiving. For by fasting, by prayer to God, by almsgiving to one's neighbor the Christian ministers to the spirit within. This means that all forms of self-mortification offered from a stricken conscience, whether "vigils, work, privation, study, prayers, abstinence from sex and pleasures, insofar as they minister to

24. Ibid., 83.
25. Ibid., 84.
26. Bainton, *Here I Stand*, 88.
27. *Luther's Works*, vol. 31, 85.

the spirit" are the result of real, inward penance.[28] And in the fourth thesis he affirms that repentance is a lifelong process, attested to by the martyrs and the saints, including such faithful Christians as St. Augustine and St. Bernard. For sin, and therefore repentance, remain "until the body of sin is destroyed," though it "diminishes daily through the renewing of the mind."[29]

The distinction between real, internal penance and sacramental, external penance was a significant step in clarifying the issues and arguments surrounding the indulgence traffic, priestly absolution, and satisfaction through works of penance. Apart from Thomas Aquinas probably no Christian theologian before Luther had dared force the distinction to such a degree, or felt compelled to do so, by stressing the high value of internal penance. Luther's inward orientation may have been sharpened by a reading of the mystics and the influence of von Staupitz during his formative years of spiritual struggle. Two years after his lectures on Romans, Luther in a dedicatory letter of the "Explanations of the Ninety-Five Theses" expresses gratitude and indebtedness to his spiritual director for pointing out the relative insignificance of sacramental penance unless preceded by internal penance and contrition. It is possible that von Staupitz had shared with Luther the sermons of Johann Tauler (1300–1361), the Dominican preacher who a century and a half earlier had captured his cloistered audiences with his appeals to a life free from self in surrender to and union with God. According to Robert Herndon Fife, Luther may have come into possession of these sermons early in 1516 while working on the Romans lectures. From the eighth chapter of Romans onward "the ideas of Tauler mingle with the quietism of Staupitz. . . ."[30] Commenting on Tauler's sermons, Luther writes to his friend Spalatin in a letter of 14 December 1516: "I have never either in Latin or in our language seen a theology which was saner and more in accord with the Evangelists."[31] Luther's own copy of Tauler's sermons was marked with comments and quotations.

Several passages in Luther's commentary with annotations of the letter to the Romans suggest the influence of Tauler and mystical thought. The struggling and fearful soul is to find release and tranquility by surrender, by a sinking and plunging into the darkness of faith and into the

---

28. Ibid., 86–87.

29. Ibid., 89.

30. Robert Herndon Fife, *The Revolt of Martin Luther* (New York: Columbia University Press, 1957), 219.

31. Ibid.

arms of a merciful God. For "we cannot overcome death and its evils by power and strength and we cannot escape them by running away from them in fear but only by bearing them patiently and willingly in weakness, i.e., without lifting a finger against them (Rom 8:5-13)."[32] About the moment of receiving God's grace repeatedly over a lifetime Luther writes: "Toward the first grace as well as toward the glory of eternal life we must always hold ourselves passive just as a woman does when she conceives. For we too are the bride of Christ. Hence, we may engage in prayer and petitions before we receive grace, yet when grace comes and the soul is about to be impregnated with the Spirit, there must be neither prayer nor any action on our part but only a keeping still"; such a holding still is fraught with "deep affliction" since "not to think and to will is for the soul the same as to go into darkness as though it were to be ruined and reduced to nothing, and this it seeks violently to avoid (Rom 8:26-27)."[33] The Christian's struggle resembles a *via negativa*, whereby our good is hidden under its opposite. "Thus our life is hidden under death, self-love [or self-respect] under self-hatred, glory under shame, salvation under perdition, the kingdom under banishment, heaven under hell, wisdom under foolishness, righteousness under sin, strength under weakness." But this is the way of following Christ to the cross and to God, "who is the negative essence and goodness and wisdom and righteousness and whom we cannot possess or attain to except by the negation of all our affirmations (Rom 9:3-5)."[34] Moreover, receiving the Gospel message presupposes a voluntary abandoning of worldly things such as the wisdom of the flesh and especially of reason, for one cannot "receive the word of Christ" unless one "humbly surrenders also the sovereignty of his reason and his whole mind (Rom 9:28-31)."[35]

The first book Luther published was from a manuscript copy by an unknown mystic. He had assumed that the book was by "the illumined Doctor Tauler of the Preaching Order,"[36] or one of his followers. In 1516 Luther wrote an enthusiastic foreword for it and published the incomplete tract dating from the late fourteenth century under the manuscript's title, *A Spiritually Noble Little Book*. Upon finding a more extensive copy

---

32. *Luther: Lectures on Romans*, translated and edited by Wilhelm Pauck (Philadelphia: Westminster, 1961), 230.

33. Ibid., 244.

34. Ibid., 264.

35. Ibid., 280.

36. Martin Luther, "Preface," *A Spiritually Noble Little Book* (*Eyn geystlich edles Buchleynn*), in *The Theologia Germanica of Martin Luther*, translation, introduction, and commentary by Bengt Hoffman (New York: Paulist Press, 1980), 42.

in a monastic library, probably the entire work, Luther republished the book in 1518 as *Theologia Germanica* or *German Theology*. In the expanded foreword Luther says that "no book except the Bible and St. Augustine has come to my attention from which I have learned more about God, Christ, man, and all things."[37] The book, attributed to an author called the Franckforter, "a German knight, a priest and a warden in the German house of knights in Frankfurt," had confirmed or perhaps clarified Luther's insight about being justified before God by grace alone, not by works or acts of satisfaction. The preface is an acknowledgment of Luther's indebtedness to this mystic for helping him formulate his theology of the cross, denoting unreserved surrender to God by crucifying the old self and negating one's will, thus allowing Christ's will to form in its place. Luther also acknowledged that he and the other Wittenberg theologians were not saying "entirely new things," but had been unable "to recognize or hear" what had been expressed by others before. Another influence the *Theologia Germanica* had on Luther was that it would shape his theology of experience, stressing an internal knowledge of the truth of the Gospel and of Christ apart from reason and learning. According to Bengt Hoffman, Luther's "kinship with the unknown author and with Johann Tauler, as well as some other mystics of the late Middle Ages, suggests a union in the Body of Christ, transcending ecclesial boundaries, through *sapientia experimentalis*, the heart's knowledge of Christ here and now."[38] In its insistence on a personal God-experience and rejection of religion as reward or punishment the book reflects the teachings of the Friends of God movement. Luther himself had lived for a year with some of the Friends of God, namely, the Brethren of the Common Life, when attending the cathedral school in Magdeburg in 1497. The movement's members considered Tauler to be one of their leading spiritual fathers, in addition to Heinrich Suso and Meister Eckhart; the last had been Suso's and Tauler's teacher and had been influenced, in turn, by the mystical orientation and teachings of the beguines, the women who had written on daily self-examination, inward repentance, and surrender in humility before God. Members of the Friends of God movement advocated inner renewal based on Scripture study, prayer, the examination of self, and a preaching that led to repentance and a renewing of the mind in union with Christ. They were clergy and laity, men and women, who practiced mutuality and equality in matters of teaching, discipline,

37. Martin Luther, "Preface to the Complete Edition of a German Theology," trans. Harold J. Grimm, in *Luther's Works*, vol. 31, 75.
38. Bengt Hoffman, "Foreword," *The Theologia Germanica of Martin Luther*, xvi.

and service to one another, engaging in what resembled a priesthood of all believers. In the first paragraph of *Theologia Germanica*'s introduction to an outline lies the watchword that signals the connection: "God the Almighty has spoken this little book through a wise, thoughtful, genuinely righteous person, a friend of His."[39]

Key concepts of Luther's theology of the cross, of experience, and of justification by faith alone are expressed in *Theologia Germanica*, including its introductory outline of the book's forty-nine chapters: "How we are not to take credit for good things we have done but acknowledge guilt for the evil we have done" (15); "How one cannot come to the true light and to the Christ life by much questioning or reading or by high natural knowledge and reason but only by renouncing oneself and all things" (17); "About poverty in the spirit and true humility and how to recognize the righteous, disciplined, truly free ones who have been made free by the truth" (24); "How one should put on the Christ life out of love and not for reward and how one should never put it aside or cast it off" (36); and "How one must believe several things pertaining to divine truth as a prerequisite before coming to true knowledge and experience" (46).[40] Among other things, it was Luther's personal experience with sin and the truth of the Gospel appeasing and cleansing his conscience that would make him distinguish between Law and Gospel, self-will and divine will, bondage and freedom, a God of wrath and a God of mercy, and external and internal repentance. To him this tension made the faithful Christian *simul justus et peccator*, both saint and sinner, both justified and sinful at the same time. While Christians had received the righteousness of Christ that made them just before God, they remained sinners because self-will persisted in them, necessitating ongoing examination of the conscience and a change of mind and heart in repentance and confession.

Following the events of 1517, Luther was hard pressed to clarify the issues surrounding the sacrament of penance. Based on his study of Scripture and Jesus' injunctions in the gospels in particular, he could retain only three of the seven sacraments: penance, baptism, and the Holy Communion. In three sermons of 1519, Luther expounded on each of the three sacraments, making their efficacy dependent on the faith by which they were received. In his sermon on "The Sacrament of Penance" Luther maintains the distinction between internal penance and sacramental penance, while adding new insights. First, the efficacy of penance and the power to receive forgiveness of sins does not rest with any

39. Ibid., 55.
40. Ibid., 55–59.

human office or authority but depends exclusively on the word of Christ and one's own faith. Priests, bishops, and the pope are only servants of the word of Christ, who extend Christ's pardon to believers. Second, whenever a priest is not available "any individual Christian—even a woman or child" can pronounce the words of forgiveness, saying "'God forgives you your sins, in the name,' etc., and if you can accept that word with a confident faith, as though God were saying it to you, then in that same faith you are surely absolved."[41] Third, forgiveness of sins does not depend on our own efforts at contrition or the amount of satisfaction we make for our sins. Instead, it comes to us through God's word in the sacrament, which we need to accept "in free and joyful faith, and never doubt that you have come to grace—not by your own merits or contrition but by his gracious and divine mercy, which promises, offers, and grants you full and free forgiveness of sins in order that in the face of all the assaults [*Anfechtung*] of sin, conscience, and the devil, you thus learn to glory and trust not in yourself or your own actions, but in the grace and mercy of your dear Father in heaven."[42] Fourth, the power and authority of the keys, the privilege of pronouncing absolution, are not given for the benefit of St. Peter or the pope or a bishop. Instead, they are given for the benefit of Christians so as to "help sinners by comforting and strengthening their conscience." For "by means of the keys the clergy should be serving not themselves but only us." One's desire for absolution should be enough evidence for the priest to grant it, regardless of how much detail has been divulged, especially since "he is not obligated to know anything." This is to uphold the value of the sacrament of penance, despite its abuses by those who have created "nothing but tyranny out of this lovely and comforting authority."[43] Finally, the Christian cannot be expected to make a full-fledged confession of the entire catalogue of sins, only those recognized as deadly, "those which at the time are oppressing and frightening the conscience." Otherwise one would be confessing all the time. Only God can properly judge concerning the distinction between venial and mortal sins except those in obvious violations of God's commandments. Even if one has not committed any mortal sins it is beneficial to confess one's minor sins simply for the hearing of absolution, which is God's word, for "the faith of the sacrament does everything, even though the confession be too much or

41. Martin Luther, "The Sacrament of Penance," in *Luther's Works*, vol. 35, *Word and Sacrament I*, ed. E. Theodore Bachmann (Philadelphia: Muhlenberg Press, 1960), 12.
42. Ibid., 15.
43. Ibid., 16–17.

too little,"[44] preferably leading to the best kind of penance and satisfaction one can offer, namely, to sin no more and do good toward both friend and foe. With these insights Luther affirms the healing power of the sacrament of penance, laying stress on the sinner's responsibility to hear in the words of absolution the very words of Christ and to trust them in faith, the possibility of other Christians functioning as confessor in the absence of a priest, and the dictates of the conscience as to what and how much to confess.

Luther sharpens these claims in his 1520 treatise titled "The Babylonian Captivity of the Church" by arguing for a priesthood of all believers in matters of hearing confession and pronouncing pardon, along with a reform of confessional practices in accordance with scriptural evidence. "As to the current practice of private confession, I am heartily in favor of it, even though it cannot be proved from the Scriptures," Luther says. "It is useful, even necessary, and I would not have it abolished. Indeed, I rejoice that it exists in the church of Christ, for it is a cure without equal for distressed consciences." For by baring our conscience in this fashion "we receive from our brother's lips the word of comfort spoken by God himself."[45] In fact, says Luther, confession of sins is necessary and commanded by God as evidenced in Matthew 3:6, 1 John 1:9-10, and Matthew 18:15-17. Private sins need not be confessed to the entire church or even to a representative, such as a priest; one's Christian neighbor suffices. Jesus' saying in Matthew 18:18 applies to "each and every Christian": that "whatever you bind on earth shall be bound in heaven, and whatever you loose on earth shall be loosed in heaven," for "where two or three are gathered in my name, there am I in the midst of them" (Matt 18:20). This means, says Luther, "that every one is absolved from his secret sins when he has made confession, privately before any brother, either of his own accord or after being rebuked, and has sought pardon and amended his ways, no matter how much the violence of the pontiffs may rage against it. For Christ has given to every one of his believers the power to absolve even open sins."[46] Instead of acting as "princes of Babylon" who hold Christians captive by their troubled consciences and inflict on them torturous, superstitious, and unscriptural means of deliverance out of greed and power hunger, bishops and priests should "permit all brothers and sisters most freely to hear the confession of

---

44. Ibid., 20–21.

45. Martin Luther, "The Babylonian Captivity of the Church," in *Luther's Works*, vol. 36, *Word and Sacrament II*, ed. Abdel Ross Wentz (Philadelphia: Fortress Press, 1959), 86.

46. Ibid., 87–88.

secret sins, so that the sinner may make his sins known to whomever he will and seek pardon and comfort, that is, the word of Christ, by the mouth of his neighbor."[47] Specific circumstances surrounding the motive and occasion of the sin, such as when, with whom, or against whom, are to be disregarded because of their enslaving effect, magnifying "the things that are nothing, to the injury of the things that are everything," namely, the value and "glory of Christian brotherhood"[48] regarding mutual forgiveness of sins in the name and on behalf of Christ.

Luther had laid the foundation for lay confession among Christians while upholding sacramental penance to a priest or minister. The requirement of annual sacramental confession implicit in the Fourth Lateran Council he rejected since inward renewal of a person's life outweighed any act of satisfaction. Those wishing to partake of Holy Communion were to notify the minister in person of their intention to do so, so that he could examine their understanding of the Christian faith and console those in trouble and temptation. There are those unable to describe "the faith, the comfort, the use and benefit of the Supper," and they "should be completely excluded and banished from the communion of the Supper," [49] while, on the other hand, there may be those who only need examination once in a lifetime or not at all. Applicants should be able to repeat the words of institution from memory and explain that they wish to partake of communion because of a troubled conscience due to sin, fear of death, or temptations of the flesh and that they now long for "the word and sign of grace and salvation from the Lord himself"[50] offered through the ministry of the priest. Blatant offenders, however, such as adulterers, gamblers, and slanderers, were to be excluded from communion until they had shown repentance of their behavior. In his order of the Mass of 1523, the *"Formula Missae,"* Luther places after the Lord's Prayer the *Pax Domini* as "a public absolution of the sins of the communicants, the true voice of the gospel announcing remission of sins, and therefore the one and most worthy preparation for the Lord's Table," provided they are received in faith as the very words of Christ.[51] Visibility of the communicants during communion is central to Luther. Communicants were to gather in one group near the altar and the chancel so as

47. Ibid., 88.
48. Ibid., 89.
49. Martin Luther, "An Order of Mass and Communion for the Church at Wittenberg," in *Luther's Works*, vol. 53, *Liturgy and Hymns*, ed. Ulrich S. Leupold (Philadelphia: Fortress Press, 1965), 33.
50. Ibid., 32.
51. Ibid., 28–29.

to be "seen and known openly" and so "that their lives may be better observed, proved, and tested."[52] Coming forward in order to receive communion was a public testimonial that the believer understood the meaning of the sacrament and that no scandalous unconfessed sin precluded participation.

In 1526 Luther commends private confession to both children and adults. According to a sermon on the sacrament of Holy Communion, the benefits are threefold. First, the absolution by the priest is "as if God himself were speaking, and that should indeed be comforting to us," especially when our conscience is burdened. Second, private confession is an opportunity for instructing people about the sacrament of Holy Communion. One can ask people what they believe and teach them to pray, "since the common herd is indolent, continually hearing sermons and learning nothing." Such instruction "can be done most conveniently in confession." Third, private confession affords the Christian the opportunity to ask for advice. "There is comfort in the fact that if anyone has an evil conscience, or some other desire or need," says Luther, "he may ask for advice here."[53] Overall, private confession, much like Holy Communion, is to be voluntary. It is only for "simple, childlike people"[54] and the devout, "and if you are not devout it is better to let it be, for then it is not righteous but damnable." Still, Luther recommends that both children and adult believers be taught about the benefits of private confession and be urged to practice it, as long as this is done "with kind words and not with coercion."[55]

By 1528, in a work on Holy Communion, Luther speaks of two sacraments only, while consistently maintaining a high regard for the ministry of confession. He himself went to confession and may have done so regularly prior to receiving communion until the end of his life. In the *Small Catechism* of 1529, Luther offers a short model for confession to a minister, placing it in his outline between the sacrament of baptism and the sacrament of the altar. The instructions of the catechism are to teach Christians, young and old, how to confess in a question-and-answer format. In confession "we confess our sins" and "we receive absolution, or forgiveness, from the confessor, as from God himself, and in no wise doubt, but firmly believe,

52. Ibid., 33–34.
53. Martin Luther, "The Sacrament of the Body and Blood of Christ—Against the Fanatics," in *Luther's Works*, vol. 36, *Word and Sacrament II*, 359.
54. Ibid.
55. Ibid., 360–61.

that our sins are thereby forgiven before God in heaven,"[56] Luther writes. To the question as to which sins to confess, the answer is that "we should plead guilty of all sins, even of those which we do not know, as we do in the Lord's Prayer. But before the confessor we should confess those sins alone which we know and feel in our hearts." In searching to list the sins, the penitent should "consider your station according to the Ten Commandments, whether you are a father, mother, son, daughter, master, mistress, a man-servant or maid-servant; whether you have been disobedient, unfaithful, slothful; whether you have grieved any one by words or deeds; whether you have stolen, neglected, or wasted aught, or done other injury." Luther then offers two examples, one of a servant, the other of a master or mistress. The servant may admit to having served the superiors unfaithfully or provoked them, exercised immodesty in word or deed, or quarreled with his or her equals. The master or mistress may admit to having neglected to properly train children, domestics, and family for God's glory, cursing, setting a bad example by rudeness in word and deed, slander, and dishonest business trade. Luther advises the penitent to address only known sins, instead of painstakingly searching one's conscience or inventing other sins. If one cannot come up with any sins (however impossible that might be), "then mention none in particular, but receive the forgiveness upon your general confession which you make before God to the confessor. The confessor is then to pray for God's mercy and the strengthening of the penitent's faith. "Dost thou believe that my forgiveness is God's forgiveness?" the minister asks, to which the penitent replies, "yes, dear sir." The concluding response and absolution of the minister is: "As thou believest, so be it done unto thee. And by the command of our Lord Jesus Christ I forgive thee thy sins, in the name of the Father and of the Son and of the Holy Ghost. Amen. Depart in peace."[57] In the Augsburg Confession of 1530 drafted by Philip Melanchthon, professor of New Testament at Wittenberg and Luther's associate, the signers profess that they are continuing the practice of private confession and absolution, usually in preparation for communion, "for it is not usual to give the body of the Lord, except to them that have been previously examined and absolved."[58]

56. Martin Luther, *The Small Catechism*, Part V, available in *Concordia: The Lutheran Confessions: A Reader's Edition of the Book of Concord*, gen. ed. Paul Timothy McCain, based on the translation by William Hermann Theodore Dau and Gerhard Friedrich Bente (St. Louis: Concordia Publishing House, 2006), and online at www.bookofconcord.org/smallcatechism.php.

57. Ibid.

58. The Augsburg Confession, available in *Concordia* (see n. 56 above), and at www.bookofconcord.org/augsburgconfession.php.

A later edition of the *Small Catechism*, adopted in 1862 in many German Protestant churches, omits the practical examples, uses twenty-two questions under the title "Teaching Simple People How to Confess," and adds theological content regarding the rite.[59] The "office of the keys" is explained as consisting of the keys of binding and loosing with a reference to John 20. Two sample confessions are offered for general, public use for those who would prefer these words to their own. And the answers to Questions 19 and 20 show the relation of the rite of confession to baptism and communion. "Where does one place this piece about confession?" the catechism asks. It belongs "to holy baptism, whose power and significance is realized in confession as a beneficial and frequent exercise." "To what does this piece about confession point also?" It points "to Holy Communion, since according to church order, when I desire to partake of communion I am supposed to make confession first."[60]

Luther loosely links private confession with the sacraments of baptism and communion in an effort to retain the importance of repentance throughout the believer's life. At the same time he ascribes to the acts of confession and absolution a sacramental significance derived from the divine word preceding these acts. Speaking of confession in the Smalcald Articles of 1537, Luther says that "the outward Word of God" comes to us in the acts of confession and absolution, filling us with the Holy Spirit and strengthening us against sin and a troubled conscience. For this to take effect, the Christian will need faith and "must firmly hold that God grants His Spirit or grace to no one, except through or with the preceding outward Word." After all, says Luther, "God does not wish to deal with us otherwise than through the spoken Word and the Sacraments." This means that the penitent coming to confession is moved to do so by the outward word that preceded the act, while the minister pronouncing absolution is speaking this outward word on behalf of Christ and because it was "ordained by Christ [Himself] in the Gospel."[61]

Linking confession with the two sacraments of baptism and communion would be a critical endeavor in later Protestant traditions, especially among Lutheran and Reformed churches. However, as confession was tied theologically to the two sacraments, the dimension of spiritual direction and pastoral counsel offered the laity during private confession and

---

59. Martin Luther, *Kleiner Katechismus mit Erklärung* (Hamburg: Helmut Korinth, 1982), 178–82.

60. Ibid., 181.

61. Martin Luther, The Smalcald Articles, art. 8, "Of Confession," available in *Concordia* (see n. 56 above), and at www.bookofconcord.org/smalcald.php.

so vital to Luther, the mystics of the fourteenth and fifteenth centuries, and among the members of the Friends of God movement diminished. As parishioners sought out the pastor for confession in order to be allowed to receive the sacraments they thought of their visit less as a time of receiving spiritual counsel and more as a means of avoiding public exclusion from the community of faith.

Luther's reforms gave subsequent generations of Protestant, or evangelical Christians the impetus to experiment with and implement confession in various ways. Theologically the practice could be easily traced in the Scriptures and Jesus' sayings and preaching ministry, thus was not only acceptable but desirable among those who considered themselves priests to one another. Liturgically the act of confession was placed in the context of communal worship, often in preparation for the sacrament of Holy Communion, or in a private setting as during home visits by either the clergy or a group of designated members and officers of the congregation. Confession was also linked with baptism, so that by witnessing a baptism one remembered one's own baptism, along with Christ's imputed righteousness, one's own baptismal death and rising with Christ, and the command to forgive others as Christ has forgiven us. A significant difference from the Roman Catholic practice of confession was the interpretation of the power of the keys. With the extension of the role of confessor to members of the laity, confidentiality was a less-guaranteed right since lay members were not obligated by vows to keep secret the sins their neighbor had entrusted to them. Also the provisional seal of confidentiality could be superseded by the faith community's right to know the sins of its members to ensure the church's health, purity, and identity. The pastor, as well as church members and ordained officers, administered the keys for the forgiveness of sins to one another as mediated through Christ. Exposing the sins of individuals to the entire community functioned also as a deterrent in implementing and enforcing communal discipline. As the practice of private confession became voluntary among Protestants, the pastor retained the primary role of confessor while ministering mostly to those whose sins and consciences were too heavy to bear on their own. By contrast, spiritual direction emerged as a form of spiritual guidance and counsel for discernment in community, practiced mostly during worship and effected by the proclamation of the Word and the administering of the sacraments. Small groups for mutual teaching, exhortation, and discipline would provide an additional locus for spiritual guidance, as did catechetical instruction; but communal worship, not private encounters between pastor and parishioner, was the primary locus for receiving divine counsel and hearing God's word. A brief overview of the variety of theological strands emerging in the wake of the Protestant Reformation and newly forming confessional practices in Protestant churches and the Roman Catholic Church will provide the salient points of distinction.

CHAPTER NINE

The Priesthood of All Believers and Mutual Confession

Pietism and Methodism

The administering of confession by the laity was developed both theologically and practically by Luther's followers. Among these was the Strasbourg reformer Martin Bucer (1491–1551), who places the responsibility for the cure of souls on all members of the Christian community. Bucer had become a Dominican in 1506 and later was drawn to the humanists, especially Erasmus. Enamored with the study of Greek and the new teachings of Luther, whom he heard speak in 1518, he obtained release from his vows in 1521 and was excommunicated in 1523 on account of his teachings. While continuing to teach and preach, he became head of the city clergy in Strasbourg in 1531, all the while seeking to reconcile the Roman Catholic and Protestant factions. In his *On the True Cure of Souls*, published in 1538 in German and Latin, Bucer concedes that the primary task of healing and administering the medicine of sins falls to ordained clergy. At the same time, every Christian has a responsibility to his or her neighbor of tending and healing by binding up the wounded and acting as a confessor to those inclined to reveal their sins. The neighbor must be led to say, "I have sinned; I seek pardon; I will amend." Inducing the sinner to reach the point of repentance and confession will require great sensitivity and compassion, as demonstrated by Paul in the case of the Corinthian offender and by Nathan in bringing David to repentance. Conveying to the sinner that God is merciful and forgiving will be essential. "For the health and life of the inner man," says Bucer, "consists in a true and living faith in the mercy of God and a sure trust in the remission of sins."[1] This is true not only of those within the church but also of those who may have become alienated. Since in many cases it is impossible to discern the difference between the two groups, Christians are to seek out all and try to reclaim, or claim, them and with gentleness bring them to repentance and into the fold of Christ.

In matters of Christian discipline Bucer sought to revive the early system of public penance in the case of severe offenses. Seven years earlier he and his Strasbourg colleagues had sought and failed to establish such a discipline, in which twenty-one elected lay officers were to assist. Apparently his methods were proposed in other parts of Europe also. The same year that Bucer's book was published, John Calvin and Guillaume Farel had been forced to leave Geneva for insisting on the exclusion from communion of those whose sins were considered scandalous and who had refused to submit to public confession. Bucer insisted that offenders were to be excluded from communion and not be readmitted until they had been publicly exposed and had repented. While the blood of Christ was sufficient for satisfaction, Bucer considered public confession as medicinal for its function as a deterrent. True penance "is not satisfaction for past sins, but medicine against those of the present and future."[2] Only those who publicly repent can be readmitted to communion. Moreover, Bucer advocates "the exclusion and separation of the he-goats" that mix with the sheep and remain unrepentant and incorrigible.[3] While Christians ought to pray for and assist the excommunicated who are suffering need, they are to avoid all social contact with them. Following numerous controversies, Bucer left Strasbourg for England in 1549 to become Regius Professor of Theology at Cambridge, serving subsequently as a consultant for the revision of the Book of Common Prayer. Meanwhile, Bucer's followers had instituted small groups in Strasbourg in which laypeople and ministers engaged in a series of catechetical exercises followed by a study of the Scriptures, mutual teaching, and exhortation.

---

1. Martin Bucer, *De vera animarum cura veroque officio pastoris ecclesiastici* (Strasbourg, 1538); text in *Buceri Scripta Anglicana fere omnia* (Basel: Ex Petri Pernae officina, 1577), 305ff.; quoted in John T. McNeill, *A History of the Cure of Souls* (New York: Harper & Brothers, 1951), 179.

2. *Buceri Scripta*, 319; quoted in McNeill, *A History of the Cure of Souls*, 179.

3. *Buceri Scripta*, 350; quoted in McNeill, *A History of the Cure of Souls*, 180.

Pietism

Seventeenth-century reformers in the Lutheran tradition continued refining and putting into practice Luther's principle of the universal priesthood of all believers. They saw each Christian as responsible for teaching, exhorting, converting, and edifying other Christians, including those in one's own home. The principle gained a high regard among members of a movement called Pietism, begun in Germany and later spreading to Holland, Switzerland, Scandinavia, and North America. Initially the movement had been a reaction to the orthodox Lutheran interpretation of justification as a forensic act whereby Christ's righteousness was considered as being imputed to the believer by faith. By contrast, Pietists claimed that justification not only freed one of the guilt of sin but added power by the experience of Christ within. Justification was seen as working in two parts: one first experienced a rebirth in Christ and then one practiced a piety that actively sought to resist evil and bring about good. The movement distinguished between an initial conversion to Christ and the ongoing work of regeneration and renovation through the workings of the Holy Spirit, between initial salvation and subsequent sanctification.

The origin of Pietism is generally linked with the city of Frankfurt and the year 1675 when the Lutheran pastor Philipp Jakob Spener (1635–1705) published Johann Arndt's sermons with a preface he entitled *Pia Desideria* ("pious desires"). At the time Spener was senior pastor of the ministerium in Frankfurt, the most prestigious pastoral position in the city. Through his pastoral duties among clergy and laity he had been made painfully aware of the laxity of Christian life in the city and throughout Germany. The writings of Johann Arndt (1555–1621), a Lutheran pastor serving in several German cities, including Eisleben and Lüneburg, had proposed to Spener concrete ways of revitalizing the Christian faith. In *True Christianity*, written between 1606 and 1610, Arndt called for repentance and sanctification that would bring the soul into living communion with God. "God is to completely possess man from within and without," Arndt writes.[4] "Thus, nothing other is to live, shine, act, will, love, think, speak, or rejoice in man except God himself."[5] While his borrowing from medieval mystics such as Bernard of Clairvaux, Johann Tauler, and Thomas á Kempis brought Arndt into repeated

---

4. Johann Arndt, *True Christianity*, trans. and introduction by Peter Erb (New York: Paulist Press, 1979), 31.
5. Ibid., 30.

conflict with his colleagues, it provided the seedbed and inspiration for pastors such as Spener in launching a new way of practicing the Christian faith. At the center of this new practice lay a personal conversion experience and a heartfelt devotion to Christ. In the preface to Arndt's *Postils*, Spener advocates, among other things, the kind of biblical preaching from the pulpit that would produce among hearers an experience of repentance and rebirth, and the founding of small prayer and study groups, the so-called conventicles (*ecclesiolae in ecclesia*), for mutual edification and exhortation of "reborn" believers, including pastors. Spener's hope was to work renewal among both the clergy and the laity. His recommendation was that all Christians immerse themselves in the Scriptures so as to be able to teach, including those under their own roof, and "to chastise, exhort, convert, and edify them, to observe their life, pray for all, and insofar as possible be concerned about their salvation."[6] Spener also advocated equality among clergy and laity in matters of correction and mutual edification. Lay members "ought to pay attention to the minister" and "admonish him fraternally when he neglects something," while assisting him in the care of souls through the ministry of mutual care. After all, "One man is incapable of doing all that is necessary for the edification of the many persons who are generally entrusted to his pastoral care."[7]

For those who wished to deepen their faith, Spener suggested working with a confessor. This confessor might be a minister or "some other judicious and enlightened Christian" with whom one entered into a confidential, ongoing relationship for reporting on one's life, reviewing opportunities for the practice of Christian love and the occasions when one had seized or neglected them. Meetings with the confessor were to be private and "should be done with the intention of discovering what is amiss and securing such an individual's counsel and instruction as to what ought now to be done."[8] Implied in the relationship with a confessor or spiritual director was that one generally accepted the advice received and followed it.

Spener stressed the need for a confessor or spiritual director especially for pastors in training. Students needed "concrete suggestions on how to institute pious meditations, how to know themselves better through self-examination, how to resist the lusts of the flesh, how to hold their

---

6. Philipp Jakob Spener, "Pia Desideria," in *Pietists: Selected Writings*, ed. and introduced by Peter C. Erb (New York: Paulist Press, 1983), 35.

7. Ibid., 36.

8. Ibid., 37.

desires in check and die unto the world . . . how to observe growth in goodness or where there is still lack, and how they themselves may do what they must teach others to do. Studying alone will not accomplish this. . . ."[9] Aspiring pastors under Spener's tutelage were also encouraged to read the *Theologia Germanica* and the writings of Tauler, which "probably made our dear Luther what he was."[10] After all, "the precious, gifted, and sainted" Johann Arndt had republished *Theologia Germanica* with a new foreword and had praised and used Tauler's writings in his book, *True Christianity*. The third book Spener commended to aspiring Protestant pastors was Thomas à Kempis's *Imitation of Christ*. The aim of such reading and instruction was the same for theology students as for all Christians, namely, to "accustom the people first to work on what is inward (awaken love of God and neighbor through suitable means) and only then to act accordingly." For what does not proceed from the "inner man" is "mere hypocrisy."[11]

The theme of the universal priesthood of all believers was central to Spener's thought and reform. In a 1677 treatise titled "The Spiritual Priesthood" he elaborated in seventy questions and answers on the theme's scriptural basis and meaning for the practices of confession, exhortation, and the giving of counsel. Every single Christian is responsible for the salvation and edification of others, Spener says. By virtue of our baptism we inherit the office of "spiritual priest," consisting of the threefold task of sacrifice, prayer and blessing, and the divine word. The office of sacrifice involves the surrender of our own will in body and soul to God; the office of prayer and blessing the care for our neighbors and making intercession for them; and the office of the divine Word the reading and studying of the Scriptures and their use for ourselves and among or with others. It is the office of the divine word in particular that relates to mutual confession and exhortation. For "the Scriptures have been given for teaching, for reproof, for correction, for discipline in righteousness (2 Tim 3:16) and also for comfort (Rom 15:4)." Therefore Christians "are to use the Scriptures to all these intents and to teach, convert from error, admonish, reprove, and comfort, as the Scriptures themselves everywhere indicate."[12] However, the laity were to exercise this office in private so as not to interfere with the public office of the pastor.

---

9. Ibid., 45.
10. Ibid., 44.
11. Ibid., 48.
12. Philipp Jakob Spener, "The Spiritual Priesthood," in *Pietists: Selected Writings*, 61.

Leading others into confession and repentance as well as reproving, exhorting, and comforting them is a form of Christian teaching. Spener distinguished between two audiences in need of teaching: the uninitiated, who should be instructed in the faith and be led to the Scriptures; and the initiated, who read the Scriptures together and who each "modestly and in love tell for the edification of the others what God has enabled him to understand in the Scriptures, and what he thinks will be serviceable for the edification of the others." In these small study groups believers will also attempt to "convert the erring" in an effort to "avert all danger of body and life from my neighbor,"[13] admonish and exhort each other "to put into practice, by God's help, what they perceive ought to be done," and reprove sinning fellow Christians "in kindness, meekness, and love, show them their wrong, and thereby try to win them over to amendment."[14] In addition, Christians will provide comfort to those who have been brought to repentance "and cheer them all they can." In cases when no ordained minister is available, Christians "may also impart the comfort of the forgiveness of sins or absolution."[15]

Spener insisted that every Christian, both male and female, has the power and the right to pronounce forgiveness of sins and absolution, along with offering teaching and exhortation. Even though women are precluded from public office they may carry out the office of the divine word in private and in small group study as do their non-ordained male brothers and, in fact, they do so already among their children and domestics. After all, the gender difference is eliminated when it comes to spiritual matters and spiritual gifts, Spener says, as is shown not only from the Scriptures but also by the example of the apostles, who worked with women and, rather than censuring them, praised them and commended their work.

Spener placed the times and occasions for exercising the three offices of the spiritual priesthood under the dictates of God's counsel and love for one's neighbor. Christians may not impose themselves on others as teachers, spiritual guides, or confessors. Instead, in small groups they may "deal only with those who are willing to accept such help in love" and come for counsel. In these gatherings no one is set above the other and appointed as leader, since "each must be just as willing to learn from others as to teach in divine order."[16] In their role as "spiritual priests" Chris-

---

13. Ibid.
14. Ibid., 61–62.
15. Ibid., 62.
16. Ibid., 62–63.

tians should avoid seeking self-glory and should focus, instead, on their own and their neighbor's edification and spiritual growth. To prevent any disorder arising from this new arrangement, pastors and laity are responsible for proper instruction and behavior. Pastors ought to teach people about the principle of the spiritual priesthood as it distinguishes between the roles of public and private ministry and encourage and, if necessary, correct members in their priestly service; lay members should associate with their ministers, be open to their counsel, facilitate the exercise of their office, and "especially refrain from all disparagement of them" and "picking flaws."[17] At the core of Spener's theology are lifelong penance, faith, and a practical obedience to God in Christ, leading to outward fruits and inner peace. The exercise of believers' gifts, particularly in regard to mutual correction and edification (*aedificatio mutua*), was expected, and it raised both the demands on and the status of the laity over against the clergy.

A generation after Spener, the Lutheran pastor and reformer August Hermann Francke (1663–1727) encouraged Christians to demonstrate boldness in rebuking others for their sin. Do "not put off the unpleasant moments because of fear or shyness," for they must be conquered in the same manner as "other evil mental turmoil must be." Preceding the rebuke should be self-examination leading to empathy and compassion toward the sinner. Christ is our role model in that regard, Francke says: he rebuked Peter with a simple glance when Peter had denied him, and he rebuked with forceful, harsh words on other occasions. Above all, "Rebuke with love and great foresight and modesty so that the other person might be convinced in his conscience . . . that he has not done right."[18] By doing so one actively bears witness to Christ and refuses to become a participant in the sins of the other, Francke says. Conversely, the Christian is to invite others' suggestions and critical evaluation of conduct, particularly in regard to the use of senseless, sarcastic, or abusive speech: "Ask others if you use such words, for habit makes one unaware that one does so."[19] Based on his own dramatic conversion experience, Francke and many Lutheran ministers under his influence conducted personal interviews to ascertain whether a believer had been truly "reborn," keeping records of the conversations and noting what was said.

Another strand of Pietism developed with Nicolas Ludwig Count Zinzendorf (1700–1760), whom Spener had blessed as a child. Raised in

17. Ibid., 64.
18. August Hermann Francke, "Rules for the Protection of Conscience and for Good Order in Conversation or in Society" (1689), in *Pietists: Selected Writings*, 111.
19. Ibid., 109.

a Pietist home and destined for a role in politics, Zinzendorf studied at the universities of Halle and Wittenberg. Not allowed to enter the Lutheran ministry by his family, he followed his late father's career in government as the king's judicial counselor at Dresden while choosing to imbue the public office with his Christian ideals. In 1722 Zinzendorf heard of the plight of the Bohemian Brethren, or Moravians, who suffered intense persecution, and offered them asylum on his newly purchased estate in Berthelsdorf. In 1727 he and his wife, Erdmuth Dorothea, moved to the estate also and named their community Herrnhut, or "the Lord's watch." While the countess took on administrative and pastoral responsibilities in the settlement, Zinzendorf provided the theological underpinnings. All the leaders of the renewed Moravian Church were in some way attached to the Pietist movement, stressing personal conversion and an experience of Christ in faith. To allay internal disputes among a community that had grown to more than three hundred by February of 1727, Zinzendorf drew up a "brotherly agreement" resembling a monastic rule and divided members into small groups, so-called bands or choirs, along lines of gender, age, and marital status; by August the community had experienced a spiritual awakening. From that time on the movement flourished and evangelists and missionaries, the first in Protestantism, carried the new practical piety from Saxony into other parts of Germany and Europe and, in particular, to the New World colonies of Georgia and Pennsylvania. As the pastor and benefactor of the Herrnhut community, Zinzendorf shaped Moravian theology to a large degree, emphasizing Luther's distinction between a hidden and a revealed God through the redemptive birth of Christ in the believer's heart, a conversion experience as assurance of one's salvation, and the process of renovation and sanctification toward increased Christ-likeness in the context of a close-knit faith community and accountability groups. Denominational differences were to be laid aside and transcended for the sake of increased focus on Christ's activity in the believer.

For Zinzendorf, saving faith occurred in two stages. The first began when a person experienced true misery and distress: "Something must happen to him which Luther calls 'the divine work in us,' which changes us, gives us new birth, and makes us completely different people in heart, spirit, mind, and all our powers. . . . If this is to begin in us, then it must be preceded by distress, without which men have no ears for faith and trust."[20] Such "faith-in-distress" contained the promise that one would

---

20. Nicolas Ludwig von Zinzendorf, "Concerning Saving Faith," sermon preached in the Brethren's Chapel in London, 6 September 1746, in *Pietists: Selected Writings*, 305.

receive grace. After that, one entered the second stage of saving faith, when one became aware of one's sin and sought the actual forgiveness of sins, "after the yearning and longing for help, for rescue, when one has time for reflection, when the distress is not too pressing."[21] The movement from the first to the second stage, from an implicit faith or *fides implicita* to an explicit one, *fides explicita*, is manifested in the Christian first by learning about Christ and then by teaching him to others. Teaching Christ to others is not a matter of the head, but of the heart, because Christians extend and exhibit him through their lives. Thus, "our entire work of the gospel is to portray Jesus," says Zinzendorf, "to paint him before the eyes, to take the spirit's stylus and etch—yes, engrave—the image of Jesus in the fleshly tablets of the heart, so that it can never be removed again."[22]

Members of the Herrnhut community practiced confession both in private to the minister and in their respective small groups. Private confession was voluntary, yet no one was allowed to receive Holy Communion without prior knowledge of the minister "in order that all confusion and levity may be prevented."[23] Confession within the small group was voluntary also and could be done during the daily meetings "given for exhortation and edification."[24] In addition, every member was allowed to rebuke and admonish others in love during the week, whether there was reason for it or not. On Sundays the elders held a conference where potential offenders were cited to appear and respond to the charges made against them in the hope that they would repent. The proper response on the part of offenders was to refrain from objecting and to willingly receive admonition and reproof; they were not to consider it "disgraceful to be spoken to on the subject"[25] nor to leave or withdraw from the community. Only in case of repeated refusal to repent and follow the admonitions of the elders were offenders asked to leave the community.

Initially Zinzendorf had drawn up the rule for the Herrnhut community to reconcile warring factions among the Moravians, seeking to identify the unifying elements of their Christian faith and to ground

21. Ibid., 307.

22. Nicolas Ludwig von Zinzendorf, "On the Essential Character and Circumstances of the Life of a Christian," sermon preached in the Brethren's Chapel in London, 25 September 1746, in *Pietists: Selected Writings*, 317.

23. Nicolas Ludwig von Zinzendorf, "Brotherly Union and Agreement at Herrnhut," in *Pietists: Selected Writings*, 326.

24. Ibid., 328.

25. Ibid.

them in the Scriptures and in Christ. By doing so he grew to embrace an active ecumenicity rooted in the conviction that the various Christian denominations were divinely instituted "schools" directing believers in the faith. His profound hope was to see the German-speaking Protestants in America united in their efforts at evangelizing and living out the Gospel. Instead, his ecumenicity would take a direction he could not have foreseen: his theological views and practices implemented among the Moravians in Germany would profoundly influence and shape the work and ministry of John Wesley and the Methodists in England and, through them, English-speaking American spirituality at large.

Methodism

The confessional practices of the Moravians, initially adopted at Herrnhut, would have a lasting impact on the founder of Methodism. John Wesley (1703–1791) first met the Moravians on his missionary trip with his brother Charles on board a ship to America in 1735. He worked with them in Georgia and following his return to England in 1737 teamed up with another Moravian, Peter Böhler, to preach and proclaim the Gospel. In 1738 Wesley went reluctantly to one of their meetings at Aldersgate Street in London, where the presider of the Moravian assembly was reading from Luther's preface to the epistle to the Romans and describing "the change God works in the heart through faith in Christ." Wesley reports in his journal that at "about a quarter before nine . . . I felt my heart strangely warmed. I felt I did trust in Christ, Christ alone, for salvation; and an assurance was given me that He had taken away my sins, even mine, and saved me from the law of sin and death. . . ."[26] Wesley had encountered great opposition to his preaching in England, being repeatedly prevented from returning to the churches where he had preached. That day he was able to forgive his opponents and adversaries: "I began to pray with all my might for those who had in a more especial manner despitefully used me and persecuted me. I then testified openly to all there what I now first felt in my heart."[27] Subsequently he went on a three-month trip to Germany, meeting with many Pietists and working out the implications and practices gleaned from them. Their impact remained in his theological and practical emphases on a religion of the heart and personal conversion, lay ministry and

---

26. John Wesley, *The Journal of John Wesley* (Chicago: Moody Press, 1951), available at www.ccel.org/wesley/journal.html.
27. Ibid.

preaching, and small groups or bands methodically organized for exercising the principle of the priesthood of all believers.

Nearly a decade earlier, in 1529, after he had been ordained a presbyter in the Church of England, Wesley had gathered a small group of scholars and fellows at Oxford who at first met on Sunday evenings and later every evening for three hours to engage in Scripture study, mutual edification, and correction. The group at Oxford became known as the Holy Club and sought to revive the practices of the early apostolic community. Members studied the Greek New Testament, read the Greek and Latin church fathers, fasted on Wednesdays and Fridays, partook of Holy Communion weekly, and prayed with and visited the sick and prisoners. By 1735 the group had grown to "fourteen or fifteen in number, all of one heart and one mind"[28]; it included students and professors from the colleges of Brasenose, Exeter, and Queens. George Whitefield had joined the group only a few months before Wesley and his brother, Charles, were called to serve as missionaries to the Indians. The reason the group came to be known as "Methodists" can easily be glimpsed from Wesley's journal chronicling the daily routine on board the ship during their three-month journey. A typical day went as follows:

> From four in the morning till five, each of us used private prayer. From five to seven, we read the Bible together. At seven, we breakfasted. At eight was the public service. From nine to twelve, I learned German; Mr. Delamotte, Greek; my brother wrote sermons; and Mr. Ingham instructed the children. At twelve, we met together. About one, we dined. The time from dinner to four, we spent in reading to those of whom each of us had taken charge, or in speaking to them severally, as need required. At four were the Evening Prayers; when either the Second Lesson was explained (as it always was in the morning) or the children were catechised and instructed before the congregation. From five to six, we again used private prayer. From six to seven, I read in our cabin to two or three of the passengers . . . . At seven, I joined with the Germans (of whom we had twenty-six on board) in the public service. . . . At eight, we met again, to instruct and exhort each other; and between nine and ten went to bed.[29]

Wesley's second stage in developing small groups took place in Savannah, Georgia, during the two years of his stay. He had "advised the serious part of the congregation to form themselves into a sort of little society, and to meet once or twice a week, in order to instruct, exhort,

28. John Wesley, "A Short History of the People Called Methodists," in *The Works of John Wesley*, vol. XIII (London: Wesleyan Conference Office, 1872), 304.

29. Ibid., 304–5.

and reprove one another." From that group he selected a smaller number, about twenty or thirty, "for a more intimate union with each other,"[30] convening them in his house each Sunday afternoon.

After his return to England, Wesley embarked on the third stage of developing small accountability groups. In 1539 he founded a "society" that initially had about sixty members, but that grew weekly and spawned new "little societies" in diverse quarters of London. More of these formed through the evangelistic preaching of Wesley, his brother, and two others, who traveled to Bristol, Bath, Wales, and other parts of Britain, calling people to repentance and urging them to form societies, or accountability groups. For the most part they preached in the open air, either because the churches denied them access over concerns of unsettling their influential members or of incurring a mob or because the churches were too small to hold the crowds. Initially small groups among the so-called Methodists were divided into societies, then classes, and eventually bands, all for the purpose of the mutual care of souls and patterned after the groups conceived by Bucer and Spener. A society constituted the overarching organizational unit, largely based on geographical proximity, whose members committed to a personal "rule" of piety and perfection. The society was divided into classes of twelve members each, men and women, under a class leader, whose role it was initially to collect financial contributions. Bands were formed along lines of gender and marital status and served as the "confessional unit," whose members assisted one another in the process of sanctification, serving as a support and accountability system in bearing one another's burdens and instructing and exhorting one another in service and piety. The bands provided a safe environment for confidential, mutual confession; the members, beginning with the lay leader, were expected to confess their faults and temptations and be receptive to criticism and counsel. They met to obey God's command to "confess your sins to one another, and pray for one another, so that you may be healed" (Jas 5:16), and they were to ask one another probing questions on a weekly basis, such as: "What known sins have you committed since our last meeting?" "What temptations have you met with? How were you delivered?" and "What have you thought, said or done of which you doubt whether it be sin or not?" In 1742 Wesley initiated weekly class meetings, where participants gave an account of their spiritual progress, discussed particular needs or problems, and received prayer support from one another. Advice or reproof was offered,

30. Ibid., 305.

quarrels were put to rest, misunderstandings cleared. In these meetings the class leader was the primary giver of pastoral care and moral discipline. Both bands and classes, with their distinct focus on confession and discipline respectively, served one overall aim: They were "to promote, as far as I am able, vital, practical religion; and by the grace of God to beget, preserve, and increase the life of God in the souls" of Christians through leaders who were qualified "to comfort, exhort, and instruct those who were athirst for God."[31] The Methodist movement was aimed at the common laborers, the working class, those untrained in and "ignorant of the things of God." Wesley reports what he saw a year after he had preached and organized the circles of piety in Kingswood: "Kingswood does not now, as a year ago, resound with cursing and blasphemy. It is no more filled with drunkenness and uncleanness, and the idle diversions that naturally lead thereto. It is no longer full of wars and fightings, of clamor and bitterness, of wrath and envyings. Peace and love are there."[32] And of the evangelistic and organizing work done in Yorkshire he reports: "Many of the greatest profligates in all the country were now changed. Their blasphemies were turned to praise. Many of the most abandoned drunkards were now sober; many Sabbath-breakers remembered the Sabbath to keep it holy. The whole town wore a new face."[33] While Wesley affirmed the Book of Common Prayer of the Church of England, which recommended private confession to a spiritual guide for the "disburdening of the conscience," the bulk of the confessional and disciplinary work took place in the small gatherings of band and class.

Wesley also encouraged a personal piety in the privacy of one's own home. For him the private journal was an indispensable tool for self-reflection, the examination of one's temptations and sins, and a contemplation of Christ and his supreme sacrifice on the cross. He himself made a habit of meticulously recording his daily dealings and exchanges with others, his reflections, prayers, acts of piety, and failures in serving God. The four volumes of Wesley's journals spanning more than twenty years offer glimpses of the journal's role as a mute confessor-friend. The spiritually significant year of 1738 Wesley begins with a description of the sins of which he feels convicted and to which he confesses: "I am convinced" of unbelief, pride, disregard for God, and "levity and luxuriancy

---

31. John Wesley, "Letter to Samuel Walker," 3 September 1756, *The Works of John Wesley*, vol. XIII, 197.
32. John Wesley, "A Short History of the People Called Methodists," *The Works of John Wesley*, vol. XIII, 309.
33. Ibid., 310.

of spirit, recurring whenever the pressure is taken off; and appearing by my speaking words not tending to edify" and "by my manner of speaking of my enemies."[34] Numerous journal entries follow through the years concerning these shortcomings, and observations and reflections on specific occurrences of the day in which he might have failed God. The journal was a tool to him for self-examination and scrutiny of the conscience. Wesley had begun such scrutiny of his conscience during his Oxford days, when he had also compiled and published a collection of prayers for each day of the week, along with several lists of questions one should be asking oneself before evening devotions and going to bed.

34. John Wesley, "Extracts from John Wesley's Journal, 8th January to 24th May 1738," in *John and Charles Wesley: Selected Writings and Hymns,* ed. and introduced by Frank Whaling (New York: Paulist Press, 1981), 99.

CHAPTER TEN

Discipline and Corporate Confession in the Reformed Tradition

Bucer, Zwingli, Calvin

The rediscovery of the early church's practice of public penance played a key role during the Reformation and would become a distinct practice in the Reformed tradition and later Puritan thought. Initially opposition had arisen against the practice among the church's flock and civic authorities. In Strasbourg, Martin Bucer had tried to preclude church members from partaking of communion until they had repented of conspicuous sinful activity and made public confession before the assembly, but he failed. Concurrently, John Calvin in Geneva had to flee the city for attempting to enforce the practice. And two hundred years later, in Georgia, John Wesley was jailed for withholding communion from a presumably errant sinner, precipitating his premature return to England. To properly appreciate this new development it is necessary to consider two factors: first, the longstanding connection of communion with penance in the early medieval church and during the period of the church fathers; and second, the groundbreaking theological reforms formulated and instituted by the second-generation Protestant theologian and pastor John Calvin in Strasbourg and Geneva.

One will recall the connection between confession and receiving communion in the order of penitents that had emerged in the third and fourth centuries. Following confession to the bishop of such sins as murder, adultery, and heresy, penitents enrolled in the penitential order and in stages, often lasting years and decades, advanced from attending worship outside the church or in the narthex to being seated within the assembly and nearer the altar, until they were finally permitted to partake of communion again. Being readmitted to communion meant being readmitted to the community of the faithful, but not without a lengthy period of penance. While private confession eventually replaced public penitential practice, the connection between penance and receiving communion remained. This is still evident in the penitentials and church decrees of the Carolingian era, roughly between 800 and 1000, suggesting that a thorough preparation for receiving the sacrament was expected. For example, a Bavarian council of around 800 decreed that Christians were to prepare themselves for receiving communion by confession and penance as well as sexual abstinence. Christians also were encouraged to receive communion every third or fourth Sunday of the month and not, as many apparently did, only once a year. According to Rob Meens, "The requirement that Christians receive communion three times a year seems to have been a minimum in Carolingian times," implying that Christians in general went to Mass at Easter, Pentecost, and Christmas, usually preceded by making private confession to a priest, but greater frequency was thought to be better.[1] The more often one went to communion, the more often one would make confession—and benefit from the healing effects of penance. It was an ingenuous way of linking a private ritual with a public declaration: while sins were revealed and penances assigned under the confidentiality of the priestly seal, the very fact that one had come to receive communion was a public declaration to all present that one had confessed shortly before. By the thirteenth century the church had accepted seven sacraments, based on the wide use of Peter Lombard's *Sentences* as a theological sourcebook. Of the accepted seven sacraments, five were generally administered only once in a lifetime, namely, baptism, confirmation, marriage, last rites, holy orders; but the two repeatable sacraments, confession and communion, were now linked without diminishing the private and the public character of each.

Among the reformers of the Reformed tradition, the Strasbourg theologian and pastor Martin Bucer formulates this connection most poignantly in his last work, "On the Kingdom of Christ." Written in 1550 in England for the successor of Henry VIII, Edward VI, the book offers Bucer's mature summary of his doctrinal and practical understanding of the Reformation, which he had developed in Strasbourg. Before we explore his treatment of confession, some background is in order. A good part of Bucer's inspiration came from the church reforms initiated by Ulrich Zwingli (1484–1531) in Zürich and carried on by Zwingli's suc-

---

1. Rob Meens, "The Frequency and Nature of Early Medieval Penance," in *Handling Sin: Confession in the Middle Ages*, ed. Peter Biller and A. J. Minnis, 35–61 (Rochester, NY: York Medieval Press, 1998), at 38.

cessor Heinrich Bullinger (1504–1575). Ordained to the priesthood in 1506, Zwingli had served parishes in Glarus and Einsiedeln as vicar and preacher before being invited to serve the principal church in Zurich in 1518. Through his study of the church fathers, his preaching on the words and miracles of Jesus, and the influence of Luther, Zwingli came to see a contrast between the Gospel and the rules of the Roman Church. When his bishop refused a review and reform of church practice, Zwingli turned to the town council. In 1523 the council called a meeting of citizens and clerics to consider Zwingli's sixty-seven theses, which proclaimed the Gospel as the only source of truth and denied the validity of any religious practice not specified in the New Testament. When the council voted in Zwingli's favor, the church reform began; over the next two years the Latin Mass was replaced by a German Eucharist in Lutheran fashion, churches were cleared of images and organs, pilgrimages were discontinued, and monasteries were secularized. Zwingli wanted to sweep away any potential obstacles to and distractions from the word read and proclaimed during worship.

For Zwingli, freeing the Gospel from external shackles and customs leading to misinterpretation and misuse of the sacraments meant placing increased responsibility on the pastor and the office of preaching and teaching. To this end he urged pastors to preach repentance from the Scriptures and to provide subsequent instruction to prevent those previously "healed" from falling into sin again. His *Commentary on True and False Religion*, published in 1525, may well be the first systematic treatment of the newly emerging Protestant theology, including a discussion of confession and penance. Here Zwingli regards private confession as a means of evangelizing unbelievers who have "not yet come to a right knowledge of grace through Christ," all those who do not yet know "the physician." To them Zwingli recommends seeking the aid of a minister, "who, like the good Samaritan, pours wine and oil into the wounds [Luke 10:34]."[2] The wine represents repentance and knowing one's own hypocrisy, "a bitter and sharp thing that you are thoroughly bad within to the very core." Then, with the wound burning, the minister pours upon it oil, which is Christ, so that those who have had this encounter "can no longer be kept from hastening" to Christ thereafter on their own accord. Auricular confession is for Zwingli "nothing but a consultation in which we receive, from him whom God has appointed to the end that we may seek the law from his lips, advice as to how we can secure peace

---

2. Ulrich Zwingli, *Commentary on True and False Religion*, ed. Samuel Macauley Jackson and Clarence Nevin Heller (Philadelphia: Heidelberg Press, 1929), 253.

of mind."[3] No amount of absolving by a priest can bring the relief and peace that comes from the certainty of knowing the physician, Christ. During private confession the minister is to act as an evangelist. "Secret confession, therefore, is a consultation," says Zwingli, "the Keys are the expounding of the gospel, and all else is mere windy gabble of the Papalists." In general Christians should confess to the Lord often and seek to "begin a new life frequently, and if there is anything not clear let us go frequently to a wise scholar who looks not at the pocket-book but at the conscience."[4]

Zwingli also wrote two treatises on the sacraments, prompted in large part by the rise of the Anabaptist movement in Zürich and other areas of Switzerland, in which he advocates infant baptism and argues against a literal interpretation of the eucharistic elements. For Zwingli the function of the two sacraments, baptism and the Lord's Supper, is not "to make us holy" and "take away our sins"; rather, it is to serve as a covenantal pledge of our faith and as a testimony. By participating in the sacraments believers inform the whole church that they are, or aim to be, Christ's soldiers. For the person "who receives the mark of baptism is the one who is resolved to hear what God says to him, to learn the divine precepts and to live his life in accordance with them. And the man who in the remembrance or Supper gives thanks to God in the congregation testifies to the fact that from the very heart he rejoices in the death of Christ and thanks him for it."[5]

Zwingli enlisted the aid of the state for the exercise of disciplinary measures, since it was in the state's interest to maintain the Christian religion. In his 1525 treatise "Advice on Excluding Adulterers and Usurers from the Lord's Supper," Zwingli argues for the state's cooperation in excluding sinners from communion or from the church. Bullinger continued strengthening relations between the church and the state in this regard. In line with Zwingli he insisted that confession and repentance begin with the faithful hearing and proclamation of the word of God. In "The Second Helvetic Confession" of 1566, Bullinger sums up the theological and practical approaches to confession in the Reformed churches: It is sufficient to make private confession to God alone or publicly during the general confession of sins in worship; private confession to a minister or other Christian is acceptable when sins and temptations are too heavy

---

3. Ibid., 254.

4. Ibid., 256.

5. Ulrich Zwingli, "Of Baptism," in *Zwingli and Bullinger*, trans. G. W. Bromiley (Philadelphia: Westminster Press, 1953), 131.

to bear. In addition to confessing our sins to God, we are also asked "to be reconciled to our neighbor if we have offended him." Repentance is brought about through preaching and is the work of the Spirit. It is "the recovery of a right mind in sinful man awakened by the Word of the Gospel and the Holy Spirit."[6] This means that Christians will need to expose themselves to the proclamation of the Word with great regularity and ministers need to preach the Gospel faithfully.

Bucer built on Zwingli's revived connection between the Eucharist and confession. Before pastors could administer the sacraments of baptism and the Eucharist, he says, they ought to "have evidence of true repentance for sins and a solid faith in Christ the Lord" among members of their flock. Otherwise they would "administer to men's judgment and condemnation what the Lord instituted for their salvation." Reading from Scripture is to precede the offering of the sacraments, and "then the people should be exhorted earnestly to a worthy reception" of them, for careful preparation for receiving the sacraments existed in the canons and laws "even from the time before Charlemagne and his sons."[7] Ministers should exercise discipline among those bearing little or no evidence that Christ is at work in them by not admitting them to the sacraments. Let penitents first attend worship services, Bucer suggests, where they hear the word of God proclaimed and are quickened to repentance and prayer, and then let them possibly seek out "mutual help from the Church and the individual brethren."[8] For these measures, says Bucer, "are heavenly remedies against sins, to bind those who have fallen into more serious sins to the doing of penance, and to loose from that bond those who have shown repentance by its worthy fruits." It is a "crime" and an "impiety against both God and his people" when ministers fail to administer the remedy of discipline commended and commanded by Christ.[9] In fact, entire churches are brought low when ministers make no effort at using "this remedy of salvation with utmost gravity and severity when it is needed."[10] The discipline of penance in connection with the Eucharist is as much for the benefit of the individual as for the community, and "those who do not labor with utmost zeal for its total

---

6. Heinrich Bullinger, "The Second Helvetic Confession," XIV in *The Book of Confessions* (Louisville: Office of the General Assembly, 1999), 76.

7. Martin Bucer, "On the Kingdom of Christ," in *Melanchthon and Bucer*, ed. Wilhelm Pauck, Book One, 174–265 (Philadelphia: Westminster Press, 1969), at 237.

8. Ibid., 243.

9. Ibid., 245.

10. Ibid., 246.

restoration according to the precepts of Christ . . . cannot say in truth that they seek the Kingdom of Christ."[11]

It remained for John Calvin (1509–1564) to lend a theological framework to the discipline of penance in the Reformed churches both in the liturgy and in catechetical instruction. Calvin's upbringing and academic training in both Roman Catholic doctrine and humanistic studies made him an ideal candidate for negotiating a mediating theological course between the Swiss reformers in Zürich (Zwingli) and Basel (Oecolampadius), and the Wittenberg reformers led by Luther and Melanchthon. Trained from the age of twelve to perform ecclesiastical duties in the cathedral of Noyon under a benefice that would finance his future university education, Calvin had entered minor orders and received a tonsure in keeping with Roman Catholic practices. At the age of fourteen he arrived in Paris to study Latin syntax and grammar and soon advanced to the College of Montaigu, where Erasmus had studied a few years earlier and where Ignatius of Loyola would arrive the same year Calvin left. By all accounts Calvin was an excellent student, moving in the circles of French humanism, refining his knowledge of theological argument and subtleties while most likely sharing Erasmus's distaste for the aims of scholastic theology and denouncing them as "mere sophistry" and "preposterous riddles" that were of little use to anyone, least of all God. In 1528 Calvin exchanged his study of theology for that of law, moving from Paris to Orléans at his father's invitation. As it turned out, the study of law involved learning Greek and reading the ancient texts as well as becoming familiar with the affairs of civic life—two useful ingredients for his later reform work. The death of his father in 1531 freed Calvin to pursue his love of classical literature and allowed him to move back to Paris and publish his first book, Seneca's treatise *On Clemency*, replete with textual commentary and gloss.

When and by what means Calvin moved from humanist to Christian humanist and church reformer, from Roman Catholic to Protestant, is unclear, due in large part to his introversion and reticence to speak about himself. It is clear that Calvin was greatly influenced by the writings of Martin Luther, which had been translated into French by the early 1520s. Calvin later addressed Luther as his "most respected father" in the faith. Calvin's first writing as a Protestant and reformer was the preface to a French New Testament, published in 1535, titled "To all Lovers of Jesus Christ and the Gospel." Also, two years prior to the French New Testa-

11. Ibid., 247.

ment publication, Calvin had been implicated in a religious controversy at the University of Paris: his friend and the rector of the university, Nicholas Cop, had delivered a convocation speech on All Saints Day in 1533, seemingly slighting and dishonoring the saints by proclaiming Christ as the sole mediator between God and human beings. Cop was forced to flee for his life, finding refuge in his home town, Basel, where Calvin, whose papers were seized in the wake of the incident, would join him shortly.

The years of Calvin's semi-exile in Basel, "hidden" and "known only to a few people," were spent in the study of biblical and patristic sources and the writing of a catechism, patterned in outline after Luther's *Small Catechism* and *Large Catechism*. Calvin's catechism, which rolled off the press in March of 1536 in the form of a little booklet, would become the pivotal text of Protestant theology in the sixteenth century. It is known as *Institutes of the Christian Religion*, but the book's full original title was "The Basic Teaching of the Christian Religion comprising almost the whole sum of godliness and whatever it is necessary to know on the doctrine of salvation. A newly published work very well worthy reading by all who are studious of godliness. A Preface to the most Christian King of France, offering to him this book as a confession of faith by the author, Jean Calvin of Noyon." Calvin saw the book's purpose as two-fold: to teach those "hungering and thirsting for Christ"[12] and to exonerate French evangelical Christians of the charges of sedition and schism—in short, to show "how God's glory may be kept safe on earth, how God's truth may retain its place of honor, how Christ's Kingdom may be kept in good repair among us."[13] The success of the *Institutes* made Calvin famous almost overnight as a proponent of the Reformation because in it he had, according to Timothy George, "presented more clearly and more masterfully than anyone before him the essential tenets of Protestant theology."[14]

In the summer of 1536 Calvin traveled from Paris to Strasbourg in hopes of pursuing a leisurely life of scholarship and study. Instead, forced to make a southern detour and being waylaid in Geneva, Calvin was visited there by Guillaume Farel, the leader of the city's Reformation movement, who implored him to stay. Only months earlier the citizens

---

12. John Calvin, "Prefatory Address to King Francis I of France," in *Calvin: Institutes of the Christian Religion*, 2 vols., ed. John T. McNeill, trans. Ford Lewis Battles, vol. 1 (Philadelphia: Westminster Press, 1960), 9.

13. Ibid., 11.

14. Timothy George, *Theology of the Reformers* (Nashville: Broadman Press, 1988), 179.

had voted to join the Protestant movement and to ban the Mass, so that much work lay ahead. When Farel realized that his pleas and arguments were lost on Calvin, he uttered an imprecation. In his preface to the commentary on the Psalms, Calvin recalls the fateful incident and the divine terror it ignited. Farel was saying "that God would curse my retirement, and the tranquility of the studies which I sought, if I should withdraw and refuse to give assistance, when the necessity was so urgent."[15] Calvin stayed in the city, becoming first a lecturer on the Bible and then a pastor at the church of St. Pierre. Subsequently a confession of faith, a catechism, and a church order were prepared in an effort to reform the people's lives and faith. However, conflict soon arose. Geneva was under the auspices of Bern, with its Zwinglian church order in regard to discipline and liturgy, to which Calvin, Farel, and their colleague Elie Coraud objected. In their view the church should be autonomous in its life, government, and worship practices rather than bowing to civic authorities. They insisted all citizens must affirm the catechism and confession of faith they had prepared. The city council refused to adopt their creed and in January 1538 denied them the power to excommunicate, a power they saw as critical to their work. Calvin and Farel responded with a blanket denial of the Lord's Supper to all Genevans at Easter services. For this the council expelled them from the city. Farel travelled to Neuchâtel, Calvin to Strasbourg in hopes of eventually settling in Basel to study and write, but he would not reach Basel since another "detention" awaited him similar to the one staged by Farel two years earlier. This time it was the local reformer Martin Bucer who urged Calvin to remain in Strasbourg and become pastor to the city's large French-speaking refugee community.

Calvin spent only three years in Strasbourg, from 1538 to 1541, before being called back to Geneva to serve there until his death in 1564, but the Strasbourg years were among the happiest and perhaps most formative of his life. He learned from and supported Bucer's work in the city and continued his own, publishing an expanded edition of the *Institutes* in 1539 (nearly three times larger than the first) and in 1540 a commentary on Romans, the first of many volumes of biblical exegesis. In his role as pastor Calvin gave considerable thought to the content and theology of worship, publishing a Sunday liturgy around 1540 (though no extant copy exists) and translating and setting to melody a number of psalms, the Apostles' Creed, the Decalogue, and the Song of Simeon. In his fore-

---

15. John Calvin, "Preface to the Commentary on Psalms," in *John Calvin: Writings on Pastoral Piety*, ed. and trans. Elsie Anne McKee (New York: Paulist Press, 2001), 61.

word to the Psalter, Calvin stresses the importance of holy liturgy and the role of music: "We know from experience that song has great force and vigor to arouse and inflame people's hearts to invoke and praise God with a more vehement and ardent zeal,"[16] functioning "like spurs" to prayer and praise and helping us "to meditate on His works in order to love, fear, honor and glorify" God.[17]

The *Institutes'* popularity had catapulted Calvin into the role of premier theologian of the Reformation age, but the theological treatise tended to overshadow his pastoral passion. Dedicated to the cure of souls in the context of worship, preaching, and catechesis, Calvin enlisted theology as a helpmate for tending to the sick in soul and body, prisoners, and the dying. Numerous prayers and letters attest to his immense efforts at pastoral care, in person or by letter, to those in distress. The primary expression of pastoral leadership lay, however, in his estimate, in the faithful proclamation of the word of God, the right administering of the sacraments, and the ordering of worship for the renewal and regenerating of God's people in their weekly gatherings of praise, prayer, and self-giving. To Calvin, corporate worship functioned as the supreme means of spiritual formation or, as he called it, "the recreating" of believers.

Not surprisingly, it is in corporate worship and the liturgy that Calvin gives the doctrine and practice of confession a prominent place. Confession is to be made any time Christians meet for worship, and preferably early in the liturgy. "In every sacred assembly we stand before the sight of God and the angels," Calvin says, and "what other beginning of our action will there be than the recognition of our own unworthiness?"[18] The implication is that in "well-regulated churches" on "every Lord's Day the minister frames the formula of confession in his own and the people's name, and by it accuses all of wickedness and implores pardon from the Lord." Such communal confession early in worship is "a key" that opens "a gate to prayer" both individually and communally.[19]

In his Strasbourg liturgy of 1539 and in that of Geneva of 1542 Calvin uses a corporate form of the confession of sins borrowed from Bucer. Corporate confession of sins is included in the service of the Lord's Day, both with the Lord's Supper and without: An opening psalm is sung, followed by the invocation and the confession of sin, given by the minister from the pulpit while the people may be kneeling from the opening

---

16. John Calvin, "Foreword to the Psalter," in *John Calvin: Writings on Pastoral Piety*, 94.
17. Ibid., 96.
18. Calvin, *Institutes* 3.4.11, in McNeill, ed., *Calvin: Institutes*, 635.
19. Ibid., 636.

Scripture sentence until after the confession of sin; another psalm follows, along with an intercessory prayer, given by the minister on behalf of the faithful for forgiveness, illumination, and the sealing of the Word read and proclaimed; after the reading and exposition of the Scripture in the form of the sermon and an intercessory prayer, the people sing a closing psalm and are dismissed by the minister with the benediction.

Calvin's service for the Lord's Day with the Lord's Supper provides worshipers with an added opportunity for repentance and self-examination. The 1562 edition of the Genevan worship order includes a confession of faith, such as the saying of the Apostles' Creed, the reciting of the Decalogue, and a sermon with exhortation prior to the administering of the Lord's Supper. Two features stand out in this service: First, the eucharistic liturgy begins with the reading of the entire passage of 1 Corinthians 11:23-29, including the portion warning members against partaking of the bread and cup in an unworthy manner or without thorough examination of self, lest they bring condemnation upon themselves; second, the Corinthians passage is followed by a sermon, in addition to the main one, on the apostle Paul's words about unworthy behavior and lack of self-examination, calling those guilty of such behavior "strangers" who cannot be admitted to the table. This sermon is to have the following admonition:

> Therefore, following that precept, in the name and by the authority of our Lord Jesus Christ I excommunicate all idolaters, blasphemers, and despisers of God, all heretics and those who create private sects in order to break the unity of the church, all perjurers, all who rebel against father or mother or superior, all who promote sedition or mutiny, brutal and disorderly persons, adulterers, drunkards, gluttons, and all those who lead a scandalous life. I warn them to abstain from this holy table, lest they defile and contaminate the holy food that our Lord Jesus Christ gives to none except those who belong to His household of faith.[20]

Calvin's phrasing of the exhortatory communion sermon reflects the penitential practice connected with the Lord's table in the Reformed churches of Switzerland and southern Germany. Its contents could have come from Bucer, whom Thomas Cranmer had invited to England to help with the *Book of Common Prayer* of the Church of England, first published in 1549 and in revised form and with Bucer's input in his *Censura*, in 1552. An English exhortatory version had been composed by Cranmer in 1549 for the *Book of Common Prayer* and reads:

20. *John Calvin: Writings on Pastoral Piety*, 131–32.

Therefore, if any of you be a blasphemer of God, a hinderer or slanderer of his word, an adulterer, or be in malice or envy or any grievous crime, bewail your sins, and come not to this holy Table, lest after the taking of that holy Sacrament, the Devil enter into you, as he entered into Judas, and fill you full of iniquities, and bring you to destruction, both of body and souls. Judge therefore your souls [brethren] that you be not judged of the Lord. Repent you truly of your sins past, have a lively and steadfast faith in Christ our Savior.[21]

This wording was adopted by John Knox (1513–1572) in his 1556 *Genevan Service Book* when working with Calvin in Geneva and was popularized by him in Scotland, where the practice came to be known as the fencing of the table. Those guilty of the offenses enumerated during the exhortatory sermon were to show repentance of their sins by making amends, seeking out the minister for confession and counsel, and offering evidence that they had reformed. Only then could they be admitted to the table without bringing "destruction" upon themselves.

Christians in Geneva who wanted to partake of the Lord's Supper were also enjoined to examine their consciences during the liturgy: "Let each one examine and prove his conscience to see whether he truly repents of his faults and grieves over them, desiring to live henceforth a holy life according to God." Such self-examination involved asking whether one had faith in God's mercy and was seeking salvation in Jesus Christ alone, in addition to "renouncing all hatred and rancor" and summoning a "high resolve and courage to live in peace" and neighborly love with others. After examination of their conscience and silent confession to God, believers were reminded of the beneficial role of the sacrament. It is "a medicine for poor sick souls" and one can be assured that "the sins and imperfections that remain in us" following repentance will not prevent Christ from admitting us to the table. The only requisite and worthiness required at this point is "to know ourselves sufficiently to deplore our sins and find all our pleasure, joy, and satisfaction in Him alone," since by coming to the Lord's table we are not testifying to our perfection, but rather are saying that "by seeking our life in Jesus Christ we confess that we are in death."[22]

In Calvin's Geneva, preparation for the sacrament of the Lord's Supper meant that worshipers reconciled with their neighbors and made

---

21. William D. Maxwell, *John Knox's Genevan Service Book 1556: The Liturgical Portions of the Genevan Service Book Used by John Knox While a Minister of the English Congregation of Marian Exiles at Geneva 1556–59* (London: Oliver and Boyd, 1931), 122–23; 130 n. 3.

22. Ibid, 133.

confession to the minister beforehand. Since the sacrament was celebrated at given intervals four times a year on set days, announced well
in advance, parishioners had weeks and even months to prepare themselves for the occasion. Calvin himself would have preferred weekly
communion, in keeping with the custom of the German church in Strasbourg and to provide for more frequent opportunities of repentance, but
he was overruled by the Genevan city council, so that he had to compromise and settle for celebrating first monthly, then only quarterly.
Preparation through private confession was to take on two forms: seeking reconciliation with a neighbor one had offended and disclosing one's
weaknesses to another, preferably the pastor, to gain solace, assurance
of forgiveness, and counsel. Calvin recommends that parishioners seek
out the pastor rather than another church member, "because the Lord
has appointed them by the very calling of the ministry to instruct us by
word of mouth to overcome and correct our sins, and also to give us
consolation through assurance of pardon [Matt 16:19; 18:18; John 20:23].
For while the duty of mutual admonition and rebuke is entrusted to all
Christians, it is especially enjoined upon ministers," since ministers are
the prime "witnesses and sponsors"[23] of the forgiveness of sins. Therefore
Christians should make ample use of this benefit and present "themselves to their shepherd as often as they wish to partake of the Sacred
Supper," and "I ardently wish this to be observed everywhere."[24]

Calvin also linked confession, or penance, with baptism, the other
so-called dominical sacrament, instituted by Christ. If Luther had said
in his ninety-five theses that our whole life was penance, then Calvin
added that this penance consisted in the lifelong practice of remembering
our baptism and understanding its meaning. In this Calvin relied on
Melanchthon's *Loci Communes Theologici*, published initially in 1521 and
revised and expanded to nearly four times its size in 1543–1544 and
again, in its final version, in 1559, one year before Melanchthon's death.
The *Loci* had resulted from Melanchthon's lectures at Wittenberg on
Paul's letter to the Romans, and they followed the letter's topical outline.
In revising the *Institutes*, Calvin had adopted Melanchthon's systematic
outline and the order of *loci*, or topics, as well as Melanchthon's view of
baptism as "the sacrament of repentance" and a sign of our "mortification and vivification."[25] Central to Calvin's view of baptism is the notion
of original sin permeating human nature: "As we are vitiated and cor-

23. Calvin, *Institutes* 3.4.12, in McNeill, ed., *Calvin: Institutes*, 636.
24. Calvin, *Institutes* 3.4.13, in ibid., 638.
25. Philip Melanchthon, *Loci Communes Theologici*, in *Melanchthon and Bucer*, 140.

rupted in all parts of our nature, we are held rightly condemned on account of such corruption alone and convicted before God, to whom nothing is acceptable but righteousness, innocence, and purity." Even infants bear this condemnation as a "seed" enclosed in them from their mother's womb.[26] Now, however, the believer had received in baptism "a token and proof of our cleansing," like a "sealed document to confirm to us that all our sins are so abolished, remitted, and effaced that they can never come to his sight, be recalled, or charged against us. For he wills that all who believe be baptized for the remission of sins (Mark 16:16)."[27] For Calvin the efficacy of baptism rested not with the act itself or the minister, but with the hearing of the Gospel message accompanying the act and received in faith by those whom God had called and elected to hear. Regardless of our age at the time of baptism, "we are once for all washed and purged for our whole life." This means that in times of doubt and troubles, "as often as we fall away, we ought to recall the memory of our baptism and fortify our mind with it, that we may always be sure and confident of the forgiveness of sins." This forgiveness of sins can never be destroyed or diminished by postbaptismal sins, says Calvin, because "Christ's purity has been offered us in it," and his purity "is defiled by no spots, but buries and cleanses away all our defilements."[28] We also recognize in this symbol of cleansing the "cloud" and the "coolness" that God gave the Israelites during their hapless wanderings in the wilderness, for "in baptism we are covered and protected by Christ's blood, that God's severity, which is truly an unbearable flame, should not assail us."[29] It is due to lack of faith, an immoderate attachment to "outward things," and a discontent with the "pure instruction of God" that the church later added the sacrament of penance: "As if baptism itself were not the sacrament of penance!"[30]

For Calvin, baptism has a dual function in regard to confession and penance and offers a "double grace." First, it provides us with the assurance that the condemnation due to us on account of our original sin has been removed, for by the sign of baptism we are assured "that full and complete remission has been made, both of the guilt that should have been imputed to us, and of the punishment that we ought to have undergone because of the guilt." While sin continues to exist "in this

---

26. Calvin, *Institutes* 4.15.10, in McNeill, ed., *Calvin: Institutes*, 1311.
27. Calvin, *Institutes* 4.15.1, in ibid., 1304.
28. Calvin, *Institutes* 4.15.3, in ibid., 1305–6.
29. Calvin, *Institutes* 4.15.9, in ibid., 1310.
30. Calvin, *Institutes* 4.15.4, in ibid., 1306.

prison of our body" as a "perversity" that ever bears new fruits through-out our life, sin cannot overcome, dominate, and rule us.[31] Second, bap-tism makes us partakers in the death and the cross of Christ, "that we may be engrafted in it" and "die to our desires" by Christ's example,[32] since in baptism believers are initiated into self-denial and bearing the cross. By remembering our baptism we again place the cross on our shoulders in the sure hope of being raised to new life in Christ by the power of the Holy Spirit. Such mortification and dying to self provides us with help to "fight against the devil, sin, and the lusts of our flesh, until we have the victory over them, to live in the freedom of His king-dom, which is the kingdom of righteousness."[33]

In Calvin's Geneva instruction on the sacraments was part catechesis and part liturgy. Worship was designed to allow for educational mo-ments, while catechetical instruction resembled a worship service. No one could call God a father without having the church as a mother, Calvin said, borrowing from Cyprian and adding that the church was not only mother but also school. As a school, the church instructed in ways that went beyond cognition: it molded the character of its members, reshaped their misguided affections, disciplined their wayward wills, and taught them to offer their gifts to God and neighbor in trust, obedience, and love. Thus worship of God as father and instruction within the womb of the church as mother were intertwined.

The weekly catechetical instruction in Geneva's parishes occurred at noon on Sundays in the context of a worship service. Instruction was based on Calvin's 1542–1545 catechism, containing fifty-five questions on faith, the Apostles' Creed, the Decalogue, the Lord's Prayer, and the sacraments. The main purpose of the service was to prepare children and others for the quarterly celebration of the Lord's Supper. On the Sundays preceding the celebration of the supper candidates were pub-licly examined on their faith. Baptisms took place on Sunday mornings or on Wednesday mornings during the morning service, which was ac-corded special status by both religious and civic laws, or during the catechetical service on Sundays at noon. The baptismal liturgy was placed at the end of the service, preceded by the reading and proclama-tion of Scripture. Private baptisms were discouraged. Baptism was a sign to the entire community of God's grace received, an exhortation to a life of self-mortification, and an opportunity for members to profess their

---

31. Calvin, *Institutes* 4.15.11, in ibid., 1311–12.
32. Calvin, *Institutes* 4.15.5, in ibid., 1307.
33. *John Calvin: Writings on Pastoral Piety*, 154.

faith to one another. By witnessing a baptism Christians not only could recall their own baptism and its pledge and promise, but be reminded by the physical outward sign of the spiritual reality underlying it. "We ought to deem it certain and proved," says Calvin, that God "speaks to us through the sign; that it is he who purifies and washes away sins, and wipes out the remembrance of them; that it is he who makes us sharers in his death, who deprives Satan of his rule, who weakens the power of our lust; indeed, that it is he who comes into a unity with us so that, having put on Christ, we may be acknowledged God's children."[34] Believers needed to be reminded of these functions of baptism. The reinterpretation of baptism as a sacrament of penance required ongoing instruction. Parents promised to give their children instruction on the Christian faith and the sacraments, including baptism, and adult believers were instructed by the pastors in sermons and through the baptismal liturgy on the baptismal call to a life of self-mortification and dying with Christ in the certain hope of being raised, transformed, and gradually regenerated throughout their Christian walk unto new life in him.

Initially the role of confessor, spiritual director of troubled souls, and enforcer of right belief and behavior in the Reformed churches fell to the pastor. In Strasbourg, and later in Geneva, Calvin personally examined all wishing to partake of the Lord's Supper. "To approach the holy Table without due consideration would be a blasphemous defilement of it," he said.[35] Calvin had observed that people thought they were saved by doing good; others were confused and so careless that they hardly knew whether they had a conscience, despising the preaching, living scandalously, blaspheming, being drunk in public, and not caring whether they had offended God, yet still eagerly coming to the Lord's table. In a letter to Farel he writes, "I have often declared to you that it did not appear to me to be expedient that confession should be abolished in the churches, unless that which I have lately taught be substituted in the place of it."[36] What Calvin set in its place was an examination with candidates for the

---

34. Calvin, *Institutes* 4.15.14, in McNeill, ed., *Calvin: Institutes*, 1314.

35. "A Sermon on I Corinthians 11:26ff," in *Ioannis Calvini Opera quae supersunt omnia*, ed. William Baum and others, Corpus Reformatorum 28 (Brunswick: C.A. Schwetschke and Sons, 1893); quoted by R. N. Caswell, "Calvin's View of Ecclesiastical Discipline," in *John Calvin*, ed. G. E. Duffield, 210–26 (Grand Rapids: Eerdmans, 1966), at 217. See also "1 Corinthians 11:23-29," in *Calvin's Commentaries*, vol. 9, eds. David W. Torrance and Thomas F. Torrance, trans. John W. Fraser, 242–54 (Grand Rapids: Eerdmans, 1960).

36. John Calvin, *Letters of John Calvin*, 4 vols., ed. Jules Bonnet, vol. 1 (Philadelphia: Presbyterian Board of Publication, 1858), 160; quoted by Caswell in Duffield, *John Calvin*, 218.

Lord's Supper to determine "whether we have a true repentance in ourselves and a true faith in our Lord Jesus Christ." It soon became clear that he needed help. In his 1537 *Ordonnances Ecclesiastiques*, Calvin requested from the city council the election and ordination of "certain persons of good life and witness from the faithful, persevering and not easily corrupted, who should be dispersed and distributed in all the quarters of the city, having oversight of the life and government of each of them; and if they see any vice worthy of note to find fault with in any person, that they communicate about it with some of the ministers, to admonish whoever it is that is at fault, and to exhort him in brotherly fashion to amendment."[37]

Upon his return to Geneva, Calvin had refined his model of church governance. In devising offices for the oversight and discipline of the church and its members Calvin had borrowed from Bucer's list of church offices, naming those of pastor, teacher, elder, and deacon. The newly recovered offices based on scriptural precedent contrasted with the Roman Church's offices of bishop, priest, and deacon, with the holders of those offices employed by the church. In the Reformed system only the pastor was employed, whereas teachers, elders, and deacons served as volunteers. It was through these four offices that the ministry of the priesthood of all believers was largely carried out. While all Christians were by virtue of their baptism of equal rank in doing the ministry of the church and entitled to teach, preach, exhort, and console one another, church officers were set apart for distinct functions within the body. Pastors devoted their time to preaching and prayer, presiding at the sacraments, and governing the church. Deacons were to oversee the church's charitable activities, and teachers were charged with the education of the young and their Christian formation; they were also those who, as doctors, held an office of theological scholarship and teaching for the training of other ministers. The responsibility of disciplinary oversight of the faith community, however, fell to the elders, who would be assigned to supervise the lives of those in a parish, visiting and examining them in their homes as to conduct and faith; once a year they would be accompanied by the pastor on these visits.

Geneva's ruling body of twelve elders was called the consistory and met every Thursday morning with the ministers to summon offenders before them. Matters ranged from trivial offenses such as making unwanted noise during worship to the more serious cases of domestic vio-

---

37. John Calvin, *Theological Treatises*, trans. J. K. S. Reid (Philadelphia: Westminster Press, 1954), 52; quoted by Caswell in Duffield, *John Calvin*, 221.

lence, fornication, and adultery. On several occasions Calvin left these meetings in disgust as rebellious citizens reviled him as the "newcomer" who wanted to rule their city or whose preaching they disdained. While the consistory had no authority to punish serious offenders, who were referred to the secular courts, it did instruct, admonish, persuade, and console the lesser offenders, seeking to settle disputes and thereby restore peace and unity in the larger community. Those who refused to submit to the consistory's discipline or who would not reform were excommunicated. But this was a last step. The goal of church discipline for Calvin was to bring about a profession of repentance for the renewal of fellowship. Unless severity was tempered by gentleness, the remedy acted as poison. "This gentleness is required in the whole body of the church," says Calvin, "that it should deal mildly with the lapsed and should not punish with extreme rigor, but rather, according to Paul's injunction, confirm its love toward them [2 Cor 2:8]." It was not the role of the church officers "to erase from the number of the elect those who have been expelled from the church, or to despair as if they were already lost." Otherwise we "claim for ourselves more license in judgment" than is appropriate and limit and confine God's law. After all, God can change the worst into the best, engraft the alien, and adopt the stranger, frustrating human opinion and restraining rash judgment. Unless "gentleness is maintained in both private and public censures, there is danger lest we soon slide down from discipline to butchery."[38]

Discipline extended also to the ministers in the Genevan churches. As the so-called company of pastors, they met weekly to stimulate one another in teaching and scriptural interpretation and quarterly to examine their behavior and correct and exhort one another on doctrine and conduct. Digressions from sound doctrine and irregularities in conduct could be referred to the elders or even the magistrates. Intrigues for better-paid posts, absences from the parish without valid reason, and favoritism were addressed, along with such moral lapses as lying, lewd behavior, and drunkenness. The ministers also oversaw and corrected one another's professional demeanor toward their flock. Strange methods of interpreting the Scriptures, negligence in study, scolding of the congregation, dress unfit for the office of pastor could be addressed in these meetings for the sake of guarding and enhancing the health of the congregation and the purity of the Gospel proclaimed.

---

38. Calvin, *Institutes* 4.12.9, in McNeill, ed., *Calvin: Institutes*, 1237–38.

CHAPTER ELEVEN

The Church of England

Reformed and Calvinist thought gained entrance and acceptance also in the Church of England, along with some of the practices of confession. While the offices of bishop, priest, and deacon were retained, Reformed doctrines and practices were applied to the sacraments and the liturgy. The ecclesiastical and liturgical reform efforts were spearheaded by Thomas Cranmer (1489–1556), archbishop of Canterbury. Sent to study at Cambridge at the age of fourteen, Cranmer became a fellow of Jesus College in 1515 and remained there teaching theology and biblical studies until 1529. In that year he came to the attention of King Henry VIII when advocating, on theological grounds, the invalidity of the king's marriage to Catherine of Aragon. Henry wished to divorce Catherine so as to marry Anne Boleyn, and he used Cranmer to that end. In 1531 Cranmer was appointed by the king as royal chaplain, a year later as archdeacon of Taunton, and the year thereafter as archbishop of Canterbury. When sent to Germany as the king's ambassador to Emperor Charles V, Cranmer came under the influence of Lutheran theology and secretly married the niece of the Lutheran theologian Andreas Osiander (1498–1552). Osiander had been a priest in Nuremberg when he came out in favor of Luther in 1522 and helped turn the city of Nuremberg to the Reformation; he also attended the disputation between Luther and Erasmus at Marburg in 1529 and the Diet of Augsburg in 1530, and was one of the signers of the Smalcald Articles, drafted by Melanchthon, in 1537. Cranmer tried to conceal his wife's ties to the famous Lutheran reformer as best he could.

Cranmer's loyalty to Henry proved invaluable in effecting the English church's split with Rome. He furthered the publication of the English Bible, granted the required decree of divorce and annulment for Henry's marriage to Catherine of Aragon, and advocated a Protestant united front by which England would join continental Europe in defeating extremist theological beliefs, even if he himself subscribed to them. With the accession of Edward VI in 1547, Cranmer began work on liturgical reform by compiling the *Book of Common Prayer* in 1549 and its revised version in 1552 reflecting Calvin's thought and Genevan worship practices.

Cranmer's reform efforts remained within the current of other English reformers. Both Hugh Latimer, bishop of Worcester, for example, and William Tyndale, Bible translator and publisher, had sought inspiration during the 1520s and 1530s from the Bible and the church fathers, and had aimed their efforts at a cure of souls. Three documents from that period address the subject of penance. In the 1536 *Articles about Religion* the ongoing requirement of penance and absolution for Christians is retained, citing that penance contains the elements of contrition, confession, and amendment of one's life. In the *Institution of a Christian Man* of 1537 confession is considered expedient but not always necessary, while the fruits of repentance, including fasting, almsgiving, restitution, and works of mercy, are required. And in *A Necessary Doctrine and Erudition for Any Christian Man* of 1543 penance is considered "an inward sorrow and grief of heart" for one's sins, with a detesting of them and a desire to recover the favor of God. During private confession sinners are to prostrate themselves before God, confess those sins dictated by the conscience as grievous, and submit to the discipline imposed by the priest in congruence with the word of God. Thus confession of grievous sins, rather than all, the authority of Scripture in regard to acts of repentance, and the definition of repentance as an inward sorrow giving expression to outward deeds are the emerging themes in early Anglican theology and practice.

On January 21, 1549, the first Act of Uniformity was passed, decreeing for all churches in England the use of *The Book of the Common Prayer and Administration of the Sacraments and other Rites and Ceremonies of the Church after the Use of the Church of England*, with the liturgy in English rather than in Latin. In Lutheran fashion the book rejected the doctrines of the real presence in the Eucharist and the sacrifice of the Mass, invocation of the Virgin and saints, prayers for the dead, the seven sacraments, and a sacrificing priesthood, and it resembled in outline Luther's Mass of 1523 and 1526. However, the call and exhortation to repentance prior to partaking of communion was thoroughly Reformed.

The opening rubric for the communion service in the 1549 version of the *Book of Common Prayer* suggests that those intending to partake of Holy Communion present their name to the priest prior to the celebration. "Notorious evil livers" who have offended the congregation or their neighbor by word or deed are to be excluded from the sacrament until they have shown repentance, amended their "former naughty life," and made restitution to the satisfaction of the people. The curate is to order those he knows to be at odds with each other to demonstrate mutual forgiveness, and if one party remains obstinate while the other repents, the repentant one is to be admitted.[1] After the opening collect, creed, Scripture readings, and sermon, the priest exhorts worshipers to receive the sacrament in a worthy manner, for otherwise "we provoke [God] to plague us with divers diseases, and sundry kinds of death. Therefore, if any here be a blasphemer, adulterer, or be in malice, or envy, or in any other grievous crime, (except he be truly sorry therefore, and earnestly minded to leave the same vices, and do trust himself to be reconciled to Almighty God, and in charity with all the world), let him bewail his sins, and not come to that holy table, lest after the taking of that most blessed bread, the devil enter into him, as he did into Judas, to fill him full of all iniquity, and bring him to destruction, both of body and soul. Judge therefore yourselves, (brethren), that ye be not judged of the Lord."[2] In cathedral churches or places where communion was served daily, a monthly exhortation was sufficient.

A second exhortation is included in the worship order for churches where attendance on communion Sundays is characteristically low, hence self-examination and repentance infrequent. Here the priest is to announce the next communion date and to admonish congregants with the following words: "Dear friends, and you especially on whose souls I have cure and charge, on [date of next communion service] next I do intend, by God's grace, to offer all such as shall be godly disposed the most comfortable sacrament of the Body and Blood of Christ, to be taken of them in remembrance of his most fruitful and glorious passion: by which passion we have obtained remission of our sins, and be made partakers of the kingdom of heaven; whereof we be assured and ascertained, if we come to the said sacrament with hearty repentance for our offences, steadfast faith in God's mercy, and earnest mind to obey God's will, and to offend no more." This sacrament is "so divine and holy a thing, and so comfortable to them which receive it worthily, and so dangerous to them that will presume to take the same unworthily." Therefore "my duty is to exhort you, in the mean season, to consider the

---

1. The communion service of the editions of the English *Book of Common Prayer* for 1549, 1552, 1559, 1604, and 1662, in modern English spelling, is available at www .commonprayer.org/pb/pb_archv.cfm.

2. Ibid.

greatness of the thing, and to search and examine your own consciences, and that not lightly, nor after the manner of dissimulers with God, but as they which should come to a most godly and heavenly banquet; not to come but in the marriage garment required of God in the Scripture; that you may (so much as lieth in you) be found worthy to come to such a table."[3]

Preparation for the next time communion would be served included sorrow over sins and tears, reconciliation with one's neighbor, and forgiveness of others as God has forgiven us. In case such turning was not possible, worshipers with troubled consciences were to seek out the pastor or "some other discreet and learned priest, taught in the law of God" and "secretly" confess in order to receive "ghostly counsel, advice, and comfort, that his conscience may be relieved, and that of us (as the ministers of God and of the Church) he may receive comfort and absolution, to the satisfaction of his mind, and avoiding of all scruple and doubtfulness."[4] Those satisfied with the general confession in worship were not to be offended by those making use of private confession to a priest, nor were those who came to private confession to be hesitant in divulging their sins. Rather, each was to follow the dictates of conscience without judging the conscience of the other.

In 1551 Martin Bucer published a critique of the first *Book of Common Prayer* at Cranmer's invitation, in which he detailed where it obscured biblical teaching. Based on Bucer's suggestions, Cranmer produced a second Prayer Book in 1552 in which the Protestant principles were more clearly adopted. During the reign of Mary Tudor from 1553–1559 the Prayer Book was prohibited, Protestants were martyred (Cranmer among them), and Roman Catholic doctrines and practices were reintroduced. In 1559 Elizabeth I restored the second book with minor alterations, so that it was in use until 1604. In 1662, after the restoration of the monarchy, the Act of Uniformity introduced another (fifth) *Book of Common Prayer*. In its theological principles and practices this edition was basically that of 1552, making it the central guide for the church's liturgical practices for more than four hundred years.

The changes of the 1552 Prayer Book compared to the earlier edition reflect an emphasis on the authority of Scripture and an avoidance of terminology reminiscent of the Roman Church. Also added to Morning and Evening Prayer are introductory sentences from the Scriptures related to sin and confession, an exhortation, a general confession, and an

3. Ibid.
4. Ibid.

absolution or remission of sins as the opening portions of the worship service. To the communion service are added the Decalogue, a new prayer of consecration, and the rubric instructing the people to kneel during communion, which was in no way to imply adoration of the host but sought to enhance penitence and reverence.

As in the Reformed churches on the continent, Christians were to prepare themselves for communion properly. Preparation involved examining one's life "and conversation by the rule of God's commandments": where one perceived to have offended "either by will, word, or deed, there bewail your own sinful lives, confess yourselves to Almighty God, with full purpose of amendment of life." One was to reconcile with a neighbor, make restitution for injuries and wrongs done to another, and extend forgiveness toward the offending party: "For otherwise the receiving of holy Communion doth nothing else but increase your damnation." In case a Christian was unable to quiet his or her own conscience and needed additional comfort or counsel, she or he was to seek out the priest "or some other discreet and learned Minister of God's word, and open his grief, that he may receive such ghostly counsel, advice, and comfort, as his conscience may be relieved; and that by the ministry of God's word he may receive comfort, and the benefit of absolution, to the quieting of his conscience, and avoiding of all scruple and doubtfulness."[5] While scriptural terminology such as "the rule of God's commandments," "minister of God's word," and "the ministry of God's word" make for a more Protestant flavor, the basic practices remain the same. Private confession is retained, but no longer required of all, and is commended to those in need of "ghostly counsel, advice, and comfort," and worshipers continue to be exhorted to examine their conscience, reconcile with and forgive their neighbor, and make restitution prior to partaking of communion. The emphasis on spiritual counsel from the minister for relieving the conscience is emphasized. The canons of 1604 make provisions for keeping the seal of confidentiality, "where we do not in any way bind the said minister by this our Constitution, but do straitly charge and admonish him, that he do not at any time reveal and make known to any person whatsoever any crime or offense so committed to his trust and secrecy" unless the minister's own life were to be put in jeopardy.

In summary, private confession as a rite rather than a sacrament was retained in the Protestant churches in the ensuing decades of the Reformation. However, it was no longer a requisite for receiving communion

5. From the 1552 edition of the *Book of Common Prayer* at www.commonprayer.org/pb/pb_archv.cfm.

nor was it necessary to make a complete confession by enumerating all sins. Christians could make confession to God directly or seek out the minister, or another Christian, for additional consolation and counsel. The latter was reserved for those unable to find relief of their troubled consciences before God and amending their lives on their own. Lutheran churches retained private confession as a rite, while Reformed churches linked confession and penance with the sacraments of baptism and communion and embedded the practice in the worship of the church. People were called on to repent of their sins in the context of Reformed worship during the opening portion with a general confession and prior to the communion service with the exhortation. A regular exhortation in worship services without communion called on worshipers to examine their life, reconcile with their neighbors, and make restitution before the next time communion was served. The catechism was critical in both Lutheran and Reformed traditions in educating children and adults on the basic tenets of the Christian faith, the sacraments, and the ongoing need for repentance. Enforcing discipline among members of Reformed churches entailed visitation by the minister and ordained officers of the church, exhortation, and the exclusion of those from communion or the church whose behavior was conspicuously offensive and showed no fruits of repentance and reform.

The Anglican church drew on both Lutheran and Reformed practices and doctrines. It retained the Lutheran practice of private confession, though with a greater emphasis on spiritual counsel given by the minister at the time. Based on the Reformed tradition, it retained sermons of exhortation on communion Sundays, excluding notorious evildoers from the table, and announcements of the next date of communion to prompt worshipers to amend their ways, forgive their neighbors, and make restitution. All three traditions, Lutheran, Reformed, and Anglican, used chapter 11 of the apostle Paul's first letter to the Corinthians prior to communion, interpreting it as a warning to avoid "damnation" when partaking of communion in an unworthy manner and encouraging the practice of examining one's heart for hidden sins, wrong motives, falsehood, and lingering anger and grudges. Both the sacraments and the proclamation of the Word in worship were to lead Christians to repentance so they could receive forgiveness from God and be restored to new life in Christ. In characterizing the Anglican practice of confession in contrast to Roman discipline, the sixteenth-century Anglican theologian Richard Hooker (1553–1600) describes it in a way that would have found approval also by Lutheran and Reformed churches of the time: "We labor to instruct men in such sort, that every soul which is wounded with sin may learn the way how to cure itself; they [Roman Catholics], clean contrary, would make all sores seem incurable, unless the priest have a hand in them."[6]

6. Richard Hooker, *Treatise on the Laws of Ecclesiastical Polity* VI, vi, 4; quoted in John T. McNeill, *A History of the Cure of Souls* (New York: Harper & Brothers, 1951), 226. Books VI–VIII did not appear in print until 1648, leading some scholars to debate their authenticity; while they reflect Hooker's style and doctrinal stance, it is possible that death prevented him from revising the last three books of a total of eight comprising the *Laws of Ecclesiastical Polity*.

CHAPTER TWELVE

Confession and Spiritual Direction in the Roman Catholic Church after Trent

In 1545 the Council of Trent was convened by Pope Paul III (1534–1549) as a form of crisis management in response to the Protestant Reformation. According to David C. Steinmetz it was generally agreed by the time of Luther "that under certain circumstances the convocation of a general council might be the church's only recourse to resolve a crisis that had proved impossible to resolve in any other way."[1] Some elements of the crisis, such as laxity on clerical celibacy and the appointment of incompetent or underage candidates to ecclesiastical offices, were old; others were new, and included the place of and relationship between the authority of Scripture and church tradition, the proper understanding of the justification of the sinner, the nature and structure of the church and its ministry, and the theology of the sacraments, especially the sacraments of the Eucharist and penance. For the most part the attempt was to purge the system of abuses without altering it in principle. In the bull *Laetare Hierusalem*, Pope Paul III had fixed the opening date of the council for March 15, 1545, and had stated the task: to settle theological disputes, to reform ecclesiastical abuses, and to begin a counterattack against dissenters and infidels.

The course of the council's history from its opening session on December 13, 1545, to its closing session December 4, 1563, was fraught with interruptions, quarrels, and tensions between the church's interests and

---

1. David C. Steinmetz, "The Council of Trent," in *The Cambridge Companion to Reformation Theology*, ed. David Bagchi and David C. Steinmetz, 233–47 (Cambridge: Cambridge University Press, 2004), at 233.

the national interests of European rulers. Roughly the council's work occurred in three stages: between 1545 and 1547 the topics of Scripture and tradition, original sin, justification, and the sacraments in general were addressed; between 1551 and 1552 the topics were the Eucharist and the sacraments of penance and extreme unction; between 1561 and 1563 the council fathers considered the Mass and the sacraments of holy orders and marriage, along with decrees on purgatory and indulgences, and the veneration of saints, relics, and sacred images.

In its fourteenth session in 1551 the council presented a repudiation of the Protestant criticism of penance and clarified penance's traditional place as a sacrament for the baptized. Penance was instituted by Christ in his postresurrection appearance according to John 20:23. The church fathers commended it "with a great and unanimous consent." And the precept of confession during Lent, commended at the Lateran Council, "should be complied with, at least once a year, by all and each, when they have attained to years of discretion."[2] Christians who had fallen after their baptism needed penance for salvation. The sacrament's traditional three parts (contrition, confession, and satisfaction) were maintained. Contrition was defined as a free and voluntary "sorrow of mind and a detestation for sin committed, with the purpose of not sinning for the future," constituting both the "beginning of a new life" and "a hatred of the old."[3] Imperfect contrition was called attrition and resulted from a consideration of the baseness of one's sin and the fear of hell or punishment; it disposed the sinner to receive the grace of God in the sacrament of penance. During the act of confession penitents were to enumerate "all the mortal sins" of which they had become aware after due self-examination.

The council also distinguished between mortal and venial sins. As a gauge of what to confess, penitents should be using the Ten Commandments with due consideration of the "two last precepts of the decalogue," involving covetousness and lust, because these "hidden" sins "sometimes wound the soul more grievously, and are more dangerous, than those which are committed outwardly." Venial sins, on the other hand, need not be confessed and could be "omitted without guilt" since they could be "expiated by many other remedies."[4] After penitents had examined their hearts with diligence and "searched all the folds and recesses"[5] of the conscience, they were to give a full account of their

---

2. *Dogmatic Canons and Decrees* (New York: Devin-Adair, 1912), 99–100.
3. Ibid., 92–93.
4. Ibid., 96.
5. Ibid., 98.

mortal sins, describing the circumstances surrounding the sin if need be. In turn, the priest functioned as both judge and physician. But if "the sick be ashamed to show his wound to the physician, his medical art cures not that which it knows not of," neither can the confessor "estimate rightly the grievousness of the crimes, and impose on the penitents the punishment which ought to be inflicted on account of them."[6]

Satisfaction is defined as "works of penitence" assigned by the confessor following absolution. These works' function is threefold: they act as a "bridle" to "make penitents more cautious and watchful for the future," as "remedies for the remains of sins" and "acts of the opposite virtues" capable of removing "the habits acquired by evil living," and as "a most sure pledge" that by suffering for our sins in penitence "we are made conformable to Jesus Christ" and "shall also be glorified with Him."[7] The council insists that works of satisfaction are not the result of one's own strength or a form of works of righteousness; rather, they are a cooperating with Christ, who strengthens us in carrying them out. Their efficacy is due to Christ, who offers them to God the Father who, in turn, accepts them from Christ. The acts of penance assigned by the priest are to be "salutary and suitable," matching "the quality of the crimes and the ability of the penitent," and are aimed at serving for "the preservation of a new life and a medicine of infirmity," along with "the avenging and punishing of past sins." In making these assignments the priest is to be guided by "the Spirit and prudence." Acts of satisfaction occur in three forms: they are those "voluntarily undertaken," those assigned by the priest "according to the measure of delinquency," and "the temporal scourges inflicted of God" on us and "borne patiently" throughout life.[8]

The council rejected the idea that the power of absolution might reside with anyone other than a priest, bishop, or the pontiff. It was erroneous to assume "that every one has the power of forgiving sins," such as when one is rebuked by another and acquiesces, or when secret sins are being confessed to another. While absolution is "the dispensation of another's bounty," namely, Christ's, personal faith alone apart from the penitential process does not provide absolution, neither is the moral disposition of the priest crucial for the sacrament to have effect.[9] In matters of grave sin, potentially leading to excommunication, bishops rather than priests are to exercise discipline as long as its intent is the sinner's edification

---

6. Ibid., 97.
7. Ibid., 106.
8. Ibid., 109.
9. Ibid., 101–2.

rather than destruction. However, to prevent any from being lost, the priest is not to withhold absolution from those who are dying. In cases without imminent danger of death, priests are "to persuade penitents to repair to superior and lawful judges for the benefit of absolution."[10]

Concerning indulgences, the council maintained their benefit and the church's authority to grant them, while forbidding their abuse for financial gain. Moderation was to be observed in granting them, and "abuses which have crept therein, and by occasion of which this honorable name of indulgences is blasphemed by heretics" are to be amended and "all evil gains for the obtaining thereof" are to be "wholly abolished." Bishops are to collect and report all abuses, such as "superstition, ignorance, irreverence" in their use, to the next provincial council for review by the Roman pontiff, so that the "gift of holy indulgences may be dispensed to all the faithful" in a holy and uncorrupted manner.[11]

On the whole, the council maintained the traditional elements of private confession in the Western church while assuming responsibility for the repentance and healthful state of believers' souls by insisting on the sacrament's healing effects. Several prominent aspects of the council's decisions would govern church life and practice for the next five hundred years: auricular confession is to precede absolution; mortal sins only are to be confessed, though the council remained vague on which sins to recount and what circumstances to report; repentance was only complete if made visible in the believer through acts of satisfaction and a changed life; and sole ecclesiastical authority in absolution was affirmed. A liturgical service order and a formula for the rite of private confession took several decades to ratify. At its final session in 1563 the council entrusted to the pope the task of liturgical reform and a reformed *Breviarium Romanum* was published in 1568 and a *Missale Romanum* in 1570; other books followed, such as the *Pontificale Romanum* in 1596 and the *Caeremoniale Episcoporum* in 1600. But it was not until 1614 that the *Rituale Romanum* containing the rite of penance was promulgated. Drafted initially by Cardinal Julius Santorio, who died in 1602, the work was completed by a commission appointed by Pope Paul V in 1612. While the use of the new manual was recommended, not mandated, local dioceses and Roman Catholic priests generally complied with it by 1650, making it the basis for the rite of penance for the next four centuries in the Western church and, with minor alterations, to this day.

10. Ibid., 104.
11. Ibid., 173–74.

The *Rituale Romanum*, or Roman Ritual, affirms penance as a sacrament instituted by Christ for those who have sinned after baptism. The essential elements of the sacrament are listed as contrition, confession, satisfaction by the penitent, and the absolution by the minister, who is to be a priest. In administering the sacrament, the priest acts as both judge and physician, and therefore needs spiritual, canonical, and doctrinal knowledge. Once the prerequisites are named, the order of the sacrament follows. The priest is to prepare himself prayerfully beforehand, asking for God's help in this ministry. He is to situate the hearing of confession in the church in an open place, namely, in a confessional with a screen between himself and the penitent, and he is to be vested with surplice and purple stole. After the penitent has approached the confessional with due humility, by kneeling and making the sign of the cross, the priest inquires about the penitent's status, the last time confession was made, the performance of the penance assigned, and whether examination of conscience has taken place. Should the penitent be under censure or guilty of a reserved sin the priest is to refer the penitent to the next higher authority, such as a bishop. If the penitent lacks basic religious knowledge the priest is to offer the necessary instruction at this time.

Once the preliminaries are settled, the penitent begins with a general confession and then makes a complete confession of the mortal sins committed. In the course of this recounting of sins the priest helps the penitent as needed, and if necessary asks clarifying questions concerning the sins' frequency and surrounding circumstances. Caution is advised in this questioning process so as not to suggest further ways of sinning to the penitent. After confession is made, the priest considers the sins and the condition of the penitent, offers counsel, and supports the penitent's contrition and resolve to make amends. He imposes a penance that will assist in the person's renewal, offers a remedy for weakness and a punishment for the sins committed, such as almsgiving, fasting, and more frequent confession and communion.

The manual explicitly forbids confessors to ask for or to accept money for themselves on account of their services. Prescribing open and public penance for secret sins is disallowed. Situations are noted for postponing or refusing absolution; these are waived if the penitent is near death. If physically unable to make confession, the penitent is to be given absolution on account of the intention to do so. Special discretion is advised when imposing penances on the sick.

Following the instruction for imposing penance is the form of absolution by the priest. The priest says: "May almighty God have mercy on you, forgive you your sins, and bring you to everlasting life." Then he raises his hand and extends it to the penitent, despite the screen preventing visibility, and makes the sign of the cross while naming the Trinity, saying: "May the almighty and merciful Lord grant you pardon, absolution, and remission of your sins. May our Lord Jesus Christ absolve you: and I by his authority absolve you from every bond of excommunication and interdict, insofar as I can and you need it. And finally I absolve you from your sins, in the name of the Father, and of the Son, and of the Holy Spirit. Amen." A final prayer by the priest on behalf of the penitent is the *passio*, which could be omitted with penitents who confessed frequently: "May the passion of our Lord Jesus Christ, the merits of the blessed Virgin Mary and all the saints, whatever good you do and evil you endure, be to you for the remission of sins, the increase of grace, and the reward of everlasting life. Amen."[12]

Implementing uniformity of penitential practices in the Roman church as decreed by the Council of Trent involved two additional teaching aids, one cognitive and the other visual: a manual, or catechism, for parish priests and the construction of a wooden confessional inside the church. The catechism was promulgated in 1566 by Pope Pius V under the title *Catechism of the Council of Trent for Parish Priests*. Its treatment of the sacrament of penance is more detailed and lengthy than the decrees of the council itself, emphasizing the authority of the priest in absolution as bearer of "the keys," urging frequent and comprehensive confession of all mortal sins in person (rather than by letter or messenger), and insisting on confessional secrecy by both the penitent and the priest. Acts of satisfaction, or penances, are listed as consisting largely of prayer, fasting, and almsgiving, while the validity of other acts, such as pilgrimages or indulgences, is implied. It was believed that regulating the use of the sacraments through educating the local parish priest would cause the lay population as a whole to be educated in keeping social discipline. Thus the use of confession aided in "the preservation of social order"; it "restrains licentiousness, bridles desire and checks wickedness," while its loss meant "you deluge society with all sorts of secret and heinous crimes—crimes too, and others of still greater enormity, which men, once that they have been depraved by vicious habits, will not dread to commit in open day."[13]

---

12. *Rituale Romanum* (1614), quoted in James Dallen, *The Reconciling Community: The Rite of Penance*, vol. 3 of *Studies in the Reformed Rites of the Catholic Church* (Collegeville, MN: Liturgical Press, 1986), 177–78.

13. *Catechism of the Council of Trent for Parish Priests*, trans. with notes by John A. McHugh and Charles J. Callan (New York: Joseph F. Wagner, 1947), 283:

Visually, the dignity of the sacrament of penance and its liturgical nature was already enhanced by the liturgical vestments of the priest. As the *Rituale Romanum* outlined, the priest was to wear a surplice and purple stole during the hearing of confession. But the more decisive visual change involved the setting of confession. Penance was not to take place in a private, secluded setting, but in a public place where both confessor and penitent could be seen. During the decades after Trent several diocesan decrees and articles addressed questions concerning the proper locale for confession, the postures of the priest and penitent, and circumstances surrounding the sacrament. For example, the *Pastorale* of Passau of 1608 and that of Freising of 1612 instructed the confessor to be seated "as a judge," expressing Trent's idea of confession as a tribunal. The Augsburg synod of 1567 referred to the priest as a spiritual judge, and the Trier *Agenda* of 1573 and the Bamberg *Agenda* of 1587 urged confessors to display proper gravity in their demeanor. In addition, the *Manuale* of Salzburg, published in 1582, urged confessors to consider sacraments as "festivals for souls"[14] to be conducted in a dignified manner and a setting befitting the solemn occasion. In his survey of confession in post-Reformation Germany, W. David Myers notes that despite these instructions the sacrament of penance "still occurred as it had during the Middle Ages: publicly, hurriedly, and under—at times—physically difficult conditions,"[15] diminishing the sacrament's dignity, infringing on its private nature, and reducing the quality of the experience for both penitent and priest. In an effort to save time due to crowded conditions, priests regularly admitted penitents in groups, heard confessions while seated within earshot of another priest, or invited scandal or suspicion of heresy by irregular behavior, improper counsel and instruction, or rushed absolution.

The confessional booth was introduced in Italy in the late sixteenth century, but its travel across the Alps and acceptance in the heartland of the Protestant Reformation was slow. Other confessional furniture was already in common use there. The oldest extant German confessional is the *Beichtstuhl* in Murau, a chair with a prie-dieu attached, dating from 1607. This chair ensured the proper posture of both penitent (kneeling) and confessor (seated), yet afforded neither privacy to the penitent nor to the sacrament the decorum fitting a "festival for souls." A similar chair

---

14. For this overview of various diocesan decrees pertaining to the setting of the sacrament see W. David Myers, *Poor, Sinning Folk: Confession and Conscience in Counter-Reformation Germany* (Ithaca: Cornell University Press, 1996), 131–33.

15. Ibid, 133.

had a table inserted between the confessor's seat and the penitent's prie-dieu, presumably for placing there the opened confessor's manual and, provided the penitent was literate, the notes of sins and circumstances to be confessed. Several synods decreed where these chairs were to be placed when in use. A decree from the diocese of Regensburg of 1589 instructs on the *Beichtstuhl*'s proper locale: The confessional table with chair and kneeler was to sit in an open space of the church visible to all, and not, as was customary in Regensburg, "in the sacristy, or behind the altars, or other obscure places and angles." If no other suitable place was found, the sacristy could be used for confession provided its door remained open and "both the confessor and the penitent can easily be seen by others in the church."[16]

The partition between priest and penitent was unknown in German lands and confession took place face-to-face in full view of other penitents. But a growing sense of individualism, producing awkwardness when penitents had to face the priest again at Mass, may have paved the way for the innovation from Italy to gain acceptance by the mid-seventeenth century. Certainly having voices from within Germany demanding anonymity helped. As early as 1591 in a treatise on church decor, titled *KirchenGeschmuck*, Jacob Müller had called for a "box" that was to be "enclosed on all sides, namely, above, below, and on both sides, but open in front." In its center, a partition the same size of the box was to be erected, containing a "four-cornered window" that was "closed shut with iron or beaten tin or even a thin wooden grate full of tiny holes the size of a pea, not shut like a small door, however, but with nails driven in all places so that nothing can pass through."[17] The grate or partition ensured anonymity between penitent and priest, while both were in public purview. The purpose of public exposure was not so much to prevent any unseemly touching or scandalous demeanor, for that was already precluded by the separating screen; instead, it was for the benefit of the other faithful who could now witness that their neighbor had gone to confession, had met the obligation for Easter, and was a practicing and loyal Catholic rather than a disloyal and heretical Protestant. In Catholic territories, making confession in the church symbolized public allegiance to church and state. Those who were suspected of Lutheran

16. See Josef Harzheim and Johannes Schannat, eds., *Concilia Germaniae*, vol. 7 (Cologne: Krakamp, 1759–90), 1065; quoted in Myers, *Poor, Sinning Folk*, 136.

17. Jacob Müller, *KirchenGeschmuck, Das ist: Kurtzer Begriff der fürnembsten Dingen, damit ein jede recht und wol zugerichtete Kirchen geziert und auffgebutzt seyn solle* (Munich: Berg, 1591); quoted in Myers, *Poor, Sinning Folk*, 136.

or Reformed loyalties could avert punitive measures, such as monetary fines or forced expulsion by the civic authorities, through being seen at confession. Only a century or so later did a shift of preference occur in German lands toward complete seclusion and privacy. By the nineteenth and early twentieth centuries privacy and concealment from public view had become central to confession. Older confessional booths were remodeled, providing complete enclosure of the penitent and the priest through the installation of either curtains or wooden doors, and new ones built did enclose both penitent and priest in a wooden box while continuing to separate one from the other by a fixed screen.

In ensuring anonymity and precluding scandalous behavior, the confessional enhanced the sacred and liturgical character of the sacrament of confession. In fact, it was the dignity of the sacrament that the inventor of the wooden confessional booth, Charles Borromeo (1538–1584), seemed to have had foremost in mind. The idea for the invention came while Borromeo was archbishop of Milan and after he had served as secretary of state to Pope Pius IV. Having helped prepare the last session of the Council of Trent (1562–1564), he was dedicated to Trent's reform decrees. Borromeo worked toward renewal among his clergy and religious, lived modestly, and visited his parishes with great frequency to observe their liturgy and vitality. After 1565 he drafted a proposal for a confessional booth that was codified in his *Instructiones*, published posthumously in 1585. By it he sought to devise an environment in which confession could be heard "in a convenient and proper way,"[18] one that would enhance the sacred nature of confession and guarantee the visible prominence of confession in the church building itself. His design not only contributed to the reverence accorded the sacrament in later times but also facilitated the long periods of patient listening involved in hearing confessions. Borromeo's confessional booth was made of wood and raised above the church floor; it was enclosed on both sides, at the back and on the top, while the front was open except in churches with heavy traffic, where a latticed door with lock was attached "to prevent laymen, vagabonds, or dirty people from idly sitting or sleeping therein, to the irreverence of the sacred function which is exercised there."[19] In addition he suggested two confessionals to keep women and men separate, for otherwise, especially in crowded conditions, "one can discern irreverence to the

18. Charles Borromeo, *Instructiones fabricae et supellectilis ecclesiasticae*, trans. Evelyn Voelker, Ph.D. dissertation, Syracuse University (Ann Arbor: University Microfilms, 1977), 297; quoted in Myers, *Poor, Sinning Folk*, 134.

19. *Instructiones fabricae*, 299; quoted in Myers, *Poor, Sinning Folk*, 134.

sacredness of the place and the sacrament as well as offense to the pious."[20] Reverence for the sacrament was also the reason railings were installed, keeping in line penitents who otherwise "would rush up without order to the sacred confessional and locate themselves too closely to the person who is making his confession, to the likely disturbance either of the penitent or of the confessor."[21] When in 1614 the *Rituale Romanum* alluded to Borromeo's confessional as the proper environment for private confession its use became binding throughout the Roman church.

The introduction of the confessional booth and the new catechism, clarifying the roles of priest and penitent, did much to make confession more attractive and accessible. Secrecy and comfort were enhanced, and like the font and the altar, representative of the sacraments of baptism and the Eucharist, the confessional pointed worshipers to the sacrament of confession in a visibly prominent way. Permanently installed in the church's worship space, it was a steady reminder to Christians to make use of the sacrament's healing powers. But more than healing and wholeness was at stake: The council had decreed confession as a stepping-stone for receiving the Eucharist. This sacramental interconnectedness forged a kinship between altar and confessional booth, meaning one knelt first in the one in order to be fed from the other. Essential to understanding one's need for making confession was the function of the Eucharist, which the council's decrees would clarify.

In October 1551 Trent affirmed the seven sacraments of medieval tradition, namely, baptism, confirmation, penance, Eucharist, orders, matrimony, and extreme unction. Of these seven the most prominent was declared to be the Eucharist, for in it Christ was really present, whereas in the other sacraments Christ's power was present. According to the council all the sacraments serve as the "symbol of a sacred thing" and are "a visible form of an invisible grace." But the Eucharist contains "this excellent and peculiar thing": while the other sacraments have "the power of sanctifying when one uses them, the Eucharist, before being used" has "the Author Himself of sanctity," for there "Christ whole and entire is under the species of bread and under any part whatsoever of that species."[22] The effectiveness of the sacrament and Christ's presence in it did not depend on the pious disposition of those who administered it (*ex opere operantis*), but depended solely on the correct performance of the rite and the spoken words of institution (*ex opere operato*). Regardless

---

20. *Instructiones fabricae*, 297–98; quoted in Myers, *Poor, Sinning Folk*, 134–35.
21. *Instructiones fabricae*, 303–4; quoted in Myers, *Poor, Sinning Folk*, 135.
22. *Dogmatic Canons and Decrees*, 72–73.

of the priest's holiness or the piety of the partakers, the elements of bread and wine were invariably transubstantiated by God into the true body and blood of Christ. Only one stipulation existed: that one approach the Eucharist in a worthy manner, as expressed in 1 Corinthians 11. The "necessary proof" for such worthiness was "that no one, conscious to himself of mortal sin, how contrite soever he may seem to himself, ought to approach to the Sacred Eucharist without previous confession." This decree was to be observed by all Christians, including priests, "provided the opportunity of a confessor do not fail them."[23] Moving from the state of sin to that of grace involved priestly absolution, so that Christians, even priests, wishing to partake of the Eucharist had to go to confession first if they were conscious of grave sin.

The relative simplicity of the order of confession facilitated implementing it uniformly in the local Catholic churches and dioceses of the West. But such simplicity also had its drawbacks. In his study of the liturgy of penance in the Roman Catholic Church, James Dallen notes the distinctive marks of the newly drafted liturgy based on the *Rituale Romanum*. The liturgy reflects "the full flowering of both individualism and clericalism," he says. Also, "it is quick, efficient, and almost aliturgical,"[24] lacking scriptural allusions and reminders of God's grace toward sinners. The elements of Scripture references and consolations, recurring elements and themes in the medieval penitentials of the eighth through the tenth centuries in particular, are almost completely missing. The liturgy "simply has the penitent express contrition, make confession, and be willing to make satisfaction, and the priest gives absolution. . . . Almost every element of praise and prayer is absent," reducing the liturgy to the basics of confession and absolution.[25] The confessional liturgy also pales by comparison with those of baptism and the Eucharist; symbolic actions and movements are few and the priest's gesture of absolution and the sign of the cross are concealed from the penitent by the screen. Not surprisingly, the sacrament could easily be seen as a transaction of sorts in which the mechanics of confession and absolution figured as a necessary means to an end, a stepping-stone and ticket for admission to the Eucharist, where Christ's true presence dwelt.

Despite the simplified liturgy, the sacramental status of confession rose after Trent. At the same time, however, the potential for dialogue between penitent and priest and the giving and receiving of spiritual

23. Ibid., 78.
24. Dallen, *Reconciling Community*, 178.
25. Ibid., 178–79.

advice and direction decreased. The trend to reduced dialogue may be attributed to three factors: first, sacraments were perceived as things done by the priest for the people, which meant in the case of confession that the penitent became the passive recipient of priestly absolution. Second, the streamlining of the liturgy of penance increased penitents' level of comfort with the sacrament and made the process more predictable and defined. Third, Catholics had learned more or less to distinguish between mortal and venial sins and understood the process of confessing according to number, species, and circumstances, so that there was, in Dallen's words, "less need for questioning and dialogue,"[26] hence a reduced perception of a need for listening and receiving spiritual counsel. The ideal of confession as a medicine for the soul, preceded by an examination of one's conscience, contrition, a heartfelt sorrow over one's sinful thoughts and deeds, and a turning to Christ in humility received less attention than it once did. With the ecclesiastical mechanics of catechetical instruction and sacerdotal decorum in place, the question of how to ensure inward repentance, self-examination, and contrition among Christians again arose. It would be a new religious order spawned during the turbulent times of the Protestant Reformation that would address this question, seeking to implement Trent's reforms by actively wooing and engaging the laity at home and abroad, its members offering spiritual direction, counsel, and religious instruction. The name of this new order was the Society of Jesus, whose members considered themselves friends and followers of Jesus—Jesuits, for short.

26. Ibid., 179.

CHAPTER THIRTEEN

Ignatius of Loyola and the Jesuits

The Jesuits were essential to the work of Trent during the council and thereafter. An important goal of the order was education and spiritual formation of the laity in the principles of the Catholic faith and its practice. In an effort to strengthen the faithful and win back those who had become Protestant, Jesuits encouraged frequent communion and frequent confession and served concurrently in the roles of priest, confessor, and spiritual director. To assess their role properly it is helpful to name this era of strident and often heavily criticized Catholic reform. Protestants generally refer to it as the "Reformation," signifying by it the work of such Protestant reformers as Luther, Bucer, Calvin, and Zwingli; Catholics are left with more ambiguous descriptors for the era within the Roman Catholic Church, such as "Counter-Reformation," "Catholic Reformation," or "Tridentine Reformation." According to church historian John O'Malley, SJ, each of these descriptors for the centuries after Trent may be "useful" but not "capacious enough"[1] because it forces "an inappropriate or inadequate interpretive framework."[2] O'Malley suggests the use of the term "Early Modern Catholicism," for balance and complementation, to describe roughly the period between the fifteenth and the late eighteenth centuries, since such a name, unlike the others, "suggests both change and continuity without pronouncing on which predominates."[3] It allows consideration of the various social, ecclesiastical, and political elites showing resistance to control; of "the negotiation that seems to have occurred at all levels"; of the fact that "religious identity might have found its genesis more in the traditional practices and the close-knit kinships of

---

1. John W. O'Malley, SJ, *Trent and All That: Renaming Catholicism in the Early Modern Era* (Cambridge, MA: Harvard University Press, 2000), 7.
2. Ibid., 10.
3. Ibid., 141.

local communities than in passive acceptance of hierarchy and of ecclesiastical disciplining"; and it "allows that popular attachment to Catholicism might sometimes be explained by the comfort people found in everyday experience of it and not always by a grudging conformity to a grid imposed from above."[4] O'Malley's considerations of the complexities of the era of Catholic reform before, during, and after Trent paint a picture from a Catholic perspective. They also show that the work of Trent was more than simply a reaction; it entailed initiative, innovation, and a new direction for the church—a direction embodied to a considerable degree by the aims of the Jesuit order.

The Society of Jesus was officially approved in 1540 by Pope Paul III after its founder, Ignatius of Loyola, and nine of his companions had submitted a draft of their constitution the previous year. Subsequent generations often viewed the order as Trent's most decisive force to combat Protestantism, when in fact it followed the ideals of a medieval monastic tradition and had been instituted mainly to do mission work and bring people to Christ. According to church historian Lewis W. Spitz, the idea of Jesuits as the "most characteristic creation of the Catholic Reformation" may have been due to the fact that they were highly effective "in polemics, education, and politics."[5] Another reason the order was viewed as the arm of Trent was its constitution. In addition to the traditional three vows of monasticism—poverty, chastity, and obedience—Jesuits took a fourth vow, that of absolute obedience to the pope. The origin of this vow goes back to 1534 and the city of Paris, where Ignatius and his companions had pledged to go to Jerusalem in an effort to evangelize the Turks but had made provisions for an alternative strategy. When stranded at Venice for a year because no ship would sail to the Near East due to war, they suspended their journey and fell back on the alternative: to go to Rome and put themselves at the service of the pope. The order's Constitutions explain the fourth vow as one made "to the sovereign pontiff as the present or future vicar of Christ our Lord. This is a vow to go anywhere his Holiness will order, whether among the faithful or the infidels, without pleading an excuse and without requesting any expenses for the journey, for the sake of matters pertaining to the worship of God and the welfare of the Christian religion."[6] It was this fourth vow that

4. Ibid., 141–42.

5. Lewis W. Spitz, *The Protestant Reformation 1517–1559* (New York: Harper & Row, 1985), 303.

6. Ignatius of Loyola, "Constitutions of the Society of Jesus I.1.7," in *Ignatius of Loyola: The Spiritual Exercises and Selected Works*, ed. George E. Ganss, SJ (New York: Paulist Press, 1991), 284.

granted the order a unique role in helping to reestablish papal authority following the Protestant Reformation, making its members uniquely available to be sent wherever there was a need for the proclamation of the Gospel and the founding of missions. "The end of this Society," wrote Ignatius in his Constitutions, "is to devote itself with God's grace not only to the salvation and perfection of the members' own souls, but also with that same grace to labor strenuously in giving aid toward the salvation and perfection of the souls of their neighbors."[7]

The religious and political climate of Spain shaped Ignatius's vision for the order. In the sixteenth century Spain had the finest army and navy in the world, controlled much of the Austrian Empire, the Low Countries, and Italy, and was virtually untouched by the Protestant Reformation. The royal palace of the king of Spain, Philip II, erected around 1560, stood as a symbol for Catholicism. It was a fortress-like construction whose baroque architecture aimed at pointing to the triumph of God through the life of the Spirit and to the people's unity born of Catholic religious devotion. In the palace's church the eucharistic liturgy and the Divine Office were celebrated throughout the day, and adoration of the blessed Host was continuous, with a hundred monks constantly employed at the task. The complex included a vast library, for God had to be served also in study and scholarship. In the midst of this splendor the king practiced the ascetic discipline of a monk, living in an austere apartment and demonstrating, in the words of George A. Lane, "greatness of soul together with religious devotion, penance, and renunciation."[8] It is little wonder that such splendor paired with religious devotion inspired the mystical ideal, the individual's interior connectedness with God in union with the spirit, generating an avalanche of mystical and devotional writings. Among them were those by Teresa of Avila, the Carmelite nun and reformer, and John of the Cross, her collaborator. The devotional writings focused on the life of Jesus and his passion, as portrayed in the gospels, and on the interior life leading to union with God. Many of them had been translated from Latin into Spanish. But the purity of such a Catholic faith had its price. The Inquisition was at the height of its power in Spain by the early sixteenth century, crusading against potential heretics among clergy and laity alike, driving declared Protestants into exile, and torturing and killing many. While Spain came to be

---

7. Ignatius, "Constitutions I.1.3," in *Ignatius of Loyola*, 283–84.
8. George A. Lane, SJ, *Christian Spirituality: A Historical Sketch* (Chicago: Loyola University Press, 1984, 2004), 52.

known as "the hammer of heretics" and the "sword of Rome,"[9] Italy seemed less concerned with keeping its people's faith pure. Finally, at the fervent campaigning of Gianpietro Caraffa, a papal nuncio to Madrid who had been impressed by Spain's Catholic discipline, the pope relented. In 1542 Paul III established the Roman Inquisition by appointing the Dominicans, former arbiters of orthodoxy, to serve as inquisitors general. Some Spaniards in Rome at the time applauded the pope's decision, Ignatius of Loyola among them, even though he himself had suffered at the hands of the Spanish Inquisition. In 1527 he had been imprisoned for over a month in Alcalá on charges of heresy and again the same year for three weeks in Salamanca. Upon his release the second time he had to promise the inquisitors to refrain from teaching on the proper distinction between mortal and venial sins until he had completed theological studies. He obediently and willingly complied.

The religious-mystical and political ideals of Spain found expression in Ignatius's spirituality and his writings. Born into a noble family at Loyola, Spain, Ignatius of Loyola (1491–1556) had embarked on the military career customary for a nobleman. When wounded in battle in 1521 and forced into a long period of convalescence, he experienced a religious conversion. His sick time was spent in prayer, note-taking, and reading two devotional classics that had been translated into numerous vernacular languages, including Spanish: *The Life of Christ* by the Carthusian monk Ludolph of Saxony, and the *Legenda Aurea* or "Golden Legend" of the lives of the saints by the Dominican Jacobus de Voragine. A year later at Manresa, Ignatius was introduced to the *Imitation of Christ*, at the time ascribed to Jean Gerson but probably compiled by Ludolph of Saxony also, rather than Thomas à Kempis; Ignatius would later commend the book "to all those with whom he dealt"[10] for its emphasis on a contempt of worldly ways, openness to divine grace, and intimacy with God. Deeply influenced by the *Imitation*, he recommended its reading during the *Exercises*, along with the life of Christ and the lives of the saints. The glowing, fanciful, and heroic tales and miracle stories of such saints as Francis, Dominic, Augustine, and the Virgin suggested to Ignatius a different kind of heroism than his military training had proposed, risking one's life on behalf not of an earthly ruler but a heavenly one. And the reflections on the life and passion of Christ, assembled with

9. Spitz, *Protestant Reformation*, 300.

10. *Fontes Narrativi de S. Ignatio et de Societatis Iesu Initiis*, 4 vols. (Rome: Monumenta Historica Societatis Iesu, 1943–65), vol. 1, 154; quoted in "General Introduction" in *Ignatius of Loyola*, 28.

a high degree of scholarship and exegetical skill, in contrast to those of *Legenda Aurea*, showed the nature and characteristics of this heavenly king during his earthly life in ways compelling enough to demand utter loyalty. The notebook Ignatius produced from his reading contained three hundred pages in which he had marked the words of Christ in red ink and the words of the Virgin in blue. It would become the nucleus of Ignatius's teaching manual for the salvation of souls, begun the following year at a yearlong retreat at Manresa, near Barcelona, and called the *Spiritual Exercises*.

The year after Ignatius's conversion is marked by a close scrutiny and examination of his sins, frequent confession and communion, spiritual listening and discernment, and acts of penance. It would be formative for his later teachings, his vision for the order, and the order's subsequent activities. Information about this period comes to us chiefly from his autobiography, dictated sometime before 1554 to Câmara and considered "a highly reliable historical source" and the "most fundamental testimony about his life."[11] After Ignatius had sufficiently convalesced from the serious injuries to both of his legs he decided to join the Lord's army, exchanging worldly honor for humble service and his soldier's uniform for a coarse beggar's robe. He wanted to make a penitential journey to Jerusalem and on his way there stopped at the Benedictine monastery of Our Lady of Montserrat, a popular pilgrims' site with the shrine of the Black Virgin, to make confession and ritually break with his old life. Upon arrival and in asking for an appointment, Ignatius was handed by the abbot a copy of the *Book of Exercises for the Spiritual Life* to help him better prepare for a general or annual confession in writing. The book, written by Montserrat's former abbot García de Cisneros, may well have been the inspiration for the title Ignatius chose for his own book, as well as for elements of the First Week. It certainly did its work in other ways, too: Ignatius's confession with the abbot lasted three days, the first two of these probably spent in self-examination designed to arouse contrition. The lengthy time of confession suggests an extensive period of dialogue and conversation between Ignatius and his Benedictine confessor. It was a method that had originated with the Benedictines and had been devoutly practiced by the contemplative Cistercian community at Clairvaux in the twelfth century. Kenneth Leech describes this method as "an institution called 'confession' which was not the sacrament of penance as we know it, but the manifestation of conscience to a spiritual guide," a

---

11. "Introduction" to the *Autobiography* in *Ignatius of Loyola*, 67.

"conversation or spiritual colloquy."[12] After the three-day experience of purgation and cleansing, Ignatius proceeded to Barcelona, stopping at Manresa for what he thought would be a brief stay, only to remain there for eleven months. Dressed in sackcloth and barefoot, he lived off alms and daily attended church for devotion, divine worship, Vespers, and Compline, and each Sunday he went to confession and communion. Ignatius would commend such frequent confession and communion to others as well, in stark contrast to the prevalent annual practice, and it would later arouse the inquisitors' suspicions at Alcalá.

At Manresa, Ignatius was plagued by the impression that his previous confession had not been complete. Wrestling with scruples, temptations, and the burden of unconfessed sins, he sought advice from spiritual men he hoped could cure him, but no cure came. Again he wrote down each sin he could remember and revealed these sins to his confessor, but the scruples returned. He prayed that his confessor would advise him to stop rummaging in his past, which he did shortly thereafter. Ignatius tried to abide by the confessor's counsel, but the burdens remained. He prayed daily for seven hours on his knees and rose for midnight vigils, but to no avail. No penitential practice and personal advice seemed to offer a cure for his scruples. "Help me, Lord," he would cry out, "for I find no remedy in men nor in any creature; yet if I thought I could find it, no labor would be hard for me." Even if it involved chasing "after a puppy that it may give me the remedy, I will do it," he said, only "Lord, show me where I may find it."[13] In his distress Ignatius contemplated suicide. He considered throwing himself down a large hole in his room, next to where he was praying. Only the thought that suicide was a mortal sin restrained him, so that he repeatedly exclaimed, "Lord, I will do nothing that offends you." Instead, upon remembering the story of a saint of whom he had read, he conceived of subjecting himself to a severe fast, eating and drinking nothing until "God succored him, or until he saw that death was quite close."[14] Starving himself thus, he continued his other exercises, going to Divine Office, saying prayers on his knees, making weekly confession prior to communion. When his confessor heard of Ignatius's resolution he ordered him to break the fast immediately, which he did and which would relieve his scruples for three days, only to have them return with greater force. "Sin after sin from his past"

---

12. Kenneth Leech, *Soul Friend: The Practice of Christian Spirituality* (San Francisco: Harper & Row, 1977), 54.

13. *Autobiography*, in *Ignatius of Loyola*, 78.

14. Ibid.

sprang to his mind, and he felt compelled to confess them again and again. Then one day he was seized by "disgust for the life he led" and experienced the impulse to give it up. The Lord had "deigned that he awake, as from sleep" and "mercifully deigned to deliver him." It was at this point that Ignatius began paying special attention to the diversity of spirits at work in his soul and mind, seeking to discern between the spirit of God and the spirit of Satan, and examining "the means by which that spirit"[15] of consolation and desolation had come to him. The experience would also curb his habitual impulse to run to "all spiritual persons to converse with them"[16] and to seek their advice, be it hermit or noted confessor, and to rely on discerning the spirits for himself, instead, and making a "good election" as guided by the spirit of God.

Ignatius recorded the *Spiritual Exercises* based on his own experience with sin, scruples, and temptation in hopes of producing a manual that would teach others to examine their consciences, discern the spirits, prepare for confession, and direct souls. According to Ursula King it is "one of the most important documents in the history of Christian spirituality," teaching "the life of the Spirit to others" and asking "the Christian disciple to reflect continuously on the life, death, and resurrection of Christ."[17] Written mostly at Loyola and Manresa, the *Exercises* were repeatedly revised by Ignatius so they would better assist others to attain to life in Christ and to undergo spiritual renewal through a firsthand experience of God. Whenever "he noticed some things in his soul and found them useful, he thought they might also be useful to others, and so he put them in writing."[18] Members of the Society were to use the exercises daily as a devotional guide, annually at a retreat, and regularly as a tool to train those to whom they ministered. From the time of the *Exercises'* rudiments in 1522 and 1523 Ignatius shared them with people or instructed others in their use: his intimate friends, the inquisitors in Spain and Paris, the students and professors at the university, those whose souls he sought to win for Christ, and those who sought him out for counsel.

The purpose of the *Exercises* is to facilitate achieving the end for which we are created. "Human beings are created to praise, reverence, and serve God our Lord, and by means of this to save their souls," Ignatius

---

15. Ibid., 78–79.

16. Ibid., 83.

17. Ursula King, *Christian Mystics: Their Lives and Legacies Through the Ages* (Mahwah, NJ: Paulist Press, 2001), 145.

18. *Autobiography*, in *Ignatius of Loyola*, 110.

says in the opening paragraph. All other things on this earth are created to help us work toward that end, meaning to employ them properly and "rid myself of them to the extent that they hinder me" (23).[19] The goal is to practice a form of detachment, making "myself indifferent to all created things" (23). Ignatius presents the practical steps one needed to take in this endeavor by formulating rules or principles defining how humans choose to think and act. The root cause and motivation for all action lies within, he says, and is governed by one's willingness to comply with spirits, both good and evil. Detecting these spirits at work, identifying their source of origin as either God or Satan, is the main task when seeking to order one's life to the purposes of God.

Designed as a retreat manual for a four-week period, the *Exercises* are divided into four "weeks," or sections, following a liturgical pattern: from preparation for the proper worship of God through self-examination one moves on to a confession of sins, then to an extended period of hearing and immersing oneself in the words of the Gospel and the life and passion of Jesus, and finally to considering the practical ways of allowing these impressions and spiritual insights to transform into love, hence self-giving service in the world. They also resemble the three stages of spiritual growth advanced by Pseudo-Dionysius in the sixth century, moving from the purgative to the illuminative to the unitive. While this pattern broadens the use of the *Exercises* from the retreat model to that of an individual and personalized setting, reading them on one's own is difficult. According to O'Malley they are "one of the world's most famous books" and "one of the least read and least well understood."[20] Three reasons may account for that: First, the *Exercises* were not a theological tract or treatise aimed at the student of the Christian faith but a set of directives and suggestions aimed at the teacher in charge of the care of souls; second, the book's diversity of genre, its mix-and-match grouping of instruction, reflection, prayers, principles, and scriptural meditations does not easily lend itself to a continuous reading; and three, critical points for understanding Ignatius's principles of the soul's movements may lie buried in supplementary sections or appendices.

The four sections of the *Exercises* can be described as follows: The first week is designated as a time of self-examination leading to contrition and involving an examination of the conscience for sins of thought, word, and deed, their contemplation, and a meditation on hell. The second

---

19. Numbers in parentheses in the text refer to paragraphs in the *Spiritual Exercises*.

20. John W. O'Malley, *The First Jesuits* (Cambridge, MA: Harvard University Press, 1993), 37.

week directs one to meditate on the lordship, public life, and teachings of Christ, and contains a number of additional rules, principles, and considerations for discernment: the two standards of Christ and Satan; three classes of persons and how they handle money; three ways of being humble; and ways and conditions for making a "good election" or choosing wisely. During the first two weeks Ignatius recommends that one meditate on the "Rules for the Discernment of Spirits," perhaps one of the most crucial, most widely explored, and best known sections of the book; these rules also address how to give alms properly; how to understand scruples and discern the enemy in them; how to regard our place in and relationship with the church universal, its liturgy, sacraments, feasts and fasts, and the spiritual practices and virtues perfected through the church, who is the Spouse of Christ. The third week invites meditation on Jesus' last days, from Bethany to Jerusalem, and the passion story, and also includes rules on ordering one's relationship with food. The fourth week concludes with meditations on Jesus' post-resurrection appearances and the mysteries of the resurrection and ascension. Other supplements, besides the one on the discernment of spirits, are a guide to the methods of praying and a compilation of scenes from the gospels, the so-called Mysteries of the Life of Christ Our Lord, divided along the stages of Jesus' "hidden" life and infancy, his public life, the passion, and his risen life as manifested by the thirteen apparitions and the ascension.

Of the four weeks, or sections, it is the first that is almost entirely devoted to an examination and scrutiny of the conscience and one's mortal and venial sins. The purpose of such scrutiny is to arouse contrition and sorrow in the soul for making a "better" confession at the end of the first week and to be "worthier and better prepared to receive the Holy Sacrament" (44). While Ignatius does not require confession and communion for those in the habit of going to confession annually (!), he heartily recommends it. Making confession may generate a "greater sorrow experienced at present for all the sins and evil deeds of one's entire life"; it generates "a deeper interior understanding of the reality and malice of one's sins"; it allows for a "worthier and better" preparation for receiving communion, which in turn offers strength to resist sin and preserves "the increase of grace" (44). For Ignatius, recognizing sin in one's past and present is a necessary step to gradually reducing the desire to engage in it. "Each time one falls into the particular sin or fault, one should touch one's hand to one's breast in sorrow for having fallen," Ignatius says. It is a physical way of making silent confession before God that can be done even in public without others noticing it.

Other methods designed to help one recognize hidden sin are preparatory prayer and employing the imagination and the senses. "Imagine
Christ our Lord suspended on the cross before you, and converse with
him in a colloquy: How is it that he, although he is the Creator, has come
to make himself a human being? How is it that he has passed from eternal
life to death here in time, and to die in this way for my sins? In a similar
way, reflect on yourself and ask: What have I done for Christ? What am I
doing for Christ? What ought I to do for Christ?" Then, "gazing on him
in so pitiful a state as he hangs on the cross, speak out whatever comes to
your mind" (53). Ignatius calls this method of speech a "colloquy" because
it resembles "the way one friend speaks to another, or a servant to one in
authority—now begging a favor, now accusing oneself of some misdeed,
now telling one's concerns and asking counsel about them" (54). For assistance in recalling one's sins Ignatius also suggests the Ten Commandments and the seven capital sins. After reviewing the commandments one
by one, "I should accuse myself accordingly and beg grace and help to
amend myself for the future" (243). For understanding better "the faults
springing from the capital sins, one should consider their contrary virtues"
(245). The review of the seven capital sins, as well as the notion of a colloquy between a guide and a seeker, is reminiscent of the desert monks'
methods of teaching a novice and the Celtic penitentials. Ignatius may
have gleaned both elements from the meditations in the *Life of Christ* by
Ludolph of Saxony, a member of the strict Carthusian order, founded in
1084 by Bruno of Cologne and strongly oriented to the desert tradition.
Unlike other Western monastics, the Carthusians lived in solitary cells,
venerated the founder of Eastern monasticism, Antony of Egypt, and
prized highly the writings of Benedict, Jerome, and Cassian.

The second exercise of week one is aimed at generating contrition,
producing a desire "for growing and intense sorrow and tears for my
sins" (55). Here one engages the memory to make a "court-record" of
"all the sins of my life, looking at them year by year or period by period."
Helpful in such a review will be recalling "the locality or house where I
lived," "the association I had with others," and "the occupation I was
pursuing" at the time (56). Such a reflection on one's own humble state
allows the attributes of God to emerge more fully, leading to "an excla-
mation of wonder and surging emotion, uttered as I reflect on all creatures and wonder how they have allowed me to live and have preserved
my life" (60). The fourth and fifth exercises involve colloquies with the
Virgin, the Son, and the Father, requesting "First, that I may feel an interior knowledge of my sins and also an abhorrence of them; Second,
that I may perceive the disorder in my actions, in order to detest them,

amend myself, and put myself in order; Third, that I may have a knowledge of the world, in order to detest it and rid myself of all that is worldly and vain" (63). The fifth exercise is designed to lead to an interior sensing of the pains of hell: To see "with the eyes of the imagination the huge fires," to "hear the wailing, the shrieking, the cries," to smell "the smoke, the sulphur," to "feel how the flames touch the souls and burn them"—not as a way of instilling fear but as an incentive to realize the great love and mercy God has granted us (65).

The first week also explores the principle of discerning spirits. The subtitle Ignatius gives this section describes its purpose: "Rules to aid us toward perceiving and then understanding, at least to some extent, the various motions which are caused in the soul: the good motions that they may be received, and the bad that they may be rejected." The rules address spiritual warfare, attack and counterattack, averting or remedying sins by the application of their opposites, and the diffusing and refuting of temptation and eradicating secret sin by bringing it to light. Again one finds here the teachings of desert wisdom in regard to the tactics of the enemy. "The enemy acts like a false lover, insofar as he tries to remain secret and undetected," wishing to seduce us by "his words and solicitations. . . . But he is displeased" when his words and designs are revealed. In like manner, the evil spirit "turns his wiles and persuasions upon a righteous person," wishing that they be received and kept secret. "But when the righteous person reveals them to his or her confessor or some other spiritual person who understands the enemy's deceits and malice, he is grievously disappointed," for now "his manifest deceptions have been detected" (326). The enemy also acts like a military commander, who attacks a stronghold at its weakest point. And he is weak when faced with strong resistance, but like a tyrant when given the upper hand.

In order to better discern good and evil spirits, Ignatius describes how they manifest themselves in a person's disposition. They either produce spiritual consolation or spiritual desolation. By spiritual consolation he means "some interior motion [that] is caused within the soul through which it comes to be inflamed with love of its Creator and Lord." The result of such a motion is orientation toward the Creator, rather than remaining stuck or focused on a thing created. Often this motion, or emotion, is accompanied by tears, grief over one's sins, and increase in a sense of "hope, faith, and charity," "interior joy," and "tranquility and peace" in the soul (316). By spiritual desolation he means the very opposite, manifested in a sense of "darkness of soul, turmoil within it, an impulse motion toward low and earthly things, or disquiet from various agitations and temptations." The result of such a motion is the absence of faith, hope, and love, and the sense of being "listless, tepid, and unhappy," while feeling separated from God (317). During a period of desolation, says Ignatius, one should not make major decisions or change former plans. The only changes permissible and even necessary are those constituting a "counterattack against the desolation, for example, by insisting more on prayer, meditation, earnest self-examination, and some suitable way of doing penance" (319), coupled with patience and trust that God has already supplied us with grace sufficient for our salvation. In times of consolation, our task is to consider how to "act in future desolation," thus storing up "new strength for that time" through acts of humility and reflection on our lowly state in times of desolation (323–324). The second week elaborates on consolation and desolation as incurred through a "preceding cause," such as "acts of understanding and willing." We may be led to make a decision based on a flash of insight, an occurrence, and think we are choosing the right course of action since it provides consolation. But not all decisions producing consolation are right. There are two types, says Ignatius, one true because generated by the good spirit, the other spurious due to the evil spirit's work. Discernment requires that we "pay close attention to the whole train of our thoughts. If the beginning, middle, and end are all good and tend to what is wholly good, it is a sign of the good angel. But if the train of the thoughts which a spirit causes ends up in something evil or diverting . . . it comes from an evil spirit, the enemy of our progress and eternal salvation" (333). After the purgative exercises of self-examination and discernment of the first week, and partially the second, the ground is prepared in the soul for the illuminative and unitive phases of the retreat experience.

Ignatius uses the model of Benedictine life in community in several ways. For one, he employs confession as a colloquy, a conversation with a friend or spiritual counselor, or with the three persons of the Trinity or the Virgin, for the purpose of self-examination, discernment, and recognition of one's temptations and evil thoughts and ways. For another, he extends the role of abbot, the one representing Christ in the monastic community to whom obedience is vowed, to that of the church. Besides the superior general of the order as spiritual leader of the Society, the pontiff as the church's earthly representative is to be given unreserved obedience in matters of conduct and precept. This model is elaborated on in his appendix to the *Exercises*, titled "Rules for Thinking, Judging, and Feeling With the Church," whose purpose is "to have the genuine attitude which we ought to maintain in the church militant." These rules were the last thing added to the *Exercises* by Ignatius, probably shortly after his stay in Paris, about 1534 or 1535. The passage that nowadays may be the most criticized by Protestants and Catholics alike appears to address the notion of papal infallibility: "To keep ourselves right in all things, we ought to hold fast to this principle: What I see as white, I will believe to be black if the hierarchical Church thus determines it. For we believe that between Christ our Lord, the Bridegroom, and the Church, his Spouse, there is the one same Spirit who governs and guides us in the salvation of our souls" (365). In saying this Ignatius may have sought to refute Lutheran tendencies he had witnessed in Paris, such as the evangelical sermon preached by Nicholas Cop the year before Ignatius arrived and in which Calvin had most certainly played a part. But the statement should not be interpreted to mean a blind obedience to the church's teachings or an exaggerated zeal to counteract Protestantism. Instead, the relative absence of controversy it aroused in the sixteenth century suggests that such an understanding of the church's supreme role as interpreter of the Christian faith was much in line with the orthodoxy of Ignatius's day. Moreover, early Jesuit commentators tended to lump together the rules on the church with those regarding almsgiving, scruples, and the use of food. "About these four the following can be said in general. They should be proposed not to everybody, but only to persons who seem to need them and for whom it is worth the effort."[21] This view implies, in O'Malley's words, that the rules were not the culmination of Ignatius's teachings, but urged the order's members and those using the *Exercises* to "a circumspect approach" in "what one said, preached, and did in ministry."[22]

The influence of the *Exercises* on people was enormous, largely due to the way the Jesuits applied the book's principles in their own lives and with those to whom they ministered. Drawing on the ancient traditions of Benedictine and desert spirituality, the *Exercises* also integrated the practices of *devotio moderna*, the movement in which Erasmus had been raised, that had influenced Luther, and whose most prominent literary expression was the *Imitation of Christ*. The movement had arisen in the early fifteenth century in the Low Countries and spread rapidly to France and other parts of Europe. Its members, both clergy and laity, men and women, were committed to regular times of prayer, ongoing consultation on one's spiritual progress, and concrete ways of translating the Christian message into service and charitable activity while maintaining a strong

21. *Monumenta Ignatiana. Exercitia spiritualia S. Ignatii de Loyola et eorum directoria*, 2nd ed., 2 vols. (Madrid: G. Lopez del Horno, 1919; Rome: Monumenta Historica Societatis Iesu, 1969), vol. 2, 292, 281; quoted in O'Malley, *First Jesuits*, 50.

22. O'Malley, *First Jesuits*, 50.

emphasis on religious experience and personal conversion. A hundred years later the movement had waned, and it was extinct by the end of the sixteenth century, perhaps in part due to the Jesuits. Many elements of *devotio moderna* would find expression in Jesuit ministry, including an emphasis on prayer, spiritual consultations, ministry in the world, and seeing God in all things. The book characteristic of the Jesuits, the *Exercises*, had its origins in personal conversion and religious experience and was aimed at producing religious experience in turn. This experiential focus of Ignatian spirituality contrasted with that of early Protestantism and its doctrinal debates on the sacraments and the role of Scripture. The major proponent of Protestantism, Martin Luther, had come to know God's grace by reading a theological treatise straight from the Bible, namely, the letter to the Romans; the guiding figure in early modern Catholicism, Ignatius of Loyola, was converted by reading *The Life of Christ*, a retelling of Christ's life, passion, and resurrection as put forth in the gospels. Both men had wrestled with scruples, a troubled conscience, and the burden of an incomplete confession; both had found deliverance, but the means had differed, leading to differing foci in their ministries and orienting subsequent generations of followers accordingly. Their differing orientation is perhaps most clearly reflected in their literary work: one wrote a handbook for guiding souls to perfection and salvation, the other wrote numerous theological treatises, catechisms, biblical commentaries, and a translation of the Bible into the vernacular. If one compares the literary work of Luther (or that of Erasmus and Calvin) with the literary work of Ignatius, the *Exercises* emerge not as "a book of dogma, but a dogmatic book"[23] urging a personal appropriation of the Gospel message and its translation into daily life and service in the world. It could be adapted in sufficiently broad ways, and people of a wide range of social status, age, and educational background could be instructed and reached by it.

Preaching and teaching were key activities of Jesuit ministry. While the Jesuits paid close attention to sermon preparation and preaching, it was also the founding of schools in the humanist tradition, paralleled by Erasmus's humanist ideals and the *devotio moderna*'s stress on education in founding schools that would make for their visibility, social prominence, and political influence. In Italy, with the support of princes, high church officials, and nobility, the Jesuits founded numerous colleges. In mostly Protestant regions they won many important ruling houses

---

23. Ibid., 42.

back to the Catholic faith through the strategy of supplying tutors for young princes such as Ferdinand of Styria and Sigismund of Poland. In the Catholic regions of Germany they strengthened the Catholic faith by founding secondary schools and colleges, such as the Jesuit Academy in Vienna and colleges at Ingolstadt and Munich. Naturally, the Jesuits made an easy transition from being the tutors of princes to becoming the confessors and confidants of rulers, and the *Exercises* lent themselves well to that end.

The Jesuits' level of academic excellence was inherent in their constitution as conceived by their founder. Ignatius himself had studied at universities in Spain and France, including the University of Paris and the College of Montaigu, where before him Erasmus and Calvin had received their theological training. Despite the embarrassment of having to share the school bench with students half his age, Ignatius had earned a licentiate in theology in 1534 and a master's degree in 1535. His own commitment to higher learning informed the admission standards of the Society. Membership was reserved only for the most intelligent men in society, those who appeared dedicated, were physically strong and attractive, and showed integrity of character. Final vows were preceded by a twelve-year preparation: two years in the novitiate, four years of studies of which the last three were in philosophy, another four years of theological studies, and two years of practical theology, preaching, and following the *Spiritual Exercises*. At the time of Ignatius's death the membership had reached over a thousand, contrary to its original limit of sixty, and Ignatius himself lived to see the founding of about a hundred colleges and seminaries.

The combined influence of the Jesuits on the students in their schools, on aristocratic families and rulers to whom they served as confessors and spiritual counselors, and on the Council of Trent, to which the pope had quickly appointed three members of the nascent religious order as official theologians, would allow for a new assessment and practical application of confession and repentance. This approach combined the external with the internal, the sacramental with the informal, the secretive with open dialogue, and the role of priestly confessor with that of spiritual director and guide. How the Jesuit approach to confession and those of early Protestant reformers, among others, would translate into the twenty-first century and into contemporary Christian theology and practices will be explored next.

PART THREE

Contemporary Practices of Confession

The preceding two parts have roughly outlined the major historical strands, turning points, and theological developments in the practice of confession and penance in the Western church. The underlying assumption has been that at the heart of the practice of confession lies repentance, a turning around, a coming clean with God, a deep sorrow over one's sins, and the possibility of a new and rekindled life in Christ. Part 3 will examine by topic contemporary expressions of confession and current frameworks for repentance within the church. The topics considered are preaching, general confession in public worship, small or accountability groups, and private confession and spiritual direction. What are their roots and biblical antecedents, what are their historical trajectories, and what are their current expressions in various Christian denominations? A brief glance at the possible causes for the declining popularity of sacramental confession will serve as the springboard into an exploration of four leading twentieth-century theologians and spiritual writers on the subject, representing both Catholic and Protestant perspectives. They are Karl Rahner, Dietrich Bonhoeffer, Eugene Peterson, and Adrienne von Speyr. It is in light of these writers' theological and spiritual reflections on confession and spiritual direction that one will attempt to construct a contemporary theology of confession from which practical considerations can be formulated for today.

CHAPTER FOURTEEN

Biblical Antecedents, Historical Trajectories, and Contemporary Expressions

In the course of its two-thousand-year history the church has conceived numerous means and mechanisms to facilitate its members' turning to and coming clean with God among its members. Some of them proved useful for a time and eventually disappeared, new ones emerged, and some have remained relatively unchanged to this day. While the history of the practice of confession is intriguing and complex, it is not enough simply to observe its scholarly complexities and concomitant theological and doctrinal disputes. For those longing for a churchwide spiritual awakening and those hungering for a deeper, intimate walk with God there remain the questions of relevance, practicality, and translation.

Making connections between the past and the present may help us discover how the various historical models of confession have emerged and to what degree they continue to inform our confessional practices today. These connections lead to the questions of how tracing and honoring historical models can enrich our understanding of confessional practices today and how to build and enlarge upon these earlier practices creatively so they prove fruitful for us. The following chapter will examine the main contexts and venues in which confession and repentance have taken place and continue to occur by tracing their biblical roots, historical trajectories, and contemporary expressions in church life. The categories examined are: preaching, general confession in public worship, small or accountability groups, and private confession and spiritual direction.

Preaching

The common means of effecting repentance and confession in biblical times was preaching. The Old Testament prophets called the Israelites by means of confrontation and exhortation to turn from their idolatrous behavior to one that honors God. The speech the prophets utter is presumably not their own but has been placed in their mouth by God. Prophetic speech is God speech. The prophet's mouth is the mouth of God. Throughout the centuries their message remains essentially the same. People have sinned, become unholy, and lost connection with their God. By their own doing they have widened the gap between a holy God and a sinful people. They have sharpened the contrast between God's holiness and righteousness and their own pride-filled and selfish lives. The prophets want to help restore people's broken connection with God and mend the marred covenantal relationship. It is up to the prophets to proclaim this severe call, and it is up to the people to yield and repent and turn around. Turning to God in repentance is more than obeying a code of law. Rather, it is behaving in a manner, exhibited for the first time or once again, that reflects God's qualities and demonstrates them in relation to others, especially in regard to the widow, the orphan, the alien, and the oppressed.

The prophets enumerate a catalogue of sins they observe among the people. These sins all reflect a failure to acknowledge people's indebtedness to God or to adopt Godlike qualities in relation to others. The prophet Amos calls Israel's sin "rebellion" (Amos 1:3, 6, 9), Isaiah "pride" (Isa 2:11, 17), Hosea disloyalty or "harlotry" (Hos 4:15), Jeremiah "whoredom" and "adultery" (Jer 3:9). Sin finds expression in disobedience (Hosea 11), idolatry (Amos 5:26; Ezekiel 8), misplaced trust (Isaiah 7), insincere and pretentious worship (Isa 1:10), and it is accompanied by the mistreatment of members of the community through acts of violence, oppression of the poor, dishonest trading, sexual immorality, bribery, and corruption.

The prophetic preaching consistently links sin and punishment. According to Gerhard von Rad "there is absolutely nothing in the thought of the Old Testament which by and large corresponds to the separation which we make [today] between sin and penalty."[1] Once committed, sin is not exhausted until it has burnt itself out in punishment. Sin has a boomerang effect; it finds its way back to the one who has committed it and trespassed. However delayed, there is punishment for sin. It is

---

1. Gerhard von Rad, *Old Testament Theology*, vol. 1 (New York: Harper & Row, 1962), 266.

this irreversibility of sin's wages that causes the prophets' urgency, their insistence on speaking and prophesying and preaching. They urge people to stop sinning, for only by bringing a halt to the ongoing sinful activity can one stem the tide of more punishment accruing over time.

The Hebrew word for "repent," *nahum*, can also mean "comfort." There exists a connection between repentance and finding comfort: those who turn and repent of their sins will be comforted and experience inner peace. They may still have to pay the price and penalty of their sin, but once they have turned to God they will do so not grudgingly but with gladness.

The Old Testament record of the Israelites' response to prophetic proclamation in repentance and confession is sparse. Nathan confronts David, who responds in tears, sorrow, repentance; later he is depicted as immortalizing his conversion experience in Psalm 51. Jonah confronts the Ninevites, and they repent. Their response may illustrate a common Middle Eastern penitential practice: "And the people of Nineveh believed God; they proclaimed a fast, and everyone, great and small, put on sackcloth" (Jon 3:5). Even the animals are included in the fast, for the king issues a decree that "No human being or animal, no herd or flock, shall taste anything. They shall not feed, nor shall they drink water. Human beings and animals shall be covered with sackcloth, and they shall cry mightily to God. All shall turn from their evil ways and from the violence that is in their hands" (Jon 3:7b-8). Under the leadership of their king the Ninevites collectively confess their sins to God and make amends. They fast as a sign of penance, and they cease committing further violence against one another and creation.

In the New Testament, preaching brings about repentance. John the Baptist calls people to repentance. Their turning and confession of sins is ritualized by the act of coming clean and stepping into the river Jordan for baptism. Likewise, Jesus calls people to repentance. The necessity of turning toward God is the new kingdom reality Jesus proclaims as imminent. In response, some leave their families and homes and follow him. The apostle Paul and the other apostles go from city to city, preaching the impending judgment of God upon the residents. They seek out Gentiles and Jews alike, lovers of God, worshipers. Those who respond are baptized and become charter members of the newly founded churches. Becoming a Christian means responding to a call to repentance. Being baptized means a turning from the ways of the devil to the ways of God. The founding of churches means that members have responded to the message preached. The message's content was the good news of God's mighty acts of salvation. The message's result was that hearers turned, confessed their sins, and professed their faith in Jesus Christ.

Preaching that aims at repentance is called evangelistic preaching. Since the word "euangelion" means good news, to evangelize means to proclaim the message and good news of salvation in Jesus Christ. Such preaching seeks to effect a decision in the hearer, a radical turning around of one's life. To take full effect, the decision has to be physically demonstrated, verbalized, and made public. Making public one's decision to turn involves confessing one's sin and professing one's faith. Evangelistic preaching is aimed at generating a decision for the faith, while expository preaching is designed to teach about the faith, instructing those who have made a decision in matters of doctrine, morality, and God.

The Acts of the Apostles gives vivid examples of evangelistic preaching. The genre was further developed by the missionary monks of England, Ireland, and Wales. Patrick, Columba, Columbanus, and Boniface effected many conversions and made converts by their preaching. Those entrusted with receiving new converts and hearing their confessions and decisions to turn from evil to God were called confessors. Confessors were mostly laypeople. They were known among the Christian community as wise men and women, excelling in piety and the ability to offer sound spiritual advice. Often they would serve as lifelong spiritual guides, or soul friends, to the new Christian converts. Their subsequent spiritual guidance complemented the change effected in the heart of the new believer through evangelistic preaching.

During the early Middle Ages preaching was not commonplace during Sunday worship. In the late eighth century Charlemagne ordered Alcuin to draw up a lectionary for all the feast days and Sundays of the year. As a result, collections of model sermons began to circulate to help priests and bishops become preachers, but generally inspired preaching was rare. Christians were converted gradually in the context of the liturgy, catechetical instruction, and the celebration of the Eucharist rather than through preaching.

With the founding of Franciscan and Dominican orders in the early thirteenth century, preaching aimed at repentance returned. The friars conducted preaching crusades in the marketplaces and churches, and afterward they would hear confessions from those moved by the preaching. The Dominican tertiary Catherine of Siena and the monks Dominic, Francis of Assisi, Albert the Great, Meister Eckhart, and Bonaventure all were outstanding preachers. Their message was aimed at producing a harvest of souls, so that when they preached confessors were often nearby to counsel those who were touched by the message, had experienced repentance, and were in need of confessing their sins.

By the later Middle Ages the seasons of Advent and Lent with their penitential emphasis became the prime preaching seasons of the year, and bishops recruited friars to assist with preaching and hearing confessions. In Italy the annual evangelistic Lenten crusade was a common feature of church life, when priests and friars worked overtime to hear penitents' confessions. In smaller churches the preacher also served as the confessor of the day. Having proclaimed the Gospel message, the priest would then witness its transforming effect in penitents' hearts and lives.

The dual role of the preacher as confessor strengthened the place of the Franciscans and Dominicans in church life and their influence on the laity. Friars became known for their engaging preaching and their ability to relate to those who came for confession. More than priests and bishops, friars could cultivate close ties with the laity among whom they served. They were less encumbered by the demands of the ecclesiastical office and its hierarchy, and unlike their secluded counterparts living behind monastic walls, they moved about freely in public. The friars' contact with the laity encouraged a new spiritual lay movement that valued the use of spiritual gifts by any Christian, not just those in religious orders or in ordained church office. In their roles as preachers, confessors, and spiritual guides the friars had a significant influence on women. They stimulated women's spiritual sensitivities, promoted their insights and writings, and equipped them for carrying out spiritual functions much like those of the friars, albeit without ecclesial sanction and recognition.

The dual role of the preacher as confessor significantly contributed to the success of the Jesuits in starting missions abroad and locally. Their excellent preaching, resulting from the order's stringent admissions requirement of lengthy studies and practical ministry experience, combined with their skilled hearing of confessions and offering spiritual guidance for new converts. The historic role of preacher as confessor also influenced the early Protestant reformers, who concluded that pastors were the most qualified among Christians for hearing confessions, providing counsel, and offering spiritual guidance. Even when confession as a sacrament was abolished in the Protestant churches, Luther, Calvin, and Zwingli would still urge congregants to seek out the pastor, rather than another church member, if they wished to make private confession or gain solace from a troubled conscience.

Not all evangelistic preaching emphasized scriptural exposition. Lutheran Pietism, for example, digressed from the scriptural emphasis and expository nature of preaching that Luther had taught. Avoiding both doctrinal theology and scriptural exegesis, Pietists focused on an inward religious experience; their preaching sought to effect a spiritual rebirth in the hearts of their listeners. Influenced by the Moravians and Pietism in his conversion experience, Anglican John Wesley stressed repentance and conversion in his preaching. Barred by bishops from preaching in churches due to what was perceived to be his harsh message, he took the Gospel to the common laborer in the streets and outside the church's institutional, traditional venues. New converts made during Wesley's preaching crusades were expected to enroll in small groups, the so-called societies or classes of Methodism, whose members served as account-ability agents, spiritual guides, and confessors one to another.

Evangelistic preaching and revival are closely linked. Through the work of Anglican priest George Whitefield, with whom Wesley had col-laborated in England, evangelistic preaching was brought to America, where it fanned the first great revival, the Great Awakening of 1739. Other revival preachers were Jonathan Edwards and Gilbert Tennent, who had already begun preaching an experiential faith under the influ-ence of Puritanism and Pietism. But preaching was not the sole element to prompt a revival. The Second Great Awakening of 1800–1810 may have had its beginnings with people gathering for prayer and fasting, fellowship, and the celebration of communion in addition to the hearing of sermons. Extending over a period of several days or weeks, the revival provided a change of pace from common daily activities and gathered people for the purpose of spiritual formation, as on a retreat. The goal of a revival was twofold: to make new converts for Christ and to strengthen those already in the faith to greater piety and maturity. Once the revival ended, Christian converts and awakened sinners testified to their faith experience in the assembly or as part of worship. During the public times of testimonial and personal witness the entire congregation served as confessors. Revival participants were also expected to share the religious experience with nonbelievers, such as neighbors or family members. Thereby they not only acted in the role of preachers, proclaim-ing God's saving activity as they had experienced it, but also as penitents who confessed to their former sinful state and actions. Giving one's testimony was preaching and confession all wrapped into one.

The two Great Awakenings in America were succeeded by a third in the late nineteenth and early twentieth centuries. Beginning in the late 1870s, Dwight L. Moody led numerous preaching crusades and revivals. Decades earlier Charles Finney had promoted revival through his preach-ing and his insistence on personal conversion. The awakening continued through World War I and thereafter. One of its key preachers in America, Billy Sunday, popularized the altar call during a public revival or cru-sade, linking revival with altar call and making proclamation and re-sponse a major symbol of American church culture. After the evangelistic sermon is delivered, people are invited to physically respond; they are to demonstrate their inward repentance by the outward act of coming forward to the chancel steps, where they either confess Christ for the first time or vocalize their decision of a renewed walk in Christian faith. Those who meet them at the chancel steps are trained lay counselors. They listen, respond, and offer guidance. Much like a traditional priestly confessor today, the counselor inquires the reason the person has come and the nature of the decision, listens to confession, and extends assurance of Christ's pardon, offers prayer, and suggests next steps.

The foremost revival and crusade preacher of the twentieth century is Billy Graham (b. 1918). He is said to have preached to more people in live audiences than anyone in history—over 210 million people in more than 185 countries and territories. Since the 1949 Los Angeles crusade that launched him into the public eye Graham has led hundreds of thousands of people to make personal decisions to live for Christ. This approach to evangelistic preaching stems from his personal experience. At age sixteen Graham made a decision for Christ through the preaching of a traveling evangelist, Mordecai Ham, who had visited Graham's home town, Charlotte, North Carolina, for a series of revival meetings. Graham was ordained as a Southern Baptist minister and served several churches before entering crusade ministry and founding the Billy Graham Evangelistic Association. The main objective of a crusade conducted by Graham is "to bring uncommitted individuals into a personal relationship with Jesus Christ and firmly establish them in a local church."[2] Through preaching, people are brought to repentance and to the point of making a decision for Christ. In accordance with the approach of eliciting a decision among the audience through preaching, the Association's radio broadcast is called "The Hour of Decision" and the monthly magazine, *Decision*.

The role of the counselor is crucial during a crusade and in follow-up. Counselors interact with those wishing to make a decision for Christ. Their demeanor affects those they counsel, making training a requisite. Before a crusade begins, prospective "counselors" from local churches are trained in five weekly sessions for interaction onsite and during follow-up. Trainees are selected on the basis of their personal faith in Jesus Christ, class attendance, and completion of their assignments. During the crusade meeting Graham presents a sermon and invites people to "come forward" to the platform area to make a commitment to Christ. Counselors, seated in a designated area, are then assigned to

2. "Crusade Facts" at www.billygraham.org.

individual "inquirers" as they move toward the counseling area, while supervisors attempt to match counselors with inquirers by sex and approximate age. After a brief talk to the inquirers by Graham and a prayer on their behalf, the personal counseling begins.

The counseling session during a Billy Graham crusade contains elements of a spiritual colloquy and private confession. The counselor asks questions to help determine the inquirer's need. Then, with open Bible in hand, the counselor attempts to help the inquirer think through what specific Scripture passages say about his or her situation and to commit the matter to God in prayer. The use of Scripture in the counseling process is to help confirm a truth revealed and "what has already been accomplished by the Holy Spirit through the preaching of the Word."[3] The counseling supervisor, who usually is a local pastor and experienced in the crusade counseling process, is available in case the inquirer wishes to address and discuss needs at a deeper level. Often the inquirer is making a first public commitment to and confession of Jesus Christ. At other times there is need for spiritual assurance or the desire to recommit one's life to Christ. Counselors are discouraged from teaching sectarian doctrines or steering inquirers toward a specific denomination. After the private counseling time the inquirer's name, address, and church affiliation (if any) are recorded on a card for referral to a local church. Later the counselor makes contact with the inquirer, either by telephone or in person, to check in regarding the person's spiritual progress and commitment, providing a time for listening, offering encouragement, and identifying further spiritual needs or problems. A letter from Billy Graham sent to all inquirers after the crusade sets the stage for measuring an inquirer's spiritual progress: Inquirers are to pray and read the Bible daily, tell others about Jesus Christ, and attend a local church. In following up with inquirers, counselors will gauge spiritual progress by the degree to which the inquirer has committed to and is practicing the spiritual disciplines outlined in the letter, while inquirers have the opportunity to review the consistency of their commitment and confess to personal shortcomings and stumbling blocks.

Despite the official designation, the crusade "counselor" functions largely as a confessor. He or she hears initial confession from the inquirer, offers assurance of salvation and pardon of sin with the help of scriptural references, and assigns a type of penance. Generally the "penance" assigned to the inquirer is that of making contact with a local church, be-

---

3. "Crusade Counseling" at www.billygraham.org.

coming active in its ministry, practicing the spiritual disciplines of daily Bible reading and prayer, and giving witness of his or her faith in Christ. During the follow-up meeting the inquirer reviews with the counselor the quality of the commitment made, opening up yet another opportunity for confession, assurance, and exhortation.

Traditionally, evangelistic preaching at revivals has had a twofold purpose: to make new converts and to rekindle the faith of the weak and lax. For a number of reasons public perception has conflated this twofold purpose into the single aim of making converts for Christ. As a result those responding to an altar call during a revival are regarded as accepting Jesus Christ as Lord and Savior for the first time, or as "being saved." It has also meant that those who have repeatedly responded to an altar call have perceived themselves as being saved again and again or, lacking the initial emotional excitement following a previous decision, they think their previous "salvation" did not "stick." Such erroneous thinking is the result of a narrow view of repentance that limits repentance to a once-in-a-lifetime event rather than regarding it as a lifelong process of conversion accompanied by the elements of private confession and public commitment. When understood properly, the altar call in the context of evangelistic preaching functions as a rite of confession and a public commitment ceremony. In addition to being the symbol of a first-time profession of faith, the altar call offers Christians a liturgical venue for experiencing and demonstrating their ongoing conversion, repentance, and renewal in Christ.

General Confession in Public Worship

By a general confession we mean here a prayer or creedal statement recited by the entire worshiping community in which sins and wrongdoing are acknowledged and God is petitioned to offer forgiveness and mercy. These confessional prayers may be said from memory or read from a printed text, such as the Scriptures, the worship bulletin, or a prayer book. Two other meanings of general confession not discussed here relate only to a private context: first, it is a standard formula used during private confession that the penitent might prefer to his or her individualized confession of sins; second, it refers to the complete recounting of one's sins spanning an entire lifetime during conversation or colloquy with a confessor.

The general confession that takes place in public worship today is recited or intoned by the entire community. It has its model in the Psalms of the Old Testament, which were hymns and prayers. The largest category of the Psalms comprises prayers for help, either on the part of an individual or the community at large. Called psalms of lament, these prayers were prayed or sung by individuals or the community during times of distress, such as sickness and adversity, betrayal and deceit, and sin and guilt. While the prayers no longer allow for a concrete connection with their original setting and the circumstances that produced them, their use of metaphor allows for a broad application to community life. Similarly, individual and corporate prayers can no longer be neatly distinguished and have become interchangeable; what used to be an individual prayer fits a corporate setting, and the other way around. The versification of the Psalms in the original Hebrew language certainly suggests corporate use during worship and may have served as a mnemonic tool. Being able to recite and sing prayers from memory was important in an oral culture, but setting prayers and hymns in verse also meant that they could be remembered outside corporate worship. They could live on in people's hearts long after corporate worship on the Sabbath had ended and they carried over into the week and into the daily life of the individual. Psalms that include a confession of sin and petition sometimes articulate the petitioner's intention and resolution of amending one's life. Psalm 51 contains all three elements: confession, petition, and resolution: "For I know my transgressions, and my sin is ever before me" (v. 3); "Create in me a clean heart, O God, and put a new and right spirit within me" (v. 10); "Then I will teach transgressors your ways, and sinners will return to you" (v. 13). And Psalm 32 teaches of the healing power of confession: "While I kept silence [about my sins], my body wasted away through my groaning all day long" (v. 3); "Then I acknowledged my sin to you, and I did not hide my iniquity; I said, 'I will confess my transgressions to the Lord,' and you forgave the guilt of my sin" (v. 5).

The early church encouraged the daily practice of confession through both private prayer and public gatherings. These confessional liturgies incorporated the Psalms and the prayer Jesus taught the disciples, the Lord's Prayer, which contains both elements of confession and petition: "And forgive us our debts, as we also have forgiven our debtors. And do not bring us to the time of trial, but rescue us from the evil one" (Matt 6:12-13). Late in the first or early in the second century the *Didachē* advised Christians to pray the Lord's Prayer three times a day during private prayer. And the *Apostolic Tradition* of about 217 CE describes seven daily hours of private prayer, the precursor of what later came to be the monastic practice of praying the Liturgy of the Hours. Evidence of daily public worship and daily communal confession in the early church is scarce. However, a few sources indicate that these were likely practices among Christians for several centuries. Commonly called the cathedral office or people's office, such daily worship services were held in the chief church of a city and contained prayer and praise, petition and intercession, readings from the Scriptures, and instruction. Since the cathedral office did not include the celebration of the Eucharist it was open to all Christians, including the unbaptized catechumens. According to a late-fourth-century source, the *Apostolic Constitutions*, Christians were encouraged to assemble twice a day for corporate praise and prayer: "assemble yourselves together every day, morning and evening, singing psalms and praying in the Lord's house."[4] Likewise, the fourth-century church father and bishop John Chrysostom (345–407) recommends that newly baptized Christians gather "in the church at dawn to make your prayers and confessions to the God of all things, and to thank him for the gifts He has already given," and then in the evening to "return here to the church, [to] render an account to the Master of [your] whole day, and beg forgiveness for [your] falls."[5] By the fifth or early sixth century the people's office had virtually disappeared and the Daily Office and the praying of the Hours had become the province and practice of monastics. No longer were Christians expected to engage in prayers of corporate confession twice a day during public worship and up to seven times daily during private devotion and confession while saying the Lord's Prayer.

New forms of corporate confession appeared when Christian worship was made truly public. Previously worship had been divided into the service of the Word and the service of the Eucharist, and only baptized Christians were allowed to remain for the latter part. By the sixth century the two services had merged into one, with the result that liturgies were expanded and new confessional elements added. One of these new elements was the introductory or entrance rite. Augustine (354–430) could still describe a simple, bare-bones beginning of worship on the Lord's Day: "I came into the church, greeted the people with the customary greeting, and the lector started the lesson."[6] Within a few decades after his death a new entrance rite had enhanced the opening of worship. It consisted of four parts: the Introit, a form of travel music accompanying the procession

---

4. *Apostolic Constitutions* II.59 in James F. White, *Introduction to Christian Worship* (Nashville: Abingdon, 2000), 135.

5. John Chrysostom, *Baptismal Instructions* VIII.17, trans. Paul H. Harkins, Ancient Christian Writers 31 (Westminster, MD: Newman Press, 1963), 126–27; quoted in White, *Introduction*, 135.

6. Augustine, "Sermon 324," PL 38 (Paris: J. P. Migne, 1863), 1449; quoted in White, *Introduction*, 155.

of the clergy to the altar table in the manner of a temple entry psalm; the *Kyrie*, a sung prayer petitioning the Lord for mercy; the *Gloria in excelsis*, a doxology; and the Collect, an opening prayer of greeting, praise, petition, and gratitude to God. The confessional element, the *Kyrie eleison* ("Lord, have mercy"), is a brief prayer that originally consisted of a litany of prayers including confession, petition, and intercession, each followed by the recurring response "Lord, have mercy." However, by the early seventh century these petitions had disappeared, so that only the *Kyrie* remained as "a tiny Greek island in a sea of Latin words."[7]

Another element of corporate confession that appeared at the time was the preparatory rite of the priest prior to leading worship and consecrating the host at the altar table. Initially a personal acknowledgment of unworthiness and a petition to be made worthy, spoken in the sacristy by those leading worship, these prayers would soon spill out into the assembly and become part of corporate worship. According to James F. White the process was marked in the Western churches and signaled "a shift in emphasis away from an assembly gathered to rejoice in what God had done to an assembly of individuals met to bemoan their sin before the Almighty."[8]

A similar fate also befell the prayer said by the priest at the foot of the altar prior to consecrating the host. The so-called *Confiteor*, a priestly prayer of confession, was converted into a corporate prayer of confession. It was spoken by the entire assembly before beginning the eucharistic celebration and was followed by the words of absolution. A thousand years later both the introductory rite and the preparatory rite would receive high marks from the Protestant reformers in their drafting of new orders of worship. Martin Bucer and John Calvin restored the penitential elements at the opening of corporate worship by including a prayer of corporate confession, followed by absolution, and the singing or saying of the Decalogue. The Reformers also expanded on the corporate preparatory rite for the sacrament of Holy Communion by adding a Scripture reading, an exhortatory sermon, and prayers of confession. Both these elements of corporate confession in public worship were included in the liturgy of the Anglican tradition. It is likely that with the abandonment of the sacrament of penance the Protestant reformers felt the need to recapture elements of confession in other ways, most prominently in corporate worship and in connection with the two remaining sacraments, especially Holy Communion. As a result, earlier litanies of

---

7. White, *Introduction*, 156.
8. Ibid., 157.

corporate confession were recovered or enlarged upon. Luther, for example, while removing the opening confessional devotion, would recover and emphasize liturgical chants and canticles from the monastic tradition, and he enhanced congregational hymnody by introducing the sung creed and hymns in the vernacular. In retaining much of Luther's order of worship, Calvin recovered corporate public confession at the opening of worship and prior to Holy Communion, added the corporate reciting of the Decalogue for self-examination of the conscience and expanding on singing by having the Psalms set to meter. It is safe to say that these liturgical innovations and recoveries in regard to corporate confession were aimed at deepening the individual's life of Christian discipleship by quickening repentance and prompting a conversion of the heart.

In today's Protestant worship some vestiges of these Reformers' efforts at corporate confession remain. For example, the Presbyterian *Book of Common Worship* includes the prayer of confession, the *Kyrie*, and the declaration of forgiveness as the opening or gathering rite for the service on the Lord's Day. While the Decalogue may be said as an exhortation following the declaration of forgiveness, the exhortatory sermon in preparation for Holy Communion has disappeared, and the Psalms, while used for the call to worship, have been largely replaced by other congregational hymns. Several liturgies for the reaffirmation of the baptismal covenant for a congregation are included also; they are modeled after baptismal liturgies of the early church and link baptism with repentance, a turning from evil to God in Christ, confession, and the forgiveness of sins. The *Lutheran Book of Worship* includes both a brief and an expanded order for corporate confession and forgiveness of sins, which may or may not precede the service of the Word or the service of Holy Communion; it may also stand alone in a penitential service. And the *Book of Common Prayer* of the Episcopal Church, in its Rite I, includes for the order of worship on the Lord's Day an exhortation, the reading of the Decalogue, and two different penitential orders preceding the celebration of the Eucharist. (Rite II retains nothing but the *Kyrie*, and that only as an option chiefly for penitential seasons; otherwise the *Gloria in excelsis* is preferred.) All of these litanies are examples of a general confession in worship aimed at repentance and conversion.

In the Roman Catholic Church the elements of general or communal confession in the divine liturgy appear less prominent today than in the fourth or fifth centuries. Vestiges of the rite of contrition remain, such as in the opening prayer of confession, the *Confiteor*, the *Kyrie*, and the *Gloria*. However, by comparison with the Reformed tradition, for example, the frequency of and emphasis on corporate confession is relatively sparse. Several reasons may account for that: First, in the Roman Catholic tradition penance exists as a separate sacrament and functions as a liturgical action; second, the Eucharist celebrated at each Mass is regarded as God's supreme demonstration of forgiveness and reconciliation, evidenced by the real presence of Jesus Christ in the elements of bread and wine; and third, despite the private nature of penance, the sacrament is considered a public action with repercussions and consequences for the entire community. Nonetheless, the Rite of Penance, promulgated in 1973 on recommendation of the Second Vatican Council and its 1963 Constitution on the Sacred Liturgy (*Sacrosanctum Concilium*), offers communal expressions of repentance. Implemented in 1977, the new rite offers three explicit forms of confession: The first is private confession to a priest either face-to-face or from behind a screen in mutual dialogue and with appropriate Scripture passages being read aloud. The second form is a "communal celebration" with Scripture readings and a homily, accompanied by an examination of the conscience in the form of a liturgy of confession into which is inserted provision for individual, private confession and absolution; at this time each church member may come forward to individually confess and be absolved, after which a common penance is given. The third form is a "communal celebration of reconciliation with general confession and general absolution," to be offered only in case of "grave necessity" and at the discretion of the diocesan bishop. Instances of grave necessity are defined as those in which imminent danger of death exists or where a shortage of confessors may result in penitents being "deprived of sacramental grace or Holy Communion for a long time."[9]

The practice of communal confession has been questioned regarding the authenticity with which the words are said. Can prayers and litanies of confession be spoken and sung with any kind of conviction and authentic verve when someone else has formulated them? Should not the expression of sorrow and contrition be spontaneous and unplanned? Can repentance be induced by a mere repeating of contrite words and phrases? To these questions the ancient practice of singing the Psalms offers some answers. These psalms continued to live on in the heart of worshipers long after worship had ended. Likewise, confessional language employed in penitential litanies and prayers of general confession can continue to live on in the memory of the individual until recalled at the time of need.

---

9. "The Celebration of the Sacrament of Penance," *Catechism of the Catholic Church* (Liguori, MO: Liguori Publications, 1994), 1483, p. 372.

Confessional litanies and prayers cultivate a posture of humility, reverence, and submission before God, and by the words that identify concrete sins in the community and the individual they stimulate worshipers to examine their consciences. Thus prayers of confession spoken in unison at set times in worship may continue to live on in our memory, prodding us to examine our consciences and providing us with the words to say in due times of contrition and sorrow. While for some the effect of these prayers and hymns may be postponed, for others it can be immediate, so that in the act of speaking words of confession a sense of contrition and sorrow is immediately felt. General confession also reminds us that sin is a universal human attribute and carries a collective effect; each of us is bound to be infected with sin and each suffers sin's consequences. The pervasiveness of sin in human nature and its unsparing effects on the community suggest the collective need for redemption and forgiveness, which the communal liturgy enacts. Also, communal confession places believers on equal footing with one another before a holy God. Through this act of solidarity there is comfort in knowing that one is not alone in the face of dejection, shame, and failure. Finally, communal confession is better than no confession at all.

The sum total of the confessional elements of worship can be greater than its parts. Prayers, litanies, and hymns of petition, confession, and intercession all combine in preparing and prompting an experience of repentance. Worshipers may be evangelized through worship as a whole rather than by its individual parts such as the sermon. In recent years the notion of worship evangelism has been advanced by Robert Webber. He suggests three types of evangelistic worship. The first is the so-called manifest-presence evangelism, in which the overall experience of worship leads to a sense of God's prominent presence and an encounter with God in Christ. The worshiper is met by God through no one particular element of worship, but rather by the confluence of several elements such as prayers, music, preaching, and the sacraments. A second form of worship evangelism is "seeker-service evangelism," where nonbelievers are exposed to spiritual themes in secular language and metaphor. The intentional absence of Christian symbols and terminology is designed to connect with the audience, while the message, songs, and prayers are aimed at conveying the spiritual principles and rudiments of the Christian message. A third form of worship evangelism originated in the third and fourth centuries. Called "liturgical evangelism," it aims at effecting a conversion regulated by the order and elements of worship and the liturgical seasons. Here "services that span the church year order the inner experience of repentance from sin, faith in Christ, conversion of life, and entrance in[to] the Christian community."[10] While used successfully by the Roman Catholic Church in teaching and initiating new members into the church through the yearlong Rite of Christian Initiation of Adults (RCIA), liturgical evangelism can be used by other denominations as well.

Liturgical evangelism involves making Christian converts gradually by first drawing them into the life of the community and then teaching them in the context of worship through the liturgies, prayers, sacraments, and rites of the liturgical year. An example of liturgical evangelism ordered by the church year is to actively invite newcomers to church during the season of Pentecost; on the first Sunday in Advent these visitors are received through a rite of welcome; from there until the season of Epiphany they are instructed in the Scriptures and holy living; on the first Sunday in Lent they participate in a rite of election, followed by a period of purification; and finally, on Easter Sunday, they are welcomed into full membership through baptism and the rite of initiation. For each segment of the cycle, prayers, hymns, liturgies, and Scriptures are aimed at marking the specific stage of the initiation process in correlation with the specific season of the liturgical year. In contrast to evangelistic preaching aimed at a quick and speedy conversion, liturgical evangelism effects a gradual and almost imperceptible conversion in the life of the seeker. The liturgy, sacraments, song, prayer, creed, and sermon all work together in offering venues for God's word to confront people and elicit the response of a changed heart and a renewed commitment to God in Christ. Thus litanies of general confession no longer stand alone but combine with other worship elements to assist worshipers in the process of self-examination, producing repentance and a first-time or renewed turning toward God.

Small or Accountability Groups

In the Old Testament the tribal clan and the extended family function as the primary small groups that hold their members accountable for their moral behavior. Both clan and family reprove, correct, and punish offenders, sometimes by expelling them from the community and, even more severely, by putting them to death, as in stoning. The evil brought into existence by an individual member is viewed as destroying the perpetrator and his or her community alike. To protect its purity and

---

10. Robert Webber, "Three Models for Evangelism Through Worship," in *The Ministries of Christian Worship*, vol. 7 of the seven-volume series *The Complete Library of Christian Worship*, ed. Robert E. Webber, 437–40 (Nashville: Star Song, 1994), at 439.

avert punishment the community cancels solidarity with the offender and severs all ties. Motivation, circumstances, or conscious awareness regarding the sinful act on the part of the offender hardly play a role in formulating a verdict. The question is simply whether the offender is a danger to the community and can be forgiven or not.

As calamities mounted for the tribes before and after the deportation into exile in Babylon, prophets rose up in Israel to function as accusers, indictors, and jury. They replaced and expanded on the clan or family's previous function, accusing and convicting the entire community rather than individuals. With the people's return from exile and the rebuilding of the temple in Jerusalem, the role of the cult as the locus for judging individual offenders and protecting the community's purity diminished. The primary accountability group during the period of Second-Temple Judaism and up to the time of Jesus was the family.

Jesus strengthened the notion of family as accountability agent, but it was a new type of family he introduced, one that has God as Father and Jesus himself as the firstborn and the one instructing the younger siblings, his followers. Those who follow Jesus and are baptized become his brothers and sisters, leaving behind their natural siblings and families to enter into a new community defined not by blood but by spiritual ties. Discipleship among Jesus' followers entails a demonstration of mutual affinity and affection for one another as members of the new family. Jesus is not the head or founder of the new community but its first exponent. He calls his disciples friends rather than servants. By their baptism they are marked as children of God, children of their father in heaven. After Jesus' death and resurrection the extended family of the church is born at Pentecost, with the local community as the smaller family unit and accountability group in matters of purity, behavior, and doctrine. The apostle Paul, along with the other apostles, teaches about this new family unit, calling it the place of sanctification where members learn "how you ought to live and to please God" (1 Thess 4:1). In this new family unit members have responsibilities for one another's behavior, though they share different gifts and offices for the purpose of building up the entire body of the church. To varying degrees members serve as accountability agents one to another, keeping the community pure and unblemished as the "bride of Christ" that anticipates his return. They do so through the reading of Scripture, exhortation, and teaching (1 Tim 4:13) within the public venue of the assembly.

In the early monastic desert communities of the East confession took on new features. During regular colloquies among the desert monastics, confessional conversations about temptation and desire were initiated by the leader. The leader and elder of the community gave testimony of personal struggles, thereby setting an example for the others to follow suit, to be unashamed in confessing their shortcomings, and to present their sins before the assembly in order to receive spiritual counsel and prayer. About a hundred years later the Benedictine rule made provisions for a chapter of faults, a regular time when members appear before the abbot and the community of their own accord to admit faults and to make satisfaction. Members take the initiative to confess their sins even before others can report them or point them out. The example of individual monks making regular confession to the entire community provides a climate of mutual compassion, accountability, and correction.

Until the sixth century, confession occurred within the community of worshipers rather than in private. Church members enrolled in the order of penitents during a communal liturgy, demonstrating their repentance by physical expressions in the form of disciplines. Liturgical rituals, such as the laying on of hands by the bishop, solemnized the stages of their development from the initial admission of fault to eventual full conversion and reconciliation with the church. Reconciliation with the church meant reconciliation with God and was marked by members' readmission to the Eucharist. However, as the church's penitential liturgies became more elaborate and worship more public, church members were less and less willing to submit to the formal institution of making confession within the assembly. By the fifth century Christianity was regarded as the religion of the state, so that being a Christian meant being a good citizen. As a result the local worshiping community lost the flavor of a close-knit family and was transformed into a public arena where social and religious values mixed. By the seventh century the order of penitents had virtually disappeared and so had the local assembly's function as an accountability group within which members publicly confessed their sins.

The thirteenth and fourteenth centuries witnessed a recovery of the small, intimate setting of an assembly where confession is made. The mobilization of laypeople pursuing practices of spiritual perfection and sanctification outside the monastery had spawned the rise of small accountability groups. Composed of members of both the clergy and the laity, these small groups met for mutual edification, teaching, and confession. They hoped to restore the earlier intimacy of the spiritual family the apostolic church had known. Members were considered equally equipped to hear confession and to pronounce forgiveness toward one another regardless of sex, age, and ecclesiastical rank. Naturally, the equality exercised in the group conflicted with the hierarchical structure of church governance and the sacramental privilege of the priest. By and large, members met covertly, and they called themselves Friends of God. They were loosely organized and established contact and community by sharing spiritual writings, often with a mystical bent. By the fifteenth century this movement had died out and was replaced by the Brethren and Sisters of the Common Life, practicing a *devotio moderna*, a newly minted "modern" way of Christian devotion whose members, both clergy and laity, met in small groups for the purpose of Scripture study, mutual edification, and exhortation. They heard and made confession and extended forgiveness, practicing the principle of the priesthood of all believers.

The Reformation theme of the priesthood of all believers was largely the result of small groups meeting in homes for mutual exhortation, edification, and confession. Martin Luther popularized the theme, which had been implemented about two hundred years earlier, in an effort to expose and redress the abuses of the sacramental system of penance by priests, bishops, and members of religious orders. But the principle of small confessional groups meeting for a deepening of Christian piety was also an important feature of early modern Catholicism. In their evangelization and mission efforts the Jesuits also made use of account-ability groups. They either revived dormant groups or founded new confraternities in villages and cities. These confraternities were modeled after religious guilds, which had begun in the late Middle Ages in Europe and had become central to remedying social evils, eliminating vice, and deepening the faith of the laity. Members of these confraternities con-sisted of both priests and laypeople, who bound themselves to daily meditation and examination of conscience, weekly confession, monthly communion, and works of charity, especially the care of the poor, instruc-tion of the ignorant in Christian doctrine, and assistance to those in prison or condemned to death. During their meetings members recited prayers, encouraged one another in the faith through exhortation and teaching, and pledged themselves to carry out certain works of mercy in the local community, the hospital, the prison, or the poorhouse. Some of these confraternities were composed of all males; others had members of both genders, though men and women met separately. Characteristic of the confraternities founded by the Jesuits was that leadership and offices were reserved for the laity, in order to ensure relative independence; also, the lay groups were not attached to a parish, so that the specific religious practices proposed were presumably chosen more freely rather than being imposed by the bishop or the local clergy. The goal was to effect and sustain an interior ethical and religious life among members, whose common goals were fundamentally shaped by the Ignatian

Exercises and who found themselves empowered to carry the Gospel into their local community.

In Protestant circles the principle of the priesthood of all believers was systematically promoted by the pastor and educator Philip Jakob Spener. More than a century after Luther, Spener commended to pastors the intentional forming of small groups within their churches. Under the pastor's leadership, members met regularly in so-called conventicles for mutual edification, exhortation, and confession. Shortly thereafter the Lutheran Pietist Count Ludwig von Zinzendorff formed small confessional groups among the Moravians and other persecuted Protestants on his estate, largely to settle conflicts and divisions. Through the Moravians the practice of confession in small groups was carried abroad. Aided by the Moravians in his conversion experience, the Anglican priest John Wesley appropriated and methodically implemented the system in England. Those converted by his and others' preaching Wesley enrolled in small accountability groups, divided by sex and marital status, for continued Christian instruction, edification, and sanctification.

Bucer and Calvin, on the other hand, sought to restore the role of the local congregation as spiritual family. Each member was held accountable for his or her moral behavior before the assembly or its representatives—the appointed leaders, the elders, and the minister. Annually, members were visited by the elders to give an account of their faith, attest to the quality of their discipleship, and confess to their shortcomings so as to make amends. Similarly, pastors were encouraged to submit to supervision in a small group of their peers, which Calvin called the company of pastors.

Today the public nature of the local congregation deters members from openly admitting their wrongdoing and seeking forgiveness. The church's function as a spiritual family is made visible mostly in small groups. While such small groups exist and meet in most local churches, their function is primarily in three areas: education (Bible and book study), mission (outreach and benevolence), and a specific task in church life (committee, board, choir). Rarely does a group meet for mutual exhortation and confession.

In recent years the vacuum is being filled by a "new" type of Christian small group that makes confession and confidentiality its central purpose. The workings and methods of these small groups are based on the twelve-step program of Alcoholics Anonymous, yet their materials are couched in Christian language and sprinkled with biblical quotations. Commonly referred to as Christian recovery groups, they aim to provide members with the means and spiritual principles for overcoming destructive dependencies and addictive behavior. An umbrella organization for these groups is the National Association for Christian Recovery, which "encourage[s] local churches to develop twelve step groups, educate and support twelve step group leaders and seek in other ways to expand the impact of Twelve Step programs within the Christian community."[11]

Among the first of Christian twelve-step groups founded is Alcoholics Victorious, begun in 1948 in Chicago as part of a rescue mission ministry and aimed at alcoholics and substance abusers. Another group is Alcoholics for Christ, founded in 1977 in Michigan, with about one hundred groups nationwide, most of them in the Detroit metropolitan area and several of them in prisons, county jails, and rehab and counseling centers. Currently one of the largest of these groups is Celebrate Recovery, headquartered at Saddleback Community Church in Lake Forest, California, and endorsed by the church's founding pastor, Rick Warren, known for his best-selling book *The Purpose-Driven Life*. Celebrate Recovery was founded in 1991 by Saddleback's associate pastor, John Baker, and has since helped establish small groups in hundreds of churches nationwide and overseas as well as in prisons nationally. Over half a million people are said to have gone through the program. At Saddleback Church all recovery small groups are gender-specific. They may be recovery groups aimed at teaching recovery principles in general or they address specific addictions and dependencies, such as abuse, anger, chemical dependency, eating disorders, finance, food addictions, love and relationship addiction, and sexual addiction. Training conferences nationwide, an annual congress held at Saddleback Church, and a multimedia curriculum for children, college students, and adults are available for equipping current and new group leaders to use and introduce the twelve-step method in local churches. Though Saddleback's program is based on the eight principles of the Beatitudes in Jesus' Sermon on the Mount, called the "Eight Ways to Be Happy," and incorporates numerous biblical quotations and scriptural references, the twelve steps are interwoven as backdrop "because so many of those attending Celebrate Recovery have come from a 12-step background."[12]

At the core of Christian recovery programs lies the method of Alcoholics Anonymous, which from its inception had relied on traditional Christian teachings, especially the principles of examining one's conscience, Christian conversion and repentance, oral confession to an individual or group, and making satisfaction and restitution to those offended. Since

11. See www.roadtoforgiveness.com, "Resources."
12. See the web site at www.celebraterecovery.com.au/johnbaker.php.

its founding in 1935, Alcoholics Anonymous has spawned 87,000 A.A. groups in 136 countries worldwide, representing 1.8 million members, leading persons to sobriety or affirming them in it. Many other lay-led groups have branched off from it and appropriated the twelve steps, raising the number of those who regularly attend such meetings to several million worldwide. One of the successes of the program has been its nonsectarian language in an intentional effort to appeal to the widest audience possible. In 1938 cofounders William Griffith Wilson and Robert Holbrook Smith, both recovering from alcoholism, published the book *Alcoholics Anonymous*, which contains the twelve steps and a spiritually based recovery program from alcoholism. Its authors chose language that would make their method accessible to atheists and agnostics, Christians and non-Christians alike. Group members are advised to talk about spirituality, not religion; sobriety, not salvation; wrongdoing, not sin; admitting, not confessing; strength and hope, not resurrection; carrying the message, not sharing the faith. However, the absence of explicit Christian references does not take away from the program's explicitly Christian roots and principles.

Among those inspiring A.A.'s methods was the Oxford Group, a Christian-based movement that had started on college campuses and focused on oral confession in a small group setting. The movement's American leader at the time was the Episcopal priest Samuel Moor Shoemaker, Jr. Between 1935 and 1937 both Wilson and Smith attended Oxford Group meetings in New York, led by Shoemaker, and based much of their program on the group's principles. Shoemaker had learned these principles from the American Lutheran pastor, missionary, and evangelist Frank N. D. Buchman (1878–1961), who is credited with inspiring the movement's inception at Oxford University, England, in 1928. Following a conversion experience in a church in England in 1908, Buchman had traveled throughout the United States, England, and Asia to share his newfound convictions. He organized local groups and urged people to surrender to God by asking for forgiveness and guidance and by confessing their sins to God and one another in group meetings. Buchman was convinced that moral compromise was destructive to human character and relationships, and that moral fortitude was a prerequisite for recovering individual wholeness and for building a just and peaceful society. To that end he conducted house parties where guests, often prominent leaders in society, were invited to examine their consciences, share their sins and temptations, and surrender to God's guidance; being repentant of one's sins also involved making restitution to those one had wronged in the past and witnessing about one's changed life in an effort to help others experience the same. The conduct of the group's members was to be marked by the four principles of honesty, purity, unselfishness, and love. Buchman also founded a center in Switzerland for the movement he called Moral Re-Armament, which had no board of officers but relied on "God control" through those who had fully "surrendered" to God's will. It was recognized for its role in post–World War II reconciliation in Europe, particularly between France and Germany.

Underlying the Oxford Group's teachings was an acute awareness of the human condition, the need to turn to God, and reliance on God for inner peace. The teachings affirm biblical principles, namely, that all human beings are sinners, can be changed, need confession as a prerequisite for that change, have access to God through a changed heart and soul, and can as God's agents positively affect the social order. Some of these teachings found their way into the practices of Alcoholics Anonymous. Today A.A. members meet regularly in recognition of their need for change, give testimony of their struggles and victories, and affirm the principle of surrender in prayer and humility to God, who brings about that change. Members are expected to observe the twelve steps of A.A., or to "work them," which means that participants routinely admit their powerlessness over alcohol, make an inventory of their defects and sins, confess them to another person in confidence, make a resolution of restitution to those they have harmed by their drinking, help other alcoholics without regard for reward or prestige by becoming a "sponsor," and pray to God for the power to practice the steps.

The twelve steps of Alcoholics Anonymous find their parallel in the Rule of Benedict and the Rule's twelve steps of humility, especially the fifth step, confessing one's defects and sins. Like monks, members entrust themselves to God in obedience and powerlessness; they make a "searching and fearless moral inventory" of their sins; they confess to God, themselves, and another person "the exact nature of my wrongs" and are willing to bear the shame and consequences of their actions; they make other members their confessors while conversely acting as confessors for others by listening and helping without the prospect of recognition. Like monks, they are "enclosed" and concealed from public view by protecting one another's confidences and identity.

The original twelve-step program designed by Alcoholics Anonymous and tailored to help with recovery from dependencies and defects other than alcoholism offers Christians the essential benefits of a personal sin inventory and confession in a small group setting. Despite the secular language, the program provides spiritual principles that are rooted in the Christian tradition and its practices. According to Ernest Kurtz, author of the history of Alcoholics Anonymous, one can recognize in the program the spirituality of the church fathers and the desert fathers and mothers, "of the monks Basil and Gregory, of the saints Augustine and Benedict and Francis of Assisi, of mystics such as Julian of Norwich, or reformers as diverse as Calvin and Luther. . . ."[13] Nevertheless, twelve-step programs using Christian language and biblical quotations may appeal to those wishing for a patently Christian approach to matters of dependency and moral defects. Members need not make the mental leap of translating A.A. wording into Christian concepts; it has already been done for them. They stand a better chance of being introduced to spiritual principles and practices they might not have discovered in traditional Bible study and worship. If their own denomination or church tradition does not have sufficient or any provisions for the face-to-face practice, they are given the opportunity to experience the benefits of confession firsthand. Finally, by exercising the varying roles of confessor, penitent, preacher (by sharing one's testimonial), and mentor (or A.A. "sponsor"), members are equipped to serve in other ministry areas of the church. The model of twelve-step recovery in churches provides Christians with the opportunity to engage in the spiritual discipline of self-examination and honesty with oneself, God, and others, and to live out the principle of the priesthood of all believers in the family-like atmosphere of a small group. Given that Alcoholics Anonymous was born at the brink of the postmodern era, which marked people's beginning disillusionment with authority, the church, and technological and scientific progress, its tenets of tolerance, humility, honesty with self, and surrender to God practiced in small groups offer Christians a venue for engaging and proclaiming the Gospel in a postmodern age.

Private Confession and Spiritual Direction

In the Old Testament the communal aspect of sin makes instances of private confession rare. If one person sins, all are affected and bear the responsibility for repentance. On occasion individuals confess to God on behalf of others, to make intercession. Moses prays on his people's behalf on Sinai to make atonement for their sins after they had worshiped a golden calf (Exod 32:31-32); later he asks to receive forgiveness for "our iniquity and our sin" (Exod 34:9). Daniel makes confession on behalf of his people and seeks God's mercy and forgiveness in a lengthy prayer

---

13. Ernest Kurtz and Katherine Ketcham, *The Spirituality of Imperfection: Storytelling and the Search for Meaning* (New York: Bantam, 1992), 6.

of confession and intercession (Dan 9:3-20). Individuals may also make private confession to a priest. The penitent approaches the priest and, without verbally admitting specific sins, offers a sacrifice, the so-called guilt offering. This guilt offering was commonly a male goat. Appearing before the priest and presenting the offering constituted admission of wrongdoing and was a physical enactment of private confession. One had incurred guilt by injuring a neighbor through such actions as fraud, robbery, lying about a lost item one had found, or swearing falsely. In addition to the guilt offering presented to the priest, the offender is also required to make restitution to the neighbor (Lev 6:1-5). While the act of making the offering and providing restitution is relatively private, the community is involved on several levels. First, the community knows of the offender's identity and offense. Second, the community takes full responsibility for the individual's offense, illustrated by the fact that the guilt offering could be presented either by the individual or by the entire community. Third, the community regards the priest as a public servant, whose role is to reconcile an entire people to God. Finally, the community determines whether a guilt offering is appropriate since it applies only to cases of unintentional sin, whereas those acting in explicit defiance and disobedience of the Lord's commandments "shall be utterly cut off and bear the guilt" (Num 15:31).

Another act of private confession involves the so-called sin offering, prompted by causing injury to one's relationship with God. People are to make a sin offering as soon as they have become aware of a particular sin. Such sins included failing to speak up at a trial, touching an unclean thing or human uncleanness, or uttering a rash oath. While the sin was not actually named, the very act of presenting oneself along with the sacrificial animal to the priest constituted a form of private confession. The sin offering was to be a female goat or sheep but, depending on one's financial resources, could also be two turtle doves or choice flour. The priest then accepted the animal or offering by placing it on the altar and burning it. Thereby "the priest shall make atonement on your behalf for whichever of these sins you have committed, and you shall be forgiven" (Lev 5:13).

Besides the ritual observance of bringing a sacrifice to a priest, there was also a verbal pronouncement, resembling an absolution. According to Gerhard von Rad this priestly declarative formula, which he also calls the *placet*, was "his sacerdotal diagnosis" of what kind of offering was required for the sin and whether the offering presented was acceptable to the Lord. Pronouncing the *placet* upon the offering "was without doubt the most important part of the whole procedure," for "only in virtue of the declarative word of the priest did the sacral event become a gracious act of God. . . ."[14] Only the addition of the word of the priest acting as God's representative made the ritual observance a saving event effecting forgiveness of sins for the one presenting the offering. While the prophets warned that the acceptability of these offerings did not depend on the priest's holiness, the greater danger was that they were regarded as a monetary payment for sins rather than as an outward sign of an inward state of repentance.

In the New Testament, Jesus is portrayed as the ultimate sin- and guilt offering. By his death he symbolizes the lamb offered on the altar that reconciles people with God. His sacrifice is acceptable and sufficient to cover the penitent's sin and guilt. He is both mediating priest and sacrificial offering, and believers receive forgiveness of sins by faith in him, by professing him to be the Christ and Lord of their lives. Those who agree to be baptized enter into God's new covenant and become part of the new family of God. Baptism means professing one's faith in Christ and confessing one's sins to God in public. As in the Old Testament, individual sin has the potential of affecting and infecting the entire community of faith. It is the community's responsibility to deal with the trespassing individual, either by exhortation, disciplinary measures, or excommunication. The apostles and overseers of the local church function as representatives of the entire community in teaching, nurturing, and disciplining its members.

Both in the Old and New Testaments spiritual formation is communal, as are spiritual direction and discipline. It occurs through religious catechesis, the liturgical order of worship, and the celebration of the sacraments. Private consultation, confession, and counsel with the overseer of the synagogue or a bishop or overseer of the local congregation carry an invariably communal dimension. For Jews it meant that the entire religious community carried out public discipline and sentencing as determined by the synagogue official. For Christians it was the local church and its baptized members who carried out the discipline ordained by the bishop or overseer. While the bishop ordered enrollment of the lapsed in the penitential order, the entire community participated in the steps of witnessing the exacted discipline, praying for penitents, and helping reconcile them with God and the church. Since the sin of the individual had communal implications, the community had a right to know who the offenders were and their stage in the penitential process. A distinct coarse garb and exclusion from the Eucharist identified penitents and distinguished them from others, and the place they were as-

14. Gerhard von Rad, *Old Testament Theology*, vol. 1, 262.

signed during worship and their proximity to the altar signaled the length of the penitential time that still lay ahead of them. In time the public humiliation connected with this process deterred Christians from making an honest confession. By the fifth century many would postpone baptism and confession of sins until shortly before death. The involvement of the entire community of believers in spiritual formation, guidance, and discipline had become more hindrance than help.

The rite of private confession among Christians was virtually unknown until the sixth century. Introduced by the Irish monks into the Western church, private confession met the need of a church that had become increasingly public. The Irish had adopted the concept from the desert fathers and mothers, who served their pupils as soul friend, trusted spiritual guide, and confidant. Desert monastics functioned as both confessor and spiritual director, hearing confessions and offering spiritual guidance. The confessor was considered a physician of the soul, who not only cauterized the wound caused by sin but gave directions on how to heal and prevent further injuries and falls. The functional relatedness between confession and spiritual guidance was largely preserved by the Irish monks. Their early guidebooks for confessors, or Celtic penitentials, regard private confession between cleric and penitent as a time of dialogue and spiritual conversation among friends. Many of the penitential books' liturgies stress prayerful preparation, empathy, and compassion on the part of the confessor, along with discernment, wisdom, and knowledge of self. Through spiritual conversation and questions asked and answered, the confessor was to discern the soul's illness and assign a penance congruent with the sin committed and the circumstances and maturity level of the penitent. A good confessor mastered the art of listening, of diagnosing the penitent's spiritual ailments, and of prescribing a penitential remedy that would send the sinner off on a path to recovery and spiritual health. Prescribing a remedy was a form of spiritual guidance, which would be offered upon confession. Thus confession was a prerequisite for spiritual guidance, and one did not exist without the other.

By the end of the eleventh century the Roman church had replaced most of the Celtic ideals and practices with its own. Equality between confessor and penitent was replaced by hierarchy and ecclesiastical prerogative. Private confession could only be made to a priest, the rite of confession and penance became a sacrament, and absolution was its lynchpin. Once considered a physician and servant of the people, the priest was now viewed more in the role of ruler and judge. The "verdict," made after investigation and questioning regarding the state of the penitent's soul, consisted in prescribing an appropriate penance and pronouncing an absolution similar to the declarative formula of the priest's *placet* in the Old Testament. As the dialogical relationship between confessor and penitent diminished, so did consideration of confession's healing function. Utility and a fixation on absolution gained prominence. Christians perceived a need for absolution to gain admittance to the Eucharist, if necessary by converting penances to monetary contributions and tariffs; bishops and priests wished to see as many parishioners as possible come for confession for the good of the church and perhaps also for reasons of added income. With the sometimes large numers of Christians in a parish, less time remained for a priest to devote to the individual in conversation and spiritual instruction. Laypeople came to supply the missing elements. Mystics, beguines, and anchorites began functioning as spiritual directors. Their popularity was in part advanced by their writings in the vernacular and they attracted those with a hunger for spiritual formation and guidance. By the thirteenth century friars supported bishops and priests in the roles of confessors and spiritual directors, but Christians could also make confession to a priest while seeking spiritual counsel from another Christian. Increasingly laywomen, accessible and unencumbered by monastic walls, became known for their wise counsel and served as spiritual guides. In time the sacramental confessor in the person of an ordained priest or bishop and the spiritual guide, often a layperson, came to be two different people. This functional division of roles produced an artificial separation between confession and spiritual guidance.

The Protestant and Catholic reformers sought to reunite private confession and spiritual direction. Luther removed the sacramental status of confession, thus opening up the possibility for all believers to exercise the joint office. Any Christian could hear confession from another, pronounce forgiveness and absolution, and offer counsel. Calvin followed suit. Nonetheless, the Protestant reformers emphasized that the person best suited to fill the joint role of confessor and spiritual guide was the pastor, who by virtue of theological training and pastoral experience was better equipped for the task of instructing and guiding souls than the laity. The Catholic reformers, particularly the Jesuits, also sought to reunite the office in their mission and ministry, carrying out both tasks with equal vigor in evangelizing nonbelievers and deepening the faith life of Christians. They offered the Ignatian Exercises, taught the discernment of spirits, and provided spiritual formation in parishes and schools. The founding of schools and colleges, where the sacraments were celebrated in chapel, ensured that young minds were shaped and trained in Christian principles and devotional practices, and new converts were made.

Today the Roman Catholic Church counts private confession, or reconciliation, as one of its seven sacraments. The new rite of penance was commissioned by the Second Vatican Council in 1963 and promulgated in 1973 by Pope Paul VI, replacing the Roman Ritual of four hundred years earlier. One-third of the committee's nine members to draft the new rite were Jesuits, Karl Rahner among them.[15] After three years of work, from 1966 to 1969, the committee submitted its final report, which sought to express more clearly the four major criteria of private confession. The committee affirmed that the nature of sin was an offense against both God and the church; that private confession allowed for a simultaneous reconciliation with God and the church; that the whole church collaborated with the sinner's effort at conversion by charity, example, and prayers; and that the sacrament of penance promoted the Christian life. In addition the committee recommended alternatives to the Roman rite of penance based on historical precedent, Eastern practice, and contemporary pastoral and theological considerations. With the dissolving of the first committee in 1969 a new seven-member committee was appointed in 1972, seating two Jesuits and one Benedictine. In the course of a year the committee made several revisions and produced the final draft of the rite, promulgated in 1973 and simply titled "Rite of Penance."

The new rite of penance could be referred to by various names, such as the sacrament of penance or reconciliation, the sacrament of confession or conversion. The names indicate the diverse functions of the sacrament and its various effects on individuals and the church at large. Among the salient features of the new rite is the recovery of patristic practices. The patristic era had emphasized the communal rather than individual nature of confession, established the connection between conversion and the sacrament of baptism and reconciliation and the Eucharist, and made confession part of the worshiping community's liturgy. Another feature of the new rite is that it incorporates practices of the Eastern church, such as balancing confession and spiritual direction, the juridical and the healing aspects of the sacrament, and the confessor's role as both judge and physician. Some of these Eastern practices, originating with the desert fathers and mothers and found also in the early Celtic penitentials, are still reflected in Eastern Orthodox churches today. There members seek reconciliation with God primarily in the communal rite prior to the

15. Besides Karl Rahner, SJ, of Münster (Germany), the two other Jesuits were Zoltan Alszeghy, SJ, of the Gregorian University (Belgium), and Louis Ligier, SJ, of the Pontifical Oriental Institute (Italy); see James Dallen, *The Reconciling Community: The Rite of Penance* (Collegeville, MN: Liturgical Press, 1986), 210.

eucharistic liturgy; if they go to private confession they do not enumerate all their sins but only those pressing on their conscience most heavily, and the priest simply prays for God's mercy and forgiveness rather than pronouncing absolution and assigning a penance. Thus the confessor acts toward the penitent as a friend, spiritual guide, and companion along the way of reconciliation and forgiveness.

The reintegration of public penitential rites and former and current Eastern practices in the new rite has put the priestly confessor in a challenging position. According to James Dallen the rite "has high expectations of the confessor, requiring much more than ordination and juridical competence. It correlates the two roles of spiritual counselor (supportive confessor or physician) and community official (absolving judge), giving primacy to the confessor's pastoral role and linking the judicial role with discernment of spirits (RP 10a), a charism traditionally associated more with the role of spiritual guide." It also "expands the roles of physician and judge to include leadership in prayer, discernment of spirits, and pastoral dedication, as well as the human warmth of a friend."[16]

Flexibility, prayer, dialogue, and scriptural references mark the new form of the liturgy of confession. In order to create an atmosphere of conversation, the new Rite of Penance allows penitents to receive the sacrament without the provision of a screen, though one is available. Priest and penitent may be seated, rather than sitting and kneeling, respectively. The chairs are arranged for making eye contact. The confessional booth is a separate room with a door, the so-called reconciliation room. And the sacrament can be referred to interchangeably as the sacrament of confession or penance, the sacrament of conversion or reconciliation, indicating its varied functions and effects. The renaming indicates a shift in focus, namely, from the penitent's activity, such as confessing and doing penance, to the activity of God in the heart of the Christian. It also directs attention away from the sin of the individual to sin's ramifications in the community and from ecclesiastical judgment to pastoral and spiritual guidance in mutual dialogue. According to Joseph Martos the new rite is "less individual and more communal, less legalistic and more liturgical, less concerned with enumeration of sins and more concerned with conversion of the heart." In addition it stresses "the idea of reconciliation rather than absolution"; it encourages "the use of scripture in addition to prescribed prayers"; and it allows for "flexibility in each of the forms."[17]

---

16. Dallen, *Reconciling Community*, 308–9.
17. Joseph Martos, *Doors to the Sacred: A Historical Introduction to Sacraments in the Catholic Church* (Liguori, MO: Liguori/Triumph, 2001), 316.

The rite's emphasis on God's activity in the heart of the believer rather than the believer's activity before God is evident also in the interpretation of the sacrament's traditional four parts. As in the medieval church and subsequent Tridentine reforms, the four parts of the sacrament still consist of contrition, confession, the act of penance, and absolution. But now the Rite of Penance[18] insists on God's activity in the life of the Christian prior to and during confession. Those who come to make private confession do so "by the prompting of the Holy Spirit" and they "should above all be wholeheartedly converted to God." Penitents are to be motivated by an "inner conversion [that] embraces sorrow for sin and the intent to lead a new life" (RP 6). Accordingly, "the most important act of the penitent is contrition, which is 'heartfelt sorrow and aversion for the sin committed along with the intention of sinning no more.'" Entering the confessional or reconciliation room means to "approach the kingdom of Christ by *metanoia*," defined as a "profound change of the whole person by which we begin to consider, judge, and arrange our life according to the holiness and love of God, made manifest in his Son in the last days and given to us in abundance" (RP 6a).

To aid Christians in preparing for the sacrament of penance, the new rite includes a form for examination of conscience.[19] The form appropriates Ignatius's method of self-examination during Week One, proposing a series of questions that, if answered honestly, help one assess potential shortcomings and sinful behavior. Adaptable to meet individual and local needs, the form offers Christians a tool for making an inventory of their sins in honest reflection and to aid in attaining to the experience of contrition prior to confession.

The self-examination is roughly divided into two parts, a set of preliminary questions concerning one's attitude toward the sacrament of reconciliation and questions in light of scriptural precepts and Christ's commands. Some preliminary questions are: "What is my attitude to the sacrament of penance? Do I sincerely want to be set free from sin, to turn again to God, to begin a new life, and to enter into a deeper friendship with God? Or do I look on it as a burden, to be undertaken as seldom as possible?" The set of questions placed in a scriptural context is divided into three parts, each preceded by one of Jesus' sayings and commands.

---

18. Rite of Penance, in *The Rites of the Catholic Church: The Roman Ritual Revised by Decree of the Second Vatican Ecumenical Council and Published by Authority of Pope Paul VI*, vol. 1 (Collegeville, MN: Liturgical Press, 1990), 519–629. Abbreviated RP.

19. For the following quotations from this form see Appendix III of the Rite of Penance, as well as Appendix III of this book.

The first part concerns love of God, the second love of neighbor, and the third love of self. Under the Lord's command to "love the Lord your God with your whole heart" the first paragraph of questions is: "Is my heart set on God, so that I really love him above all things and am faithful to his commandments, as a son his father? Or am I more concerned about the things of this world? Have I a right intention in what I do?" Other questions relate to the practices of worship and devotion, such as morning and evening prayers, attendance at Mass, annual confession and communion, and the place of money or superstition in one's life. The second part concerns the love of neighbor and is by far the longest of the three parts. "Have I a genuine love for my neighbors? Or do I use them for my own ends, or do to them what I would not want done to myself? Have I given grave scandal by my words or actions?" Other areas of neighborly relations are one's family, the less fortunate and oppressed, the church's mission, the local community, work ethics, and honest and just relations in dealing with others, including a willingness to make restitution and extend forgiveness. The third part concerns love of and respect for self and the practices of sanctification and perfection, for "Christ our Lord says: 'Be perfect as your Father is perfect.'" Topics include the practice of virtues and spiritual discipline, such as the use of one's time and talents, patience, fasting and abstinence, chastity of the senses and the body, and the purity of one's conscience. The opening set of questions is an invitation to review the direction of one's life along with its ambitions and passions: "Where is my life really leading me? Is the hope of eternal life my inspiration? Have I tried to grow in the life of the Spirit through prayer, reading the word of God and meditating on it, receiving the sacraments, self-denial? Have I been anxious to control my vices, my bad inclinations and passions, e.g., envy, love of food and drink? Have I been proud and boastful, thinking myself better in the sight of God and despising others as less important than myself? Have I imposed my own will on others, without respecting their freedom and rights?" Engaging these questions is meant to help Christians better prepare for confession. It also can make the experience of confession more meaningful and life-changing, for confession will have sprung from a true sense of contrition as the "most important act of the penitent" in the sacrament.

The dynamics of the sacrament of private confession are couched in the language of the desert tradition and the patristic period. Sin causes "wounds" for which the sacrament is a "saving remedy" providing "healing." The sacrament is beneficial in enabling one to confess both "grave" and "venial" sins. After an examination of conscience, penitents "must confess to a priest each and every grave sin that they remember," for by doing so they are able to return "to the life they have lost." Making confession of venial sins is not necessary but "useful," since it constitutes "not a mere ritual repetition or psychological exercise, but a serious striving to perfect the grace of baptism so that, as we bear in our body the death of Jesus Christ, his life may be seen in us ever more clearly" (RP 7).

The rite affirms confession as a ministry of the entire church. While only bishops and priests may administer the sacrament of penance, the whole church, "as a priestly people," carries out the ministry of reconciliation. The church does so by preaching the word of God, making intercession, and helping sinners "to acknowledge and confess their sins and to obtain the mercy of God, who alone can forgive sins" (RP 8). The penitents themselves also play a significant part. By approaching "this saving remedy instituted by Christ," penitents allow that "their own acts become part of the sacrament itself." As they experience and proclaim the mercy of God in their own lives they also "are with the priest celebrating the liturgy of the Church's continual self-renewal" (RP 11).

The liturgy of the rite of private confession is patterned after that of Trent. Called the Rite for Reconciliation of Individual Penitents, it incorporates elements of early medieval penitential liturgies, such as prayers, Scripture readings, and reminders to the priest to show compassion and exercise discernment in counsel. For example, there is an optional reading of the word of God by the priest, either read or recited from memory. Upon reception of the penitent, "the priest welcomes him warmly and greets him with kindness" (RP 41). If needed, the priest "helps the penitent make an integral confession and gives him suitable counsel." The priest urges the penitent "to be sorry for his faults, reminding him that through the sacrament of penance the Christian dies and rises with Christ and is thus renewed in the paschal mystery." Finally, "the priest should make sure that he adapts his counsel to the penitent's circumstances" (RP 44). After confession the penitent expresses sorrow over his or her sins in the form of a prayer; in response, the priest pronounces absolution. The penitent's prayer and the priestly absolution form a unit in the liturgy and show the dialogical nature of the sacrament. Similarly, the formula of absolution does not stand alone, but is preceded by a trinitarian statement and a petition on behalf of the penitent: "God, the Father of mercies, through the death and resurrection of his Son has reconciled the world to himself and sent the Holy Spirit among us for the forgiveness of sins; through the ministry of the Church may God give you pardon and peace, and I absolve you from your sins in the name of the Father, and of the Son, and of the Holy Spirit," to which the penitent says "Amen" (46).

The format of the new rite of confession seeks to promote dialogue between priest and penitent along with the giving and receiving of spiritual direction and counsel, and assurance of God's pardon and absolution. The penitent can choose between protecting his or her anonymity and participating in the rite while kneeling behind a screen, or be seated face-to-face with the priest. The aim of the rite is inner conversion, a returning to God, and the cultivation of holiness. With its elements of self-examination, prayer, Scripture, and dialogue, the liturgy provides a safe, confidential setting in which sins can be acknowledged and freely confessed and the wounds caused by sin dressed for healing. Both priest and penitent share responsibility for facilitating the healing experience, one by skilled listening, coaxing, and guiding; the other by careful preparation and examination of the conscience, prayerful reflection on one's sins and the forgiveness received in Christ, and the living out of that experience of forgiveness in daily life.

Only two of the denominations that are heirs to the Reformation, Lutherans and Anglicans, afford sacramental or near-sacramental status to private confession, calling it a rite and offering private confession to parishioners. Lutherans most often confess their sins (and receive forgiveness) publicly in preparation for Holy Communion, using a Brief Order for Confession and Forgiveness. Nevertheless, private confession is available to those who have a troubled conscience or who wish individual absolution. The *Lutheran Book of Worship* offers a liturgy of Individual Confession and Forgiveness.[20] Whatever the penitent reveals during private confession "is protected from disclosure" and "the pastor is obligated to respect at all times the confidential nature of a confession" (1). After a greeting and as soon as the penitent is kneeling, the pastor asks whether the penitent is ready to make a confession. Then pastor and penitent together say a portion of Psalm 51. The pastor invites the penitent to confess with the following words: "You have come to make confession before God. In Christ you are free to confess before me, a pastor in his Church, the sins of which you are aware and the sins which trouble you." The penitent then confesses those sins of which he or she is aware and that are troubling or disturbing, concluding with the words: "For all this I am sorry and I pray for forgiveness. I want to do better." Depending on the nature of the sins confessed, the pastor may "engage in pastoral conversation, offering admonition and comfort from the Holy Scriptures" or spiritual direction. No penance is assigned; rather, the

---

20. "Individual Confession and Forgiveness" in *Lutheran Book of Worship*, Minister's Desk ed. (Minneapolis: Augsburg Publishing, 1978), 322–23.

penitent's resolve "to do better" constitutes penance. Then both pastor and penitent pray together from a portion of Psalm 51 before absolution is pronounced. Facing the penitent while either standing or remaining seated, the pastor asks: "Do you believe that the word of forgiveness I speak to you comes from God himself?" Then the pastor "lays both hands on the head of the penitent" (6) and pronounces the absolution: "God is merciful and blesses you. By the command of our Lord Jesus Christ, I, a called and ordained servant of the Word, forgive you your sins in the name of the Father, and of the Son, and of the Holy Spirit," to which the penitent responds "Amen." A closing prayer of thanksgiving, based on Psalm 103, may be said by the penitent in silence or together with the pastor. The pastor then sends the penitent off with a blessing and benediction: "Blessed are those whose sins have been forgiven, whose evil deeds have been forgotten. Rejoice in the Lord, and go in peace."

The Lutheran liturgy of private confession is divided into two parts, confession and absolution; contrition and an act of penance are implied. Since private confession is optional, those seeking out the pastor for private confession are assumed to have experienced sorrow (and contrition) over their sins; penance is exercised by sinning no more. Both Scripture and prayers play a significant role in the liturgy. Spiritual guidance and direction given to the penitent following confession is to devolve from the Scripture's providing "admonition and comfort" (4). The pastor's authority to pronounce forgiveness or absolution is derived from his or her ordination to the office, but the penitent should think of the words pronounced as the very words of Christ. This authority or power of the keys is visually affirmed by the pastor's posture during confession: being seated while the penitent is kneeling, and standing over the penitent during the laying on of hands. The *Lutheran Book of Worship* does not specify the place where confession is to occur or require the pastor to wear vestments or a stole.

The rite of private confession in the Episcopal Church incorporates and combines elements of both Lutheran and Roman Catholic practices. Showing a Roman Catholic influence, the *Book of Common Prayer* calls it the rite or "ministry of reconciliation," indicating its communal nature and function. Another Roman Catholic trait is that the rite contains all the traditional four elements of contrition, confession, penance, and absolution. The penitent is to give "evidence of due contrition" and "the priest may assign to the penitent a psalm, prayer, or hymn to be said, or something to be done, as a sign of penitence and act of thanksgiving"; absolution "may be pronounced only by a bishop or priest"; and the sins the penitent is expected to confess are "all serious sins troubling the conscience." Lutheran elements included in the Episcopal Church's rite are the freedom to make confession, the locale, and the occasion. The rite is not an obligation but "available for all who desire it" and as need may arise. And "confessions may be heard anytime and anywhere," either in the church or outside of it.[21]

The Episcopal rite of private confession has several elements in common with the Lutheran and Roman Catholic practices. There is the secrecy of a confession, which is "morally absolute for the confessor, and must under no circumstances be broken"[22]; the order and general outline of the liturgy, which includes prayers and Scripture; and an opportunity for the priest to "offer counsel, direction, and comfort."[23]

Several aspects are unique to the Episcopal rite of private confession. First, the *Book of Common Prayer* offers two forms of The Reconciliation of a Penitent, a shorter and a longer one. The longer version contains additional prayers and Scripture references, and offers two questions addressed to the penitent. The first question, "Will you turn again to Christ as your Lord?" is reminiscent of the early baptismal formula; the second question, "Do you, then, forgive those who have sinned against you?" relates to the Lord's Prayer and mutual reconciliation.[24] Second, two formulas of absolution are offered from which the priest may choose. Third, the liturgy of private confession may be used by a deacon or a layperson rather than the priest or bishop. The only alteration for the use by laity is the omission of a formula of absolution. Instead of saying "by [our Lord Jesus Christ's] authority committed to me, I absolve you from all your sins: In the Name of the Father, and of the Son, and of the Holy Spirit," the layperson simply declares forgiveness. Bound by the same requirement of secrecy, laypersons and deacons may hear private confession; offer counsel, direction, and comfort; and declare to the penitent forgiveness of sins. The layperson or deacon says, "Our Lord Jesus Christ, who offered himself to be sacrificed for us to the Father, forgives your sins by the grace of the Holy Spirit," to which the penitent replies, "Amen."[25]

Since the early 1980s the penitential liturgy of parts of the Anglican Communion has provided laypeople with the opportunity to hear pri-

---

21. "Concerning the Rite" in *The Book of Common Prayer and Administration of the Sacraments and Other Rites and Ceremonies of the Church* (New York: Church Publishing, 1977), 446.

22. Ibid.

23. Ibid., 447.

24. Ibid., 450–51.

25. Ibid., 448; cf. 451–52.

vate confession and offer Christ's words of forgiveness, counsel, and direction. This provision may have significantly contributed to the singular rise and popularity internationally of one aspect of the penitential process, namely, spiritual direction. Since the 1980s, training centers and seminaries in the United States have begun offering students certificates and degrees in spiritual direction. Completion of the requirements does not include ordination to the priesthood or an advanced degree in theology. As a result, spiritual direction programs have been particularly attractive to women, who due to prior family responsibilities may not have had the opportunity for higher theological education or who by virtue of their gender are excluded from priestly ordination. Thus the lay spiritual director complements and enhances the functional office of the priest. Yet much like a priest, the spiritual director serves as confessor, soul friend, and guide, who traditionally has listened, extended forgiveness on behalf of Christ, and offered remedies for the soul.

CHAPTER FIFTEEN

The Decline of Confession in the Church

Several factors have led to the decline of confession in the church. Prominent among them are the availability of secular or clinical "confessors," such as psychotherapists and psychologists, as well as practitioners in the fields of clinical pastoral psychology, pastoral counseling, and social work. Often their roles overlap with those of spiritual directors in seeking to offer patients, clients, and counselees a cure for the soul. At the same time, there are distinctions. The Anglican priest Kenneth Leech may have been among the first to examine the historical significance of spiritual direction in the twentieth century. To him "spiritual direction, or the cure of souls, is a seeking after the leading of the Holy Spirit in a given psychological and spiritual situation," with the spiritual director assisting the directee in the process of seeking and discernment.[1] In comparing the roles of the spiritual director and the psychotherapist, and the spiritual director and the pastoral counselor, Leech points out the following: First, both psychotherapist and pastoral counselor tend to focus on crisis moments in a person's life, resulting in states of emotional distress that focus on problems and problem solving. Thus they are primarily concerned with the immediacy of the sickness rather than the ongoing maintenance of health. This has led to the dictum that sinners, or those in a state of maladjustment and disintegration, stand in need of counseling, while saints, or those whose spiritual health appears to be relatively stable, are in need of spiritual direction or confession. Second, psychotherapy and pastoral counseling have tended to become specialized, hence detached from the moral and spiritual framework of

---

1. Kenneth Leech, *Soul Friend: The Practice of Christian Spirituality* (San Francisco: Harper & Row, 1977), 34.

ethical principles, the Jewish and Christian traditions, or the church. "Spiritual direction, on the other hand," says Leech, "is firmly located within the liturgical and sacramental framework, within the common life of the Body of Christ," or should be. Third, psychotherapy and counseling have tended to focus prominently on a person's individual problems of adjustment and adaptation to society. Thereby "social adjustment is frequently seen as an objective, while issues of social criticism are ignored." Spiritual direction, on the other hand, places personal problems in the context of spiritual principles and a discernment of God's activity in a person's life without making adjustment to society the sole venue for solving the effects of personal crisis moments such as discontent, emotional upheaval, and lack of inner peace.

Making a clear distinction between the psychological models of psychotherapy and confession is difficult. Psychoanalysis, psychotherapy, and counseling all incorporate elements of confession and aspects of remorse or contrition in their approaches. In fact, confession is considered essential to treating the troubled soul. According to Carl Gustav Jung, one of the founders of modern psychotherapy and psychiatry, "The first beginnings of all analytical treatment are to be found in its prototype, the confessional." Even though no "causal connection" may exist, there is a close relationship "between the groundwork of psychoanalysis and the religious institution of the confessional."[2] What the church may call concealing one's sin, the psychoanalyst calls "repression." According to Jung such repression involves the maintaining of secrets, and it "acts like a psychic poison which alienates their possessor from the community." Secrets function differently in groups and individuals. Sharing secrets with several persons, for example, can create a sense of "differentiation of the individual" and prevents one from "dissolving in the unconsciousness of mere community life." The secret rituals of the Christian sacraments of the early church give evidence of the constructive power of shared secrets. On the other hand, "a merely private secret has a destructive effect" and "resembles a burden of guilt which cuts off the unfortunate possessor from communion with his fellow-beings."[3] For Jung the higher the degree of awareness of these secrets and concealments, the less harm they can cause. For when one is unaware of one's concealment, what is repressed is allowed to split off "from consciousness as an independent complex, to lead a separate existence in the

2. Carl Gustav Jung, *Modern Man in Search of a Soul*, trans. W. S. Dell and Cary F. Baynes (New York: Harcourt Brace Jovanovich, 1933), 31.
    3. Ibid.

unconscious, where it can be neither corrected nor interfered with by the conscious mind."[4] This means that "an unconscious secret is more harmful than one that is conscious," and "every personal secret has the effect of a sin or of guilt,"[5] regardless of how the larger society may judge it. The illness of the soul is manifested in what psychotherapy and psychiatry call a neurosis. Healing the psyche, or soul, involves the revealing and confessing of personal secrets or at least bringing their repressed existence to the client's or patient's awareness, thereby dissolving their harmful effects.

In building on Jung's findings, the psychiatrist William Glasser advanced the idea that healing the psyche involves encouraging patients to take responsibility for their wrongdoing by facing "reality." Glasser calls his approach "reality therapy," which insists on a close scrutiny of the person's behavior not as a victim of circumstance or heredity but as a person with moral responsibilities. Glasser's approach is marked by the "three R's" of responsibility, reality, and right and wrong: one faces reality, rejects irresponsible behavior, and learns better ways to behave. In this approach an implicit confession is made when one acknowledges wrongdoing and accepts responsibility for the action.

By contrast, explicit confession as part of therapy is suggested by psychiatrist O. Hobart Mowrer. A former follower of Sigmund Freud, Mowrer had been in psychotherapy for several years and been repeatedly treated for depression. His personal struggles led him to conclude that psychoanalysis, with its emphasis on removing guilt, was wrong. Instead, guilt could fulfill a necessary function in bringing about the healing of the psyche: it could serve as a reminder of past misdeeds and prompt one to make them known. When shortcomings were concealed they would continue to give rise to discomfort, uneasiness, and depression. When they were divulged to significant people in one's life they lost their effect and the discomfort disappeared. Guilt then was not an enemy but a friendly, motivating force that could induce confession. Mowrer calls his therapeutic approach "integrity therapy," a way of integrating and enlisting one's feelings of guilt in a way that prompted one to admit wrongdoing, take responsibility for past actions, and adjust one's behavior to reduce the frequency of further guilt-inducing actions. A key practice in integrity therapy is confession to the therapist and in a small group. The psychologist and pastoral counselor John W. Drake-

4. Ibid., 31–32.
5. Ibid., 33.

ford[6] has identified the distinguishing marks of such a confession: It is not complaining or blaming other people for problems; it avoids boasting of one's virtues and focuses on one's weaknesses, instead; it is for one's own benefit, rather than that of others; it is not indiscriminate but made only to "significant others," who keep confidentiality; and it shows a willingness to come under others' judgment.

Distinguishing between pathological and beneficial guilt is the province of both the therapist and the pastor. But establishing the distinction is fraught with difficulties. All too often pastors have misjudged their parishioners' guilt by suspecting psychological illness and referring them to a psychotherapist. By doing so they miss the opportunity for spiritual guidance at a crucial juncture in a person's life. Leech suggests patience and discernment. Pastors will need to recognize that all Christian experience involves a cycle of death and rebirth, "alien mental contents which are being ejected in the course of sanctification,"[7] and distinct movements of the Holy Spirit that may appear troubling and disconcerting at first sight. Another difficulty is the definition of the concept of "guilt." A common misconception has been to distinguish between guilt and sin. The use of the term "guilt" has been viewed as value neutral and fit for the clinical setting, while sin, with its implication of belief in a divine presence and the divine-human relationship, has been reserved for pastoral counselors and pastors. Prominent among those calling the linguistic distinction into question has been the psychiatrist Karl Menninger. In his book *Whatever Became of Sin?* Menninger argues for a return to the concept of sin in clinical psychotherapy. In observing the symptoms of sin in his patients, Menninger calls it a behavior that is characterized by a defiant withdrawal from relationships and community, supererogation, and a preoccupation with self. Menninger also offers a study of the seven deadly sins as a guide for self-examination and diagnosis of sin in the patient's life. Sin, he says, is "at heart a refusal of the love of others."[8] Mowrer, on the other hand, uses the terms guilt and sin interchangeably and infuses his therapeutic approach with theological terminology. "As long as a person lives under the shadow of real, unacknowledged and unexpiated guilt, he . . . will continue to hate himself and to suffer the inevitable consequences of self-hatred. But the moment he . . . begins to accept his guilt and his sinfulness, the possibility of radical reformation opens up,

6. See John W. Drakeford, *Integrity Therapy* (Nashville: Broadman Press, 1967), 100.
7. Leech, *Soul Friend* (1977), 120.
8. Karl A. Menninger, *Whatever Became of Sin?* (New York: Hawthorn Books, 1973), 19.

and a new freedom of self-respect and peace."[9] The appropriation of the concept of sin by psychotherapy, along with the elements of confessional practice in clinical analysis and treatment, seemingly diminish the need for people to seek out a pastoral confessor or priest.

Why do Christians prefer to see a clinical psychologist rather than their pastor when experiencing problems of the soul or psyche? Considerations may be related to the differing perceptions one has of these two professional groups. First, there is the value one generally attributes to a service for which one pays. Services rendered by a psychologist, psychiatrist, or professional counselor, to whom one pays a (significant) hourly fee, might be valued more highly than those offered by a pastor or priest who is expected to render these services for free. From the health-care profession people know that health comes at a price; and it is assumed that the higher the cost, the more valuable the service. In the case of pastors, such a service "fee" is hidden. Parishioners who make regular financial contributions to the parish and its programs may not be consciously aware that they are also paying for the priest's or pastor's salary, along with his or her counsel and spiritual guidance. Second, patients and clients who seek the services of a health-care professional or psychotherapist understand from the outset that payment is involved, and the more they pay, the more they may value what is received. Finally, payment for services implies that certain professional ethical guidelines are kept, especially the obligation to confidentiality. The client has enlisted and "hired" the professional, who, in turn, is obligated to abide by professional standards, including the secrecy of what has been discussed. People may not be so certain about the professional obligation of a priest or pastor to keep the conversation confidential. By and large, Catholics know their priests to be bound by the seal of confession by virtue of the ordination vows and the sacrament of holy orders; Protestants, with their denominational variants and differing standards of ordination, may be uncertain of the degree of confidentiality the pastor will exercise. This uncertainty may have contributed to Protestants' preference for "confessing" to a certified professional in the fields of medicine, psychotherapy, or social work, rather than to their own pastor.

The roots of the decline of confession in the Roman Catholic Church are of a somewhat different nature than those in Protestantism. Certainly parishioners need not fear that their confidences be divulged. Priests face grim penalties for breaking the confessional seal, ranging from

---

9. O. Hobart Mowrer, *The Crisis in Psychiatry and Religion* (Princeton, NJ: Van Nostrand, 1961), 54–57; quoted in Leech, *Soul Friend* (1977), 119.

temporary censure by the bishop to excommunication and discharge from priestly office on papal authority. While the clinical and medical professions may have drawn Catholics away from the confessional to the therapist's couch or the chair across from the psychotherapist, concerned observers have looked also at internal changes in the Roman Catholic Church. Only a few decades ago confessionals in the United States were full during the penitential seasons of Lent and Advent. Today's picture is quite different: they remain, for the most part, empty. According to a 2005 survey by the Center for Applied Research in the Apostolate, 42 percent of Catholic adults "never" went to confession and 32 percent of Catholics said they confessed their sins to a priest "less than once a year." Only 12 percent of Catholics went to confession more than once a year. By 2008 these figures were respectively "never," 45 percent; "less than once a year," 30 percent; and "once a year," 12 percent, with "once a month or more" remaining steady at 2 percent.[10]

Several internal reasons have been identified as leading to the decline of confession among Catholics, and their convergence has produced a cumulative effect. First, Catholics are less inclined to view themselves as sinners who stand in need of forgiveness and absolution pronounced on Christ's behalf by a priest than they were prior to Vatican II. In a mere thirty years there has been a marked shift among members from formerly being obsessed with sin and the proverbial Catholic guilt to being almost oblivious to, or "liberated from" it. This has made church officials pay closer attention to the place of catechetical instruction of children and adults and the seminary training of priests. Second, the changes of Vatican II, with its communal emphasis, have allowed priests to focus increasingly on social sins such as racism, sexism, the arms race, and economic and ecological ills; this refocusing has caused a shift away from the individual to society at large and social and political structures. In addition, the introduction of the three-year cycle of the lectionary with its stories of Jesus demonstrating forgiveness and portraying a God of grace may have relativized members' sense of sin in their own lives. Also, the ecumenical stance of the Vatican Council may have produced the impression that if members of other denominations are not expected to go to confession, Catholics should not be expected to do so. A third reason for decreasing lines at the confessional is often traced to the time when the Catholic Church lost credibility with many of its members in defining sexual sin. The 1968 publication of the papal encyclical *Humanae*

---

10. Mark M. Gray and Paul M. Perl, *Sacraments Today: Belief and Practice Among U. S. Catholics* (Georgetown, DC: Center for Applied Research in the Apostolate, 2008), 57.

Vitae, declaring as sinful the use of contraceptives by married couples, weakened the church's credibility on matters of sexual morality in general. Joseph Martos explains the process this way: "Women who began using the pill for reasons they considered legitimate felt obliged to discuss it in confession, but many confessors believed there was nothing to discuss: if women wanted to be forgiven they would have to renounce their sin." Given the global population explosion, many Catholics viewed birth control as a virtue rather than a vice, leading Catholics to stop mentioning birth control in the confessional, so that "the image of the priest as the final arbiter in moral matters began to be discarded."[11] An associate editor of *America*, James Martin, SJ, puts it similarly: "Catholics began to doubt not only the need to confess sexual sins but also the moral authority of the church, whose representatives would absolve them from these sins."[12] Uncertainty among priests in matters of sexual morality heightened the debate, leaving laypeople wondering what to confess, with many of them deciding to judge their own moral actions for themselves rather than according to the church's moral precepts. These reasons, along with increasingly busier lives of American families, with both spouses working and children engaged in numerous activities, have decreased the chances that Saturday afternoon can be reserved for going to confession with the entire family.

Apart from the counselor's office, the confessional or pastor's study has received competition from the meeting room of the spiritual director. The role of the spiritual director is to assist another in attending to God's presence and call. While this practice has continued from its ancient roots in Eastern and Celtic expressions to modern monastic communities and the Roman Catholic Church, Anglican and Protestant churches have begun to recover it more fully only in the past twenty years. Formerly a part of the rite or sacrament of confession and administered by ordained clergy, today's spiritual direction is offered outside the confessional by laypeople and those who evidence spiritual maturity in the Christian faith. But spiritual direction is not limited to the churches and is being offered in other faith traditions also. Current issues discussed among spiritual directors are the place of spiritual direction from a non-Christian perspective within the church, group spiritual direction, certification, and remuneration for services rendered. The popularity of enlisting a

---

11. Joseph Martos, *Doors to the Sacred: A Historical Introduction to Sacraments in the Catholic Church* (Liguori, MO: Liguori/Triumph, 2001), 317.

12. James Martin, SJ, "Bless Me, Father," *America* (May 21, 2007), at http://www.americamagazine.org/content/article.cfm?article_id=5483.

spiritual director for personal spiritual growth and spiritual companionship is growing among Christians and non-Christians alike. This popularity is reflected in the trend among mainline denominational seminaries to offer degrees or certificates in spiritual direction for the laity, which has opened the door for a lively debate on the place, function, and need of spiritual direction within the life of the church. To what degree does the spiritual director complement, to what degree compete with the pastoral office and the responsibilities of individual members to one another in regard to spiritual formation and Christian education?

The professional organization Spiritual Directors International addresses emerging issues surrounding the role and function of spiritual direction and offers resources for support of its members. Founded in 1989 in a gathering of spiritual directors of Christian faith at Mercy Center in Burlingame, California, Spiritual Directors International (SDI) today includes people from many faiths and traditions. Designed as a network for those "who share a common concern, passion and commitment to the art and contemplative practice of spiritual direction," SDI seeks "to foster the transformation of individuals, organizations and societies in light of the holy" by providing a forum for the "exchange of perspectives, contemplative practices and patterns of expansive thinking."[13] The idea of such a network was developed by Mary Ann Scofield, RSM, who had been on the board of the West Coast branch of the National Federation of Spiritual Directors, an association of those working in Roman Catholic seminaries. In an effort to strengthen ecumenicity, the initial steering committee included three Roman Catholics (Mary Ann Scofield, Lucy Abbott Tucker, and Janet Ruffing), a Methodist psychiatrist (Gerald May), and an Episcopal priest (Donald Schell). What began with four hundred applications for membership in the newly formed international association of spiritual directors in 1990 had grown to 4,650 members in the United States and sixty-five other countries on five continents in 2002.[14] SDI offers numerous resources for seasoned and aspiring spiritual directors from various Christian denominations as well as for members of other faiths.

The growing interest in spiritual direction worldwide has had consequences for other helping professions. Parishioners may prefer to see a spiritual director rather than their pastor for spiritual counsel and dia-

---

13. "Purpose and History of Spiritual Directors International" at http://www.sdiworld.org/index.pl/purpose_and_history.html.
14. "A Brief History of Spiritual Directors International, Part I" at http://www.sdiworld.org/index.pl/purpose_and_history.html.

logue; they might think their pastor too busy and occupied with other functions of church life, insufficiently equipped in matters of spiritual discernment, or unavailable for other reasons. The fact that a spiritual director can be a layperson might enhance the sense of mutuality and dialogue between director and directee. And the rationale for seeking a spiritual director is generally less associated with a psychological crisis and distress, and hence has positive, rather than negative overtones. Going to see a spiritual director may be more appealing and less threatening than visiting the sacramental confessor or pastor. Another profession affected by the emerging popularity of spiritual direction is that of the counselor and psychotherapist. Clinical psychologist Larry Crabb believes that clinical therapy and pastoral counseling should be oriented along the lines of spiritual direction, if not by it entirely. Since pastoral care models have tended to imitate secular models, the antidote is to enlist ancient Christian disciplines, including prayer, silence, solitude, and discernment of spirits, in the hope of restoring their uniquely Christian vantage point. Spiritual direction is superior to psychotherapy, says Crabb, because at the heart of a psychological problem lies a spiritual problem that only spiritual direction can address.

Among the first to address the growing popularity of spiritual direction with Protestants and Roman Catholics in the twentieth century were the Jesuits William Barry and William Connolly. In their classic *The Practice of Spiritual Direction*, published in 1982, the authors define the purpose: spiritual direction "proposes to help people relate personally to God, to let God relate personally to them, and to enable them to live the consequences of that relationship."[15] The spiritual director aims at helping the directee discern the movement of the Holy Spirit and to act on that discernment. The focus is on intimacy with God, not on solving clinically identified psychological problems; on the whole sinful orientation of the self, not any particular dysfunction; on the ways in which one has pushed God aside by substituting other resources for God and thereby recognizing and recovering the right path with the Spirit's guidance. The director's role is one of companioning, rather than dictating; of being a "soul friend" or *anamchara*, as in the Celtic ideal, rather than of acting as a detached clinical observer, though the nurture tends to flow mostly one way. Barry and Connolly propose that spiritual direction be considered the core of all forms of pastoral ministry. All forms of pastoral care and counseling are aimed "at helping people to center their

---

15. William A. Barry, SJ, and William J. Connolly, SJ, *The Practice of Spiritual Direction* (San Francisco: Harper & Row, 1982), 136.

lives in the mystery we call God,"[16] but spiritual direction does so with an intense focus. Therefore "it is startling . . . that help directly aimed at the personal worship of God in spirit and in truth should ever have been regarded as only one of many pastoral concerns, and a somewhat esoteric concern at that."[17] It is precisely through spiritual direction that people are helped "to recognize and focus their lives as response to God's loving, creative, and saving action." Unless Christians have had the experience of such a reorientation and focusing they will continue to treat interior movements as if they were "objective data" that could be read like "an almanac list of historical events."[18] By contrast to counseling and psychotherapy, spiritual direction is engaged in a triadic relationship. Both director and directee seek to discern the movement and "direction" of God in the directee's life. The relationship between the directee and the director can be instrumental "for the development of the relationship of the directee and God," but the latter relationship exists prior to and is independent of the former.[19]

Catholics and Protestants have different responses to the rising popularity of spiritual direction and its availability to the laity. Since the time of Ignatius of Loyola and the ministry of the Jesuits, Catholics have become familiar with the practice. In increasing numbers, however, they have exchanged their priestly confessor for a lay spiritual director. Protestants, on the other hand, have emphasized the direct, unmediated nature of the Christian's relationship with God in Christ, thus tending to be suspicious of the function of any individual serving in a spiritually mediating role. Now, however, their suspicion is offset by a growing dissatisfaction with the standard means of spiritual growth, such as moral attentiveness, church attendance, and involvement in a series of church activities and programs. The perceived need for a person to whom one can entrust personal spiritual struggles and who allows for discerning the movement of the Spirit is felt more acutely among church members whose tradition makes no other explicit provision for an ongoing intimate spiritual exchange. Apart from the therapist, the spiritual director is the most likely person to help Protestants experience the dynamics of confession and spiritual guidance.

More recently, clinical counselors and psychotherapists have attested to a thirst for spiritual direction among their clients. According to

16. Ibid., 11.
17. Ibid., 44.
18. Ibid.
19. Ibid., 31.

psychiatrist Len Sperry, "recent research and clinical experience suggest that clients are increasingly expecting that psychotherapists will deal with their spiritual concerns that are traditionally addressed in spiritual direction. This expectation has already begun to impact the practice of psychotherapy by increasing interest in the 'spiritually-oriented-psychotherapies.'"[20] Increasingly, people are experiencing a "spiritual homelessness," an experience of no longer feeling at home in one's own religious tradition or unease with and disconnectedness from church staff and professionals in ministry. Many are turning to psychotherapists rather than ministers for spiritual advice, expecting therapists to focus on spiritual concerns in addition to, or rather than, the traditional crisis management of symptom relief, problem resolution, and restoration of one's psychological health. In anticipation of this demand, Sperry advocates an approach to psychotherapy that incorporates at least two outcomes traditionally attributed to spiritual direction: spiritual assessment and advisement. In Sperry's view, "even a brief spiritual assessment can reveal the client's current spiritual practices, image of God, and past and present religious and spiritual concerns. Based on this assessment the therapist, in collaboration with the client, can choose to focus therapeutically on an issue that has spiritual meaning, refer the client to a minister or other spiritual guide, or consider a spiritual practice."[21] Another element to be incorporated in therapy is advisement, where "the therapist might prescribe, monitor, and offer advice and feedback" on certain spiritual practices. Such practices might include meditation, fasting, reading sacred writings, healing prayer, forgiveness, moral instruction, and service, and can be "utilized as an intervention within a treatment session or prescribed as an intersession activity" in an effort at "cognitive restructuring and guided imagery strategies."[22] While health-care professionals recognize the importance of tending to the spiritual dimension of the person, the traditional education and training of those in the health-care field has not been adequate in this regard. Moreover, there are clear distinctions between the two approaches. According to Siang-Yang Tan, faculty member of the school of psychology at Fuller Seminary, psychotherapy should keep in mind its goals of ame-

---

20. Len Sperry, "Integrating Spiritual Direction Functions in the Practice of Psychotherapy," *Journal of Psychology and Theology* (March 22, 2003), at http://www.thefreelibrary.com/Integrating+spiritual+direction+functions+in+the+practice+of...-a0100230873.
21. Ibid.
22. Ibid.

liorating symptoms of psychological distress rather than seeking to replace therapy with spiritual direction. Only "when the goals of psychotherapy per se are achieved," he says, and when only spiritual direction is desired, should psychotherapy be terminated.[23] Tan also cautions against transgressing ethical boundaries, such as displacing or usurping religious authority, violating the work setting and insurance guidelines regarding the separation of church and state, and overstepping one's professional competence.

The blending of psychotherapy with spiritual direction and confession is not only a trend taking place in the clinical setting. It is also part of people's perception of their own life experiences, where the areas of the secular and the sacred blend or become interchangeable, as do the means of mental and spiritual health, such as in confession and spiritual direction. Catholics in particular may feel that the psychologist or the spiritual director meets the same needs the confessor once did. Protestants, who generally have no conception of what a confessor is, tend to view the role of the spiritual director through the lens of that of counselor or psychotherapist, a role, in short, with which they are most likely familiar. Either way, both Catholics and Protestants lose the element of sacramental confession and its sacerdotal and liturgical dimension; they either replace the confessor with a therapist or spiritual director or they view the spiritual director as a therapist with a Christian focus. This blending occurs especially as psychoanalysis integrates spiritual direction in its therapeutic approaches, pushing sacramental and liturgical rites of healing, such as confession, even farther to the sidelines. The increasing secularization and marginalization of the church in the postmodern and post-Christendom eras contribute to making psychotherapy the prime locus and most accessible venue in people's search for spiritual healing and wholeness. Given that there are currently about half a million psychotherapists in the United States, including psychologists, social workers, psychiatrists, marital and family therapists, and mental health counselors, the number of spiritual directors comprises only a fraction of that, perhaps slightly more than one percent. If even a small percentage of these psychotherapists were to practice a form of spiritually sensitive psychotherapy they would far exceed the number of available spiritual directors. In addition, clients can expect that these psychotherapists have more

23. Siang-Yang Tan, "Integrating Spiritual Direction into Psychotherapy," *Journal of Psychology and Theology* (March 22, 2003), at http://www.thefreelibrary.com/Integrating+spiritual+direction+into+psychotherapy%3a+ethical+issues...-a0100230874.

specialized training in dealing with complex psychological issues involving spiritual aspects than most spiritual directors do.

We conclude, then, that declining numbers in the church's confessionals are the result of a complex web of issues. Among the leading causes for the decline are the rise of psychotherapy and spiritual direction, which have rivaled or supplanted the function of the minister as primary confessor and dialogue partner in matters of spiritual guidance and direction. The integration of spiritual direction into psychotherapy is likely to cast the therapist even more in the functional role of confessor, while the sacramental and sacerdotal side of confession and the pronouncement of forgiveness with subsequent penance receives short shrift or is virtually nonexistent. For Protestants the emergence of spiritual direction as a venue for one-to-one dialogue in matters of the spirit is a welcome step toward what might approximate the hitherto unfamiliar setting of and experience associated with the confessional process. This is especially true for members of church traditions without private confession, such as the Presbyterian and Reformed churches. However, neither spiritual director nor psychotherapist can sufficiently substitute for the sacramental and sacerdotal elements inherent in the church's rite of confession and the traditional role of confessor. What is needed more among parishioners, pastors, and Christian psychotherapists is a theological understanding of confession rather than the mere conviction of confession's positive functional outcome; a concrete venue for placing oneself in the way of Christ and his forgiveness at a cost, rather than the aim of evading or circumventing Christ and sustaining a personal level of comfort; a nudge to reveal one's ugly and sin-tainted self and to overcome personal pride in the company of another, rather than premature assurances of personal wholeness; and a glimpse of interconnectedness within the body of Christ, the church rather than a focus on sin's individuality and the exceptionality of the person's spiritual experiences. In order to highlight such an understanding of confession we turn next to a brief theological exploration of the inner dynamics of confession by some leading Christian theologians and thinkers of the twentieth century.

CHAPTER SIXTEEN

A Contemporary Theology of Confession

Rahner, Bonhoeffer, Peterson, von Speyr

The selection of representative twentieth-century Christian thinkers who have explored the dynamics of confession, and particularly private confession, in the Christian tradition is aimed at highlighting distinct theological approaches. Guiding considerations in regard to selection have been twofold: first, to allow for theological voices of both Protestant and Catholic thinkers, as well as clergy and laity; second, to offer theological approaches that are sufficiently different from one another to invite further reflection on the meaning and practices of sacramental and liturgical confession and its possibilities for the church of the twenty-first century. The theologians discussed are Karl Rahner, a Jesuit priest; Dietrich Bonhoeffer, a Lutheran pastor; Eugene Peterson, a Presbyterian pastor; and Adrienne von Speyr, a Roman Catholic layperson, physician, mystic, and the spiritual directee of the Jesuit priest Hans Urs von Balthasar.

Karl Rahner, SJ (1904–1984)

Born on March 5, 1904, in Freiburg im Breisgau, Germany, as the fourth of seven children, Karl Rahner grew up in a traditional Catholic family. His father was a teacher and later professor of German, French, and history at the teachers' college in Freiburg. Following in the footsteps of his brother Hugo four years earlier, Rahner joined the Jesuits at age eighteen and was ordained a Roman Catholic priest in 1932. Interested in mystical theology, he devoted considerable time to the study of prayer, the history of penance, and historical theology, particularly in regard to the sacraments. The blending of mystical and experiential theology with the study of philosophy and the history of doctrine would significantly influence his thought and would remain a lifelong thread in his writings.

After doctoral studies in philosophy at Freiburg, where one of his teachers was Martin Heidegger and where he submitted a dissertation in philosophy, Rahner completed his doctoral degree in theology at the University of Innsbruck in 1936 and began teaching there the following year. When in 1938 and 1939 the faculty and the Jesuit seminary, respectively, were closed by the Nazis, Rahner was forced into exile, first moving to Vienna, where he taught on a freelance basis, then in 1944 to Bavaria, where he served as a parish priest until 1945. Following a three-year stint at the Jesuit philosophy faculty in Pullach, near Munich, he returned to Innsbruck in 1948, where he remained as a professor of theology until 1964.

In 1959 Rahner was invited by Cardinal König of Vienna to be his personal advisor when he was called by Pope John XXIII to be part of a preparatory commission for the Second Vatican Council. In 1961 Rahner was made a consultant to the Congregation for the Discipline of the Sacraments by Pope John XXIII (though never invited to any of its meetings), and in 1962 became one of the theological advisors, or *periti*, for the Second Vatican Council, which took place between 1962 and 1965. It was largely due to Rahner's work on the council's theological commission, which dealt with church and sacraments and the role of the laity in the groundbreaking conciliar documents *Lumen Gentium* and *Gaudium et Spes*, along with his subsequent writings that sought to interpret and explain the changes the council called for, that he gained worldwide fame. Particularly the idea of the church as sacrament for the salvation of all yet ever standing in need of repentance and renewal, advanced in *Lumen Gentium*, has been referred to as bearing Karl Rahner's "trademark image"[1] and stamp. "He became a symbol, a point of reference for a convulsive institutional change in an institution that had thought it could not change," says Philip Endean, SJ, in his introduction to Rahner's selected spiritual writings. As a "kind of intellectual icon for the forces of change in Roman Catholicism"[2] Rahner was greatly admired by many and even idolized. After teaching at the universities of Munich (1964–1967) and Münster (1967–1971), Rahner retired and lived in Munich for ten years, continuing to write and giving lectures in Europe and the United States. He returned to Innsbruck in 1981, where he previously had experienced the "most work intense" and "possibly most

---

1. See Richard Lennan, *The Ecclesiology of Karl Rahner* (Oxford: Oxford University Press, 1995), 18.
2. Philip Endean, SJ, "Introduction," in *Karl Rahner: Spiritual Writings*, ed. Philip Endean (Maryknoll, NY: Orbis Books, 2004), 12.

fruitful"[3] period of his life, with nine honorary doctorates from U.S. universities alone received between the years 1966 (Notre Dame) and 1980 (Fordham). In 1984, fewer than four weeks after his eightieth birthday, Rahner died in Innsbruck, where his body is buried, with those of many other Jesuits, in the crypt of the Jesuit University Church.

The scope of Rahner's writing is immense, comprising a bibliography in German alone of more than sixteen hundred entries. It includes the sixteen volumes (twenty-three in English) of his *Theological Investigations* (*Schriften zur Theologie*), several books on prayer and the sacraments, collections of sermons, letters to young people, a book on Ignatian spirituality and the Exercises, a treatise on confession, and his *Grundkurs des Glaubens*, translated into English as *Foundations of Christian Faith: An Introduction to the Idea of Christianity*; this last comes closest to a systematic theology. It was written or dictated at the forceful insistence of the publisher Herder and is based on courses Rahner taught at Munich and Münster. Most of his writings are shorter essays addressing a particular situation, issue, or question in the life of the church, doctrinal matters, or specific aspects of the Christian faith. In addition, Rahner edited or co-edited the thirteen-volume *Lexikon für Theologie und Kirche* (1957–1968); the Herder series *Quaestiones Disputatae* (1958–1984), containing 101 volumes at the time of his death; the five-volume *Handbuch der Pastoraltheologie* (1964–1969); the four-volume commentary on sacramental theology *Sacramentum Mundi* (1967–1969); and the thirty-volume encyclopedia *Christian Faith in Modern Society* (1980–1983). He also coauthored with Herbert Vorgrimler, one of Rahner's first doctoral students, the popular *Dictionary of Theology* (1961) and a commentated collection of the conciliar documents of Vatican II, called *Kleines Konzilskompendium* (1971). The distinctive traits of his theological thought and writings are well outlined by former student and fellow Jesuit Harvey Egan, who calls Rahner an Ignatian theologian, a mystic, a teacher of prayer, a preacher of the Gospel, a follower of Jesus Christ, a teacher of church and sacraments, and a guide to the Christian life and the last things.[4] At an early age Rahner read the *Imitation of Christ* by Thomas à Kempis and was inspired particularly by its fourth chapter, a meditation on the Eucharist. He also translated hymns by Thomas Aquinas from Latin into German. His early theological studies at the Jesuit theologate in Valkenburg, Holland, from 1929 to 1933, sparked

3. Karl Lehmann, "Karl Rahners Bedeutung für die Kirche," *Stimmen der Zeit*, special Rahner edition 1 (2004), 7.

4. See Harvey D. Egan, SJ, *Karl Rahner: Mystic of Everyday Life* (New York: Crossroad, 1998), esp. 19–27.

his interest in "theological questions, above all in spiritual theology, in the history of piety, in patristic mysticism, and also in Bonaventure."[5] This interest is reflected in his first significant publications, dealing with Origen's and Bonaventure's notions of the spiritual senses (1932–1934) and his 1939 book *Aszese und Mystik in der Väterzeit* (*Asceticism and Mysticism in the Patristic Era*), a translation of a 1930 French book by fellow Jesuit Marcel Viller on the mysticism of the first six hundred years of Christian thought and practice with emendations and elaborate bibliographical references by Rahner, making it nearly double in size of its French original. He also collaborated with his brother Hugo, professor of church history and patristics and later dean of the theological faculty and president of the University of Innsbruck (1949–1950), on a collection of prayers, patristic studies, and the spirituality of Ignatius of Loyola. It was especially Ignatius who would, in Egan's words, "indelibly [stamp] Rahner's theology of grace, repentance, prayer, discernment of spirits, and existential ethics."[6]

Central to Rahner's thought on confession is his understanding of the sacraments as a whole. In his 1974 book *Die siebenfältige Gabe* (*The Sevenfold Gift*), which was translated into English in 1977 as *Meditations on the Sacraments*, Rahner explores the nature of the church and its sacraments. To him, Jesus Christ is the primordial sacrament (*Ursakrament*), while the church is the basic sacrament (*Grundsakrament*) and the visible and sociohistorical continuation of the Christ event. The church, as the basic sacrament and sign that perpetuates Christ's presence in the world, administers the seven particular sacraments or "performs" these sacred signs to effect and enhance the Christian's salvation. The traditional understanding of sacrament is that it functions as an isolated event that happens to the believer. Through the single action of the sacrament, "God reaches into space and time to confer grace under signs instituted by Christ." Rahner suggests a new understanding of sacrament that "contrasts with the traditional understanding while remaining entirely within the bounds of orthodoxy."[7] The key to his new concept of sacrament is grace. For Rahner, grace does not happen only in isolated instances, such as when the sacraments are administered or during so-called graced

5. Karl Rahner, *Faith in a Wintry Season: Interviews and Conversations with Karl Rahner in the Last Years of His Life, 1982–84*, eds. Hubert Biallowons, Harvey D. Egan, SJ, and Paul Imhof, SJ (New York: Crossroad, 1990), 16.

6. Egan, *Karl Rahner: Mystic*, 22.

7. Karl Rahner, *Meditations on the Sacraments*, trans. Salvator Attanasio, James M. Quigley, SJ, and Dorothy White (New York: Seabury, 1977), xi; published originally as *Die Siebenfältige Gabe* (Munich: Verlag Ars Sacra Joseph Mueller, 1974).

events in the course of one's life, where one happens to recognize and accept grace. Instead, grace is everywhere, "whether in the mode of merely preceding the act, or in the mode of acceptance, or in the mode of rejection."[8] This preceding grace and its acceptance is most readily observed when the church pledges itself to people as the basic sacrament of salvation in word and deed and when people in turn accept this pledge and act on it. The act of the church's pledging occurs through the sacraments, while the act of people's acceptance of that grace and their living it out occurs both within the church and in the world. Thus the sacraments are "in the first place" the "ecclesial manifestations and historical incarnations of *that* grace which is at work everywhere in the history of mankind and manifests itself historically, though in highly diversified ways," including in those moments when people do good and act morally.[9] Second, the sacraments are the manifestations of "that mysterious grace which inconspicuously governs our whole life, the celebration in the community of the Church of that which wills to find its victory in the monotony and pain of daily life."[10]

Since grace is everywhere and not limited to the sacraments or spiritual turning points, Rahner urges one to look to everyday life in order to find the experience and presence of God's grace and its eternal dimension. "Where an ultimate responsibility is assumed in obedience to a person's own conscience," he says, "where ultimate selfless love and fidelity are given, where an ultimate selfless truth regardless of self is lived out, and so on, at this point there is really in our life something that is infinitely precious . . . that is able to fill out an eternity."[11] It is grace, then, that one finds operative in the selfless acts of everyday life as life's eternal dimension and as the self-communication of God, available to all people.

God is ever communicating Godself to all persons, and this self-communication is experiential. Rahner considers the experience of God (*Gotteserfahrung*) innate in human nature, so that all people do experience God. Some do so in passing or fleetingly; others are aware of God's presence and grace more intensely. The more free, conscious, and self-aware people are, the more they will sense God on a regular basis as "experienced grace." Rahner maintains that the fulfillment of human existence

8. Rahner, *Meditations on the Sacraments*, xi.

9. Ibid., xvi.

10. Ibid., xvii.

11. Karl Rahner, "Eternity from Time," in idem, *Theological Investigations* 19, trans. David Morland, OSB (New York: Crossroad, 1979), 77; quoted in Egan, *Karl Rahner: Mystic*, 58.

consists in receiving God's self-communication, and that the human being is actually constituted and made truly human by this divine self-communication. The reception of God is only full or complete at the end of time in the beatific vision, but it is present now in seminal form as grace. The key theme of "experienced grace" is, according to Egan, "Rahner's entire theological enterprise" and its summation.[12] While God's self-communication lies at the heart of human existence, people have the freedom to receive or reject this self-communication and to make a decision for or against God. By saying "no" to God the person affirms and denies God at the same time, producing a seeming contradiction that manifests itself in one's conscience as the experience of guilt.

Rahner's interest in confession and the theology of the sacrament of penance has a long history. In 1948 he had published a review of Bernhard Poschmann's book on the history of absolution and subsequently began lecturing at the University of Innsbruck on the history of penance from its biblical origins to the church fathers and up to the Reformation. Rahner offered a course on the historical development of penance regularly, almost annually, during his tenure at Innsbruck,[13] and a single volume of shorter articles on the early history of penance was published in *Schriften zur Theologie* in 1973 as volume XI. According to Herbert Vorgrimler, "The subject of penance is one of [Rahner's] most fundamental interests."[14] Between 1966 and 1969 Rahner also collaborated on the initial draft of what would become the Rite of Penance. Rahner's view of confession was shaped by his understanding of the dialectic and experiential relationship of humans with God. To him there are two formative movements and mysteries in people's lives: the first is the "complete and enduring incomprehensibility" of the mystery of God to whom one entrusts oneself "through faith and hope and love"; the second is "the ever deepening guilt [*Schuld*] of man who has not achieved the objective of his personal freedom within the incomprehensibility of God" and who can conceive of this mystery of guilt only by turning to God "in a true conversion."[15] The experience of both mysteries, that of God and that of guilt, is a fundamental characteristic of and a driving force in human beings.

---

12. Egan, *Karl Rahner: Mystic*, 55.

13. Rahner lectured on the history of the doctrine of penance between 1949 and 1963/64, and his "Codex de paenitentia" is the most comprehensive of the three lecture manuscripts he created. For a detailed course and seminar schedule of Rahner's lectures on penance and related topics see Herbert Vorgrimler, *Karl Rahner: Gotteserfahrung in Leben und Denken* (Darmstadt: Primus Verlag, 2004), 67–70.

14. Ibid., 68.

15. Rahner, *Meditations on the Sacraments*, 42.

Rahner defines guilt as the human "no" to God's self-communication. Its effect is that it destroys the relationship with one's self, one's neighbor, and the outside world. This "no" to God "strives in isolation toward its own finality and irrevocability," and when prematurely cut off through the person's death results in what is called "judgment and definitive perdition."[16] Guilt is not, as is often assumed, a series of specific violations against an authority with punitive powers, or the collective infractions and transgressions of human norms and the law. Likewise, it is not an error in judgment or a failure to act on moral obligation. Rather, guilt is "an ultimate, irrevocable protest, stemming from the rejection of life itself, of an act against oneself as a whole person and against God"[17] Guilt is not even an entity unto itself, as in the case of certain violations and legal infractions, but is always "guilt before God." In fact, guilt escapes being localized as one particular sinful act and a particular event in a person's life or a group of people at a specific point in history. Too many factors influence one's actions, including heredity, social upbringing, and other circumstances. "Therefore, no one can say with absolute certainty and cocksureness, whatever appearances may suggest in a particular case, that one is really guilty or not guilty" before God, for "an absolute judgment on a real guilt before God in a determined individual case is not possible" for human beings to make.[18] "And precisely because evil cannot be totally isolated nor limited to wholly particular individual points in the history of the individual or mankind the human situation is difficult to deal with,"[19] Rahner says. The elusiveness of evil leaves us in constant uncertainty and shackled with the burden of the "uncancellable dark situation of our existence" in which both what has been done and what "remains forever dark is entrusted silently and hopefully to God."[20]

The problem with guilt is that people no longer acknowledge it as a tangible reality of their consciences. People no longer fear God, so that the issue of justification before God and its means, so vividly addressed by Augustine and again by Luther during the time of the Reformation, is seldom raised. "[I]n everyday life people today have no clear consciousness that they stand before God burdened by guilt and blame which cannot be shifted and as people deserving condemnation, but

16. Ibid., 42–43.
17. Ibid., 43.
18. Ibid., 46.
19. Ibid., 47.
20. Ibid., 48.

who nevertheless are saved by the incalculable miracle of God's pardon, by God's grace alone,"[21] Rahner says. The former sentiment is gone. Still, people experience their own finality, brokenness, and ambiguity. They are by no means oblivious to moral demands and social norms and desensitized to moral maxims. Rather, people have come to interpret the unpleasant thoughts that arise from their reality in a different way. "The modern social sciences have a thousand ways and means to 'unmask' [as an illusion] the experience of [human] guilt before God and to demolish it as a false taboo,"[22] Rahner says. There is a clear gap between what one should be and what one is, what should be and what exists. In light of the experience of "evil of apocalyptic proportions in the world," people have become distrustful of themselves, their vision and insights sharpened by the "eye of the psychologist, the analyst and the sociologist." They consider what once was "called guilt as a part of that universal misery and absurdity" where people are no longer the subject, but the object, "and this all the more so as biology, psychology, and sociology investigate the causes of what is called moral evil."[23] It is why people have the impression that it is God who needs to be forgiven and justified and that God's actions need explaining, not they themselves or their actions. People see themselves as the victims, not the causes or agents of moral evil, and even when they inflict harm on others they explain and seek to justify those actions as the result of their physical or genetic makeup and social condition. Even death has been reinterpreted "as the point at which all of the confusion of human existence is finally resolved, or as the final and naked climax of the absurdity of existence, for which there is no resolution."[24] This "epochal difficulty" would give rise to the question whether perhaps the Christian message about people as sinners is valid after all, despite the illusion that people are harmless. Even if people do not hear the Christian message that identifies them as sinners, they should be able to gain that same insight from "hearing it in the innermost center" of their being and their conscience.[25]

Another characteristic of human guilt is that it cannot be humanly canceled. Even the distancing of oneself from the transgression and its acknowledgment "does not bring about a cancellation of the guilt." In-

---

21. Karl Rahner, *Foundations of Christian Faith: An Introduction to the Idea of Christianity*, trans. William V. Dych (New York: Crossroad, 1982), 91.

22. Ibid.

23. Ibid., 92.

24. Ibid.

25. Ibid.

stead, true forgiveness becomes possible only when a person does not look upon previous transgressions as an isolated and "completed corruption" of the past and, at the same time, "does not consider them cancelled simply because he now plans to do" better. The word of forgiveness can only be heard by those who do not "exaggerate" the importance of the past and are able and willing to experience "the reality and mystery" of human freedom in the present.[26] It comes to those who have understood guilt "as both a possibility or as a terrible reality," those who know "how hopeless real guilt before God (deriving from man alone) really is."[27] This word of forgiveness "pertains to God alone," and "it is God's love that really [remits][28] the guilt itself, a guilt whose incomprehensibility pertains to the incomprehensibility of God."[29] Such forgiveness "is the greatest and most incomprehensible miracle of the love of God because in it God communicates Himself to a human being who in the seeming banality of everyday life has had the effrontery to say *No* to God."[30]

Just as people can hear the message of their guilt by listening to their consciences, they can also hear there the word of forgiveness. "This gentle word of forgiveness," says Rahner, "can be heard in the depths of the conscience because it already dwells in it as supportive ground in that trusting and loving turning back of man to God"—a turning back whereby, in self-reflection and self-judgment, the person "honors the merciful love of God."[31] In addition to human conscience, God's word of forgiveness has become concrete in history and in "space and time." It "has found its total expression and its rich historical irrevocability in Jesus Christ, the crucified and risen Lord. He, the Loving One of God, became one with all sinners and His final act of faith, hope and love experienced in the darkness of His own death the darkness of our guilt and accepted for us God's word of forgiveness." God's word of forgiveness given to Jesus Christ is unconditional, "historically evident and irrevocable," and it remains present within the community of those who believe in this forgiveness, namely, the church. For Rahner, "the Church is the fundamental sacrament of this word of God's forgiveness."[32]

26. Rahner, *Meditations on the Sacraments*, 50.
27. Ibid., 51.
28. The English translation uses "cancels" the guilt, while the German word *aufheben* used in the text (*die Schuld selbst wirklich aufhebende Liebe*) might be better translated as "remitting" guilt.
29. Ibid.
30. Ibid., 52.
31. Ibid.
32. Ibid.

The word of God's forgiveness heard in the human conscience is complemented by the word of forgiveness uttered by the church. The church offers this word in several ways. It does so in its proclamation, such as in the Apostles' Creed concerning "the forgiveness of sins"; it does so with baptism, which "remains basic and decisive for the whole history of an individual"; and it does so through its prayers of intercession and petitions, in which it solicits "the mercy of God for every individual and thus everywhere and always," accompanying people's conversion and making it "more complete" until death. A most specific mode of this word of forgiveness is the one spoken after the individual has acknowledged to the church his or her "great guilt" or "wretchedness" either in private confession to a representative of the church or "in a common confession of a community" before God and Christ.[33] Through the word of forgiveness that has been entrusted to the church by Christ, the church forgives the one who, though a vital part and member of the church by virtue of baptism, has offended it. It is in accordance with the church's essence that the word of forgiveness is pronounced in a concrete guilt situation of the individual, because when it does this the word of forgiveness "is not only a verbal utterance of the forgiveness of God, but rather its actuality," which means that "this word is really a sacrament." As this human word functions as a sacramental sign, "great mercy is declared and effected." But such mercy can also be effected and be offered by God whenever people listen to the "holy dictates of their conscience."[34]

Rahner insists that the effect of this word of forgiveness in the sacrament of penance is not the cancellation of guilt. Rather, guilt before God is *overcome*, sins are remitted, grace is received. Moreover, this sacrament, like the others, not only points to some possible grace and God's salvific will but it "*is* the tangibility and the permanence of this grace and salvation."[35] This concrete event of grace takes place only as both God and the person meet in the point of mutual encounter. It takes place in a concrete relationship between God and the person, namely, when the Christian "validly" and "fruitfully" receives the word of forgiveness and responds to God's self-communication "in the depths" of one's graced human existence at a specific time and place.[36] Thus the sacraments are "tangible word" and "tangible response" and "dialogue" and "partner-

33. Ibid., 53.
34. Ibid., 54.
35. Rahner, *Foundations of Christian Faith*, 427.
36. Ibid.

ship"[37] between God and the person. The "tangibility" of such grace received is made possible also when one makes confession to God directly. However, people tend to be less critical of themselves in their direct dialogue with God than they might be before God in the presence of another. "Have you never heard," Rahner writes to a young person who preferred to confess his sins directly to God in private and regarded sacramental confession as meaningless, "how many contemporary people are able to cope with their inner difficulties and troubles only when they try to clarify for themselves and to render surmountable their inner state of things by speaking about them to a psychologist or psychiatrist?"[38] Moreover, "all faults, however hidden they may seem to be in the inmost recesses of the heart, are also faults against our neighbor"; they all "ultimately affect and influence the behavior of a human being in his or her relationship to others," which means they assume a social dimension and hence are "also directed against the holy community of the Church," which makes "a forgiving word of the Church" both "meaningful and important."[39]

The primary aim of sacramental confession is conversion to God. The outward act has to be preceded and accompanied by the inner disposition of the individual and a willingness to encounter God and receive God's grace. As in the ancient church, the word of absolution cannot "replace the inner, authentic and very real turning away from guilt."[40] Therefore no duty exists to make a sacramental individual confession or annual confession unless the individual is certain of an "objective" or "subjective" personal guilt. The "cry for help" has to be authentic, not mere ritual. In addition, "mere regret over our earlier deeds" is not enough.[41] What is needed is "a very sober and realistic effort to bring about more justice and love in everyday life" in regard to one's neighbor. This includes acknowledging the "great amount of injustice and lovelessness" that exists in the world "for which we are responsible, but which do not all become discernible in the average everyday consciousness of man and of society: the exploitation of social power for one's own advantage, the culpable economic advantages which play into the hands of the unjust structures of our society and are all too matter-of-factly and

37. Ibid., 427–28.

38. Karl Rahner, *Is Christian Life Possible Today?* trans. Salvator Attanasio (Denville, NJ: Dimension, 1984), 95; quoted in emended translation in Egan, *Karl Rahner: Mystic*, 167.

39. Rahner, *Is Christian Life Possible Today?* 96.

40. Rahner, *Meditations on the Sacraments*, 57.

41. Ibid., 55–56.

selfishly absorbed." Otherwise, participation in the sacrament of penance remains "a fruitless ideology" and "a liturgically pre-planned ritual."[42]

The sacrament of penance invites us to make a repeated choice between being trapped in our guilt and being liberated from it. Those who allow themselves to experience their guilt, and choose to overcome it in a surrender of self, experience the liberating grace and mercy of God. Making confession and receiving the word of forgiveness consists in the "ever-renewed self-surrender of the total person to the merciful grace of God." In this act of self-surrender the person "does not want to judge himself nor justify himself before God, but rather to let true justice be promised and granted to him as the mercy of God." Scrupulosity in the examination of one's sins, their precise listing, is not necessary, for the sacrament is not a matter of individual sins but is about the sinful person as a whole, "who is encompassed by God's mercy and who can grasp, who can accept, historically and socially, this situation in the word of forgiveness of the Church, coming from God, and superabundantly overcoming all his guilt."[43] Thus in our freedom we continue to have two choices regarding God: we may surrender to the mystery of God and God's grace in order to find our true selves in God, or we may live with the oppressive and "dark" mystery of guilt and the refusal to be loved. The Christian message says that "we should allow ourselves to be forgiven" and "to be loved by an infinite and all-forgiving love." We do so by our flight from guilt and from ourselves in the act of self-distancing and by "the flight to God's word of forgiveness, which is most distinctly spoken through the word of Jesus in the Church"[44] in the sacrament of penance.

Despite the human need to hear the words of forgiveness spoken to us by another on behalf of Christ, the recognition that God ever seeks to communicate Godself to us is paramount to Rahner. In the 1984 lecture titled "Experiences of a Catholic Theologian," given at the University of Freiburg on the occasion of his eightieth birthday, shortly before his death, Rahner sums up his thoughts regarding confession and grace. "I think that a Christian theologian is permitted to regard the subject of human sinfulness and the forgiveness of sins by means of sheer divine grace as somewhat secondary compared to the radical self-communication of God,"[45] he says. This is not to deny or downplay our ingenious ways

42. Ibid., 56.

43. Ibid., 57.

44. Ibid., 58–59.

45. Karl Rahner, "Erfahrungen eines katholischen Theologen," in *Vor dem Geheimnis Gottes den Menschen verstehen: Karl Rahner zum 80. Geburtstag*, ed. Karl Lehmann (Munich: Schnell und Steiner, 1984), 111.

of sinning, our consciously ignoring God's efforts at reaching out to us, our own experience at reaching for God in an act of utter freedom that God permits, and our need for God's forgiveness. Rather, there are two reasons that speak for emphasizing God's self-communication over against the forgiveness of sins: first, people have a hard time grasping the doctrine of justification and its related doctrine of the forgiveness of sins; and second, this Catholic theologian views the giving of Godself to humanity as an act of pure grace, as "an unexpected miracle of God, who spends himself and who makes the adventure of such love his own history." It is in light of these considerations that "I think one is entitled to regard God's self-communication toward the creature as more central than sin and the forgiveness of sin." After all, deliberating too much about sin in light of God's love toward the sinner may lead to hubris, a tendency to "take sin too seriously and to forget that what terrifies us most about human history is more the result of the creatureliness of humans, their guileless stupidity, their weakness, and their lustfulness, rather than the sin itself that will have to be accounted for at the divine tribunal." This, in addition to the positive witness of Christian faith history, makes it seem plausible "to place greater importance on faith in God's self-communication as freely received grace than in a faith that professes human sinfulness."[46]

Still, making confession is a beneficial practice. In a 1980 article on "why one ought to confess nonetheless" ("Warum man trotzdem beichten soll"), Rahner acknowledges the decline of confession in the Roman Catholic Church without considering it a catastrophe.[47] The decline may be largely due to a shift in reinterpreting the duty to confess, away from a moralistic to a devotional consideration; it does not signal society's moral demise. Since only grave sins require sacramental confession, the number of Christians thus obligated is relatively small, yet precisely these are probably least likely to be found waiting outside the confessional. Throughout church history the sacrament has presupposed the penitent's cooperation in the form of an inner disposition of repentance, without which it remains mechanical and ineffectual. Thus the primary reason for making confession today is not its sacramental obligation but its devotional nature. The act of confession gives bodily expression to

---

46. Ibid., 111–12.

47. Karl Rahner, "Warum man trotzdem beichten soll," *Entschluß* (Vienna) 35, no. 9 (1980) [English: "The Status of the Sacrament of Reconciliation," *Theological Investigations* 23 (New York: Crossroad, 1992)]; cf. "Zur Situation des Bußsakramentes," in idem, *Schriften zur Theologie* 16 (Einsiedeln: Benziger, 1984), 18–37.

an inner attitude and "strengthens and deepens" it. The act may also generate and "awaken" the attitude of repentance that did not exist to the same extent prior to the act. "This is the strange human characteristic—that the body forms the soul and the soul the body" in a mutual dialectic in which the physical action may give rise to a new inner disposition, and vice versa. Moreover, making private confession, which goes beyond the kind of confession commonly made in the Lord's Prayer, at the beginning of Mass in the general confession, in a worship service of penance, or during evening prayer, is helpful to Christians in making physically concrete "this inner disposition of an ever-turning-away from guilt and one's turning toward God."[48] To Christians who are neither priests nor members of a religious order and who desire to confess more frequently than necessary through *"Andachtsbusse"* (devotional confession), Rahner suggests making a "wise choice" in regard to the confessor.[49] The "good confessor" will be willing to engage in dialogue, be sensitive to what is not said out loud, refrain from acting as a psychologist or advice-giver or an "absolution-machine," and allow for the other's "inner personal collaboration" in the sacramental process. How to find such a confessor and how to enable the confessor to carry out a truly pastoral function in the confessional process will depend on the individual situation and should be left up to the one wishing to make devotional confession.

Dietrich Bonhoeffer (1906–1945)

Dietrich Bonhoeffer was born on February 4, 1906, in Breslau, Germany, the sixth of eight children—minutes before his twin sister. His father was one of the leading physicians and neurologists of his time, and his mother was a teacher and came from a long line of theologians and artists. They were well off, with a staff of servants, and the mother homeschooled the children in their early years. When, in 1911, his father was offered a newly founded professorship in psychiatry at the University of Berlin, the Bonhoeffers moved to the capital city. Even as a child Dietrich occupied himself with questions concerning death and eternity. While his father was uninvolved with religion, his mother raised the children in the Christian faith, though they rarely attended worship. As a high school student Bonhoeffer read widely in the areas of church his-

---

48. Rahner, "Warum man trotzdem beichten soll," 11 ["The Status of the Sacrament of Reconciliation," 217].

49. Ibid., 218.

tory and philosophy of religion; he chose Hebrew as an elective and voiced his intention to become a theologian and pastor, much to the family's surprise. At the age of seventeen, Bonhoeffer graduated, two years earlier than was the custom, and began theological and philosophical studies at the University of Tübingen. After a brief visit to Rome he transferred to Berlin, where at age twenty-one he presented his doctoral thesis on the communion of saints, and after three years his inaugural dissertation, "Act and Being," which defined the position and relevance of dialectical theology and secured him a position on the theological faculty. Too young to be ordained to the pastorate—the minimum age was twenty-five—Bonhoeffer served as a curate to a German-speaking church in Barcelona, Spain. Thereafter he was awarded a fellowship to attend Union Theological Seminary in New York for the academic year 1930–1931. Here he became acquainted with the churches in Harlem and witnessed the effects of the economic crisis, especially on African-Americans and farmers. Influenced by the Social Gospel and the two Niebuhr brothers, African-American spirituals, and discussions of pacifism, Bonhoeffer began to study the theme of peace from a theological perspective.

Following his return to Germany, Dietrich Bonhoeffer was ordained as a Lutheran pastor and taught at the University of Berlin from 1931 to 1933. His first lecture was on the history of systematic theology in the twentieth century, his first seminar on the idea of philosophy and Protestant theology. In subsequent years he lectured on the nature of the church and Christology. His first book, *Schöpfung und Fall* (*Creation and Fall*), grew out of his lectures and was a theological exposition of the first three chapters of Genesis. At the time he also taught confirmation classes in a poor section of Berlin, coauthored a new catechism for his students entitled "Glaubst Du, so hast Du" ("If you believe, you have"), and founded a gathering place for unemployed youth and young adults. In 1932 Bonhoeffer, using his own funds, bought a cottage near Berlin as a place where students could gather for meditation and religious discourse. From this circle emerged his subsequent allies in the resistance movement. His reputation spread, drawing considerable numbers of people to hear him preach.

Between 1933 and 1935 Bonhoeffer served as pastor of two German-speaking Protestant churches in London, visited India to study the non-violent resistance methods of Gandhi, and returned to found a seminary for pastors who had joined a movement that opposed the Nazi regime. This movement, called the Confessing Church, was a small but influential resistance movement among German-speaking Protestant pastors. It was founded by Martin Niemöller and Karl Barth, among others, and Bonhoeffer played a key role in it. To avoid being discovered by the Nazis, the seminary was moved from Zingst to Finkenwalde; eventually, in 1937, it was shut down. Upon its closing Bonhoeffer wrote *Gemeinsames Leben* (*Life Together*), published in 1938, an exposition of the life of the Christian community based on biblical insights and his personal experience of living in intentional community in makeshift housing with some twenty-five student vicars. Shortly thereafter he wrote *Nachfolge* (*The Cost of Discipleship*). Both books were "the distillation of his fundamental message—What it means to live with Christ."[50] From 1937 also survives a manuscript entitled *Versuchung* (*Temptation*), presented in the form of a Bible study at a five-day reunion of the clergy who two years earlier, under Bonhoeffer's leadership, had established the Confessing Church's seminary and had finished the first course. With the seminary's closing by the Nazis, Bonhoeffer was banned first from preaching, then from teaching, and finally from any kind of public speaking.

In 1939 Bonhoeffer visited the United States again and was urged by his friends to stay and use his gifts as a scholar there. He refused, acting "in accord with his fundamental view of ethics, that a Christian must accept his responsibility as a citizen of *this* world where God has placed him."[51] Upon his return to Germany he joined a secret group based in the military intelligence office, who hoped to overthrow the National Socialist regime by killing Hitler. In his spare time between tasks on behalf of the Confessing Church and the resistance movement Bonhoeffer wrote chapters for his book *Ethics*, some penned in the Benedictine Abbey at Ettal and other temporary places of refuge. He intended the book to be the summation of his life's work and he continued writing it in prison; while a preliminary outline and numerous chapters and essays survive, it was never completed to the degree Bonhoeffer had hoped. Arrested in April 1943 after money used to help Jews escape to Switzerland was traced to him, Bonhoeffer was charged with conspiracy and imprisoned in Berlin for a year and a half. During this time the prison guards permitted a courier system to his family and friends, thereby preserving many of his papers, essays, and poems, including portions of his *Ethics*. The collected prison writings were published posthumously by his friend and colleague Eberhard Bethge, first in 1950 and 1951 and then in an expanded version in 1970, translated into English as *Letters and Papers from Prison* (*Widerstand*

---

50. John W. Doberstein, "Introduction," in Dietrich Bonhoeffer, *Life Together*, trans. Doberstein (San Francisco: Harper & Row, 1954), 11.

51. Ibid., 12.

und Ergebung: Briefe und Aufzeichnungen aus der Haft). After the failure of the plot on Hitler's life in 1944, Bonhoeffer's connections with the conspirators were discovered. He was moved to a series of prisons and concentration camps, ending at Flossenburg, where he was executed by hanging on April 9, 1945, just three weeks before the liberation of the city. Also hanged for their parts in the conspiracy were his brother Klaus and his brothers-in-law Hans von Dohnanyi and Rüdiger Schleicher.

Theologically, Bonhoeffer counted among his strongest influences Karl Barth (1886–1968), whom he had met in Bonn during a theological seminar and with whom he remained in contact thereafter, and Adolf von Harnack (1851–1930), his early childhood mentor and his teacher at the University of Berlin. Bonhoeffer sees as the main tasks of the church to orient Christians to the Sermon on the Mount and to teach practical discipleship of Jesus Christ. The church as the body of Christ, made up of Christ's disciples, is commissioned to solidarity and reconciliation with the world. Christian ethics are always governed by the individual's membership in the Christian community. Central to Bonhoeffer's theology is Jesus Christ, the sole savior of the world in whom God took on human form. Departure from this center of human existence, whether in dialogue with other religions, ideologies, or daily life means refusing to be a Christian. The radius and extension built around the center that is Christ is the church. It exists for the sake of the world and others, not for its own benefit, and its aim is to proclaim and work toward reconciliation between the world and God. Therefore the kingdom of God and the world are not separate entities; the former exists within the latter and must take an active stand and play a redemptive role in it. Guilt is generated when Christians and the church as a whole fail to act on or act counter to Christ's commands of radical discipleship in the world and when, aware of their guilt, they fail to fall back on Christ's "costly grace" by asking for forgiveness and making confession. Rather than pointing and accusing, Christians, individually and as the church, assume and bear the guilt of the world as their own guilt. Whenever we as individuals and as a church have failed Christ, we must acknowledge and confess this guilt to the world.

Bonhoeffer's most detailed reflections on confession are formulated in *Life Together*. His theological approach to it, however, finds expression in his university lectures on the first three chapters of Genesis, *Creation and Fall*, and it is summed up again in the opening chapters of *Ethics*. In his biblical exegesis of the Fall, Bonhoeffer notes that in its first biblical depiction, the human experience of guilt manifests itself in shame. The first man and woman show their shame by sowing fig leaves together and making themselves aprons (Gen 3:7). Their nakedness means innocence. It reflects "the essence of unity and unbrokenness, of being for the other, of objectivity, of the recognition of the other in his right, in his limiting me and in his creatureliness."[52] Covering oneself, on the other hand, means recognizing a world that is veiled, divided, split into good and evil, into *tob* and *ra*, where limits are set and transgressed. The contradiction here is "that man, who has come to be without a limit, is bound to point to his limit without intending to do so" by the act of covering himself. "Man's shame is his reluctant acknowledgment of revelation, of the limit, of the other person, of God." Shame, then, and "its preservation in the fallen world is the only—although a most contradictory—possibility of acknowledging the original nakedness" and its "blessedness."[53]

The step following shame is flight and the birth of the conscience. Aware of *tob* and *ra*, Adam has "fallen from unity into division" and "can no longer stand before his Creator. He has transgressed his limit and now he hates his limit, he denies it, he is like God, without a limit."[54] By fleeing from God, Adam unwillingly agrees with God his Creator. This flight is prompted by the voice of conscience, which did not exist before the Fall. And this conscience drives Adam away "from God into a secure hiding place," where he "plays the judge himself and just by this means he escapes God's judgment" and lives by his own definition of good and evil, "from the innermost division within himself."[55] Bonhoeffer defines conscience not as "the voice of God to sinful man" but as "man's defense against it," while pointing to it. "Conscience is shame before God in which at the same time our own wickedness is concealed, in which man justifies himself and in which, on the other hand, the acknowledgment of the other person is reluctantly preserved." When God calls Adam out of his hiding place it is a call to come out of his conscience and to stand before the Creator. Not permitted to stand alone in his sin, Adam is stopped in his flight by God, who says: "Come out of your hiding place, from your self-reproach, your covering, your secrecy, your self-torment, from your vain remorse . . . confess to yourself, do not lose yourself in religious despair, be yourself, Adam . . . where are you? Stand before your Creator." It is as this point that Adam could make an honest confes-

---

52. Dietrich Bonhoeffer, *Creation and Fall: A Theological Interpretation of Genesis 1–3 and Temptation—Two Biblical Studies* (New York: Macmillan, 1959), 79.

53. Ibid.
54. Ibid., 80.
55. Ibid., 81.

sion before God, for "he knows he has already been apprehended."[56] Instead, Adam blames Eve, and Eve blames the serpent, which is another form of flight. "Adam has not surrendered, he has not confessed. He has appealed to his conscience, to his knowledge of good and evil, and out of this knowledge he has accused his Creator," Bonhoeffer says. Instead of recognizing "the grace of the Creator" shown by calling out to him and refusing to let him flee, "Adam sees this grace only as hate, as wrath, and this wrath kindles his own hate, his rebellion, his will to escape from God."[57]

Shame, then, is the sign by which humans demonstrate that they know something has been lost, namely, their wholeness, their nakedness. Rather than knowing themselves only in their origin through relationship with God, they now know themselves in their origin by relationship with themselves, which implies their awareness of living under the constant threat of death. Shame lies at the heart of the "dialectic of concealment and exposure"; however, this dialectic cannot be ultimately overcome, so that death remains. "Shame can be overcome only when the original unity is restored, when man is once again clothed by God in the other man, in the 'house which is from heaven,' the Temple of God (2 Cor 5:2ff.)." Shame can only be overcome "in the enduring of an act of final shaming," says Bonhoeffer, "namely the becoming manifest of knowledge before God."[58] This ultimate act of shaming occurs "through the forgiveness of sin, that is to say, through the restoration of fellowship with God and men." It "is accomplished in confession before God and before other men," for only in this act is one "clothed with the forgiveness of God, with the 'new man' that [one] puts on, with the Church of God, with the 'house which is from heaven.'"[59]

In *Life Together*, Bonhoeffer devotes the entire fifth and final chapter of the book to "Confession and Communion." The reflections are based on the actual practice of private confession Bonhoeffer had introduced at the seminary in 1935 in connection with celebrating Communion. Before receiving the sacrament students were to confess their sins privately to one another or else to him as the director of the community. The procedure was conducted without vestment or formal liturgy. Despite initial protests about what to them resembled a non-Protestant

---

56. Ibid., 82.
57. Ibid.
58. Dietrich Bonhoeffer, *Ethics*, ed. Eberhard Bethge, trans. Neville Horton Smith (New York: Macmillan, 1955), 23.
59. Ibid.

monastic discipline, seminarians began to embrace the practice that same summer, especially after Bonhoeffer himself set the example by asking one of them to hear his confession. The first inspiration for the practice may have come during his 1924 visit to Rome, where he had observed people of all ages going to confession in the church of Santa Maria Maggiore. As early as 1932 Bonhoeffer speaks to his students in Berlin of oral confession as "an act to be carried out in practice." And his essays on *Spiritual Care* (1935–1939), resulting from life in community at the Finkenwalde seminary, make private confession a prerequisite for creating true Christian community.[60] In *Life Together*, Bonhoeffer commends to believers the frequent use of private confession to another Christian, not necessarily a pastor, and briefly touches on the relationship between confession and the sacrament of Holy Communion.[61] While many Christians may be "unthinkably horrified when a real sinner is suddenly discovered among the righteous," says Bonhoeffer, it is a fact "that we *are* sinners," though we would prefer to "remain alone with our sin, living in lies and hypocrisy."[62] In Christ, however, "the love of God came to the sinner," so that "all sham" could be ended. It is the reason "he gave his followers the authority to hear the confession of sin and to forgive sin in his name." By doing so he made both the church "and in it our brother, a blessing to us."[63] The brother or sister in Christ "hears the confession in Christ's stead," "forgives our sins in Christ's name," and "keeps the secret of our confession as God keeps it," so that by going to another Christian to confess "I am going to God" and to the entire church.[64]

Bonhoeffer lists several benefits of private confession for the individual. First, sin loses its power over the individual when the secret sin is revealed, thereby restoring authentic fellowship with other believers. "The sin concealed separated him from the fellowship, made all his apparent fellowship a sham," while "the sin confessed has helped him to find true fellowship" in Christ.[65] It is not necessary to confess the sin to the entire

---

60. See Jeffrey B. Kelly, "Editor's Introduction to the English Edition," in Dietrich Bonhoeffer, *Life Together*, trans. Daniel W. Bloesch, in *Dietrich Bonhoeffer Works*, vol. 5 (Minneapolis: Fortress Press, 1996), 16–17; for further reflections on the history and practice of confession in Luther and among the Benedictines, as well as practical advice for contemporary Christians, see Dietrich Bonhoeffer, *Spiritual Care*, trans. Jay C. Rochelle (Minneapolis: Fortress Press, 1985), 60–65.

61. In linking confession with Holy Communion, Bonhoeffer follows the pattern of the Protestant reformers, most notably Luther and Calvin.

62. Bonhoeffer, *Life Together*, 110.

63. Ibid., 111.

64. Ibid., 112.

65. Ibid., 113.

church, since the other Christian hearing confession acts on behalf of the Christian community. Second, confession acts as an antidote to pride, which is the root of all sin and produces one's self-elevation to the place of God. Confession in the presence of another "is the profoundest kind of humiliation. It hurts, it cuts a man down, it is a dreadful blow to pride." In this "ignominy that is almost unbearable," the old self "dies a painful, shameful death before the eyes" of another Christian. The discomfort and humiliation associated with the act of private confession blind us to seeing "the promise and the glory in such abasement."[66] Third, the promise confession holds is the breakthrough to new life. "Confession is conversion," whereby "Christ has made a new beginning with us." It delivers us "out of darkness into the kingdom of Jesus Christ," while restoring, as a type of second baptism, our baptismal joy.[67] Fourth, confession in the presence of another Christian delivers us from the illusionary benefits of self-forgiveness and self-absolution. The presence of another "breaks the circle of self-deception" and generates certainty of one's forgiveness before God. The concrete presence of the other corresponds with the concrete reality of God's forgiveness. In addition, a confession in the company of another person invites us to address concrete sins we can name. Despite the seeming benefits of a general confession, the naming of specific sins has the effect of plunging us into "the utter perdition and corruption of human nature." Due self-examination using the Ten Commandments prior to confession reduces the chances of falling into hypocrisy and mere ritual. Bonhoeffer commends confession as a Christian discipline especially for those who have been lacking the experience of the abundant life in Christ. It is for those who "cannot find the great joy of fellowship, the Cross, the new life, and certainty."[68]

Knowledge of psychology or psychiatry does not qualify one as a good confessor. For Bonhoeffer there is a distinction between scientific, that is, psychological or medical, and sacred knowledge. "The most experienced psychologist or observer of human nature knows infinitely less of the human heart than the simplest Christian who lives beneath the Cross of Jesus," he says. "Worldly wisdom knows what distress and weakness and failure are, but it does not know the godlessness of men," neither does it know "that man is destroyed only by his sin and can be healed only by forgiveness. Only the Christian knows this." In the eyes of the psychiatrist "I can only be a sick man; in the presence of a Christian

66. Ibid., 114.
67. Ibid., 115.
68. Ibid., 118.

brother I can dare to be a sinner"; the psychiatrist may search the other's heart without finding its depth, the Christian knows instinctively: "here is a sinner like myself, a godless man who wants to confess and yearns for God's forgiveness."[69] Therefore "it is not lack of psychological knowledge but lack of love for the crucified Jesus Christ that makes us so poor and inefficient" in hearing confessions. In addition, only those should hear confession who themselves practice it, and neither should one individual in a community function as the primary and sole confessor, as it may be too much of a burden on the individual, lend itself to becoming "empty routine," or lead to "the disastrous misuse of the confessional for the exercise of spiritual domination of souls." Those making confession should beware of taking pride in it as a "pious work." Otherwise "it will become the final, most abominable, vicious, and impure prostitution of the heart" and "idle lustful babbling." One should always keep in mind the "sole ground and goal of confession," namely, "the promise of absolution" and "the forgiveness of sins."[70] This is also true as regards one's preparation for the sacrament of Holy Communion. While prior to celebrating this sacrament Christians "will beg the forgiveness of the others for the wrongs committed" as a conciliatory act, such begging still falls short of confession. The certainty of knowing that particular sins known only to God are forgiven and that one is approaching the Lord's table with a pure heart comes only through confession. For it is here that the Christian "forgives the other all his sins in the name of the triune God."[71]

Seeking to obtain forgiveness in Christ on account of sin applies not only to the individual Christian but also to the church. As the living body of Christ, the church lives with the mandate to work reconciliation between the world and God, and it stands in need of confession for having failed Christ in discipleship, loyalty, and courage. By its failure it carries "the entire guilt of the world" in the same way as Christ did for the church. Bonhoeffer includes a confessional litany in his *Ethics*, a sobering wake-up call to the church entitled "Confession of Guilt." Probably written in September 1940 "when Hitler had achieved his most astounding victory,"[72] the confession covers nearly three pages and begins by saying:

---

69. Ibid., 118–19.
70. Ibid., 120.
71. Ibid., 121.
72. Eberhard Bethge, "Editor's Preface to the Newly Arranged Sixth German Edition," in Bonhoeffer, *Ethics*, 12.

The Church confesses that she has not proclaimed often and clearly enough her message of the one God who has revealed Himself for all times in Jesus Christ and who suffers no other gods beside Himself. She confesses her timidity, her evasiveness, her dangerous concessions. She has often been untrue to her office of guardianship and to her office of comfort. And through this she has often denied to the outcast and to the despised the compassion which she owes them. She was silent when she should have cried out because the blood of the innocent was crying aloud to heaven. She has failed to speak the right word in the right way and at the right time. She has not resisted to the uttermost the apostasy of faith, and she has brought upon herself the guilt of the godlessness of the masses.[73]

The church's confession of guilt does not exempt individual Christians from seeking confession. Rather, by the church's own confession "she calls them into the fellowship of the confession of guilt," summoning them by example with the message that they are sentenced in their guilt, "and as such they are justified by Him who takes upon Himself all human guilt."[74]

The hope of Western civilization, and in fact of all nations, does not lie with a strategic change of direction commanded by the nations' leaders but with the confession of the guilt of the church. For Bonhoeffer it is only the church that can work its transformative powers among both leaders and nations because Christ empowers the church to do so. Thus "the justification of the western world, which has fallen away from Christ, lies solely in the divine justification of the Church, which leads her to the full confession of guilt and to the form of the cross. The renewal of the western world lies in the divine renewal of the Church, which leads her to the fellowship of the risen and living Jesus Christ."[75] Bonhoeffer establishes a direct link between the redemption of the world from sin and the church's willingness to confess its own sins and transgressions. The church plays the leading role in the process of a worldwide transformation from violence to justice, lawlessness to order, war to peace. "The western world, as a historical and political form, can be 'justified and renewed' only indirectly, through the faith of the Church," he says. While for the church there is the "experience in faith [of] the forgiveness of all her sins and a new beginning through grace," the nations will only experience "a healing of the wound, a cicatrization of guilt, in the return to order, to justice, to peace, and to the granting of

73. Bonhoeffer, *Ethics*, 113.
74. Ibid., 116.
75. Ibid., 116–17.

free passage to the Church's proclamation of Jesus Christ."[76] Thus the church is "the fountain-head of all forgiveness, justification and renewal"[77] and has the potential by its own confession of guilt to lead and bring about the transformation of the entire Western world toward a societal structure that promotes justice, order, and peace, not only among its own members but throughout the world. Much more is at stake than the church's own purity and the individual's well-being. Individual and collective confession of guilt is the ongoing task of the church so that the reconciling powers of Christ may come to fruition in the world.

The church's divine mandate in regard to its reconciling mission in the world expresses itself is two ways: preaching and confession, or ecclesiastical discipline. They are public or private, directed at the entire assembly as in preaching, or at the individual as in private confession. Both tasks belong together, and neglect of one or the other weakens the church's mission. "If confession or church discipline is lost," says Bonhoeffer, "then the commandment of God in preaching will be understood as no more than a proclamation of general moral principles which in themselves are devoid of any concrete claim." On the other hand, "if public preaching is entirely relegated to the background and attention is concentrated on the confessional," there "arises a dangerous legalistic casuistry which destroys liberty of faith" and tends "to establish the absolute authority of the mandate of the Church."[78] The result of this unbalanced favoring of one task over the other is borne out by the Protestant and Roman Catholic churches, respectively. As Protestant ministers were no longer "constantly confronted by the problems and responsibilities of the confessional," they evaded their "responsibility of concrete proclamation of the divine commandment" and "ceased to posses a concrete ethic." The Protestant Church "can find its way back to a concrete ethic such as it possessed at the time of the Reformation" only when it has rediscovered "the divine office of confession."[79] Conversely, Roman Catholic priests are prepared for the office of confession "by discussing innumerable 'cases'" on which to make a decision, involving the "very serious danger" of "reducing the divine commandment to a mere code of laws and pedagogic method." The Roman Catholic Church can overcome this concrete danger "only by a rediscovery of the Christian office of preaching."[80]

---

76. Ibid., 117.
77. Ibid., 119.
78. Ibid., 292.
79. Ibid.
80. Ibid., 293.

Either office, that of preaching as well as that of confession, is "the proc-lamation of divine revelation." And in either office "the word which came from heaven in Jesus Christ desires to return again in the form of human speech." The principal agent of proclaiming this divine revelation is the pastor, who stands before the congregation "in the place of God and of Jesus Christ." As a "spokesman of God," not of the congregation, the pastor then "is authorized to teach, to admonish and to comfort, to forgive sin, but also to retain sin,"[81] and this authorization comes directly from Jesus Christ. The audience includes both believers and unbelievers and the message directed to them is uniform, namely, "the one commandment of God which is in Jesus Christ." There ought not to be "a message of universal reason and natural law for unbelievers, and a Christian message for believers," for that would be "pharisaical self-conceit."[82] When faith-fully delivered as "the testimony of Jesus Christ" and "inseparably bound up with Holy Scriptures," such proclamation will have the effect that "life is infused into all the other offices of the congregation,"[83] including that of confession.

Eugene H. Peterson (1932–)

Eugene H. Peterson was born in East Stanwood, Washington, on November 6, 1932. The oldest of four children (he had one brother and two sisters, of whom the older died when he was three), he grew up in Kalispell, Montana. His father was a butcher by trade and owned a local butcher shop where Peterson worked in his youth; it would shape his understanding of Old Testament ritual, temple sacrifice, and the priestly office. The family attended a Pentecostal church, where both parents were active members, frequently welcoming traveling evangelists and preachers into their home and inviting Eugene to accompany his mother on evangelistic preaching outings. In 1954, Peterson earned a bachelor's degree in philosophy from Seattle Pacific University, followed by a de-gree in sacred theology (STB), the equivalent of a master of divinity degree today, from New York Theological Seminary. In 1957 he matricu-lated at Johns Hopkins University, planning to pursue doctoral studies, and earning a master's degree in Semitic languages in 1958. But at that point Peterson sensed a call to parish ministry and was ordained in the

81. Ibid., 293.
82. Ibid., 295–96.
83. Ibid., 294.

United Presbyterian Church, USA, in 1958.[84] After four years of service at churches in New York state he founded a new church development, Christ Our King Presbyterian Church, in Bel Air, Maryland, in 1962. Twenty-nine years later, Peterson retired from the church and the pastorate, at which time the congregation had grown to about five hundred members. During his pastorate Peterson also served as adjunct faculty member at St. Mary's Seminary in Baltimore, the first Roman Catholic seminary established in the United States, which was operated by the Sulpician Fathers, priests dedicated to priestly formation. Through teaching and study Peterson developed aptitude and fluency in the biblical languages of Hebrew and Greek and the subtleties of scriptural translation and interpretation. Guided by a desire to pursue writing and teaching full time, he retired from pastoral ministry to become writer-in-residence at Pittsburgh Theological Seminary in 1992. Some of the initial work on his translation of the Bible into contemporary English, *The Message*, took place while he was at Pittsburgh, though translating the entire Bible would take a total of ten years. In 1993 Peterson became the James M. Houston Professor of Spiritual Theology at Regent College, Vancouver, British Columbia, where he served for five years and continued teaching as professor emeritus until 2006. He is married to Janice Stubbs and they have three adult children. The Petersons now live in Montana, where he works as a writer and poet.

Widely known for *The Message*, a translation of the Bible into contemporary American English with over ten million copies in print, Peterson is author or coauthor of more than thirty books. Their topics range from expository studies on the Psalms, the prophets of the Old Testament, the book of Revelation, and the Pauline epistles to the themes of prayer, spiritual formation, spiritual theology, and spiritual direction. Peterson's early works focus on coaching pastors to be prophets in Christ's service in a consumerist and numbers-driven culture, urging them to desist from a performance-driven and program-obsessed compulsion and to subject themselves, instead, to the practice of prayer and their consciences to the word of God as revealed in the Scriptures.

Often described as a pastor to pastors, Peterson calls pastors to repentance of their ego-drives, self-absorption, and compromise with culture's fads. Lodging his argument in a scriptural exegesis that is nurtured by the poetic imagination and enhanced by personal narrative, Peterson calls on pastors to return to the service to which they have pledged

84. The denomination is now the Presbyterian Church (USA).

themselves by their ordination vows: serving the people so that the people, and pastors themselves, can serve God. Since the mid-1980s Peterson has challenged pastors with the truths of their sacred calling by such works in pastoral theology as *Five Smooth Stones for Pastoral Work; The Contemplative Pastor: Returning to the Art of Spiritual Direction; Under the Unpredictable Plant: An Exploration in Vocational Holiness; Working the Angles: The Shape of Pastoral Integrity;* and *The Unnecessary Pastor: Rediscovering the Call* (coauthored with Marva Dawn). Calling pastors to repentance and renewal by an exposition of the Scriptures as God's word in which Christ is revealed, Peterson seeks to rekindle a passion for the Gospel and its prophetic themes of covenant and creation, price and promise, death and resurrection. Once pastors have begun to reflect contemplatively on Scripture they are better equipped to lead members into an equally transformative experience of connectedness with God in Christ and bring familiarity with the contemplative practice to the service of their congregants.

In recent years Peterson has undertaken the task of outlining the principles of spiritual theology, a thematic approach to understanding and fostering the life of Christian discipleship, Christian formation, and the Christian spiritual disciplines. In the five-volume series subtitled "Conversations with Eugene H. Peterson" and published between 2005 and 2009 Peterson engages spiritual theology, spiritual reading, the ways of Jesus Christ, language, and spiritual maturity. For Peterson the church's role and that of every Christian is to claim and proclaim the risen Christ, whose message is bound to and mediated through the words of Scripture as the word of God in Christ and whose presence and commands are lived out in the midst of Christ's community, the church. Peterson draws on his pastoral experience to carry out the tasks of prophet, poet, and preacher; he convicts by charting a prophetic vision with discernment, clarifies by the use of potent poetic and metaphorical imagery, and woos readers into a new kind of seeing by the narrative discourse of a preacher who tells the divine-human story and tells it well.

At the heart of Peterson's theology lies the conviction that the Scriptures reveal the word of God, which in turn allows people to act on Christ's calling for their life and become active participants in God's work in the world. The Scriptures function as a means of spiritual formation and spiritual direction within the heart of the community that contemplates them and appropriates their meaning by translating them into action. Much depends on the right translation, the right reading, the right understanding of the Scriptures and the Christ event as their center.

Like Martin Luther before him, and Karl Barth and Dietrich Bonhoeffer in the twentieth century, Peterson locates the prophetic and divine power in the word of God, read and proclaimed rightly as the word of Christ, by which the new creation takes form in people's hearts and minds, convicting, transforming, and leading them to repentance and into a direction that is in accordance with God's ways. "As a reader working with the words of Scripture," says Peterson, "[I am] determined to recover the words of Scripture as a *templum*, [a temple and place of observation], and then live these words that I read 'in the presence of a god,' in my case the God and Father of Jesus Christ." Such reading is proposed by *lectio divina* and requires contemplation, which is "submitting to the biblical revelation, taking it within ourselves, and then living it unpretentiously, without fanfare." It "means living what we read, not wasting any of it or hoarding any of it, but using it up in living," so that from it springs a "life formed by God's revealing word, God's word read and heard, meditated and prayed."[85] This kind of hearing, reflecting on, and reading of the Scriptures will "become formative in the Christian church and become salt and leaven in the world" in ways that no "doctrinal disputes and formulation," "strategies" of subduing "the barbarians," or "congregational programs" aimed at educating the laity "in the 'principles and truths' of the Scriptures" could ever manage.[86] For Peterson, appropriating the Scriptures as the word of God means "performing the score, eating the book, embracing the holy community that internalizes this text," and, as a result, being "released into freedom"[87] with God and for God. Barth had viewed the Bible as a "different" type of writing than one normally read, so that it required "a different kind of reading," namely, one that was "receptive and leisurely instead of standoffish and efficient," one that took into account the Bible's character as "revelatory and intimate instead of informational and impersonal."[88] With Barth, Peterson believes that facilitating for contemporary readers, preachers, and hearers the right reading, translating, and hearing of the Scriptures will make for a gradually life-changing, formative, and transformative experience in which God plays the leading role in believers' lives.

Sin is what separates us from God and others, and this is a theological, not a moral assessment, Peterson says. Sin results from misreading,

---

85. Eugene H. Peterson, *Eat This Book: A Conversation in the Art of Spiritual Reading* (Grand Rapids: Eerdmans, 2006), 111–13.
86. Ibid., 116.
87. Ibid., 77.
88. Ibid., 6.

misjudging, and failing to hear and act on God's ever-operative and subtle voice of love that comes to us prominently in the Scriptures and enables us to live in community and relationship. Sin is also failing to yield to soul friends and wise guides along the way who might expose our self-delusion, wrongheaded self-interests, and the lustful substituting of our ego and self-engineered directions for the God-place in us. "People don't reckon with sin as that total fact that characterizes them," says Peterson, "nor do they long for forgiveness as the effective remedy." They prefer to live a life "without grace," trusting in their own resources and strengths. Thus "the Word of God to which pastoral ministry is committed loses propinquity the moment a person is not understood as a sinner."[89] Moreover, "sin is not simply a failure in relation to God that can be studied lexically; it is a personal deviation from God's will" residing "within the chronological boundaries of a person's life and in the geographical vicinity of his or her street address."[90] Pastoral ministry, and ministry to one another as sinners, means being interested in the details of "how people are sinners," discerning and discriminating the various faces and forms of sin, and then loving, praying, witnessing, conversing, and proclaiming "the details of grace appropriate to each human face . . . ."[91]

Fundamentally, sin is a break in relationship—with God, others, creation. The remedy for this broken relationship lies not in providing more teaching, moral training, or punitive measures, such as exclusion from the community, but in the recognition that God wishes to be in relationship with us and that from this elemental relationship all other relationships are principally defined and governed. Based on his exposition of the first letter of John, Peterson identifies love as the defining mark of the Christian community, so that the absence of love is sin. Christians are "given the responsibility for telling one another that God loves them, that he commanded every one of us to love one another," and to "assume responsibility for giving guidance and instruction in the life of love."[92] To cultivate "our identity as children of God" means "to refuse ever to sacrifice our commitments as a community to Jesus' love command in favor of a simpler and more readily achieved identity based on a common

89. Eugene H. Peterson, *The Contemplative Pastor: Returning to the Art of Spiritual Direction* (Grand Rapids: Eerdmans, 1989), 120.

90. Ibid., 121.

91. Ibid.

92. Eugene H. Peterson, *Christ Plays in Ten Thousand Places: A Conversation in Spiritual Theology* (Grand Rapids: Eerdmans, 2005), 311.

creed or a common cause," he says. With baptism our new life is defined by repentance, conversion, and an immersion in the Trinity of Father, Son, and Holy Spirit, at the same time redefining "our lives in the love-defined community of the beloved—God's loved children, love-created and love-commanded brothers and sisters" in Christ.[93] Since sin is relational, "a refusal to deal with sin is a refusal to deal with relationships. And if we don't deal with relationships, we can't love." For Peterson "love is the relational act par excellence just as sin is the de-relational act par excellence," so that by saying that "I do not sin or that sin is a minor issue for me, in effect I am saying that love is not high on my agenda."[94] The opposite of love is "a silent wasting of love," a being "incapacitated for what we are created and saved to do best, to love: to love God, to love Henry, to love Emily."[95]

One of the aspects of sin as lovelessness, derived from the first letter of John, is perfectionism. "It is one of the deadliest sins in the book for resurrection communities," since "those who pursue this way are convinced that it is possible, if only they try hard enough and find the right principles and techniques, to live without sin."[96] It is "deadly because it anaesthetizes any awareness of personal sin and therefore any awareness of Jesus in his primary and essential work of forgiveness on the cross, the unprecedented miracle of expiation (*hilasmos*)." Workaholics illustrate the principle: "by ignoring the ubiquity of sin they persist in the illusion that if they accomplish just one more mission, master just one more act of devotion . . . , they will emerge head and shoulders above the others." While they may masterfully perform, "they also end up without friends, often without family, without forgiveness because they never need it, and without love."[97]

Another result of a lack of love is that the "antichrist" is allowed to enter the community and one's mental picture. This happens when we believe in a "superspiritual" or "dehumanized" Jesus, who "allows us to develop a practice of love that has nothing to do with actual people" and "consists of a mix of music, mountains, and stories that fills our hearts with inspiring thoughts and feelings without all the distraction and bother of people." Belief in this type of Christ makes us "become lovers of ideas and feelings, lovers of ecstasy and novelty," but "not

93. Ibid., 314–15.
94. Ibid., 316.
95. Ibid., 319.
96. Ibid., 320.
97. Ibid.

lovers of the God who so emphatically revealed himself in human flesh and blood" and "certainly not lovers of our brothers and sisters."[98] It reduces people to objects one can manipulate or condescend to, and it dehumanizes them so that one need not be in relationship with them. It also reduces God to an abstract idea so we do not have to be in relationship with God.

Finally, the lack of love transforms into the worship of idols. According to Peterson, "an idol is god with all the God taken out. God depersonalized, God derelationalized, a god that we can use and enlist and fantasize without ever once having to . . . receive or give love, and then go on to live, however falteringly, at our most human." Since the idol requires no personal relationship, it "is a form of divinity that I can manipulate and control" and where the God-creature relationship is inverted: "now I am the god and the idol is the creature."[99] Thus a broken relationship with God leads to a dehumanizing of God who took on human form in Christ, a depersonalizing of others, and an idol-making by which God and our neighbor are enlisted to serve and bow down to us.

The Christian community is, or ought to be, the very place where sin is taken seriously because its members live in the reality of the ever-present forgiveness of God. "A life of love in the community is secured by a life of forgiveness by God," says Peterson; this is "the only foundation, on which a community of love can be formed."[100] This means that the community is also the place where we are "trained to recognize sin as an unwillingness to live in relationship and therefore in love," "to recognize the unrelational ways set before us in community," and to "see them for what they are, substitutes for love." When we see that, "we can confess our sin and receive absolution—return to our knees over and over again and receive Jesus' forgiveness and cleansing and get up off of our knees and love one another."[101]

Confession is carried out mostly as confession before God in private and in the act of reconciliation with the person one has offended or with whom there exists a broken relationship. It is returning "to our knees" and receiving "Jesus' forgiveness and cleansing" and then getting off our knees and going back "to our families and friends afresh to love them,"[102] as well as reconciling with those with whom relationships are

98. Ibid., 322–23.
99. Ibid., 325.
100. Ibid., 319–20.
101. Ibid., 324.
102. Ibid., 325.

severed or strained. These two basic forms of confession are complemented by a third, in which one "confesses" or admits to another person
one's difficulties with or questions concerning certain aspects of the life
of faith, family, relationships, and God. It is the type of confession that
is prompted by prayerful exposure to and meditation on the Scriptures
and life in the community of faith and is made to those who serve as
soul friends and confidants along the way of Christ in the context of
spiritual direction.

A pioneer among Protestant theologians in the twentieth century in
advocating for spiritual direction in the pastorate and among congregants, Peterson has written on the subject for nearly three decades.
As the word of God comes to people during the proclamation of the
Scriptures and upon prayerful meditation on and in dialogue with them,
so also it comes through those with practice in discipleship and a willed
discipline of living the Christ way of love in community. The manner of
this exchange between two people is called spiritual direction, though
better terms to describe it might be spiritual counsel, holy conversation,
or a colloquy aimed at the cure of the soul. The main vocation of the
pastor is that of spiritual director, not program manager or messiah. As
spiritual director the pastor makes possible "sanctification in progress"
by "the act of paying attention to God, calling attention to God, being
attentive to God in a person or circumstances or situation."[103] Part of this
role involves standing back and engaging in the act of "unknowing" and
"uncaring,"[104] getting out of the way and being unimportant, being "(really) present without being (obtrusively) present." Spiritual direction is
looking for God in others in an attentive, worshipful, loving way that
helps them become what they already know and helps them "enter into
the reality that is already God in and around"[105] them.

Peterson's treatment of spiritual direction is important to the subject
of confession. The exchange with a spiritual director in the person of the
pastor or another mature Christian may be the closest most Protestants
will ever come to experiencing the confidential atmosphere and Spirit-
guided conversation of private confession. While the element of forgiveness in the form of a spoken formula of absolution and a clearly discernible
liturgical outline are missing, there are traces of a pronounced forgiveness
in the prayerful presence of the other, reminders of God's grace and the

---

103. Eugene H. Peterson, *Under the Unpredictable Plant: An Exploration in Vocational
Holiness* (Grand Rapids: Eerdmans, 1992), 181.

104. Ibid., 186.

105. Ibid., 188–89.

reconciling activity of the Spirit operative in the directee's life, as well as the liturgical movement of the Holy Spirit that organically guides and directs the back and forth flow of the exchange. Other elements of private sacramental or liturgical confession are discernment, exhortation, and counsel. In a series of letters to the fictional Gunnar Thorkildsson, a recent Christian convert seeking spiritual guidance, Peterson illustrates the nature and process of spiritual direction. "In the verbal triad of biblical speech," of which the other two elements are preaching and teaching, it lacks the authority of the one and the precision of the other, hence occupying "a far more modest place," namely, one that is "reticent, shy, awkward,"[106] but important nonetheless. The primary role of spiritual directors and guides is to help recognize and name the "work of God the Spirit in you" and "[to prevent] you from taking on the Christian life as your project," because "God has already taken you on" and "you are His project."[107] Spiritual directors are to help us see "who God is and what he is doing in and among us; what it means to be created and chosen by God and how we get in on what he intends for us." They are theologians by nature because they "have disciplined their mind to think *God*" and they help us think "not just *about* God, but in terms of God, with God as our presupposition." It may be fashionable for Christians to seek out "counselors, psychologists, and psychiatrists" in matters of the soul, thus gaining something "along the lines of the therapeutic." But it takes a theologian when it comes to the Christian life and prayer, not a psychologist, "to help us *start* with God, not just end up with God as a court of last resort." Therefore, "If you're trying to understand yourself, go ahead and consult a psychologist, but if it's God you're after, get a theologian," for many "difficulties in prayer come from paying too much attention to ourselves—our moods, our feelings, our fitness to pray," when prayer means "paying attention to God"; as Christians we "need theologians far more than we need psychologists."[108] The task of the theologian, as well as that of the spiritual guide, is "to help us to pray to God—pray to the God revealed biblically in Jesus, and not just piously grovel around in some figment of our idolatrous imaginations."[109]

The spiritual guide or director assists one to recover prayer as ongoing conversation with and immersion in God, possibly leading to reconciliation,

---

106. Eugene H. Peterson, *The Wisdom of Each Other: A Conversation Between Spiritual Friends* (Grand Rapids: Zondervan, 1998), 20.
107. Ibid., 32.
108. Ibid., 49–50.
109. Ibid., 61.

forgiveness, and a strengthening of broken or tense human relationships. Recovering prayer does not mean scheduling it at various intervals throughout the day, but exercising one's imagination by reconceiving the day as a "ritual—a rhythmic sequence of movements in a sacred space and time" into which one enters, responds, and participates "in the ways of God."[110] The result may be "persistent and prayerful strategies of reconciliation" on the part of the one who has begun to pray and engage in the Spirit's movement. In this way "good and holy counsel" may transform "bitterness and recrimination" toward certain people into being on speaking terms and in renewed relationship with them. Where such mending seems impossible, "mature love" is called for, a love that accepts and embraces the other "without conditions." One is "now working out of a context of prayer, God's love," and one's "own obedience," which may mean "to live as courteously as you can manage." This type of reconciliation involves sacrificing dreams, illusions, and hidden expectations so one can "enjoy the accomplishments of successful courtesy," Peterson says, "instead of the guilty or angry frustrations of unreciprocated love."[111] The act of reconciliation flows, then, from one's immersion in prayer, a disciplined and willed availability to God's reconciling activity toward the world in Christ through the one who seeks to follow Christ and do things in Jesus' way.

Peterson cautions against the professionalization of spiritual direction, its functionalist, problem-solving tendency, and its emergence as a specialized area of ministry. Pastors as well as laypeople should be about spiritual direction, seeking and exercising this form of ministry one to another as conduits of God's word. Spiritual directors can be found in one's immediate vicinity. They are not necessarily those with a certificate in hand, but those who exhibit the characteristics of integrity, practiced prayer, and "seasoned Christian wisdom." Their role is not problem solving or giving advice, but a willingness to "show up and shut up" for monthly meetings, serving as "an honest, prayerful presence"[112] and taking the person seriously as a soulful creation of God for whom prayer should be the most natural language. By this form of ministry the two sources of preaching and teaching in which God's word reaches us are complemented by a third, namely, a prayerful listening that, like the other two, may lead to conversion and confession, a reorientation toward God and reconciliation with one's neighbor.

---

110. Ibid., 78–79.
111. Ibid., 62–63.
112. Ibid., 68.

Adrienne von Speyr (1902–1967)

Adrienne von Speyr was born on September 20, 1902, into a Protestant family in La Chaux-de-Fonds, Switzerland. Her father was an ophthalmologist whom she accompanied on his rounds at the hospital; her mother was the descendant of a family of noted watchmakers and jewelers. She raised the four children, of whom Adrienne was the second. Influenced by the Christian faith of her grandmother, von Speyr early developed sensitivity for the needs of the poor and sick and had experiences of divine mystical visions in which Roman Catholic imagery, Ignatius, and the Jesuits figured prominently. Despite her mother's opposition, Adrienne, with the support of her father, aspired to become a doctor. On her own she studied Greek, Russian, German, and English. Shortly after her father's death in 1917, von Speyr was diagnosed with tuberculosis in both lungs and was expected to die within the year. Instead, she recovered and pursued her studies and a medical internship, supporting herself through tutoring. Her decision to enter the medical field led to a break with her mother. In the summer of 1927 she married the dean of the department of history at the University of Basel, Emil Dürr, a widower with two young sons. Shortly after her marriage von Speyr passed the medical exams, making her the first woman in Switzerland to be admitted to the medical profession. Two years after Dürr's death in 1934 she married Werner Kaegi (1901–1979), who had taken over Dürr's post at the University of Basel. In the spring of 1940, after several failed attempts at converting to Roman Catholicism, von Speyr was introduced to the Swiss priest Hans Urs von Balthasar, SJ (1905–1988). Von Balthasar had recently been appointed campus chaplain at Basel and instructed von Speyr in the teachings of the Roman Catholic faith. The same year, von Speyr was baptized on the feast of All Saints, despite her baptism as a child in the Protestant Church, leading to a further disruption of the relationship with her mother and family. While working at her medical practice and seeing as many as sixty to eighty patients a day, von Speyr also came in contact with such prominent Roman Catholic theologians as Romano Guardini, Hugo Rahner, Henri de Lubac, and Gabriel Marcel.

From 1940 on, von Speyr had von Balthasar, who lived nearby, as her lifelong confessor and spiritual director. Despite her frail health, a heart attack, severe arthritis, and diabetes that lead to her eventual blindness in 1964, von Speyr worked actively as a physician, supporting the poor and those unable to pay for her services, and founding, together with von Balthasar, a publishing house and a religious lay community. Almost daily between 1940 and 1953 she dictated to von Balthasar her theological meditations while in a trance, resulting in sixty-two books ranging from contemplative reflections on the gospels, most epistles of the New Testament, and the Old Testament prophets, to theological works, such as treatises on the church, the Trinity, prayer, theological aesthetics, the sacrament of confession, the Mass, and the evangelical counsels of poverty, celibacy, and obedience. Dictations usually lasted for about half an hour at a time, and between two and three hours during vacation times. Due to her illness, von Speyr discontinued her medical practice in 1954, spending hours in prayer and reading the Bible and French authors. She died on September 17, 1967.

Von Balthasar both legitimized and promoted von Speyr's writings and visions. Their relationship was reminiscent of those emerging in the thirteenth century between a male spiritual director/confessor who was both a priest and a member of a religious community and a female lay directee whose theological training was largely the result of private scriptural study and who experienced mystical visions. Von Balthasar lent credibility to von Speyr's work through his prominence in theological circles. The Johannes Verlag was founded primarily to publish and promote her work. At the same time, von Balthasar was greatly influenced by von Speyr's spirituality and mysticism, insisting that her thought was a major source of inspiration for his own writings and that her work could not be separated from his. The notoriety von Balthasar gained for his writings and their recognition among major theologians in the West continue to this day. Author of more than one hundred books and several hundred articles, von Balthasar came to be highly regarded during his lifetime by such theologians as Karl Rahner, Cardinal Henri de Lubac, and Pope John Paul II. The current endorsement of his writings by Pope Benedict XVI contributes to his growing recognition in theological circles and among the wider public today. Having studied in Vienna, Berlin, and Zürich, von Balthasar completed his doctoral dissertation in German literature in 1928 and entered the Society of Jesus the following year. In 1936 he was ordained to the priesthood and in 1937 he declined a teaching position at the Gregorian University in Rome in order to work as campus chaplain at Basel, where he met von Speyr. His study of theology and philosophy led him away from scholasticism to the thought of Reformed theologian Karl Barth, with whom he struck up a friendship at Basel, and to a conviction that Scripture and the church fathers were the primary sources for theological reflection. His studies of Irenaeus, Origen, Augustine, Gregory of Nyssa, and Maximus the Confessor attest to this conviction.

In the mid-1940s von Balthasar and von Speyr founded a religious community, a so-called secular institute, whose members were laypeople and priests who had consecrated themselves to a life of vowed poverty, celibacy, and obedience and who were devoted to the sanctification of the world through their own Christian discipleship. This religious community, the Johannesgemeinde (Community of St. John), which exists to this day, came into conflict with the Jesuits. The Jesuits were hesitant to take responsibility for the lay community or its publishing house, nor would they validate the reports of von Speyr's mystical visions until further examination by the church. After years of delay by the Order and a growing conviction of his mission in regard to von Speyr's writings, von Balthasar left the Jesuits in 1950. This would leave him without a pastorate, teaching post, place to live, and income. Eventually he found refuge and an ecclesiastical home in the diocese of Chur, supporting himself by giving lectures and continuing to write. In 1972 von Balthasar founded the journal *Communio: International Catholic Review* with Cardinals Jean Daniélou, Henri de Lubac, and Joseph Ratzinger, later Benedict XVI. Between 1961 and 1987 von Balthasar produced the fifteen-volume trilogy *The Glory of the Lord*, *Theo-Drama*, and *Theo-Logic*, a systematic theological exploration from the Christian perspective of the principles of beauty, goodness, and truth. He died in 1988, two days before he was to be made a cardinal by Pope John Paul II.

After more than twenty-five years of collaboration, van Balthasar summarized von Speyr's theological perspective in *Erster Blick auf Adrienne von Speyr*. The book was published by the Johannes Verlag a year after her death and appeared in a 1981 English translation published by Ignatius Press as *First Glance at Adrienne von Speyr*. It provides an overview of von Speyr's theology, showing its consistency amid a diverse range of topics she had addressed over the years; it also includes descriptions of her practices of prayer and scriptural contemplation, an annotated bibliography that includes her posthumous works, and the method by which the works had come into being. As her confessor, van Balthasar provides glimpses into von Speyr's joyous and cheerful personality, her early childhood experiences of mystical insights and the subsequent manifestations of the stigmata on her body, and her willingness to submit to the spiritual exercises and disciplines assigned by her confessor and patterned after Ignatius's Exercises. With regard to the sessions of dictation, von Balthasar notes von Speyr's complete self-forgetfulness in obedience to the mission set before her. "It is characteristic that when Adrienne had 'transmitted' some commission she had received—to her confessor, who was for her the representative of the Church—the matter was completely finished as far as she was concerned, so much so that it usually disappeared completely from her consciousness," he says. "She could not remember the contents of her books and it would never have occurred to her to open one of them."[113] Usually her trancelike states were induced by a simple prayer and they closed the same way. When in this state she became "the mere vehicle of a truth which had to be communicated and explained" to someone, in this case her confessor, "who understood nothing to begin with" and whom she did not recognize.[114]

Von Balthasar admits to difficulties in his role as a confessor who had to impose penitential exercises. "I was obliged to impose the program 'with authority' (a penance for me, since I would have much rather done the penance myself than demand it from her)"; and for the sake of the overall mission "it was often necessary for me to turn myself into 'sheer authority' in my behavior towards Adrienne."[115] But von Balthasar concedes that his role in what he calls a "play before God" was "infinitely easier" than that of von Speyr, "who always had to preserve absolute interior willingness, readiness, availability for any mission—however adverse—as an inner attitude."[116] Von Balthasar insists that von Speyr's mysticism was not a series of private revelations separate from Scripture and tradition but an ecclesial mysticism that supported and clarified the doctrines of the church in light of the Scriptures. Charismatics and mystics of earlier ages "were meant to set aglow the core of the faith in a new way under the promptings of the Holy Spirit," and the significance of von Speyr's life and work had to be regarded as part of "this central enlivening of Christian revelation."[117] After the dictations were made, von Speyr would review the notes to elaborate on points that seemed unclear or imprecise.

A key theme in von Speyr's thought is the person's absolute surrender and consent to the will of God. Sin is a refusal to give such consent and an insistence on being guided by one's own will in time and space. The Virgin Mary is a role model of complete surrender for Christians. By her "yes" to God she binds herself to God and thus becomes entirely free in God. This "yes" is "the highest [human] achievement made possible by grace" and it is an "unconditional, definitive self-surrender" to God. As a "synthesis of love and obedience—of John and Ignatius," this consent constitutes "the original vow, out of which arises every form of Christian

113. Hans Urs von Balthasar, *First Glance at Adrienne von Speyr*, trans. Antje Lawry and Sr. Sergia Englund, OCD (San Francisco: Ignatius Press, 1981), 53.

114. Ibid., 67.

115. Ibid., 70.

116. Ibid., 71.

117. Ibid., 58.

commitment to God and in God."[118] In fact, Mary's consent "is the archetype of Christian fruitfulness," first by the Son of God being born in Mary, then by being born "anew in each one who attempts to join in her consent."[119] In this "pure emptied space for the Incarnation of the Word, and in this state of emptiness, obedience, poverty, and virginity all are one." Such consent begins with baptism, where the believer makes an irrevocable vow to God, and it continues as an ongoing invitation in the Christian's life to respond to God's call.

In several books written largely for the consecrated lay community of St. John's, von Speyr explores the nature of this consent and its consequences for the believer. Her 1955 book *They Followed His Call: Vocation and Asceticism* (originally published as *Sie folgten Seinem Ruf*) describes the Christian vocation as an irrevocable commitment of discipleship. To her, consent to God's call, which resounds always like a voice "in the background,"[120] makes grace "palpable."[121] The call from God may come mediated by a sermon, in confession, at communion, during private prayer, or in the context of the liturgy. "As soon as the call resounds, there takes place a sort of veiling of the personality," rousing the person "to a new liveliness."[122] The call and consent do not belong to the person, however, but to the church and the church's tradition. The consent "becomes integrated with the Son's consent to the Father, the Mother's consent to the angel and with those called in both the Old and New Testaments." Hence "there is a sum of all consents which radiates a certain energy and which takes each consent spoken anew and draws it into itself," she says. The result is a "transformation," the direction of which has little to do with the person and everything to do with God. The one who has consented to God's call only has to "limp along, full of gratitude, since he has entered not the harsh impartiality of a worldly school, but the source of unheard-of graces, whose essence seems to consist in surpassing his understanding."[123] Moreover, the consent has an immediate and unexpected effect and "strips him of all that is superficial, but it burdens him heavily with new things that begin to transform him and his life in the direction of the choice."[124] Consenting to God means for the believer that "the whole of Scripture

118. Ibid., 51.
119. Ibid., 53.
120. Adrienne von Speyr, *They Followed His Call: Vocation and Asceticism*, trans. Erasmo Leiva (New York: Alba House/Society of St. Paul, 1979), 3.
121. Ibid., 6.
122. Ibid., 7.
123. Ibid., 9.
124 Ibid., 12.

now becomes a living reality" and the "Word becomes flesh in him."[125] Such consent cannot be given as a "temporary commitment" or a testing of the waters, but only as an unreserved "yes" into uncertainty. In *The Christian State of Life*, published as *Christlicher Stand* in 1956, von Speyr reflects on the use of the Ignatian Exercises in making a choice and saying one's "yes" to God. She acknowledges that the choice involves renunciation, such as in a commitment to poverty, celibacy, and obedience. But it also "gives us an opportunity to transcend our nature once and for all so that we need not wither in it forever," for by making our choice "we give the Lord the keys that enable him to be active in us in accordance with his choice." Then, when we have renounced our own "efficacy in favor of God's efficacy," God returns it to us as though it were our own. Renunciation means uncertainty, but this uncertainty is "the truth and the certainty of God" into whose hands we have now placed ourselves.[126] Making a choice before God and surrendering to God also involves complete transparency. Whereas sinners seek to cover their nakedness, as shown in the biblical account of the Fall, penitents who return to God uncover themselves completely and become transparent. Such uncovering and transparency before God, resulting from a self-surrender through which God's word can fill the void that has been prepared, takes place in confession.

Perhaps the best known of von Speyr's books is *Confession*, first published in 1960 as *Die Beichte*. It may also be the most central, since the subject of confession constitutes a focal theme in her biblical commentaries, her book on prayer, and that on Mary. What is the act and attitude of private confession, and what is the nature of the liturgical-sacramental encounter between sinner and God? she asks. Von Speyr's answers to these questions anticipate in some ways the resolutions made at the Second Vatican Council (1962–1965) with regard to interpreting the sacraments of the church, the role of the believer's active cooperation in them, and the sacraments' significance for Christians as the locus of the divine-human encounter. Noteworthy in her view of confession is the strongly dialogical nature whereby penitent and confessor engage with one another under the express guidance of and in the presence of a triune God and in joint obedience to him. Unique to von Speyr's treatment of confession is its trinitarian and christocentric character and the vivid depictions of the roles each person of the Trinity is assigned in relation to human sin, in the hearing and witnessing of confession, and in the

125. Ibid., 13.
126. Adrienne von Speyr, *The Christian State of Life*, ed. Hans Urs von Balthasar, trans. Sr. Mary Frances McCarthy (San Francisco: Ignatius Press, 1986), 156–57.

pronouncing of absolution and the obtaining of forgiveness of sins. Von Speyr begins her discourse by outlining the shortcomings of traditional psychoanalysis and psychotherapy, whose clinical methods resemble the confessional conversation. Discussion in dialogue with the therapist may foster self-expression and a degree of introspection and new insights. However, few of those seeking treatment are inclined to change anything about themselves. People seek affirmation rather than a confrontation with and exposure to the areas in their lives that need changing. Therapy often offers people a new weapon in their struggle with the environment without expecting them to understand "inwardly the lives of others and to share life with them in love." Feeling the need "to talk about how badly things are going for them," patients and clients "want to be pitied," "they want support in their rejecting attitude toward others," and in general "they care nothing about real change." The result is that "most encounters of this sort are nothing but so much prattle about oneself and about what one believes to be one's own state of affairs,"[127] providing temporary relief only and a grid that is to be rigorously followed thereafter and that "abbreviates and explains away everything that does not fit into the rigid method of analysis." Despite the positive aspects of therapy resulting in increased social responsibility or greater self-awareness, for example, "all these techniques remain human techniques, prescriptions someone has invented, to be applied in a more or less flexible or rigid fashion to as many cases as possible," yet able to "comprehend and cure only a very limited side of the human Thou," regardless of whether religious tools such as prayer are being used.[128]

Only the creator of the human soul can treat and cure the soul properly, and only God can know, disclose, and prescribe what is needed for healing. Such disclosure, along with the prescription offered, takes place when both penitent and confessor submit themselves in obedience to God. Confessors do not hear confession out of a personal need, and penitents to do not go to confession for that reason either; they do so out of obedience to God. God has already pointed to "the locus where he intends to practice psychoanalysis on sinners," and this locus is the cross and confession.[129] Even a person of simple faith can understand himself or herself as being created by God and redeemed by Christ, who has opened for humans the way to the Father. If then "he unconditionally

127. Adrienne von Speyr, *Confession*, trans. Douglas W. Stott (San Francisco: Ignatius Press, 1985), 13.
128. Ibid., 15.
129. Ibid., 16.

feels himself to be a sinner" who is living "between the two poles" of life and death, "he will expect confession with a kind of necessity." In other words, "he will expect that God offers him the possibility to return again and again to a center which God himself points out and makes accessible." The person will also sense to talk "something out according to his own or someone else's formula and to burden someone else with the problem is not enough if he wants to find his way back to that most profound correctness, the straight line connecting his birth and death."[130] While psychological sessions may be able to alter modes of behavior, confession confronts a person "with his divine destiny and places him directly within it" and within what "is final and ultimate."[131] Such a process is humbling for several reasons: first, one cannot divulge selectively what is troublesome and embarrassing, but has to reveal oneself completely; second, one is put on the same level with other sinners, regardless of social status, and the particulars and circumstances of "my case" that one might wish to elaborate on no longer matter; and third, one cannot separate the spheres of "fate" and one's "faultiness" but is forced to see one's life as a whole before God because "God himself holds the mirror before us" during confession.[132]

Confession is to be understood in light of the dynamic interrelatedness of the persons of the Trinity. Underlying the triune relationship is the principle that God takes pleasure in revealing Godself to God. Each person of the Trinity shows complete openness to the other two. This means that "God shows God what he does, and by revealing his actions he reveals himself, shows the effect of his existence as God within those actions and awaits recognition, affirmation and encouragement in order to proceed further in this exchange of revelation and self-understanding."[133] Jesus Christ is the very "prototype" of the act and attitude of confession by virtue of his relationship with the Father and the Holy Spirit. As the self-revelation and expression of the Father on earth, Jesus is also an ongoing "response to the Father." Jesus "expects a response from the Father so that he can orient himself toward the Father ever anew." This expectant responsiveness presupposes that the Son continually reveals himself to the Father while ever anticipating the intervention and directives of the Holy Spirit. With that, each person of the Trinity "is wholly himself for the sake of the other two, and for the sake of the others he

130. Ibid., 16–17.
131. Ibid., 18.
132. Ibid., 20.
133. Ibid., 21.

reveals himself completely to them."[134] Jesus lives on earth before the Father in an attitude of dependency and utter nakedness, and it is the same attitude the penitent should seek in relation to her or his confessor, the church, and God. It is an attitude of "complete openness, concealing nothing, always ready in every moment to expect the intervention of the Holy Spirit, drawing security from the Father and his Spirit instead of from within himself."[135]

The task of Jesus during his entire earthly life is that of witnessing and gathering up the sins present in the world. From the moment of his birth, through his childhood, temptation, baptism by John, and during his earthly ministry all the way to the cross, "the Son will increasingly gather sin upon himself." But because he is not touched by sin, he can "recognize, bear and confess all sin."[136] It is a gathering of sin "in anticipation of confession."[137] To Jesus, sin gradually manifests itself in its many hues and appearances, becoming ever more tangible and differentiated as his life progresses. "Each gives him pain in a different way," exposing "countless vulnerable surfaces" and "in places in his soul he never suspected were there."[138] The experiences in the wilderness and in the garden on the Mount of Olives are periods of pause and contemplation. Here "the will of the Father is accepted in a fresh and explicit way" and Jesus makes "fresh contact with the Father."[139] These periods in Jesus' life resemble one's making a general confession "in which the entirety of one's life is spread out and presented so that God may arrange it in a new way." Meanwhile, absolution is delayed because the hour of the cross has not yet come.[140]

On the cross Jesus is completely naked and exposed to the forces of sin. By being in this vulnerable state he reassumes Adam's nakedness, not "because of innocence, but rather because of sin, for his arms embrace all that is, was and will be." When he is on the cross, "everything, completely exposed and in all its truth, is thrust upon the Naked One."[141] What Jesus had initially gathered in a more or less orderly manner "now suddenly turns against him in all its weight like an alien external power, and it seems to him that he does not have the slightest thing in common

134. Ibid., 22.
135. Ibid., 23.
136. Ibid., 32.
137. Ibid., 45.
138. Ibid., 47.
139. Ibid., 48–49.
140. Ibid., 49.
141. Ibid., 51.

with all that he has taken upon himself." While he is vulnerable, extended, and naked, "every spearhead of every sin is pointed toward him and wounds him," and the cry of his confession is "Everything!" When "here and there something specific appears and acquires contours . . . then his cry becomes 'That, too!'"[142] Meanwhile, the Father participates in the Son's suffering, though the Son, in his agony of absorbing sin in its totality, is no longer aware of the Father's participation and "no longer comprehends his own intention" of seeking to redirect "the spearhead of sin," originally aimed at the Father, "toward himself." It may be that it is "this meaninglessness that kills him."[143] Thus Jesus suffers from his alienation from the Father and the alienation of the sinner from the Father as "the mediator between the two."[144] Jesus' complete openness and exposure to sin models the attitude one should assume in the act of confession. The movement of carrying our sins to confession is "comparable to the movement of the Son carrying all sins to the cross," whereby each sin is "the coarse, rough, raw element comparable to the beams of the Cross." Similarly, the confessor who hears them and "accepts them in the commission of the Holy Spirit" acts in a mode similar to that of the Father, who "accepts them at the behest of the Son on the Cross."[145]

During Jesus' descent into hell, sin takes on a new proportion. On Good Friday the Son bore unto his own death "the sin of every individual," whereby "each sin appeared bound to the sinner and bore the characteristics of the subject that had committed it." But on Holy Saturday, during the descent into hell and "from the perspective of the underworld, sin extricates itself from the subject of the sinner until it is only the hideous, amorphous element that constitutes the terror of the underworld and elicits the horror of the observer."[146] Sin now appears "in its final, eternal ineluctability"; it is an anonymous mass, detached from the individual sinner.[147] In a similar way the confessor hears the sins of the penitent, but they stand "objectified between the confession itself and the absolution"; they are "seemingly measured out, yet immeasurable,"[148] for that is how sin looks when separated from the human being.

With the resurrection, Jesus' body is raised from death and out of hell. This raising "comes like a bolt of lightning" to him and "it is the abrupt

142. Ibid., 52.
143. Ibid., 53.
144. Ibid.
145. Ibid., 53–54.
146. Ibid., 57–58.
147. Ibid., 58.
148. Ibid., 55.

absolution." In the same way, the penitent surrenders "the finished confession into the hands of the confessor," focusing attention only on the sin committed with no concern for what the confessor may do with it. The penitent does not anticipate absolution, so that when it comes, "it comes to him like a bolt of lightning."[149] Resurrection, like absolution, is the "reacquisition of all that had been suspended" in the Son, namely, union with the Father and divinity. When the Son, who had taken on sin for all humanity, receives absolution as humanity's representative, he also experiences the joy of all those who are redeemed and forgiven. Thus the Son sees in everyone whom he has redeemed "someone filled with joy in whom, as part of the Father's mission, he may dwell." With the resurrection, Jesus "thus discovers himself in a person," or, as the apostle Paul describes it, "it is no longer I who live, but it is Christ who lives in me" (Gal 2:20). On the cross Jesus could only see the sin of the human being he was carrying and he "breathed his own spirit, the Holy Spirit of love, back to the Father." With the resurrection, however, he "has new powers of disposition over his own love, and all humanity is itself new, mature, fruitful and loving in the triune God."[150] Thus those who willingly and expectantly confess their sins and receive absolution in the name of the triune God reacquire what has been lost through sin, namely, the indwelling of the Holy Spirit manifested in love of neighbor, Christ being alive in the believer as the divine nature inhabiting the human, and a union with the Father through the Son's confession and the absolution he has received from the Father on behalf of and as a representative of all humanity.

Jesus invents, models, and institutes confession for us and imparts it to the church. The purpose of confession is bound up with the life of Jesus Christ and the incarnation. Both are aimed at glorifying the Father. Jesus' mission is the "ultimate glorification of the Father, and its most sublime expression is the Son's glorification of the Father's creation." With the redemptive act of taking on the sins of the world he "so glorifies something that belongs to the Father that the Father experiences the splendor of this something which is his and which has been taken out of him."[151] Confession, then, is not only an act of obedience in openness to God; it is an act of love by which we allow that through our bodies, now cleansed of sin through absolution, God may be glorified in and through us for the sake of others and the world.

---

149. Ibid., 59.
150. Ibid., 60.
151. Ibid., 61.

Summary

What do these theological considerations suggest for the practice of private confession in the twenty-first century? Is there still a place for private confession and, if so, what form might it take and in what context might it be carried out? Based on the above theological reflections and findings, four guiding observations emerge. First, the frequency with which Christians go to confession in the Catholic Church, for example, is in decline, resulting largely from a changed perception of the "need" for the sacrament. In Rahner's words, this is not a catastrophe but an invitation to pay more attention to the ever-present self-communication of God and the mystery of God's grace in all things, made evident in the centrality of the Christ event, rather than a categorical need to be justified before God or having one's guilt removed. Confession is a sacrament because it offers a locus in which God's self-communication is made tangible, so that going to confession enriches the individual's knowledge of God and the experience of grace. The sacrament is less obligatory than revelatory, a means of awakening and strengthening one's God-awareness; by demonstrating responsiveness to the mystery of God in the act of confessing, one returns to God and is allowed to experience God more deeply in turn. Going to confession is largely an act of devotion. When doing so, believers are encouraged to choose an experienced and sensitive confessor who can carry out the pastoral function toward which the confessional process is aimed. The principal sin is saying "no" to God's self-communication while being cognizant and aware of it.

Second, Dietrich Bonhoeffer reminds us that turning toward God in repentance and humility is a lifelong process. In Bonhoeffer's view both individuals and the church as a whole always stand in need of God's forgiveness and should feel compelled to repent and give visible outward expression to an inner attitude. To that end believers may seek out another fellow believer, someone designated by the community perhaps and not necessarily the pastor, to whom to confess regularly, particularly in preparation for Holy Communion, and from whom to receive directly the words of God's forgiveness in Christ. The confessor is to be a mature Christian who practices confession himself or herself. The church or the entire community of Christians should also make public confession whenever it has failed God's ordinances as Christ's reconciling body and witness in the world. The course of nations and the world's history depend on the church's and the individual's willingness to confess. Sin is, above all, flight from God and establishing one's own ordinances and laws, thereby reneging on the responsibility of being God's witness and active agent in the world and shaping a course of history aligned with God's designs of peace, order, and justice.

Third, Eugene Peterson speaks of confession as made to God directly or to another Christian, perhaps accompanied by visible acts of submission and contrition. In Peterson's view discerning the activity of the Spirit as God's self-disclosure to us is the lifelong task of the Christian. The Scriptures and preaching are the supreme vehicles by which God speaks to humans, but another Christian may serve as a third, though somewhat subordinate, source of divine revelation, especially in the context of spiritual direction. Here Christians are guided in praying rightly and discerning the movement and the "direction" of God's Spirit for their lives at a particular time and place. The primary sin is lovelessness toward neighbor and idolatry—putting the ego, along with its self-interest, in the place reserved for God.

Fourth, Adrienne von Speyr's mystical insight shows us that confession has been supremely modeled for us by Jesus Christ, who in continuous communication with the Father through the Spirit "confessed" the sin witnessed during his earthly life to the Father and made atonement for it by means of his suffering on the cross on our behalf. Jesus models confession for us by his intimate exchanges with the Father, so that confessing is a form of Christian discipleship that places us within the dynamic interior life of the trinitarian God. The major sin is withholding our "yes" from God who is seeking to come to us bodily and who, as in the case of Mary, wishes to birth in us the new creation physically and visibly as testimony of God's glory to others, and who wishes to draw us into intimate union with God.

These theological observations offer us entry points for constructing an approach to confession that may prove helpful to Christians within the context of their own denominational affiliation or apart from it. The next step will be to outline concrete ways of encouraging private confession among church members and within the Christian community. The topics to be addressed are questions surrounding the choice of a confessor, serving as confessor to others, the particular sins to be confessed, the nature of one's penance, the frame of a litany that might guide the confessional dialogue between believer and the one hearing confession, and catechetical considerations.

PART FOUR

Why Confession Matters
Practical Considerations

In recent years spiritual disciplines and devotional practices have gained increasing popularity with Christians, both Catholics and Protestants. Among them are contemplative prayer, guided meditation, *lectio divina*, spiritual direction, silence, solitude, and directed retreats. The burgeoning interest in spirituality has rediscovered ancient Christian disciplines, monastic observances, and spiritual formation. The reason for this cultural orientation may lie in the outlook the current postmodern era shares with Christians living prior to the age of Emperor Constantine: the emperor had not yet joined the church, the military forces of the kingdom and the institutional church had not yet merged into the powerful movement of Christendom, and citizenship and being Christian were not yet synonymous. In the words of Robert E. Webber, "The cultural situation of the current church is much like the culture in which Christianity emerged in the first three centuries," a culture defined, in short, by "competing religions, a marginalized church, [and] pagan values."[1] This new cultural era, commonly described as post-Christendom or postmodernity, has not only seen the rediscovery of ancient spiritual practices but has also threatened the church's identity and changed what it means to be a Christian.

One of the leading Christian thinkers of the postmodern era is pastor and author Brian McLaren, who sees "a new kind of Christian"[2] emerging.

1. Robert E. Webber, *Journey to Jesus: The Worship, Evangelism, and Nurture Mission of the Church* (Nashville: Abingdon, 2001), 18–19.
2. As the founding pastor of Cedar Ridge Community Church in the Baltimore-Washington area, Brian McLaren has been active in networking with and mentoring church planters and pastors since the mid-1980s and has assisted in the development of

This "new kind of Christian" is shaped by two losses: of an objectifiable truth and of the church's authority and credibility in society. As lone voices in a plurality of many, postmodern Christianity and a marginalized church have lost their former status as society's trendsetting agents of moral values and authorities on divine truth. Even more important, they have lost the certainty of modernity's belief that faith could be interpreted and validated by the categories of reason, science, and empiricism. Whereas once modernity relied on the sciences and reason for making truth claims, postmodernity rejects the notion that truth claims can ever be affirmed with certainty or that an objective, independent type of truth exists at all. This has had far-reaching consequences for the church and its efforts in evangelization and mission. While in the era of modernity it was believed that Christian truth existed and could be transmitted, often in an effort to wield control and elicit consent among current and prospective church members, postmodernity no longer leaves one that option: it only knows a truth that is "my truth"—one experienced by interaction with and immersion in the concrete life and fabric of the community of faith. This community is made up of a mosaic of distinct voices, each valid and equal in weight, that together hint at the larger picture, namely, that of Christ's incarnate presence and face. For postmodern Christians it is impossible to know the truth of Christ apart from the community that seeks to live in his company and be sustained by his Spirit. One has to enter and engage with communal life to hear spoken and learn to speak a distinct reality-shaping language and see there a Christian message embodied in the way members act and interact. In this situation spiritual practices have come to play a leading role as ways—the only ways—of offering access to an experience defined as the power and presence of Christ.

Postmodern Christians have put in the place of their losses a truth that is experiential, tangible, and embodied. The losses of no longer being able to lay claim to objective truth and of being among those who have a powerful institution behind them as backing are also gain and blessing. Deprived of these two "powers," postmodern Christians are left little

---

several new churches, largely aimed at reaching the unchurched. Author of numerous books on being Christian in the postmodern era, he is a popular speaker and leader in the church's postmodern ministry. His third book, *A New Kind of Christian*, published in 2001, is the first in a trilogy aimed at exploring the distinction between modernity and postmodernity and its implications for the church's mission and ministry in the twenty-first century; this book, like its two sequels, takes the form of a novel prominently featuring two friends, one functioning as teacher, the other as student. For the odyssey of his convictions and the books' chosen format see *A New Kind of Christian: A Tale of Two Friends on a Spiritual Journey* (San Francisco: Jossey-Bass, 2001), xiii–xxii.

choice but to locate their power and identity in the immediate source of their faith, namely, Jesus Christ. Bereft of propositional truths, they are thrust into living an incarnational, embodied truth if sharing the good news of the Gospel with others is to be relevant and convincing at all. As a result they look to the Scriptures as God's testimony of Godself, the incarnation of Jesus Christ as God's supreme self-revelation in history, and the Gospel as the message of salvation offered to all. They also look to the tradition of the church throughout history, in particular that of the church fathers, in which Christians were still novices at describing the new kingdom reality that had come upon them and in which the entire world had been made subject to Christ's reign and final judgment. In seeking to recover the original enthusiasm of early Christians and the closeness to their source of faith, these Christians attempt to relive the method of Christ's early followers: being a community that testifies to Christ's rule among them in word and deed and perceives its own role and mission in the world as that of Christ's reconciling body. It is not surprising, then, that we are witnessing the reemergence of Christian spiritual practices, since they both enable and enhance the Christian experience and are venues for unbelievers and believers alike to be overcome in the here and now by the revealed mystery of a living God.

Among the spiritual practices and disciplines that have been commonly appropriated by the Christian community of the postmodern era, private confession still remains among the least explored and perhaps most underrated. One reason for this neglect might be that during the first three centuries of the pre-Constantinian era private confession among Christians was virtually unknown except when an occasional visitor sought out a hermit or desert monastic; it was introduced by the Celtic monks and adopted by the larger church only some two hundred years later. Nonetheless, the devotional nature of private confession holds a promise similar to contemplative prayer, worship, silent retreats, or the frequent reception of communion for deepening the Christian faith and attaining to its experiential truth. Another reason for the neglect, particularly in Protestant churches, may be that the practical steps of making private confession available to members and reflecting theologically on its benefits have not been sufficiently explored. It is these aspects in particular that will be addressed in what follows.

CHAPTER SEVENTEEN

The Choice of a Confessor

To whom do I want to entrust my deep, occasionally dark secrets, thoughts of anger and despair weighing on my conscience, making me unsettled, restless, and rough? Who will speak to me the words of forgiveness that resound as if they were spoken to me by Christ? And where am I reassured that these confidences will not be betrayed and backfire with missile power? These are difficult questions to answer if we believe that the word of forgiveness does not find an easy substitute in psychotherapy, private prayer, or the common confessional liturgy. Yet if we believe that the words spoken to us by a brother or sister are to be like Christ's words of forgiveness spoken to us directly, we will be looking for this brother or sister within the community of faith, the church.

Priests and Friars

It seems obvious to consider those first who have been trained to hear confessions, are professionally obligated to keep confidences, and are steeped in the long ecclesial tradition of this practice. Both priests and friars—male members of religious communities ordained to the priesthood—are expected to participate in confession themselves and are able to administer the sacrament by pronouncing the words of absolution. Since the twelfth century Roman Catholics have been given the freedom to choose a priest other than their own for confession, which might preclude a subsequent awkwardness in encounters outside the confessional or reconciliation room. Most parishes list in their bulletin, the phone book, or on their web site, the times during the week when confessions are being heard so that it is relatively easy to make a selection. This regular and ready availability of the sacrament of confession is one of the great services the church offers people seeking to live a more holy and devout life before God. The service is not limited to Roman Catholics. Rather, by its public nature it constitutes a standing invitation to Protestants, who might be unfamiliar with the sacramental process yet desire a closer relationship with God. Thus they can make their first acquaintance with this devotional practice and experience its benefits for the life of faith. Why, indeed, should Protestants not engage in one of the oldest penitential practices during the seasons of the church year that have been designated for it? During Lent and Advent, prior to Easter or Christmas, they might join their Catholic brothers and sisters in a devotional discipline that has been practiced for more than fifteen hundred years. They might enter a Catholic church, knock on the door of the reconciliation room or confessional whose green light is signaling entry, and be guided by the priest through the litany of prayer, confession, and absolution. Before entering the room Protestants should know, as most Catholics already do, that they have the choice of remaining anonymous by kneeling behind a screen or being seated in the room facing the priest. Lack of familiarity with the litany and what to do or say is hardly an issue: The priest will guide in the confessional litany, prompting the believer when to begin the confession, opening and closing with prayer, assigning a penance, pronouncing absolution, and offering the benediction.

Catholics may be more comfortable choosing a diocesan priest other than their own. However, they should be aware of the limitations on the amount of time the priest can give, especially if the confessional dialogue is to be more frequent and regular. Given the demands made on diocesan priests by the complexities of today's parishes, believers may prefer to visit a friar or monastic at a religious community nearby. Often these communities also house retreat centers with overnight accommodations for visitors, and they may offer retreats during which confession is available. Among the houses and centers operated by such religious orders as the Benedictines, the Dominicans, and the Franciscans—(whose abbreviations are OSB, OP, and OSF, respectively), one might consider Jesuit centers in particular. By virtue of the order's history and the aims of the Society of Jesus (members have an SJ after their name) and of their founder, Ignatius of Loyola, Jesuits are uniquely trained and equipped to hear confession and offer spiritual counsel. Found mostly in bigger cities and near or on university campuses, Jesuit churches and centers offer regular hours for confession and spiritual consultation with a priest. Jesuits also make available retreats on the Spiritual Exercises of Ignatius, a method of guided meditation on the mysteries of Jesus' life, death, and resurrection, including the practice of discernment of spirits, making an election, and an examination of the conscience with the possibility of private confession.

Women and Men Religious

Members of religious communities who are not ordained to the priesthood are precluded from administering the sacraments. In regard to confession this means specifically that they cannot pronounce the formula of absolution. However, they can make themselves available to hear confessions in the larger sense, opening and closing the confessional dialogue with prayer, offering words of forgiveness on Christ's behalf, and following the general outline of the rite (Appendixes IV and V). Since by virtue of their religious vows they are expected to go to confession themselves and live by the rule of their community, vowed religious bring a wealth of depth and experience in matters of the spirit. It is probably no exaggeration to say that male and female religious are the most overlooked and underused when it comes to this devotional practice. This is especially deplorable given the fact that among the members of the body of Christ they may be some of the most qualified for doing so. From their own lives in consecrated communities they know the spiritual struggles that come with seeking to discern the will of God, are acquainted with the darker and oppressive sides of human nature and the conscience, and have learned to persevere against the obstacles of a society and culture that know little about vowed commitment to God in pursuit of a holy life. Since the church does not recognize vowed religious as confessors in the strict sense, they have taken on the title of spiritual director, even though they may function as the former. When someone seeks out a religious for confession, the spiritual director and directee may want to discuss the intended format of their meeting to provide sufficient flexibility. Their conversation may contain elements of both spiritual direction and confession, not unlike the colloquy that was customary in the early stages of the history of private confession between a wise man or woman and one seeking spiritual guidance. The conversation's confidentiality, which is binding for priests by nature of their ordination vows, should be agreed upon from the outset. Information about monastics who offer spiritual direction may be obtained from the diocesan office, the local parish, or the religious houses themselves.

Protestant Pastors and Church Officers

Some Protestant denominations offer members the opportunity for private confession with absolution. In the liturgies of the Lutheran and Episcopal churches for this rite it is the pastors or priests who serve as confessors. One can speculate about the reasons for the decline of the practice. They may be similar to those among Roman Catholics: other alternatives, such as psychotherapy and spiritual direction, are seemingly meeting the need for sharing confidences and receiving guidance in matters of the spirit and the soul; an awareness of the complex demands of a parish may make parishioners reluctant to take up more of the pastor's time; the shame associated with divulging intimate details of one's weaknesses and failings is a deterrent to parishioners, especially those in positions of active leadership and prominence in the life of the church. While the pastor may be best equipped for hearing confession by virtue of his or her theological training and pastoral experience, parishioners often prefer someone other than the pastor. Since the period of the Protestant Reformation some Protestant denominations have assigned select ministerial roles to ordained officers of the church, such as elders (in the Reformed tradition) or deacons (in some Baptist and Congregational traditions), commissioned by the congregation to facilitate pastoral ministry. One of these roles has been that of confessor. During annual home visits, elders, for example, might inquire of members about the quality of their Christian discipleship and faithfulness regarding morality, tithing, and discipline. The purpose of such an organized "confrontation" was to give the wayward and the weak the opportunity to confess their wrongdoing and amend their ways. Even though the tradition has nearly disappeared in church life today, it has left unpleasant memories associated with the office of elder or deacon in regard to private confession. Moreover, the confidentiality of confession is no longer a given in such an arrangement since officers are likely, and even obligated in some cases, to report their findings to the pastor, local judicatory, and even the entire congregation.

Fellow Parishioners

It may seem logical to suggest that each parishioner, each member of a Christian community, is qualified to serve as confessor to another by listening, exhorting, and pronouncing the words of forgiveness on Christ's behalf. Luther certainly had suggested as much in principle, so that even a child, should the situation require it, could serve in that role. The practice, however, has shown different developments. While Calvin had sought to maintain the principle of the priesthood of all believers, specific pastoral functions such as preaching, interpreting the Scriptures, offering pastoral counsel and guidance, had been reserved as the pastor's province. Others, including Philipp Jakob Spener in the late seventeenth century, sought to revive Luther's idea of the role of confessor as one shared by all members of a community. When this principle worked, as in the case of Spener's conventicles or Wesley's societies or classes, it was in the context of a small and intimate group—a circle, in short, whose members were committed to meeting regularly for edification and counsel, Scripture reading and exposition, and mutual exhortation. A version of private confession to another Christian—if one can call it that—took and continues to take place in instances of reconciliation between two parties at odds, the offender and the offended, where a transgression is admitted, forgiveness extended, and reparations made. Dietrich Bonhoeffer's underground seminary community at Finkenwalde proves an exception to the pattern of private confession among Protestants: some members of this close-knit community were appointed as private confessors to the others. In addition, there have existed throughout the church's history Christians who, through a holy life lived often in solitude and silence, came to the attention of their fellow Christians. Considered worthy guides in matters of the soul, these men and women were called hermits, beguines, or anchorites, depending on their habitation and living conditions. Committed to Christian discipleship and the pursuit of holiness and perfection, they rose to unwitting prominence as those whose counsel could be relied upon, whose hearts would keep safe the secrets entrusted to them, and whose directives would bring to the soul healing and health. Such hermits and people devoted to Christian discipleship who are living in relative isolation are found today as well.[1]

Given the relatively easy access to those professionally trained and experienced at hearing confession, such as priests, friars, and members of religious communities, one might wonder what would warrant seeking out another lay member to function as confessor and spiritual guide. Based on the developments of the past five centuries, three occasions when a parishioner might hear private confession suggest themselves: one, in cases where an individual or a group is in a state of crisis and under imminent threat; two, where the dictates of the Holy Spirit suggest hearing confession and extending the words of forgiveness; and three, where special provisions and preparations have been made for laypeople to function temporarily in that capacity. In the first instance crisis and threat may preclude seeking out an experienced confessor, such as a priest; the individual may be at the point of death, or a community may be in hiding and under threat of persecution by the state. In these cases it is only appropriate that laypersons should hear confession and extend the reassuring and healing words of forgiveness on Christ's behalf. A similar scenario exists when parents baptize a newborn child that is at

1. For an example see www.stillsonghermitage.org.

the point of death or when soldiers in battle administer last rites to one another. The seminary community at Finkenwalde is an example of a group in crisis; under the threat of persecution and the prospect of death at the hands of their persecutors they felt compelled to train their own for the hearing of private confession.

Second, there may be instances in which one is placed in the involuntary role of confessor and the situation may warrant a symbolic act of absolution. One can think of situations when strangers on the airplane and in the subway pour out their life story and reveal a state of their soul's agitation that calls for the spoken words of Christ's forgiveness and cleansing. A spontaneous intercessory prayer offered and the Lord's Prayer said together will serve as an incarnational sign and a sacramental presence of Christ's succor and healing.

Finally, there are special occasions in the church's life and ministry that might call for enlisting the help of laypeople to hear confession. Such occasions are evangelistic crusades or mission events, for example, when lay counselors are trained for this specific task. To argue on the basis of the principle of the priesthood of all believers that the ministry of confession should be extended to other occasions and to all members of the body at all times seems more legalistic than pastoral and practical; it would certainly not be in the best interest of those in need of spiritual counsel and consolation. The answer the Carmelite reformer and mystic Teresa of Avila (1515–1582) gave when asked about the type of confessor to look for, a holy or a learned one, is still valid today: "My opinion has always been and always will be that every Christian should try to consult some learned person if he can, and the more learned the person the better."[2]

---

2. Teresa of Avila, *Life*, 13; quoted in Kenneth Leech, *Soul Friend: Spiritual Direction in the Modern World* (Harrisburg, PA: Morehouse, 2001), 62.

CHAPTER EIGHTEEN

Serving as
(a Good) Confessor to Others

Training in preparation for hearing confession is a required course in Roman Catholic seminaries. Prospective priests learn about the dynamics of the confessional dialogue through instruction in sacramental theology, case studies, and mutual practice sessions. What are the questions to anticipate, what the responses, what the follow-up questions, what the attitude to keep in mind throughout the process? An inside look at a seminary course on confession is *A Confessor's Handbook* by Kurt Stasiak, OSB. Stasiak teaches such a course, among others in liturgical and sacramental theology, at Saint Meinrad's School of Theology. His book explores the basic theological principles underlying the confessional dialogue and offers practical suggestions and case studies, illustrating what the confessor is to keep in mind and what to avoid. What is it that makes for an effective confessor? The confessor's effectiveness, says Stasiak, "is never measured entirely by how well one knows 'what to do,'" but depends on the degree to which one is "credible." The confessor "is credible when he knows from his own experience as penitent the fear and the courage with which his people approach the sacrament. He is credible because he has experienced, with another minister, both the embarrassment of his sin and the gift of God's grace." While knowing human behavior and being familiar with the art of pastoral counseling is helpful, the effective and credible confessor is first and foremost the one who "knows what it is to confess to another and have another minister to him."[1] No amount of seminary training and education can substitute for the experience of regularly submitting to the discipline of

1. Kurt Stasiak, OSB, *A Confessor's Handbook* (New York: Paulist Press, 1999), 96–97.

confession, repeatedly mustering in humility the courage to admit to another person one's wrongdoing and experiencing the grace of God's forgiveness in the words spoken to us on Christ's behalf.

Pastors in the Protestant tradition, including those with a tradition of private confession, would benefit from having a general understanding of the theological principles of confession. During pastoral consultations and home and hospital visits with parishioners they are bound to hear stories filled with expressions of remorse, guilt, self-reproach, and shame. In many ways these conversations resemble sacramental confession. The pastoral role is one of careful and emphatic listening, while allowing Christ to enter into the conversation and acting as representative and spokesperson on Christ's behalf. The preparation of prospective pastors for the role of confessor during seminary education may take place in the context of a course on pastoral care and counseling and during clinical pastoral education. The disadvantage of placing such training strictly in the practical areas of a seminary education is that the principles of confession, based on its theological, sacramental, and liturgical foundations and developments in church history, are not sufficiently addressed. To complement the theoretical understanding of confession, students could be introduced also to the experience of confession. This might happen in a small group patterned after Spener's or Wesley's confessional groups, whose members submit themselves to the making and hearing of mutual confession, edification, and exhortation over the length of a semester or quarter. Once introduced to the practice in seminary, ministers might be more likely to continue it when actively serving a parish. Calvin's company of pastors is an example of a confessional group whose members meet for mutual edification and exhortation. A reasonable fear among Protestant pastors is that the group's members will break confidentiality and professional lives will be ruined as a result. This fear is legitimate. Without the "seal" of confession by which Roman Catholic and Episcopal priests are obligated to keep confidential the information shared, Protestant pastors may be skeptical of sharing with denominational peers their wrongdoing and sinful behavior. Thus limited in observing and participating in the practice of confession, they are potentially less equipped for serving as confessors than are those with the experience. Regular meetings with a spiritual director or a priestly confessor outside one's own denomination can offer the experience of coming before another in humility and have the potential of making one a more "effective" pastor.

CHAPTER NINETEEN

What to Confess

Most people tend to talk to God somewhat spontaneously, if only under their breath. Saying a prayer of gratitude or uttering a cry for help seems to come naturally and no long preparation or deliberation is needed. Baring our soul in the company of another and in the presence of God is a form of prayer, though one involving some prior reflection. What is it I want to tell God in the company of another, and from what burden do I need to be freed? Into what segments have I sliced my time, my attention, my activities? What are my life's priorities and what its recurring joys and repeated frustrations? There are times throughout the day when I do not like myself. Where am I true to myself and where am I marring the image God intended for me to demonstrate?

Deliberating on our priorities in life and trying to see ourselves from the perspective in which God sees us is an exercise in contemplation. Such contemplation takes time. For some it may happen during worship or at Mass; hearing a thoughtful sermon, allowing ourselves to be carried away by the tune of a melody, the words of a hymn, an anthem, may set in motion a tiny prayer wheel. For others a walk in the park or on the nature trail will do infinitely more for allowing life's questions to sprout and come to the fore so we can ponder and compose the answers. It is these answers that tend to point us to the shortcomings and failures we have known all along but have pushed back. Such contemplation is preparation for prayer in someone else's company, prayer that finds utterance in the act of resolving to go to confession, sitting or kneeling in the reconciliation room, and saying what the silence in us has produced.

Over the centuries the church has composed lists, columns, and eventually catalogues of sins and vices to help prod our poor memories and make us take responsibility for some at least. These catalogues were divided into sins that would lead to eternal damnation should one die before having confessed and received absolution for them, and those that were less grave and would allow for entry into the heavenly realms, albeit with some discomfort. The distinction between mortal and venial sins goes back to St. Augustine (354–430), who differentiated between sins unto death and pardonable sins.[1] The definition was adopted by St. Thomas Aquinas (1225–1274) and clarified in his *Summa Theologiae*, then ratified at the Council of Trent in the sixteenth century and again at the Second Vatican Council in the twentieth. Even though Luther and other reformers had protested the intelligibility and practicality of such a distinction it remains the traditional classification of sins to this day. According to the *Catechism of the Catholic Church*, "All mortal sins of which penitents after a diligent self-examination are conscious must be recounted by them in confession, even if they are most secret and have been committed against the last two precepts of the Decalogue, for these sins sometimes wound the soul more grievously and more dangerously than those which are committed openly."[2] Also carried over from the Council of Trent, but formulated as early as the twelfth century at the Fourth Lateran Council, comes the stipulation that those "aware of having committed a mortal sin must not receive Holy Communion" until they have made confession.[3] Thus the types of sins that will need confessing are those violating the commandments of the Decalogue, better known as the Ten Commandments. Reviewing the Ten Commandments prior to confession is intended to raise awareness of potential violations. The last two sins the *Catechism* highlights are committed in secret and reside in the heart. Their concealment is considered "dangerous" because the heart is the seedbed and source from which spring the desire and the will to go against the design of God. For a list of the Ten Commandments, see Appendix I.

The second type of sin, according to the *Catechism*, comprises "everyday faults," called "venial sins."[4] Assuming that people do not commit mortal sins very often, venial sins tend to be those confessed by people who go to confession frequently, perhaps once a week or a few times a month, and for whom doing so has become a devotional practice. This practice, says the *Catechism*, "helps us form our conscience, fight against evil tendencies, let ourselves be healed by Christ and progress in the life

1. See John Paul II, *Reconciliation and Penance (Reconciliatio et Paenitentia): Post-Synodal Apostolic Exhortation, December 2, 1984* (Washington, DC: United States Catholic Conference, 1984), 31, III.

2. *Catechism of the Catholic Church* (Liguori, MO: Liguori Publications, 1994), 1456, p. 365.

3. Ibid., 1457, p. 365.

4. Ibid., 1458, p. 366.

of the Spirit." By receiving and experiencing God's mercy more regularly "we are spurred to be merciful as he is merciful." Or, as it was poignantly put by Augustine, "The beginning of good works is the confession of evil works."[5] Thus confession may make mention of both the sins named in the Ten Commandments and those that constitute everyday faults. The distinction between mortal and venial sins may be more important to canon lawyers and theological experts than to people in the pews. Knowing the distinction and differentiating accordingly is not necessary during the confessional dialogue. More important is to have searched one's conscience with honesty and being willing to lay bare those areas in one's life that the conscience has identified as standing in need of correction, forgiveness, and healing.

Another way of identifying what to confess may be less abstract or theoretical since it begins with everyday human experience. The approach comes from Karl Rahner, who suggests that we look not at sins, which can be isolated and detached from human beings and sorted by degrees of severity and attributed to various circumstances, etc., but at the experience of human guilt. Guilt is never isolated or individualist but is always guilt before God. Rahner distinguishes between objective and subjective guilt before God. Objective guilt results from actions that are considered wrongful behavior by common moral standards, while subjective guilt is produced by those actions the person considers wrong even though others, including the church, might not. The ability to identify guilt before God, whether objective or subjective, is inherent in human nature. No code of law or catalogue of sins is needed to impart the knowledge that one has sinned; rather, conscience reveals it innately. This is not say that the Ten Commandments or the Sermon on the Mount, for example, are superfluous; it only means that human beings have the capacity to know, even subconsciously, that they have resisted God and uttered their "no" to him. The Scriptures, the prayers of the church, the proclamation of God's word, and the sacraments are ways of quickening the conscience toward realizing, admitting, and confessing that one has resisted God; they make tangible and experiential in the present this "no" one has spoken in the past. At the same time, they offer an equally tangible and embodied way of experiencing the forgiveness of God, of which the most concrete is the sacrament of penance. Thus searching one's conscience in light of the Scriptures and one's life as part of the church and the church's actions as the body of Christ in the world will

5. Ibid.

suggest and reveal the areas where we have refused grace, which is God's ongoing self-communication to us. Our ability to confess is caused by grace preceding it, but the actual doing of it, from our end, requires cooperation and partnership in dialogue with God. We know what to confess when we allow ourselves to be exposed to the mystery of God's grace, tangibly revealed in the life of the church and the sacraments, thereby participating in life with God and responding to God.

An easy way of helping us identify what to confess is the practice of examining our conscience at the end of a day. This daily exercise, practiced perhaps unconsciously by many during evening prayers, helps us to reflect on God's activity in a given day and is the cultivation of a habit that will prove useful in preparing for confession. The method comes from the founder of the Jesuits, Ignatius of Loyola (1491–1556), and is called the examen prayer or "Daily Particular Examination of Conscience."[6] The word "examen" refers to the examination of conscience, or one's consciousness, another word for translating the Latin *conscientia*. In his book *My Life With the Saints*, James Martin, SJ, describes the daily practice in five simple steps:[7] First, ask God to be with you. Then recall the events of the day for which you are grateful, such as "a phone call from a friend, an enjoyable meal, a tough job finally completed." Then review the day as if it were "a movie" being replayed in your head, "seeking an awareness of where you accepted (or did not accept) God's grace." For example, "When you recall someone offering you a kind word, you might say to yourself, 'Yes, there was God,'" and "when you recall treating someone with disrespect, you might say, 'Yes, there I turned away from God.'"[8] Then one asks God for forgiveness for the particular ways in which one has turned away from God that day. The prayer is concluded by asking God for the grace to follow God more closely the next day and, as Ignatius suggests, the Lord's Prayer. Following the steps of the examen prayer is designed to raise our awareness of God's presence in everyday events, at the same time raising our awareness of where we repeatedly avoid or run counter to God's ways for us.

6. Ignatius of Loyola, "Spiritual Exercises," in *Ignatius of Loyola: The Spiritual Exercises and Selected Works*, ed. George E. Ganss, SJ (New York: Paulist Press, 1991), 24–31, 130–31.

7. This approach to the examen prayer is actually the collapsing of the daily examination of conscience and the general examination of conscience, which in recent years has become common practice; see Katherine Dyckman, SNJM, Mary Garvin, SNJM, and Elizabeth Liebert, SNJM, *The Spiritual Exercises Reclaimed: Uncovering Liberating Possibilities For Women* (New York: Paulist Press, 2001), 114.

8. James Martin, SJ, *My Life With the Saints* (Chicago: Loyola University Press, 2006), 87–88.

A more comprehensive method of preparing for confession is to review the entirety of one's life by using steps similar to those outlined in the examen prayer. The practice is known as making general confession and, again, Ignatius's Exercises are its model. At the beginning of the first week of the four-week-long Exercises, participants make a comprehensive inventory of their life in preparation for confession at week's end. Ignatius himself had done so on starting his Christian journey at the monastery at Monserrat. A review of one's life may be particularly appropriate in preparing for "first confession," as in "first communion" in the Roman Catholic Church. Preparing for first confession is a way of discerning lifelong patterns of resistance to and cooperation with God, enhancing future examinations of the conscience and discerning (bad) habits of the will and heart. In *Reconciliation: Preparing for Confession in the Episcopal Church*, Martin L. Smith, SSJE, suggests preparing for first confession by taking a life inventory. Obviously, doing so will involve prior consultation with one's confessor or spiritual director. Making a covenant beforehand and setting a date by when the exercise is to be completed will ensure some measure of accountability. It is well known that Ignatius's confession lasted three full days. Today a general confession might take at least a few hours. Smith gives an overview of the preparatory process and its practical steps. These steps proceed in three stages. The first stage is the process of reviewing one's life without aids, where the conscience is allowed to be at work. It is suggested here to divide up one's life into five or six phases, where one recalls the experiences of those years and allows the particular sins to emerge in the conscience. Smith calls this stage "the biographical backbone of the confession."[9] The second stage involves reviewing one's life and its stages in light of the Scriptures, along with answering some questions designed to focus the "awareness of sin more sharply." It is intended to help one "articulate more sins that were not seen before" and make note of them. The third stage is a reflection "on the patterns of sinning," such as common "faults and threads of behavior running through the various phases" of one's life. This last stage allows for identifying "our root sins and putting our finger on the inner motivation underlying some of our sinful behavior."[10] Laying the preparatory work may take between three and six weeks, according to Smith, during which time one takes notes. These notes should be brought along as a memory prop when making

9. Martin L. Smith, SSJE, *Reconciliation: Preparing for Confession in the Episcopal Church* (Cambridge, MA: Cowley Publications, 1985), 71.

10. Ibid.

first confession, but they should be destroyed afterward, symbolic of a "truly letting-go of our sins and handing them all over to God."[11] As part of these exercises in self-examination Smith offers thirteen sets of questions, patterned after Jesus' summary of the Law, the Ten Commandments, the Sermon on the Mount, and other Scripture texts. A sample of two sets of questions is found in Appendix II.

The Rite of Penance of the Roman Catholic Church also offers lists of questions intended to aid Christians in searching their consciences and preparing for confession. Reminiscent of Ignatius's examen prayer and the practices of the Eastern church, the questions are an aid in taking stock of one's life direction as well as stimulating preparation for the sacrament of confession. Incidentally, they would lend themselves also to a small group study during the season of Lent, for example, when participants could, if comfortable, reflect on and share their reactions, thoughts, and responses to the questions raised. Two of a total of three sets of questions contained in the manual for self-examination are found in Appendix III.

11. Ibid., 70.

CHAPTER TWENTY

The Nature of Penance

As naturally as guilt arises in (most) humans when they have engaged in unjust or wrongful behavior, so also is it natural for them to expect punishment. Such punishment is considered just when it is commensurate with the crime or misdeed committed and unjust when disproportionate to it. To speak of someone deserving punishment means that the person has committed an act that has harmed others for which he or she should pay or make amends. This legal principle of crime and punishment has carried over into the history of the sacrament of confession and the role given to acts of penance. Mistakenly, Christians perceived their long prayers, ascetic practices, self-exile, money donations, and measures of self-chastisement as acts that had to be "paid" in order to obtain divine forgiveness and to satisfy a wrathful God. Often the officials of the church and priors of monastic communities did little to clear up the misunderstanding, even exploiting the masses' ignorance and superstition in an attempt to fill their own coffers and enlarge upon power and influence. However, it is a mistake to say that the teachers of the church and early church fathers interpreted the role of good works or the aim of penitential practices as payment made for sins committed. Rather, penitential practices were understood as remedies for the soul. As spiritual practices and disciplines they were aimed at healing the soul's sickness, preventing the repeating of sinful acts, purifying the mind and the heart, and encouraging Christians to do good in imitation of their Father in heaven. Rather than being an attempt to save oneself through good—and often painful—works, doing penance was the human response to God's mercy, goodness, and grace.

Even today the word "penance" conjures up associations of pain, torment, and punishment. This is not surprising, given that the root of the English word "penance" is derived (via the French *peine*, meaning penalty, pain) from the Latin word *poena*, penalty or punishment, hence pain and torment. Even during the centuries of public penance bishops and synods were intent on pointing Christians to look past the pain penitents might have experienced and the implied punishment they received to the ultimate aim of penance, namely, its healing effects on the soul. The reason these Christians underwent a public discipline, they said, was not in the first place to suffer pain and punishment, but to allow for their soul's healing, conversion, and increase in holiness. Among the masses these interpretive words went largely unheeded. The image of penance's temporary side effects of pain inflicted and punishment doled out—a lively picture to be sure!—was retained more easily than that of the discipline's intended sustained effects and ultimate aim, a holy life before God. The Fourth Lateran Council of 1215, the Council of Trent, and the Second Vatican Council all sought to correct and restore the understanding of penance's original aim. This aim is clarified by the current Rite of Penance, interchangeably also called the sacrament of reconciliation, and the acts of penance recommended.

What type of penance can one expect to receive today? According to the rite, the penance "must be suited to the personal condition of penitents so that they may restore the order that they have upset and through the corresponding remedy be cured of the sickness from which they suffered."[1] This means concretely that the act of penance prescribed serves as "a remedy for sin and a help to renewal of life." Thereby "penitents, 'forgetting the things that are behind' (Philippians 3:13), again become part of the mystery of salvation and press on toward the things that are to come."[2] Emphasis is placed on the healing and remedial character of penance, intended to facilitate one's renewed participation in "the mystery of salvation." Typically, priests and confessors assign prayers, perhaps some Scripture reading, attendance at Mass, or a devotional practice such as a period of fasting or abstinence. The rite suggests that the penance "may suitably take the form of prayer, self-denial, and especially service to neighbor and works of mercy" to make clear the social aspect of "sin and its forgiveness."[3] Certainly these practices do not readily suggest pain or punishment. However, concern has been raised about another matter, namely, the proper fit of a penance with the

---

1. Rite of Penance, in *Rites of the Catholic Church: The Roman Ritual Revised by Decree of the Second Vatican Ecumenical Council and Published by Authority of Pope Paul VI*, vol. 1 (Collegeville, MN: Liturgical Press, 1990), 517–630, at 529.

2. Ibid., 529–30.

3. Ibid., 535.

penitent's situation and its intended healing effect. According to David M. Coffey, "to give no penance at all or to give the same for all comers, are equally abuses crying out for remedy."[4] Often a confessor's mechanical assigning of penances may betray lack of imagination. A cursory glance at the early penitential liturgies of private confession and the Celtic penitentials could quicken the imagination and serve as a reminder to confessors to be relevant, specific, and direct. In *A Confessor's Handbook*, Kurt Stasiak suggests three ways of assigning penances that relate to the individual. The first is to give a standard penance in a way that is creative, personalized, and concrete. Examples are:

- Pray the Our Father once. But pray it slowly. Try really to pay attention to the words.
- Tell your wife you are sorry. (Tell your wife that although you don't always say it, you do love her.) Is there something you can take home to give her that will help you say that?
- Put your Bible (or prayer book) next to your coffee pot, and for the next week read (pray) from it for a few minutes while you are having that first cup.[5]

A second way of assigning a penance relates to the hurt and harm the penitent has caused by his or her actions, and the making of restitution. In Stasiak's opinion "the seriousness of the offense—in some cases, the crime—need not take away from the respectfulness of our approach."[6] Examples of such penances are:

- You have admitted that you have really done some damage to this person's reputation, and you are sorry about that. You have taken the first step. But that damage is still out there. What do you think you need to do to help this person? What can you do?
- You have confessed stealing a large amount of money. As you yourself have said, this is a serious sin. You have taken the right first step, but this is one of those times when it is important to think about how you can make up for the loss you have caused another.[7]

A third way of assigning a penance is already hinted at in the previous approach, namely, doing so in dialogue with the parishioner. What do

---

4. David M. Coffey, *The Sacrament of Reconciliation* (Collegeville, MN: Liturgical Press, 2001), 118.
5. Kurt Stasiak, OSB, *A Confessor's Handbook* (New York: Paulist Press, 1999), 35.
6. Ibid., 36.
7. Ibid., 36–37.

you think would be an appropriate penance? This approach is particularly advised for those who come to confession frequently and are inclined to reflect intently on their relationship with God and other people, including their adversaries. Encouraging them to develop the habit of taking responsibility for their attitudes and pondering the possible remedies that might help strengthen relationships is bound to enhance spiritual development and maturity.

The confessional litany's sequence, in which the assigned act of penance precedes absolution (or forgiveness of sins) is critical for understanding the inherent activity of God and the gift of grace in the penitential act: First comes the act of penance, then absolution. One may recall that during the centuries of public confession in the church the process of penance had to be completed before Christians obtained absolution from the bishop and were justified before God. When private confession was introduced, and especially when commutations and indulgences became available, penitents were seemingly absolved first and then "paid" for the services rendered, even though bishops and councils denounced such a practice. Nonetheless, the impression remained that the act of penance followed absolution. With that, God's activity and grace appeared to play a minor role in the salvific process, and the sacrament was seen as a transaction whose effectiveness depended mostly on the penitent's works. Today's rite seeks to clarify God's salvific purposes toward humans: the act of penance is given first and then absolution is pronounced, as had been the case in early days. Even before the penance is technically completed and humans have done their part, God in Christ, through the person of the confessor, grants forgiveness, stressing God's supreme grace toward sinners. This grace continues to be at work by preceding and equipping penitents to cooperate with God in the process of a "true conversion." They participate with God, whose grace goes before them, through "amendment of life" and "by rectifying injuries done."[8] God's grace had been stressed over against human works by the Protestant reformers in matters of salvation. The unfortunate result was that penance as a sacrament, along with acts of penance, was dropped almost entirely. Reintroducing the practice among Protestants will mean combating the misconception that penance, including its association with pain and punishment, is a form of works righteousness. It also needs to be made clear to Christians, not just to Protestants, that carrying out the acts of penance after one has received absolution does

8. Rite of Penance, 529.

not mean making satisfaction in the literal sense, even though the phrase is used in traditional terminology. In the words of Pope John Paul II, the acts of satisfaction "are not the price one has to pay in order to be absolved from sin and obtain forgiveness." Rather, they are "the sign of the personal commitment that the Christian has made to God in the sacrament to begin a new life."[9] Speaking from an Anglican perspective but writing with "an ecumenical aim,"[10] theologian John Macquarrie says succinctly and emphatically what bears frequent repeating: Penance "is in no sense a way of 'earning' forgiveness. Neither penance itself nor any of its expressions is a 'work,' but only a response to the proclamation of God's forgiveness, [God's] acceptance of Jesus Christ as the representative of all humanity, and the consequent justification of all men and women in him."[11]

9. Pope John Paul II, *Reconciliation and Penance (Reconciliatio et Paenitentia): Post-Synodal Apostolic Exhortation, December 2, 1984* (Washington, DC: United States Catholic Conference, 1984), 31, III.

10. John Macquarrie, *A Guide to the Sacraments* (New York: Continuum, 1997), viii.

11. Ibid., 97.

CHAPTER TWENTY-ONE

A Litany of Private Confession

The order for the sacrament of confession follows a clear outline. This outline is called a litany to indicate that confession is part of the larger church's worship and liturgy. Despite the private nature and the confidentiality of what is shared, confession is one aspect of the church's overall ministry and mission in the world. The order of today's litany and its parts were defined during the early centuries of the church. According to the rite of the Roman Catholic Church the four elements are contrition, confession, act of penance, and absolution or forgiveness. The first three parts are named for the actions the penitent carries out, while the fourth is named for what the confessor does. In contrition the Christian admits to a "heartfelt sorrow and aversion for the sin committed along with the intention of sinning no more."[1] In confession the Christian names those sins, both mortal and venial, that have come to the fore in the conscience through an "inner examination of the heart." In the act of penance the Christian agrees before God to certain acts of penance proposed by the confessor as "remedy for sin and a help to renewal of life."[2] The last part, absolution, is reserved for the confessor; by it "God grants pardon to sinners who in sacramental confession manifest their change of heart to the Church's minister."[3] According to the rite, this minister has to be an ordained Catholic priest.

Could a litany like this be used by other denominations as well as by people not ordained to the priesthood? Both Lutherans and Episcopalians have adopted the outline of the Catholic litany of confession, renamed

---

1. Rite of Penance, in *Rites of the Catholic Church: The Roman Ritual Revised by Decree of the Second Vatican Ecumenical Council and Published by Authority of Pope Paul VI*, vol. 1 (Collegeville, MN: Liturgical Press, 1990), 517–630, at 529.

2. Ibid.

3. Ibid., 530.

the sacrament a "rite," and substituted one of their own pastors or priests for the "ordained Catholic priest." In 1979 the Episcopal Church in the United States (the offshoot of its Anglican mother church, the Church of England) went one step further: it adopted a rite of reconciliation that allowed laypeople, meaning those not ordained to the priesthood, to administer the entire rite. Only one change was made: Instead of the formula of absolution, the layperson would recite a formula of forgiveness. With this change the church recognized the calling and gifts of select members to hear confession, offer spiritual guidance and counsel, suggest a penance, and pronounce forgiveness. In Macquarrie's words, the change was "a useful reminder that we have to be reconciled not only to God but to the church, and that in the earliest days, it seems that confession might be made to any fellow-Christian, clerical or lay."[4]

The change is an opportunity for enhanced ministry whereby members may more fully share their spiritual gifts for the benefit of the larger church. This point is especially important in regard to members of religious orders, both in the Roman Catholic and in Protestant traditions, and their unique calling to the evangelical counsels of poverty, celibacy, and obedience. One of the key documents of the Second Vatican Council acknowledges and commends the unique gifts and responsibilities of men and women religious. According to the Dogmatic Constitution on the Church, *Lumen Gentium*, promulgated by Pope Paul VI in 1964, vowed religious have "greater stability in their way of life [and] sound teaching on striving after perfection" (*LG* 43). Thus they are "consecrated more closely to [God's] service" (*LG* 44) than other Christians. Their vowed profession is "a sign that can and should effectively inspire all the members of the church to fulfil indefatigably the duties of their Christian vocation" and the religious state "reveals with greater clarity to all believers the heavenly blessings that are already present in this world" (*LG* 44). Men and women religious are urged to "see to it that through them the church may truly and ever more clearly show forth Christ to believers and unbelievers alike." Since the evangelical counsels "contribute in no small measure to the purification of the heart and to spiritual freedom" and "continually urge one to more fervent charity," they "have the power to conform the Christian person to the kind of virginal and poor life" that Jesus chose for himself, as did his mother (*LG* 46).

Typically the life of vowed religious includes regular hours of daily prayer, frequent communion, and frequent confession. Previously those

---

4. John Macquarrie, *A Guide to the Sacraments* (New York: Continuum, 1997), 95.

with significant experience in going to confession were excluded from hearing confession because they were not ordained priests. Now their experience can be profitably shared. As lay confessors they can offer the gifts of discernment, knowledge, and spiritual counsel gained with years and often decades of living by the evangelical counsels of poverty, celibacy, and obedience, and other Christians can benefit from being guided by their wisdom and their example of holy living. The litany offers a format for hearing confession, offering spiritual direction, suggesting acts of penance, and extending the words of forgiveness on Christ's behalf. As this ministry is made available, parishioners need to be assured of the rite's confidential nature and told of the fact that forgiveness is being granted, not absolution. The *Book of Common Prayer* includes two litanies, a longer and a shorter one, both patterned after that of the Roman Catholic Church, but called the Reconciliation of a Penitent. For the shorter version see Appendix IV; for the Roman Catholic litany, adapted to a lay confessor, see Appendix V.

CHAPTER TWENTY-TWO

Catechetical Considerations

Naming an activity or process intends to teach about its meaning and effects. The name of the sacrament of confession has undergone numerous changes since its origins in the fifth century. It is alternately called by one of its parts: *confession* (after its second part—which has been the most popular name of the sacrament in the church's history), *penance* (after its third part), and *reconciliation* (after the fifth part, where the Christian makes good on the act of penance through conversion and renewal of life with God's help, leading to reconciliation with God and neighbor). Since Vatican II the two preferred names are reconciliation and penance. It is no coincidence that Pope John Paul II's 1984 apostolic exhortation on the sacrament is titled *Reconciliation and Penance*, nor is calling the place where confession is made the "reconciliation room." There is purpose and intent behind the use of the new names for a sacrament that among Catholics, and some Protestants, is simply known as confession. The intent is catechetical, related to instructing the faithful about the meaning and theology of the sacrament. While parishioners prefer to identify an activity, their activity—which presumably has cost them some effort at self-examination and the conquering of embarrassment—the church's bishops and cardinals insist on naming the sacrament by its effect: reconciliation with the church, God, and neighbor. This effect can only be understood in light of theological reflection and theological explanations. What the change in the name of the sacrament indicates is the hope of moving people's associative thinking from activity to theology, from a focus on doing to a focus on experiencing what the sacrament can do, from their own work to the work of God, from autonomy before God to partnership with God. Whether the new name will be embraced and become standard parlance among Christians is perhaps not very likely, but its embracing is less relevant than the degree to which theological reflection occurs and Christians begin asking the questions of how, with whom, and through whom the reconciliation for which the sacrament is named is brought about.

What is a sacrament, how does it function, and what are its effects? These questions require ongoing exploration in the life of the church and its teaching ministry. Invariably, discussion will point to mystical theology, from the original Greek word for sacrament, *mysterion*. Today the Roman Catholic Church acknowledges seven sacraments, while Protestants have only two, baptism and Holy Communion. In the sacraments the church offers signs of God's self-communication in concrete ways, such as through elements and embodied actions that can be felt, tasted, and seen and by which people can experience God's presence and transformative activity. However, by Karl Rahner's definition one has to enlarge the meaning of sacrament to include the entire body of the faithful, the church as the community of the saints in heaven and on earth. The church is founded by and derives its authority and power from yet another sacrament, namely, Jesus Christ. As the primary sacrament, Jesus Christ is the historical reality of God made flesh. In him the divine and human natures are made visible, tangible, and concrete. This means that those in whom Christ's reconciling work is active are indwelled by his sacramental presence as they carry out the work of service, making it sacramental also. By their activity God's presence and activity are revealed, made tangible and concrete. In confession, then, the confessor or spiritual director acts as sacramental presence and tangible sign of God's self-communication to the penitent. The confessor facilitates God's forgiving, transforming, and redemptive activity, allowing for the penitent's participation, dialogue, and partnership with God. Subsequently the penitent participates in the steps of contrition and true sorrow over sins, the confession of concrete sins, the act of penance to which one agrees before God, the absolution (or forgiveness of sins), which one accepts as pronounced by the confessor in Christ's stead, and the response of carrying out penance with God's grace preceding it so that the beginning of a new life and a true turning, one's "yes" toward God, is actualized and made concrete. This process is sacramental because God's presence in the form of grace is recognized, received, and responded to.

The two sacraments that directly relate to confession are those commonly recognized by all Christian churches, baptism and Eucharist. These two sacraments function as bookends for confession, stabilizing, propping, and framing it. Without them confession collapses, becoming an exercise in self-absorbed navel-gazing, psychoanalysis, and therapeutic counseling. To use another analogy: confession sits on the foundation of baptism as the beginning of and initiation into the Christian life.

From this position it looks back or down on baptism as an event of the past that through confession is made concrete in the present; at the same time it looks ahead or up to Holy Communion, the Eucharist, Christ's presence manifested in the elements of bread and wine, the banquet in which the saints in heaven and on earth are participating and attending as guests, along with the heavenly host. In preparation for this festive event one gets dressed for the occasion, thus honoring the other guests and especially the host: one takes a bath, becomes clean, prepares ahead. Thus confession is a preparatory act in anticipation of the festive celebration and joyous occasion of Holy Communion, where the host of the feast is present. One might also say that confession forms the vital link between the original innocence of the first man and woman in paradise and the eschatological expectation, the original guiltlessness and the anticipated restoration of this freedom from guilt in ultimate union and communion with Christ and the heavenly host. Thus it is a looking back and a looking ahead, a looking down and a looking up by which what is lost is regained and what is not yet is foreseen. The tension of these two gravitational poles is not resolved by confession but rather brought into focus, making the gravitational power of each pole more concrete in the present moment. Thus Rahner can say that in confession guilt is not canceled, but rather is overcome, remitted, and transformed. Confession heightens the awareness of our original innocence before God and the anticipated deliverance from guilt's burden in the last days. At the same time it makes guilt bearable by pointing toward hope, expectation, transformation through a renewed confidence in the mercy and goodness of God, made concrete in history and redemptive in Jesus Christ.

With the new Rite of Penance, Catholics are offered the opportunity of participating in communal services of penance. The hope of the council was to point to sin's social ramifications and the responsibility of an entire community to submit to penance. Communal expressions of confession, including those at the beginning of Mass or during a worship service, have their precedents in the Hebrew tradition and that of the early church. Perhaps they can point to private confession, but they cannot substitute for it. It is a positive characteristic of the rite that it reserves a place for private confession in the context of the communal liturgy of penance. In the penitential services of the Protestant tradition the element of private confession is missing, and it is doubtful that communal services of penance or the repeated use of general prayers of confession in the liturgy will somehow suggest to Christians to consider private confession as an alternative or option. Teaching about private confession, its benefits, its nature has to be more concrete and intentional. What actually happens there? The personal and private encounter in the confessional dialogue involves the concrete naming of "my" sorrow over "my" sins, the counsel I obtain in concrete reference to them, the acceptance of "my penance," the receiving of the words of absolution or forgiveness for "my" transgressions. In this encounter God speaks through another, who has been called and equipped for this office in ministry, to me alone and no one else. And it is in the presence of another, who serves as witness of my attitude before God, that I am held accountable for the response I offer God—as my gratitude cooperating with God's grace.

The supreme teacher and role model for confession and its principles is Jesus Christ. During his earthly ministry Jesus witnessed the sins of a people to make complete "confession" of them to the Father. As Adrienne von Speyr says, Jesus gathers up the sins present in the world to "recognize, bear and confess all sin"[1] to the Father. Her approach illustrates how confession begins with Jesus Christ and relates to the inner workings of the Trinity. Jesus' complete exposure to sin shows us the attitude to have during confession: taking the sin that is ours and handing it over to God, the Father. As the self-revelation and expression of the Father on earth Jesus lives in an ongoing response to God as Father, so he can orient himself toward God while ever anticipating the intervention and directives of the Holy Spirit. Before the Father he lives in an attitude of dependency and nakedness, and it is the same attitude the Christian should seek in relation to the confessor, the church, and God. Jesus' death is the result of the gravity of sin and the hopelessness and separation from God it produces. The resurrection is analogous to the Son's receiving absolution from the Father for the sins he took to the cross, so that Jesus, as humanity's representative, also experiences the joy of all those who are redeemed and forgiven. Thus the Son sees in everyone whom he has redeemed "someone filled with joy in whom, as part of the Father's mission, he may dwell" by the power of the Holy Spirit. Upon his resurrection Jesus "discovers himself in a person," or, as the apostle Paul says, "it is no longer I who live, but it is Christ who lives in me" (Gal 2:20). Those who willingly and expectantly confess their sins and receive absolution or forgiveness in the name of the triune God reacquire what has been lost through sin: the Holy Spirit manifested in love of neighbor, Christ made alive as the divine nature inhabiting the human, and a union with the Father through the Son's confession and the absolution by the Father on behalf of and as a representative of all humanity. Thus Jesus

1. Adrienne von Speyr, *Confession*, trans. Douglas W. Stott (San Francisco: Ignatius Press, 1985), 60.

invents, models, and institutes confession for us and imparts it to the church. By following him we engage in an act of obedience and an attitude of utter openness and nakedness before God. At the same time we carry out an act of love by which we allow that through our bodies, now cleansed of sin by absolution and forgiveness of sins, God may be glorified in and through us for the sake of the reconciliation of the world with God.

Conclusion

This historical overview of some of the fundamental practices and theological principles of confession in the life of the Western church and its Christian traditions may allow for a brief closing observation. It seems significant that among the church's various confessional practices, private confession has continued from its humble informal beginnings in the third or fourth centuries to today. In its many secular or religious guises, taking the form of psychotherapy or of spiritual direction, for example, private confession points to a basic human need for disclosure, the release and making known of one's innermost secrets, the unburdening of the conscience, and a hunger for forgiveness. Based on the long and sustained history of private confession and its development into sacrament and rite one can safely say that those who have engaged in the practice must have benefited, that their hunger was met in some way, that their conscience was unburdened, that they gained at some level a reassurance of their own human dignity, and that by it faith in a benevolent God was either birthed or strengthened.

While it is possible to observe practices and their liturgical settings throughout the church's history and their extension into other areas of the helping professions, it is not possible to assess concretely the human benefit of the experience, to measure the long-term results, to know and examine in detail the contents of what was revealed. By its very nature the process of confessing remains secret, confidential, concealed, and so are, to some degree, its effects on those who engage in it. What remains is simply the human experience, and what can be said about this experience is, again, rather tentative, vague, and subjective. One might try to describe it in human language as something that was liberating, freeing, reassuring, but the exact "what" and "how" remains a mystery, pointing to the meaning of the word "sacrament." Or, from a theological perspective, one might call it the experience of grace, of God's presence, of God's goodness and redeeming love and reconciling activity. Still, putting into human words what has been revealed at the initiative of the divine will always remain difficult and will be only an insufficient, unsatisfactory approximation of the true, the real, the concrete. Thus one could say that the experience of confession as grace is mystical, a dark and mysterious matter, something that ultimately escapes analysis and defies definition. Like any experiential knowledge of God, it confronts us, in the words of Rahner, with a dual problem: "one cannot talk about it when one has not had the experience, and one *will* not talk about it when one has."[1] What remains in the end is the courageous jump, the embarrassing leap into uncertainty, into the unknown, into the silent mystery that is waiting to offer this experience of grace to those willing to submit to it. By chronicling private confession's developments in history and theology, context and litany, human activity and ecclesial response, this book has tried to serve as an encouragement and a gentle invitation to readers to make such an experience of grace their own.

---

1. Karl Rahner, *Alltägliche Dinge* (Einsiedeln: Benziger, 1964), 26.

Appendix I

The Ten Commandments

A Traditional Catechetical Formula

1. I am the Lord your God; you shall not have strange Gods before me.

2. You shall not take the name of the Lord your God in vain.

3. Remember to keep holy the Lord's Day.

4. Honor your father and your mother.

5. You shall not kill.

6. You shall not commit adultery.

7. You shall not steal.

8. You shall not bear false witness against your neighbor.

9. You shall not covet your neighbor's wife.

10. You shall not covet your neighbor's goods.

Appendix II

Exercises for Self-Examination[1]

4. The Lord's Summary of the Law: Part C

"You shall love the Lord your God with all your heart, and with all your mind."

> The commandment reveals that the mind is an instrument of love. Are there ways in which you sin by refusing to give your whole mind to your relationship with God?
>
> Have you ever been content with agnosticism as a way of avoiding the challenges of faith?
>
> Have you been intellectually lazy in your faith, never asking questions or showing any interest in developing your understanding of God?
>
> Do you read the Scriptures? Do you do other reading which makes you think hard about interpreting God's will in the issues of modern life and discuss them with others?
>
> If there are particular beliefs and principles in Christianity with which you have problems, have you had the courage to investigate them with the help of a priest or some other competent Christian?
>
> Are you prepared to let God change your mind and do you pray to be open to new light, or have you got everything "sewn up?"
>
> Have you clung on to immature and childish ways of imagining God, or of praying?

1. Excerpted from Martin L. Smith, SSJE, *Reconciliation: Preparing for Confession in the Episcopal Church* (Cambridge, MA: Cowley Publications, 1985), 82–83, 95; quoted are two exercises of a total of thirteen.

Do you openly profess your faith or do you conceal it?

Are you prepared to talk about the gospel to others and commend it to them with a real interest in their discovery of God's wonderful grace?

11. Sinning Against Your Own Life

A major way of refusing God's love for us is to counteract it by self-hatred. What are the ways in which you have gone against your own life, the life of God within you?

Have you neglected or abused your body by overeating, lack of exercise, or poor nutrition? Do you accept your body as God's creation and give thanks for who you are, or are you consumed with dissatisfaction?

Have you endangered your health by neglecting medical care, or through the abuse of alcohol, drugs or tobacco? Have you taken steps to curb harmful addictions?

Have you risked throwing your life away by ignoring safety precautions?

Have you wallowed in self-loathing or punished yourself?

Have you attempted to kill yourself?

Have you ever withdrawn into isolation and self-pity?

Have you buried your talents?

Have you allowed yourself to be a victim of another's mistreatment without seeking a remedy?

Have you exhausted yourself by not recognizing or honoring your limitations?

Have you ignored spiritual longings within you?

Have you degraded yourself by feeding on "entertainment" that is trashy, perverted or involves sexual exploitation? Have you taken part in sexual acting-out in groups, or been involved in prostitution, sado-masochism, or trivial sex outside a context of love and commitment?

Have you been untrue to yourself, or insincere?

Have you sacrificed your integrity to keep a relationship you didn't want to lose?

Have you made a fetish of being independent and self-sufficient, and thus dishonest about your need for others?

Have you blighted your humanity by being negative about your sexuality, or rejecting the challenges and joys of friendship?

Have you used sexual fantasizing and masturbation as an escape into self away from the reality of relationship?

Have you sought help from God to grow in knowledge and understanding of yourself?

Appendix III

Form of Examination of Conscience[1]

I. The Lord says: "You shall love the Lord your God with your whole heart."

    1. Is my heart set on God, so that I really love him above all things and am faithful to his commandments, as a son loves his father? Or am I more concerned about the things of this world? Have I a right intention in what I do?

    2. God spoke to us in his Son. Is my faith in God firm and secure? Am I wholehearted in accepting the Church's teaching? Have I been careful to grow in my understanding of the faith, to hear God's word, to listen to instructions on the faith, to avoid dangers to faith? Have I been always strong and fearless in professing my faith in God and the Church? Have I been willing to be known as a Christian in private and public life?

    3. Have I prayed morning and evening? When I pray, do I really raise my mind and heart to God or is it a matter of words only? Do I offer God my difficulties, my joys, and my sorrows? Do I turn to God in time of temptation?

    4. Have I love and reverence for God's name? Have I offended him in blasphemy, swearing falsely, or taking his name in vain? Have I shown disrespect for the Blessed Virgin Mary and the saints?

    5. Do I keep Sundays and feast days holy by taking a full part, with attention and devotion, in the liturgy, and especially in the Mass?

---

1. From the Rite of Penance in *The Rites of the Catholic Church*, vol. 1 (Collegeville, MN: Liturgical Press, 1990), Appendix III (excerpted are Parts I and III of a total of three parts and an introduction).

Have I fulfilled the precept of annual confession and of communion during the Easter season?

III. Christ our Lord says: "Be perfect as your Father is perfect."

1. Where is my life really leading me? Is the hope of eternal life my inspiration? Have I tried to grow in the life of the Spirit through prayer, reading the word of God and meditation on it, receiving the sacraments, self-denial? Have I been anxious to control my vices, my bad inclinations and passions, e.g., envy, love of food and drink? Have I been proud and boastful, thinking myself better in the sight of God and despising others as less important than myself? Have I imposed my own will on others, without respecting their freedom and rights?

2. What use have I made of time, of health and strength, of the gifts God has given me to be used like the talents in the Gospel? Do I use them to become more perfect every day? Or have I been lazy and too much given to leisure?

3. Have I been patient in accepting the sorrows and disappointments of life? How have I performed mortification so as to "fill up what is wanting to the sufferings of Christ"? Have I kept the precept of fasting and abstinence?

4. Have I kept my senses and my whole body pure and chaste as a temple of the Holy Spirit consecrated for resurrection and glory, and as a sign of God's faithful love for men and women, a sign that is seen most perfectly in the sacrament of matrimony? Have I dishonored my body by fornication, impurity, unworthy conversation or thoughts, evil desires, or actions? Have I given in to sensuality? Have I indulged in reading, conversation, shows, and entertainments that offend against Christian and human decency? Have I encouraged others to sin by my own failure to maintain these standards? Have I been faithful to the moral law in my married life?

5. Have I gone against my conscience out of fear or hypocrisy?

6. Have I always tried to act in the true freedom of the sons of God according to the law of the Spirit, or am I the slave of forces within me?

Appendix IV

The Reconciliation of a Penitent[1]

P: Bless me, for I have sinned.

C: The Lord be in your heart and upon your lips that you may truly and humbly confess your sins: In the Name of the Father, and of the Son, and of the Holy Spirit. *Amen.*

P: I confess to Almighty God, to his Church, and to you, that I have sinned by my own fault in thought, word, and deed, in things done and left undone; especially _____. For these and all other sins which I cannot now remember, I am truly sorry. I pray God to have mercy on me. I firmly intend amendment of life, and I humbly beg forgiveness of God and his Church, and ask you for counsel, direction, and absolution.

Here the [confessor] may offer counsel, direction, and comfort.

Declaration of Forgiveness to be used by a Deacon or Lay Person

C: Our Lord Jesus Christ, who offered himself to be sacrificed for us to the Father, forgives your sins by the grace of the Holy Spirit. *Amen.*

C: Go (or abide) in peace, and pray for me, a sinner.

---

1. From *The Book of Common Prayer and Administration of the Sacraments and Other Rites and Ceremonies of the Church* (New York: Church Hymnal Corporation, 1986), 447–48: Form One (the shorter of two forms), here showing the case in which the confessor (C) is a layperson hearing the confession of the penitent (P). (See the rubric on p. 446.)

Appendix V

A Sample Rite for Reconciliation Adapted for a Layperson Serving as Confessor

Drawing on the general outlines for the rites of reconciliation in the Roman Catholic Church and the Episcopal Church in the United States, respectively, I offer here a litany formulated in my own words and in reliance on Scripture. The rite should not be understood as a sacrament or as a venue for pronouncing absolution (reserved for Roman Catholic or Episcopal/Anglican priests and bishops). Rather, it is to be an aid to help facilitate conversation of a confessional nature taking place in the context of spiritual direction or pastoral care between a layperson (someone not ordained to the priesthood), a spiritual director, or a spiritual guide (L) and the person (P) who seeks to hear Christ's words of forgiveness.

L: In the name of the Father, and of the Son, and of the Holy Spirit. Amen.
May God, who is our light and truth, help us know our sins and trust in his mercy.

P: Amen.

L: *A short reading from Scripture is offered. Suggested readings: Ezekiel 11:19-20; Matthew 6:14-15; Mark 1:14-15; Luke 6:31-38; Luke 15:1-7; John 10:19-23; Romans 5:8-9; Ephesians 5:1-2; Colossians 1:12-14; Colossians 3:8-10, 12-17; 1 John 1:6-7, 9. The reading may be introduced with the words:* Let us listen to God's word to us. *Then the lay pastor/spiritual director/ guide will prompt the person to make confession with such words as,* You may now make your confession to the Lord.

P: *The person highlights specific incidences of wrongdoing and the sense of a troubled conscience.*

331

L: *The lay pastor/spiritual director/guide offers words of comfort, counsel, and direction. Then he or she invites the person to say the following prayer:*

P: Lord Jesus Christ, have mercy on me, a sinner (cf. Luke 18:13b).

L: Our Lord Jesus Christ came into the world to save sinners. He himself bore our sins in his body on the cross. Through him, God forgives your sins by the grace of the Holy Spirit. (cf. 1 Tim 1:15; 1 Pet 2:24; 2 Cor 5:19)

P: Amen.

L: Blessed are those whose sins have been forgiven,
whose evil deeds are remembered no more.
Rejoice in the Lord, and go in peace. (cf. Ps 32:1, 11)

Bibliography

Anchorite Spirituality: "Ancrene Wisse" and Associated Works. Translated by Anne Savage and Nicholas Watson. New York: Paulist Press, 1991.

Ancrene Riwle: Introduction and Part I. Edited and translated by Robert W. Ackerman and Roger Dahood. Binghamton, NY: Medieval and Renaissance Texts and Studies, 1984.

Arndt, Johann. *True Christianity.* Translation and Introduction by Peter Erb. New York: Paulist Press, 1979.

Ashley, Benedict M. *Spiritual Direction in the Dominican Tradition.* Mahwah, NJ: Paulist Press, 1995.

Athanasius. *The Life of Antony* and *The Letter to Marcellinus.* Translated and introduced by Robert C. Gregg. New York: Paulist Press, 1980.

Augustine. *Confessions.* In vol. 1/1 of *The Works of Saint Augustine—Translation for the Twenty-First Century.* Edited by John E. Rotelle. Translated by Maria Boulding. Hyde Park, NY: New City Press, 1997.

Bagchi, David, and David C. Steinmetz, eds. *The Cambridge Companion to Reformation Theology.* Cambridge: Cambridge University Press, 2004.

Bainton, Roland. *Here I Stand: A Life of Martin Luther.* Nashville: Abingdon, 1950.

Balthasar, Hans Urs von. *First Glance at Adrienne von Speyr.* Translated by Antje Lawry and Sergia Englund. San Francisco: Ignatius Press, 1981.

Barry, William A., and William J. Connolly. *The Practice of Spiritual Direction.* San Francisco: Harper & Row, 1982.

Bayonne, Emmanuel-Ceslas. *Lettres du B. Jourdain de Saxe, deuxième général de l'ordre des Frères-Prêcheurs, aux religieuses de Sainte-Agnès de Bologne, et à la b. Dianae d'Andalo, leur fondatrice (1223–1236).* Paris and Lyons: Bauchu, 1865. Reprinted in *The Catholic Encyclopedia,* vol. 12. New York: Robert Appleton Company, 1911.

Bilinkoff, Jodi. *Related Lives: Confessors and Their Female Penitents, 1450–1750.* Ithaca: Cornell University Press, 2005.

Biller, Peter, and A. J. Minnis, eds. *Handling Sin: Confession in the Middle Ages.* Rochester, NY: York Medieval Press, 1998.

Bonhoeffer, Dietrich. *Life Together*. Translated and with an introduction by John W. Doberstein. San Francisco: Harper & Row, 1954.

———. *Ethics*. Edited by Eberhard Bethge. Translated by Neville Horton Smith. New York: Macmillan, 1955.

———. *Creation and Fall: A Theological Interpretation of Genesis 1–3 and Temptation— Two Biblical Studies*. Translated by John C. Fletcher. New York: Macmillan, 1959.

———. *Spiritual Care*. Translated by Jay C. Rochelle. Minneapolis: Fortress Press, 1985.

———. *Dietrich Bonhoeffer Works*, vol. 5. Edited by Jeffrey B. Kelly. Translated by Daniel W. Bloesch. Minneapolis: Fortress Press, 1996.

Book of Common Prayer and Administration of the Sacraments and Other Rites and Ceremonies of the Church. New York: Church Hymnal Corporation and Seabury Press, 1977.

Book of Common Worship: Prepared by the Theology and Worship Ministry Unit for the Presbyterian Church (U.S.A.) and the Cumberland Presbyterian Church. Louisville: Westminster John Knox, 1993.

Book of Concord: The Confessions of the Evangelical Lutheran Church. Edited by Robert Kolb, Timothy J. Wengert, and Charles P. Arand. Minneapolis: Augsburg Fortress, 2000.

Borromeo, Charles. *Instructiones fabricae et supellectilis ecclesiasticae*. Translated by Evelyn Voelker. Ph.D. dissertation, Syracuse University. Ann Arbor: University Microfilms, 1977.

Bucer, Martin. *Buceri Scripta Anglicana fere omnia*. Basel: Ex Petri Pernae officina, 1577.

———. "On the Kingdom of Christ." In *Melanchthon and Bucer*. Edited by Wilhelm Pauck. Philadelphia: Westminster Press, 1969.

Bullinger, Heinrich. "The Second Helvetic Confession." In *The Book of Confessions*. Louisville: Office of the General Assembly, 1999.

Bynum, Caroline Walker. *Jesus as Mother: Studies in the Spirituality of the High Middle Ages*. Berkeley: University of California Press, 1982.

Cahill, Thomas. *How the Irish Saved Civilization: The Untold Story of Ireland's Heroic Role From the Fall of Rome to the Rise of Medieval Europe*. New York: Random House, 1995.

Calvin, John. *Letters of John Calvin*. Edited by Jules Bonnet. 4 vols. Philadelphia: Board of Publication, 1855–1858.

———. *Theological Treatises*. Translated by J. K. S. Reid. Philadelphia: Westminster Press, 1954.

———. *Calvin: Institutes of the Christian Religion*. Edited by John T. McNeill. Translated by Ford Lewis Battles. 2 vols. Philadelphia: Westminster Press, 1960.

———. *The First Epistle of Paul the Apostle to the Corinthians*. In vol. 9 of *Calvin's Commentaries*. Edited by David W. Torrance and Thomas F. Torrance. Translated by John W. Fraser. Grand Rapids: Eerdmans, 1960.

———. *John Calvin: Writings on Pastoral Piety*. Edited and with translations by Elsie Anne McKee. New York: Paulist Press, 2001.

Cassian, John. *Conferences*. Translated by Colm Luibheid. Classics of Western Spirituality. New York: Paulist Press, 1985.

———. *Institutes*. In vol. 11 of *A Select Library of Nicene and Post-Nicene Fathers of the Christian Church*. Edited by Philip Schaff and Henry Wace. Grand Rapids: Eerdmans, 1986.

Catechism of the Catholic Church. Liguori, MO: Liguori Publications, 1994.

Catechism of the Council of Trent for Parish Priests. Translated with notes by John A. McHugh and Charles J. Callan. New York: Joseph F. Wagner, 1947.

Catherine of Siena. *The Dialogue*. Translated by Suzanne Noffke. Classics of Western Spirituality. New York: Paulist Press, 1980.

———. *Letters of St. Catherine of Siena*. Translated by Suzanne Noffke. Binghamton, NY: Medieval and Renaissance Texts and Studies, 1988.

Chittister, Joan. *Wisdom Distilled From the Daily: Living the Rule of St. Benedict Today*. San Francisco: Harper & Row, 1990.

Clement of Alexandria. *Stromata, or Miscellanies*. In vol. 2 of *The Ante-Nicene Fathers*. Edited by Alexander Roberts and James Donaldson. 1868–1873. 24 vols. Repr. Peabody, MA: Hendrickson, 1999.

Coffey, David M. *The Sacrament of Reconciliation*. Collegeville, MN: Liturgical Press, 2001.

Concilia Germaniae. Edited by Josef Harzheim and Johannes Schannat. 11 vols. Cologne: Krakamp, 1759–1790.

Concordia: The Lutheran Confessions: A Reader's Edition of the Book of Concord. General editor Paul Timothy McCain. Based on the translation by William Hermann Theodore Dau and Gerhard Friedrich Bente. St. Louis: Concordia Publishing House, 2006.

Constitutions of the Holy Apostles. In vol. 7 of *The Ante-Nicene Fathers*. Edited by Alexander Roberts and James Donaldson. 1868–1873. 24 vols. Repr. Peabody, MA: Hendrickson, 1999.

Cyprian. *Treatise III: On the Lapsed*. In vol. 3 of *The Ante-Nicene Fathers*. Edited by Alexander Roberts and James Donaldson. 1868–1873. 24 vols. Repr. Peabody, MA: Hendrickson, 1999.

Dallen, James. *The Reconciling Community: The Rite of Penance. Studies in the Reformed Rites of the Catholic Church*. Vol. 3. Collegeville, MN: Liturgical Press, 1986.

Davies, Oliver, and Thomas O'Loughlin, eds. *Celtic Spirituality*. Classics of Western Spirituality. New York: Paulist Press, 1999.

Devotio Moderna: Basic Writings. Translated and introduced by John van Engen. Mahwah, NJ: Paulist Press, 1988.

Didache. In vol. 7 of *The Ante-Nicence Fathers*. Edited by Alexander Roberts and James Donaldson. 1868–1873. 24 vols. Peabody, MA: Hendrickson, 1999.

Dogmatic Canons and Decrees. New York: Devin-Adair, 1912.

Drakeford, John W. *Integrity Therapy*. Nashville: Broadman Press, 1967.

Duffield, G. E., ed. *John Calvin*. Grand Rapids: Eerdmans, 1966.

Dyckman, Katherine, Mary Garvin, and Elizabeth Liebert. *The Spiritual Exercises Reclaimed: Uncovering Liberating Possibilities for Women*. New York: Paulist Press, 2001.

Egan, Harvey D. *Karl Rahner: Mystic of Everday Life*. New York: Crossroad, 1998.

Erb, Peter C. *Pietists: Selected Writings*. Edited and introduced by Peter C. Erb. New York: Paulist Press, 1983.

Erikson, Erik H. *Young Man Luther: A Study in Psychoanalysis and History*. New York: W. W. Norton, 1958.

Fife, Robert Herndon. *The Revolt of Martin Luther*. New York: Columbia University Press, 1957.

Fleming, David L. "Reconciliation." In *The Complete Library of Christian Worship*. Vol. 6. Edited by Robert E. Webber, 321–25. Peabody, MA: Hendrickson, 1993.

Fontes Narrativi de S. Ignatio et de Societatis Iesu Initiis. 4 vols. Rome: Monumenta Historica Societatis Iesu, 1943–1965.

Furlong, Monica. *Visions and Longings: Medieval Women Mystics*. Boston: Shambhala, 1996.

George, Timothy. *Theology of the Reformers*. Nashville: Broadman Press, 1988.

Gerson, Jean. *Opus tripartium II*. Cologne: Ulrich Zell, [1470?].

Gray, Mark M., and Paul M. Perl. *Sacraments Today: Belief and Practice Among U.S. Catholics*. Georgetown, DC: Center for Applied Research in the Apostolate, 2008.

Grundmann, Herbert. *Religiöse Bewegungen im Mittelalter*. Hildesheim: G. Olms, 1961.

Hadewijch. *The Complete Works*. Edited by Columba Hart. New York: Paulist Press, 1980.

Hellwig, Monika K. *Sign of Reconciliation and Conversion*. Wilmington, DE: Michael Glazier, 1982.

Hinnebusch, John Frederick, ed. *The Historia Occidentalis of Jacques de Vitry*. Spicilegium Friburgense 17. Fribourg, Universitätsverlag, 1972.

Hippolytus. *The Apostolic Tradition of Hippolytus*. Translated and with an Introduction and Notes by Burton Scott Easton. Cambridge: Cambridge University Press, 1934.

Hoffman, Bengt R. *Luther and the Mystics: A Re-examination of Luther's Spiritual Experience and His Relationship to the Mystics*. Minneapolis: Augsburg, 1976.

Ignatius of Antioch. *The Epistle of Ignatius to the Ephesians*. In vol. 1 of *The Ante-Nicene Fathers*. Edited by Alexander Roberts and James Donaldson. 1868–1873. 24 vols. Repr. Peabody, MA: Hendrickson, 1999.

Ignatius of Loyola. *Ignatius of Loyola: The Spiritual Exercises and Selected Works*. Edited by George E. Ganss. New York: Paulist Press, 1991.

John Chrysostom. *Baptismal Instructions*. Translated by Paul H. Harkins. Ancient Christian Writers 31. Westminster, MD: Newman Press, 1963.

John Paul II. *Reconciliation and Penance (Reconciliatio et Paenitentia): Post-Synodal Apostolic Exhortation, December 2, 1984.* Washington, DC: United States Catholic Conference, 1984.

Julian of Norwich. *Showings.* Translated by Edmund Colledge and James Walsh. New York: Paulist Press, 1978.

Jung, Carl Gustav. *Modern Man in Search of a Soul.* Translated by W. S. Dell and Cary F. Baynes. New York: Harcourt Brace Jovanovich, 1933.

Kierkegaard, Søren. *Purity of Heart Is To Will One Thing: Spiritual Preparation for the Office of Confession.* New York: Harper & Brothers, 1938.

King, Ursula. *Christian Mystics: Their Lives and Legacies Through the Ages.* Mahwah, NJ: Paulist Press, 2001.

Koch, Ludwig. *Graf Elger von Holmstein: der Begründer des Dominikanerordens in Thüringen; ein Beitrag zur Kirchengeschichte Thüringens.* Gotha: A. Perthes, 1865. Reprinted in *The Catholic Encyclopedia,* vol. 12. New York: Robert Appleton Company, 1911.

Kurtz, Ernest, and Katherine Ketcham. *The Spirituality of Imperfection: Storytelling and the Search for Meaning.* New York: Bantam, 1992.

Labriolle, P. de. *The Life and Times of St. Ambrose, by P. de Labriolle.* Translated by Herbert Wilson. St. Louis: Herder, 1928.

Lane, George A. *Christian Spirituality: A Historical Sketch.* Chicago: Loyola University Press, 1984, 2004.

Lawrence, Clifford H. *Medieval Monasticism: Forms of Religious Life in Western Europe in the Middle Ages.* London and New York: Longman, 1984.

Leclercq, Jean, François Vandenbroucke, and Louis Bouyer. *The Spirituality of the Middle Ages.* History of Christian Spirituality 2. London: Burns & Oates, 1968.

Leech, Kenneth. *Soul Friend: The Practice of Christian Spirituality.* Introduction by Henri J. M. Nouwen. San Francisco: Harper & Row, 1977. Revised ed. entitled *Soul Friend: Spiritual Direction in the Modern World.* Foreword by George Carey, Archbishop of Canterbury. Harrisburg, PA: Morehouse Publishing, 2001.

Lennan, Richard. *The Ecclesiology of Karl Rahner.* Oxford: Oxford University Press, 1995.

Lives of the Desert Fathers. Translated by Norman Russell. Introduction by Benedicta Ward. SLG. Kalamazoo: Cistercian Publications, 1981.

Long, Thomas G. *Testimony: Talking Ourselves into Being Christian.* San Francisco: Jossey-Bass, 2004.

Luther, Martin. *Works of Martin Luther.* Edited and translated by Adolph Spaeth, L. D. Reed, Henry Eyster Jacobs, and others. 6 vols. Philadelphia: A. J. Holman, 1915.

———. *Luther's Works.* General editor Helmut T. Lehmann. 55 vols. Philadelphia: Muhlenberg Press, 1955–1986.

———. *Career of the Reformer I.* In vol. 31 of *Luther's Works.* Edited by Harold J. Grimm. Philadelphia: Muhlenberg Press, 1957.

———. *Sermons I.* In vol. 51 of *Luther's Works.* Edited and translated by John W. Doberstein. Philadelphia: Muhlenberg Pres, 1959.

————. *Luther: Lectures on Romans*. Translated and edited by Wilhelm Pauck. Philadelphia: Westminster Press, 1961.

————. *Liturgy and Hymns*. In vol. 53 of *Luther's Works*. Edited by Ulrich S. Leupold. Philadelphia: Fortress Press, 1965.

————. *Word and Sacrament II*. In vol. 36 of *Luther's Works*. Edited by Abdel Ross Wentz. Philadelphia: Fortress Press, 1959.

————. *Word and Sacrament I*. In vol. 35 of *Luther's Works*. Edited by E. Theodore Bachmann. Philadelphia: Muhlenberg Press, 1960.

————. *The Theologia Germanica of Martin Luther*. Translation, introduction, and commentary by Bengt Hoffman. New York: Paulist Press, 1980.

————. *Kleiner Katechismus mit Erklärung*. Hamburg: Helmut Korinth, 1982.

————. *Luther's Small Catechism*. Minneapolis: Augsburg Fortress, 2001.

Lutheran Book of Worship. Minneapolis: Augsburg Publishing House, 1978.

Mackey, James P., ed. *An Introduction to Celtic Christianity*. Edinburgh: T & T Clark, 1989.

Macquarrie, John. *A Guide to the Sacraments*. New York: Continuum, 1997.

Martin, James. *My Life with the Saints*. Chicago: Loyola University Press, 2006.

Martos, Joseph. *Doors to the Sacred: A Historical Introduction to Sacraments in the Catholic Church*. Liguori, MO: Liguori/Triumph, 2001.

Maxwell, William D. *John Knox's Genevan Service Book 1556: The Liturgical Portions of the Genevan Service Book Used by John Knox While a Minister of the English Congregation of Marian Exiles at Geneva 1556–59*. London: Oliver and Boyd, 1931.

McGinn, Bernard. *Meister Eckhart and the Beguine Mystics*. New York: Continuum, 1994.

————. *The Flowering of Mysticism: Men and Women in the New Mysticism—1200–1350*. Vol. 3 of *The Presence of God: A History of Western Christian Mysticism*. New York: Crossroad, 1998.

————. *The Harvest of Mysticism in Medieval Germany*. Vol. 4 of *The Presence of God: A History of Western Christian Mysticism*. New York: Crossroad, 2005.

McGrath, Alister E. *Reformation Thought: An Introduction*. 3d ed. Malden, MA: Blackwell, 1999.

McLaren, Brian. *A New Kind of Christian: A Tale of Two Friends on a Spiritual Journey*. San Francisco: Jossey-Bass, 2001.

McNeill, John T. *A History of the Cure of Souls*. New York: Harper & Brothers, 1951.

————, and Helena M. Gamer. *Medieval Handbooks of Penance: A Translation of the Principal* Libri Poenitentiales *and Selections From Related Documents*. New York: Columbia University Press, 1938, 1990.

Meister Eckhart. *The Essential Sermons, Commentaries, Treatises, and Defense*. Translated and introduced by Edmund Colledge and Bernard McGinn. Mahwah, NJ: Paulist Press, 1981.

Melanchthon, Philip. *Loci Communes Theologici* in *Melanchthon and Bucer*. Edited by Wilhelm Pauck. Philadelphia: Westminster Press, 1969.

Menninger, Karl A. *Whatever Became of Sin?* New York: Hawthorn Books, 1973.

Merton, Thomas. "The Spiritual Father in the Desert Tradition." *Cistercian Studies* 3, no. 1 (1968): 3–23.

Monumenta Ignatiana. Exercitia spiritualia S. Ignatii de Loyola et eorum directoria. 2nd ed. 2 vols. Madrid: G. Lopez del Horno, 1919; reprinted Rome: Monumenta Historica Societatis Iesu, 1969.

Mortimer, Robert C. *The Origins of Private Penance in the Western Church.* Oxford: Clarendon Press, 1939.

Mowrer, O. Hobart. *The Crisis in Psychiatry and Religion.* Princeton, NJ: Van Nostrand, 1961.

Müller, Jacob. *KirchenGeschmuck, Das ist: Kurtzer Begriff der fürnembsten Dingen, damit ein jede recht und wol zugerichtete Kirchen geziert und auffgebutzt seyn solle.* Munich: Berg, 1591.

Murk-Jansen, Saskia. *Brides in the Desert: The Spirituality of the Beguines.* Maryknoll, NY: Orbis Books, 1998.

Myers, W. David. *Poor, Sinning Folk: Confession and Conscience in Counter-Reformation Germany.* Ithaca: Cornell University Press, 1996.

O'Malley, John W. *The First Jesuits.* Cambridge, MA: Harvard University Press, 1993.

————. *Trent and All That: Renaming Catholicism in the Early Modern Era.* Cambridge, MA: Harvard University Press, 2000.

Oberman, Heiko A. *Luther: Man Between God and the Devil.* Translated by Eileen Walliser-Schwarzbart. New Haven: Yale University Press, 1989.

Origen, *De Principiis.* In vol. 4 of *The Ante-Nicene Fathers.* Edited by Alexander Roberts and James Donaldson. 1868–1873. 24 vols. Repr. Peabody, MA: Hendrickson, 1999.

Peterson, Eugene H. *The Contemplative Pastor: Returning to the Art of Spiritual Direction.* Grand Rapids: Eerdmans, 1989.

————. *Under the Unpredictable Plant: An Exploration in Vocational Holiness.* Grand Rapids: Eerdmans, 1992.

————. *The Wisdom of Each Other: A Conversation Between Spiritual Friends.* Grand Rapids: Zondervan, 1998.

————. *Christ Plays in Ten Thousand Places: A Conversation in Spiritual Theology.* Grand Rapids: Eerdmans, 2005.

————. *Eat This Book: A Conversation in the Art of Spiritual Reading.* Grand Rapids: Eerdmans, 2006.

Porete, Marguerite. *The Mirror of Simple Annihilated Souls.* Translated and edited by Ellen Babinsky. New York: Paulist Press, 1993.

Rad, Gerhard von. *Old Testament Theology.* 2 vols. Translated by D. M. G. Stalker. New York: Harper & Row, 1962.

Rahner, Karl. *Alltägliche Dinge.* Einsiedeln: Benziger, 1964.

————. *Meditations on the Sacraments.* Translated by Salvator Attanasio, James M. Quigley, and Dorothy White. New York: Seabury, 1977; originally published as *Die Siebenfältige Gabe.* Munich: Ars Sacra Joseph Mueller, 1974.

————. "Eternity from Time." In *Theological Investigations* 19, 169–77. Translated by David Morland. New York: Crossroad, 1979.

————. "Warum man trotzdem beichten soll." *Entschluß* (Vienna) 35, no. 9 (1980), 4–12. English: "The Status of the Sacrament of Reconciliation." In *Theological Investigations* 23, 205–18. Translated by Joseph Donceel. New York: Crossroad, 1992.

————. "Erfahrungen eines katholischen Theologen." In *Vor dem Geheimnis Gottes den Menschen verstehen: Karl Rahner zum 80. Geburtstag.* Edited by Karl Lehmann. Munich: Schnell & Steiner, 1984.

————. *Is Christian Life Possible Today?* Translated by Salvator Attanasio. Denville, NJ: Dimension, 1984.

————. "Zur Situation des Bußsakramentes." In vol. 16 of idem, *Schriften zur Theologie.* Einsiedeln: Benziger, 1984, 18–37.

————. *Foundations of Christian Faith: An Introduction to the Idea of Christianity.* Translated by William V. Dych. New York: Crossroad, 1987; originally published as *Grundkurs des Glaubens: Einführung in den Begriff des Christentums.* Freiburg: Herder, 1976.

————. *Faith in a Wintry Season: Interviews and Conversations with Karl Rahner in the Last Years of His Life, 1982–84.* Edited by Hubert Biallowons, Harvey D. Egan, and Paul Imhof. New York: Crossroad, 1990.

————. *Karl Rahner: Spiritual Writings.* Edited and with an introduction by Philip Endean. Maryknoll, NY: Orbis Books, 2004.

Raymond of Capua. *The Life of Catherine of Siena.* Translated, introduced, and annotated by Conleth Kearns. Preface by Vincent de Couesnongle. Wilmington, DE: Michael Glazier, 1980.

Rites of the Catholic Church: The Roman Ritual Revised by Decree of the Second Vatican Ecumenical Council and Published by Authority of Pope Paul VI. Vol. 1. Collegeville, MN: Liturgical Press, 1990.

Rule of St. Benedict 1980. Edited by Timothy Fry. Collegeville, MN: Liturgical Press, 1982.

Salvian, *On the Government of God.* Translated by Eva M. Sanford. New York: Octagon Books, 1966.

Sayings of the Desert Fathers: The Alphabetical Collection. Translated by Benedicta Ward. Kalamazoo: Cistercian Publications, 1975.

Sellner, Edward C. *Wisdom of the Celtic Saints.* Notre Dame, IN: Ave Maria Press, 1993.

————. *The Celtic Soul Friend: A Trusted Guide for Today.* Notre Dame, IN: Ave Maria Press, 2002.

Smith, Martin L. *Reconciliation: Preparing for Confession in the Episcopal Church.* Cambridge, MA: Cowley Publications, 1985.

Spener, Philipp Jakob. *Pia Desideria.* In *Pietists: Selected Writings.* Edited and introduced by Peter C. Erb. New York: Paulist Press, 1983.

Speyr, Adrienne von. *They Followed His Call: Vocation and Asceticism.* Translated by Erasmo Leiva. New York: Alba House/Society of St. Paul, 1979.

———. *Confession*. Translated by Douglas W. Stott. San Francisco: Ignatius Press, 1985.

———. *The Christian State of Life*. Edited by Hans Urs von Balthasar. Translated by Mary Frances McCarthy. San Francisco: Ignatius Press, 1986.

Spitz, Lewis W. *The Protestant Reformation 1517–1559*. New York: Harper & Row, 1985.

Stasiak, Kurt. *A Confessor's Handbook*. New York: Paulist Press, 1999.

Tauler, Johann. *Sermons*. Translated by Maria Shrady. Introduction by Joseph Schmidt. Preface by Alois Haas. New York: Paulist Press, 1985.

Tentler, Thomas N. *Sin and Confession on the Eve of the Reformation*. Princeton, NJ: Princeton University Press, 1977.

Tertullian. *On Repentance*. In vol. 3 of *The Ante-Nicence Fathers*. Edited by Alexander Roberts and James Donaldson. 1868–1873. 24 vols. Repr. Peabody, MA: Hendrickson, 1999.

Thomas Aquinas. *An Apology for the Religious Orders*. Translated and edited by John Procter. St. Louis: Herder, 1902.

Thomas of Eccleston. *Tractatus de Adventu Fratrum Minorum in Anglicam*. Edited by Andrew G. Little. Manchester: Manchester University Press, 1951.

Trilhe, A. *Statuta Capitulorum Generalium Ordinis Cisterciensis*. Edited by Joseph Marie Canivez. Louvain: Bureaux de la Revue, 1933.

Vetter, Ferdinand. *Die Predigten Taulers*. Deutsche Texte des Mittelalters 11. Berlin: Weidmann, 1910.

Vorgrimler, Herbert. *Karl Rahner: Gotteserfahrung in Leben und Denken*. Darmstadt: Primus Verlag, 2004.

Waal, Esther de. *Seeking God: The Way of St. Benedict*. Collegeville, MN: Liturgical Press, 1984.

Waddell, Helen, trans. *Beasts and Saints*. London: Constable, 1934; new ed., with introduction by Esther de Waal. Grand Rapids: Eerdmans, 1934, 1995.

Walsh, John R., and Thomas Bradley. *A History of the Irish Church 400–700 A.D.* Dublin: Columba Press, 1991.

Ward, Benedicta. *The Desert Fathers: Sayings of the Early Christian Monks*. New York: Penguin Putnam, 2003.

Watkins, Oscar D. *A History of Penance*. London: Longmans, 1920.

Webber, Robert E., ed. *The Complete Library of Christian Worship*. 7 vols. Nashville: Star Song, 1993–1994.

———. *Journey to Jesus: The Worship, Evangelism, and Nurture Mission of the Church*. Nashville: Abingdon, 2001.

Wesley, John. *The Works of John Wesley*. 14 vols. London: Wesleyan Conference Office, 1872.

———. *The Journal of John Wesley*. Chicago: Moody Press, 1951.

———. *John and Charles Wesley: Selected Prayers, Hymns, Journal Notes, Sermons, Letters, and Treatises*. Edited and with an introduction by Frank Whaling. New York: Paulist Press, 1981.

White, Carolinne. *Early Christian Lives*. New York: Penguin Books, 1998.

White, James F. *Introduction to Christian Worship*. Nashville: Abingdon, 2000.

Whitelock, Dorothy, Rosamond McKitterie, and David Dumville. *Ireland in Early Medieval Europe*. Cambridge and New York: Cambridge University Press, 1982.

Workman, Herbert B. *The Evolution of the Monastic Ideal*. Boston: Beacon Press, 1962.

Zum Brunn, Emilie, and Georgette Epiney-Burgard. *Women Mystics in Medieval Europe*. Translated by Sheila Hughes. New York: Paragon House, 1989.

Zwingli, Ulrich. *Commentary on True and False Religion*. Edited by Samuel Macauley Jackson and Clarence Nevin Heller. Philadelphia: Heidelberg Press, 1929.

———. *Zwingli and Bullinger*. Selected translations with introductions and notes by G. W. Bromiley. Philadelphia: Westminster Press, 1953.

Index

343